THE CHURCH OF WOMEN

THE
CHURCH
OF WOMEN

INDIANA UNIVERSITY PRESS
BLOOMINGTON AND INDIANAPOLIS

GENDERED ENCOUNTERS BETWEEN MAASAI AND MISSIONARIES

Dorothy L. Hodgson

This book is a publication of

Indiana University Press
601 North Morton Street
Bloomington, IN 47404-3797 USA

http://iupress.indiana.edu

Telephone orders   800-842-6796
Fax orders   812-855-7931
Orders by e-mail   iuporder@indiana.edu

© 2005 by Dorothy L. Hodgson

The paper used in this publication meets the minimum requirements of American National Standard for Information Sciences—Permanence of Paper for Printed Library Materials, ANSI Z39.48-1984.

Manufactured in the United States of America

Library of Congress Cataloging-in-Publication Data

Hodgson, Dorothy Louise.
    The church of women : gendered encounters between Maasai and missionaries / Dorothy L. Hodgson.
        p.   cm.
    Includes bibliographical references and index.
        ISBN 0-253-34568-5 (alk. paper)—
        ISBN 0-253-21762-8 (pbk. : alk. paper)
            1. Catholic Church—Missions—Tanzania.
    2. Women, Masai—Religious life—Tanzania.
    3. Masai (African people)—Tanzania—Religion.
    4. Congregation of the Holy Ghost—Missions—Tanzania.   I. Title.

BV3625.T4H63 2005
266'.2678'082—dc22
                                            2004022320
1   2   3   4   5   10   09   08   07   06   05

For Rick, with love

CONTENTS

PREFACE • ix

NOTE ON MAASAI TERMS • xvii

Introduction: Gender, Power, and
the Missionary Encounter • 1

1. "Oh She Who Brings the Rain" • 19

2. Men of the Church • 68

3. Evangelizing "the Maasai" • 106

4. The Church of Women • 145

5. Being a Man in the Church of Women • 188

6. Possessed by the Spirit • 210

7. Toward a Maasai Catholicism? • 230

Conclusion • 256

NOTES • 261

BIBLIOGRAPHY • 281

INDEX • 299

PREFACE

Sometimes, although we listen, we do not hear. Fortunately, one of the many benefits of longitudinal research in the same area is that finally, if we are lucky, our ears (and eyes and other senses) become unplugged and we can begin to hear and see in new ways. Such has been my experience studying, living, and working with Maasai in Tanzania since 1985. In 1985, I was hired by the local Catholic Diocese of Arusha to work for the new Arusha Diocesan Development Office (ADDO) for three years and to teach for one year at Oldonyo Sambu Junior Seminary (where I also lived). During these years as a development practitioner, and then later as an anthropologist, I heard many Maasai women complain bitterly about their loss of economic and political rights, a historical process of disenfranchisement that I documented in great detail in my first book, *Once Intrepid Warriors*. I included research on missionaries, the church, and religious experience as part of the original study of gender and social change that informed that book, but decided, after some reflection, that the missionary encounter deserved a book of its own. Why?

Over the course of the years, in my many conversations, interviews, and experiences with Maasai women and men, it eventually became clear to me that although women were very concerned about the political and economic changes that they had experienced in their lives (and that I had documented)—the loss of shared rights to cattle and often smallstock, the consolidation of formal political authority by Maasai men, the replacement of the female barter trade with male-dominated cash transactions, the targeting of development interventions to men as the presumed "experts," "household heads," and "livestock owners," to mention just a few—the arena of their lives that they considered most important to their power and identity as women in general and Maasai women in particular was what we might call the "religious" or "spiritual" domain. Maasai women prized their special relationship with their divinity, Eng'ai. They were proud of their spiritual practices and powers in cultivating and maintaining this relationship in the interests of their children, families, herds, and households. They also believed that their relationship with Eng'ai made them responsible for ensuring the moral order of their daily world, and protesting and remedying any transgressions to that order. As such, they cast men's historical usurpation of political and economic power as not just an affront to the privileges of Maasai women, but to the precepts and moral vision of Eng'ai.

The more I came to understand the centrality of spiritual power to Maasai women's sense of themselves, the more I was forced to rethink some of my own assumptions and beliefs as a secular feminist scholar. In my work, I have tried to explore the relationship of culture and political economy, of meaning and materiality, in dynamic, complicated ways that do not prejudge or presume a given causality between how we understand our world and how we act in it. Merging anthropological and historical theories, epistemologies, and methodologies has helped me produce analyses of gender, ethnicity, development, pastoralism, and other subjects that are sensitive to the complex (and often unpredictable) interplays of culture, power, and history. But, frankly, the world of religion, or spirituality, or what some have called the "supernatural," never entered into my secular theoretical and empirical frameworks. The beliefs and practices of Maasai women therefore challenged my ideas not only about power, but about gender as well. Attention to their world of faith, religious belief and practice, moral authority, and spiritual power has made me consider how to reconcile the moral world with the material one, how to incorporate and analyze spiritual forms of power with political and economic ones, and how to understand the relationship of spirituality to the production, reproduction, and transformation of gender relations among women, among men, and between men and women.

My early work in Tanzania also introduced me to the Catholic Church and to the Congregation of the Holy Spirit, or Spiritans as they are more familiarly known. Although I was raised an Episcopalian, the Spiritans kindly agreed to sponsor my work for ADDO, paying me a small monthly stipend, return airfare to the United States, and a modest resettlement allowance once I completed my contract. I became one of several "Spiritan Associates," lay people (including nuns) who worked in various capacities—primarily as teachers, development workers, and pilots—with the Spiritans in Arusha Diocese. At the time, the Bishop of Arusha Diocese was an American Spiritan, many of the missionary priests whom I worked with were American Spiritans, and almost all of the Spiritan Associates were also

Americans. Most of the Spiritan Associates lived, as I did, at Oldonyo Sambu Junior Seminary, where they worked as teachers for the primarily Maasai boys who attended the school in Form I through Form VI. We lived with several Tanzanian diocesan priests and lay people who also taught at the school, sharing meals, social activities, and public spaces in common.

Thus, at the same time that I was traveling throughout Maasailand meeting with Maasai men and women, listening to their concerns, and co-ordinating the design and implementation of a range of community-based development projects, I was also meeting, talking to, and learning about Spiritan missionaries. I quickly came to know many of them on a personal level, and several became dear friends. Pat Patten shared his caches of American junk food with me, as well as his sometimes offbeat but always passionate ideas on social justice and social change. Ned Marchessault introduced me to aspects of Maasai life and belief that I had not encountered before, and gained my continuing admiration and respect for his courageous work educating Maasai girls. The late Coleman "Shorty" Watkins taught me about the exhilarating and sometimes painful transformations in missionary practices produced by Vatican II. Don McEachin became a fast friend, and shared the highs and lows of my personal life at the times when I needed him most. The list goes on, but the point is that I came to know these missionaries as human beings, as men with a range of talents and temperaments, of quirks and quibbles. We may have disagreed about many things, but they were hardly the monsters caricatured by some scholarly works on missionary evangelization. This book represents my efforts to come to terms with the questions and issues raised by my unique access and insights into the lives of Maasai and Spiritans, and the history and contours of their encounter.

And so I am indebted, as with my first book, to many, many people in Tanzania, the United States, and elsewhere. Residents of Emairete, Mti Mmoja, and Embopong', where I first began living and studying in 1991, have graciously allowed me to pester them with questions and participate in and observe their daily lives for over a decade. My rapport with and research in these communities was greatly enabled by the adept assistance, insights, friendship, and sense of humor of Morani Poyoni, my long-time research assistant. Mwalimu Moses Lengaa also helped me with introductions and interviews in Mti Mmoja in the summer of 2000, for which I am very grateful. Many other friends in Tanzania have provided personal, emotional, intellectual, and logistical support for this project, including Saning'o Milliary, Alais ole Morindat, the Peterson clan (especially Dave, Thad, and

Robin), Trish McCauley and Kees Terhell, Jo Driessen and Judith Jackson, Leo Fortes, Marian Fortes, Dick Bakker, and Marjorie Mbilinyi. I received research permission from the Tanzanian Commission on Science and Technology, where the late Professor Cuthbert Omari served as my local sponsor for many years. He was a generous and helpful colleague, and is sorely missed. I would also like to thank Professor Anku Sanga, who kindly agreed at the last minute to serve as my local sponsor after Professor Omari's death.

Many Spiritans in Tanzania and the United States have also kindly allowed me to interview them, review their files and archives, and discuss my arguments. Father Gerry Kohler has been an especially engaging interlocutor, and I appreciate his interest and respect his criticisms. I learned tremendously from my interviews with him, as well as with Father Gene Hillman and Father Bill Christy. Father Hillman generously let me copy some of his pictures to use in this book and patiently answered my occasional email queries. The late Father Henry Koren helped me navigate the Spiritan archives in Bethel Park. I also benefited from his astounding memory and published histories of the Congregation.

Several institutions and individuals have generously supported the research and writing of this book at different stages. My early work was financed by an International Doctoral Research Fellowship funded by the Joint Committee on African Studies of the Social Science Research Council and the American Council of Learned Societies with funds provided by the Rockefeller Foundation, a Fulbright-Hays Doctoral Dissertation Abroad Award, a National Science Foundation Doctoral Dissertation Improvement Grant (BNS #9114350), an Andrew W. Mellon Candidacy Fellowship, an Andrew W. Mellon Dissertation Fellowship, a Rackham Predoctoral Fellowship, a Margaret Wray French Foundation Grant, a Center for Afroamerican and African Studies—Ford Foundation Grant, several Rackham Travel Grants from the University of Michigan, and a Jacob J. Javits Fellowship from the U.S. Department of Education. Subsequent research was funded by a Richard Carley Hunt Memorial Postdoctoral Fellowship from the Wenner-Gren Foundation for Anthropological Research, a Fellowship from the American Philosophical Society, and Faculty Research Grants and research allowances from the Research Council and Faculty of Arts and Sciences at Rutgers University. A residency fellowship at the Center for the Advanced Study in the Behavioral Sciences (CASBS) in Palo Alto in 2001–2002 enabled me to read much of the relevant literature and write an early draft of chapter 1. Perhaps more importantly, I had the opportunity to discuss the project with some very smart and opinionated people from diverse disciplines. I am especially indebted to the Feminism group at CASBS, particularly Judy Walkowitz, Jenny Mansbridge, Suman Veerma, Sergio Miceli, and Susan Hanson for an extremely helpful brainstorming session.

I have presented selections from the book to audiences at Tulane University, Stanford University, Miami University at Ohio, Rutgers University, Colby College, Columbia University, the African Studies Association, the American Anthropological Association, and the Society for the Anthropology of Religion. In addition, I presented early chapters at two small conferences: "African Expressions of Christianity in East Africa," sponsored by the University of Wisconsin–Madison and the University of Dar es Salaam in 1996; and "Africans Meeting Missionaries: Rethinking Colonial Encounters" sponsored by the University of Minnesota and the MacArthur Foundation in 1997. Fellow participants in the "Symposium on Contemporary Perspectives in Anthropology" organized by Brad Weiss in 2001 and 2003 also read selected chapters. The lively debate and intellectual interactions with colleagues in anthropology, history, and other disciplines at each of these venues shaped this project in important ways.

Many colleagues read all or parts of the manuscript at different stages, and the book is far better thanks to their critical insights and encouragement. Misty Bastian, Barbara Cooper, Richard Schroeder, and Richard Waller read and commented on the entire manuscript, taking time from their overburdened schedules to offer wise advice, gentle suggestions, and insightful critiques. As the reader for the press, Misty Bastian offered comments that were especially detailed and helpful—she understood my purpose in writing the book and helped me make it stronger, clearer, and more compelling. Tom Spear and Richard Waller were early and constant supporters, and I only hope that I can be as generous with my time, advice, and encouragement as they have been. Barbara Cooper pushed me to restructure several chapters and write a few more, for which I am now, many months later, grateful. T. O. Beidelman offered lengthy commentaries on an early paper and the book's prospectus. Bill Taylor shared advice and suggested sources from his voluminous work on Catholicism in Mexico. At a lovely lunch where I nervously outlined my argument, Steve Feierman challenged me to think more about the relationship between spirituality and healing. Marcia Wright kept me honest about my historical sources and resources for studying gender relations in the past. Jean Comaroff graciously probed my arguments and suggested sources at breakfast one day. Judy Walkowitz patiently read, listened to, and commented on various iterations of early chapters over lunch and on our walks at CASBS; I am sure that she learned far more about

Maasai religion and the Catholic Church than she ever needed (or wanted) to know. Other friends and colleagues who offered suggestions, comments, and critiques include Susan Andrade, Vigdis Broch-Due, Manuela Carneiro da Cunha, Fred Cooper, Elliot Fratkin, Tamara Giles-Vernick, Deborah Gordon, Robert Gordon, Maria Grosz-Ngate, Susan Hanson, Mary Huber, Pier Larson, Fletcher Linders, Julie Livingstone, Ron Kassimir, Cindi Katz, Nancy Lutkehaus, Greg Maddox, Adeline Masquelier, Sheryl McCurdy, Saning'o Milliary, Alais Morindat, Jane Parpart, Peter Pels, Steven Pierce, Neil Smith, Bilinda Straight, Bill Taylor, Danny Walkowitz, Brad Weiss, Dick Werbner, and Eric Worby.

Many of my colleagues, friends, and students at Rutgers University in anthropology, African studies, and women's and gender studies have been wonderful sources of inspiration and encouragement. I am especially grateful to Laura Ahearn, Ousseinna Alidou, Mona Bhan, Abena Busia, Ethel Brooks, Sue Cobble, Rebecca Etz, Jack Harris, Alan Howard, David Hughes, Jessica Morales-Libove, Julie Livingstone, Leslie McCall, Bonnie McCay, Michael Moffatt, Nia Parson, Paige West, and Carolyn Williams. Andy Bickford and Lisa Vanderlinden translated and verified translations from Moritz Merker and Oscar Baumann.

Dee Mortensen, my editor at Indiana University Press, has supported and encouraged (and patiently waited for) this book since its beginning. Dee is simply the most wonderful editor I can imagine working with, and I am only afraid that if I sing her praises too loudly she will be flooded with excellent manuscripts from other authors and forget about me. Jane Lyle, the managing editor, has been extraordinarily efficient in coordinating the production process. Carol Kennedy, the copy editor, had a keen eye for sharpening my prose.

I am most grateful, however, for the support of my extended family. My parents, sisters, brothers, nieces, nephews, and in-laws have all kept my spirits up when writing got me down, especially during our holidays and annual reunions. But it has been Rick Schroeder—my husband, in-house editor, and love of my life—and our two sons, Luke and Toby, who have borne the daily brunt of the research and writing of this book. In the summer of 2000, Rick and Luke (and Toby, in utero) sat through innumerable church services and suffered my frequent absence. Since then, they have allowed me the space and time to write, but always reminded me to play as well. Without Rick's generosity in sharing the daily burdens and joys of juggling family, work, and household, however, none of this would have been possible. And so I dedicate the book to him, in thanks and love.

*   *   *

I am grateful to the following publishers for permission to republish selections, often revised, from the following: "Embodying the Contradictions of Modernity: Gender and Spirit Possession among Maasai in Tanzania," in *Gendered Encounters: Challenging Cultural Boundaries and Social Hierarchies in Africa*, ed. Maria Grosz-Ngate and Omari Kokole, pp. 111–129, reprinted with the permission of Taylor and Francis; "Engendered Encounters: Men of the Church and the Church of Women in Maasailand, Tanzania, 1950 to 1993," *Comparative Studies in Society and History* 41(4), pp. 758–783, reprinted with the permission of Cambridge University Press.

Note on Maasai Terms

Maa is primarily an oral language with different diale
orthography. I have kept the original spellings of Maa
from primary and secondary sources. In my own writi
sistent, simplified spellings based on the dictionaries co
(1977, 1996), but occasionally have adapted them to
nunciation and spelling. Since the issue of translation
understanding is a key aspect of the encounters betwe
sionaries, I have used many Maa words in the text, with
glosses. Moreover, since gender is a key theme of this b
the gender prefix on nouns that designate masculine (s
ir) and feminine (sing. e/en/eng/er; pl. i/in/ir) forms. I
included tonal marks, hyphens, and other linguistic mark
trophe marks.

THE CHURCH OF WOMEN

INTRODUCTION:
GENDER, POWER, AND THE
MISSIONARY ENCOUNTER

A significant paradox of the missionary endeavor in many parts of Africa, as elsewhere, is the preponderance of female adherents to Christianity despite concerted efforts by most mainstream missionary groups to convert men.[1] "Again and again in a mission history," notes Adrian Hastings, "the early significant baptisms were mostly of women" (Hastings 1993: 112). Much of the ethnographic and historical literature on missionization in Africa corroborates Hastings's findings (Barrett 1968: 148; Isichei 1995; Landau 1995: 197; examples discussed in Hastings 1993: 112–114). Although not self-evident, such an outcome is of course more understandable for missionary groups who directed their efforts at converting and training African women to be the "good wives and mothers" necessary for the propagation of the Christian family and the "domestic" duties of the Christian home (Gaitskell 1979; Hunt 1990; Labode 1993; Kanogo 1993). But how do we explain the predominance of women in churches where missionaries did not, in general, seek their participation or encourage their involvement?

Consider the case of Maasai in Tanzania, where Catholic missionaries from the Congregation of the Holy Spirit, also called Spiritans, have spent over fifty years trying to evangelize Maasai men. In vain they have tried to convert men first through schools, then in their homesteads, and finally in individual instruction classes. Maasai women were restricted from attending school, tolerated but not encouraged to attend homestead instruction and services, and dissuaded from holding formal leadership positions in the church. Despite these gendered evangelization strategies and objectives, however, significantly more Maasai women than men have sought instruction and baptism in the Catholic Church. Conversion to Catholicism was never easy for these women, as they had to overcome not only the reluctance of the missionaries but also the objections of their husbands and fathers. Yet they persevered, and now comprise the majority of practicing Catholics. Intent on creating Christian communities premised on male leadership and patriarchal authority, the men of the church have instead facilitated the creation of a "church of women."

The most basic purpose of this book is to use ethnographic and historical data, methods, and theories to explain this paradoxical outcome: Why have so many Maasai women and so few men converted to Catholicism, despite sustained missionary efforts to evangelize men? *How* and *why* did Maasai women overcome the cultural, social, and institutional barriers to their participation in the Catholic Church? How do Maasai women and men, and Catholic catechists and priests, understand and worship in the contemporary "church of women"? To address these questions, the book analyzes how gender has shaped the terms, contours, and outcomes of the missionary encounter between Maasai and Spiritans. As such, it examines how spirituality and conversion serve as sites for the negotiation of gender and ethnic identities, the relationship between spirituality and other domains of power, and religion as a source of personal, political, and collective empowerment for women.

Gendered Perspectives in the Study of Mission

The study of gender in Africa and elsewhere has flourished in recent years, building on the important insights of anthropologists, historians, and other scholars as they have explored the everyday lives, ideas, practices, and relationships of men and women across the globe. In Africa, new sources and the creative, critical use of older sources have enabled scholars to rethink certain prior assumptions, such as the universal subordination of women, and analyze new topics, such as the study of masculinities, local-global interactions, and gendered forms of modernity and agency.[2] As a result, gender itself has become a much more sophisticated concept and category of analysis, requiring attention to culture and political economy, agency and structure, processes of social change, relationships of power, and other forms of social difference. It is therefore much more than just the study of "women" (with which it is still too often conflated), or, more recently "men." Instead, it explores the relationships among and between men and women, probing how these relationships are produced, reproduced, and transformed, and thus how the very categories and meanings of being a "man" or a "woman" in different societies and at different times are configured and reconfigured. Central to these dynamic relationships are the intersections, articulations, and mutual constitution of gender with other forms of social difference such as ethnicity, "race," sexuality, religion, class, and nationality.

An important theme in recent work has been the centrality of power to the production of gender and to gendered relationships. Drawing on the insights of Foucault (1972, 1978 [1976], 1979), Scott (1988), Connell (1987), di Leonardo (1991), Dirks et al. (1994), and others, scholars have analyzed how various dimensions of power—including economic, political, social, and cultural—interact to shape gender and gender relationships, and are, in turn, themselves gendered. Here, attention to scale has been crucial, as people, practices, processes, and power move across the boundaries of, and come together at, the level of the locality, region, nation, and globe. Gender relations are never the result simply of "local" ideas and practices, as these in turn shape and are shaped by, to varying degrees, "non-local" factors such as nationalist ideologies, capitalist ambitions, rural-urban interactions, transnational institutions, and the international media. The temporal dimension of power is also important, as it exposes the dynamism of gendered meanings, practices, and relationships by challenging static, essentialist, ahistorical assumptions about, for example, the "proper" roles of men and women. Moreover, a historical perspective on gender and power captures the agency of all actors, men and women, in shaping the terms of their lives and interactions, within certain structured, but also dynamic, constraints and opportunities.

The problem is that this rich work on gender and power has focused primarily on political, economic, and social relationships as the primary sites for analyzing gender. It has generally ignored or dismissed the growing literature on spirituality as a domain of power for women in diverse religious contexts. Among other issues, these studies have explored female representations of the divine, sacred images, and religious cosmologies; the centrality of women as intermediaries with the divine, including their roles as priestesses and ritual experts; female forms of worship and reverence; and the general devaluation of these female roles and realms under the influence of Christianity, Islam, and other so-called world religions.[3]

These studies pose important empirical and theoretical challenges to dominant understandings of gender and power: How do we trace the articulation of all aspects of power in the production and negotiation of gender? How do we assess, for example, gender inequality, when men dominate the political and economic spheres but women dominate the spiritual? Does the "material world" matter more than the "moral"? Or vice versa? How do we analyze shifts over time, especially in the relative significance of one domain of power over another? How do we reconcile divergent perspectives among our informants, but also between our findings and their claims? Can scholars whose work is premised on concepts of rationality, science, and secularism even "see" the sacred in its own terms, especially if they are non-believers themselves?

One arena where the relationship of spirituality to other domains of power is often studied is that of missionary evangelization (Comaroff and Comaroff 1991, 1997; Landau 1995; Peel 2000). There is, however, a surprising neglect of gender analysis in these studies of mission, especially in Africa. As Adrian Hastings mused, "All in all, African society was apparently so male-dominated that the impact of Christianity upon it has been treated overwhelmingly in male terms . . . the social analysis has stopped well short of a gender analysis" (Hastings 1993: 110). Those scholars who do consider gender in their analyses of missionization usually focus on only one side of the equation: the missionaries or the "missionized." They examine the different roles of men and women in the missionary group (Beidelman 1982, 1999; Brusco 1994; Huber 1988; Klein 1994; Swaisland 1993; Williams 1993), the gendered ideologies conveyed by missionary teachings (Hunt 1990; Labode 1993; Musisi 1999), or the "impact" of missionization on the gender roles and ideologies of the "missionized" (Bowie 1993; Bowie et al. 1993; Hinfelaar 1994; Isichei 1993; Kanogo 1993; Moss 1999). Although these studies contribute to our understanding of gender in aspects of the missionary enterprise, most privilege the agency and intentionality of the missionaries over the "missionized" (but see Green 2003; Huber and Lutkehaus 1999; Peel 2000).

Similarly, few scholars have explored the gender dynamics that produce and are reflected in conversion, that is, the conscious shift from (or incorporation of) one set of religious beliefs and practices to another, especially in the mission context. Near the end of his remarkable synthesis of the vast literature on conversion, Lewis Rambo notes the scarcity of studies of women's conversion experiences "to offset the assumed generic (but almost always male) research to date" (Rambo 1993: 174).[4] Important issues remain to be addressed, including "Do women experience conversion differently than men? If so, what are those differences? To what extent are women's experiences distorted, denigrated, or denied by patriarchal requirements of the conversion stereotype?" (Rambo 1993: 174). Such questions, Rambo concludes, "have scarcely even been raised in the literature to date, much less adequately addressed" (Rambo 1993: 174).[5] One wonders, in fact, whether explanations of conversion as "the desire for security, material or psychological" (Etherington 1977: 35), the lure of "socio-cultural inducements which the mission presented" (Carmody 1988: 193), as a "rational adaptation of existing beliefs to a changed social situation" (Horton 1975a: 234; see also Horton 1975b), or as the "production of the modern subject" (van der Veer 1996: 20) fully embrace the conversion experiences of women (or men).[6]

Larsson's (1991) study of Haya women in the Catholic Church in Tanzania is an important exception. She examines the "response" of Haya women to Christianity and social change, particularly their attraction to a Roman Catholic mission station run by White Fathers and White Sisters in the early 1900s and the Lutheran Revival movements of the 1940s and 1950s. The Haya situation differed markedly from that of Maasai, however, since the White Fathers and Sisters who worked in the area encouraged women to convert and ran a residential mission station that offered education to both boys and girls. Another important exception is the vast literature on independent religious movements in Africa such as Jules-Rosette (1979, 1987), Comaroff (1985), Hackett (1987, 1995), Peterson (2001), and especially Hoehler-Fatton (1996). Although many of these movements arose from encounters with missionary churches, the studies themselves explore the conversion of women to these movements, not to mission Christianity.

In contrast to explanations that attribute female conversion to women's motivations as economically and politically subordinate members of their societies, I argue that any explanation of conversion must attend to meaning as well as motivation, to culture as well as political economy. Instrumental explanations that reduce the complex articulations of culture, power, and history that shape the experience of conversion in the missionary context to political and economic variables alone are inadequate to fully explain the resonant appeal of Christianity to some groups of women. Furthermore, they presume that religious expressions and experience of power are subordinate to and determined by political and economic ones. In contrast, this book explores how gender differences in the meaning and experience of conversion interacted with gendered political and economic dislocations to compel Maasai women to surmount the restrictions on their involvement with the Catholic Church and shape the terms and outcomes of the missionary encounter. As such, I argue that attention to spirituality and morality as domains for the experience and expression of power challenges analyses that exclusively privilege economic and political domains.

Such a gendered understanding of conversion challenges the prevailing literature on Maasai engagement with Christianity. Most scholars write bluntly of Maasai "resistance" to Christianity, which they variously attribute to the innate, almost primordial cultural conservatism of Maasai (Gulliver 1969), the ideological presuppositions of pastoralism as a mode of production (Rigby 1981, 1985, 1992), and, more recently, the socialization and encul- turation of young boys to become the fierce, independent, self-reliant men necessary to survive the hardships of pastoralism (Neckebrouck 1993, 2002).[7] Not only are these arguments simplistic, essentialist, and ahistorical, but they are premised (like much research on Maasai and other pastoralist and agro- pastoralist groups) on an understanding of "Maasai" that is not just homog- enous but deeply androcentric. The experiences and perspectives of Maasai men, usually elders but sometimes junior men, are taken as normative and definitive for all Maasai, while the potentially different ideas and practices of Maasai women are at best ignored and at worst disparaged. By taking gender (and other social differences) seriously, my study, like the detailed historical work of Richard Waller (1999), presents a much more nuanced, complicated analysis of the variable reasons that shape why some men and women convert and others do not that challenges such a crude dualism as "resistance" and "adaptation."[8]

Gendered Tensions: Becoming and Being Maasai in the 1950s

In order to make sense of the missionary encounter as it took place between Maasai and Spiritans, I would like to draw from my book, *Once Intrepid Warriors* (Hodgson 2001a), to provide a brief overview of the changes and continuities that had shaped Maasai life until the 1950s, when the Spiritans began to live and work full-time in Masai District.[9] As will become clear in this section and chapter 1, gender was a central organizing principle of Maasai life, as reflected in their language, social organization, mode of production, and religious beliefs and practices. Moreover, by the 1950s, Maasai life and gender relations had undergone significant changes since their first encounters with early missionaries and travelers in the mid nineteenth century.[10] In fact, the history of Maasai has been defined by flux and flexibility—of people and their self-identifications, livelihoods, spatial movements, and social relations among themselves and with others.

Scholars still debate the origins of Maasai as an ethnic group and their relationship with other groups.[11] Contemporary Maasai attribute their ori- gins to their migration *opa* ("long ago"), from "Kerio," a legendary place somewhere to the north, perhaps in Sudan. Although the archeological, linguistic, and oral historical data is sparse and sometimes conflicting, much of it suggests that the ancestors of contemporary Maa speakers moved down the Rift Valley into present-day Kenya during the latter part of the first millennium A.D.[12] Through social, political, and cultural processes of fission and fusion, groups of Maa-speaking peoples came together and moved away, formed and reformed, expanded and contracted. Some groups, such as Samburu and Parakuyo, eventually developed distinct social identities and dialects. Eventually, in about the fifteenth century, a large group of Maa-speakers moved further southward into present-day northern and central Tanzania. Their expansion into Kenya and Tanzania was achieved in large part by the conquest and incorporation of other pastoralist and agricultural groups. Maasai willingly assimilated any non-Maasai willing to adopt their cultural and social practices and allegiances, and incorporated others through marriage, conquest, and child adoption.

Most early Maa-speakers were agro-pastoralists, cultivating sorghum and millet and raising cattle and smallstock. Eventually, however, a group of Maa-speakers emerged that specialized in pastoralism, taking advantage of certain material, political, cultural, social, and ecological changes that enabled such specialization (Hodgson 2001a: 24). By the early nineteenth century, therefore, communities of Maa-speakers existed with different primary livelihoods—pastoralism, agro-pastoralism, farming, and hunting and gathering. But the association of the ethnonym "Maasai" as a designation for pastoralist Maa-speakers did not come into being until the late nineteenth century. According to Bernsten (1980), "Maasai" was initially used to refer to a place-based identity (that is, that Maasai lived in certain areas, Iloikop/Kwavi in others). In the 1870s, however, it shifted to become associated (at least in the minds of European onlookers) with the pursuit of a distinct livelihood—pastoralism (with Iloikop and Kwavi seen as agro-pastoralists).

Maasai social relations were at once united and divided by both vertical and horizontal principles of social organization. They were divided into patrilineal descent groups comprising moieties (*Orokiteng'*, of "the black cattle" and *Odomong'i*, "of the red cattle"), clans (*olgilata*, pl. *ilgilat*), and sub-clans (*enkishomi*, pl. *inkishomi*) that shaped the rules of marriage (clan exogamy was the ideal norm), descent, inheritance, and conflict resolution and compensation.[13] These vertical groupings were cross-cut by male age-sets (*olaji*, pl. *ilajikin*) that united men of similar ages (and divided men of different ages) into a common, uniquely named group based on the period in which they were circumcised.[14] As a named group, these men then moved together through a cycle of age-grades, from *ilmurran* (*olmurrani,* often glossed as "warriors"), to junior elders, elders, senior elders, and venerable elders. Age-sets shaped the rules of sexual access, dietary regulations, the timing of marriage and procreation, and male rights and responsibilities. Women also gained power and prestige with age, but the transformation of their status was an individually rather than collectively marked occasion. Finally, the clan and age-set systems were further complicated by the geographical division of Maasai into politically and ritually autonomous sections (*olosho*, pl. *iloshon*) and localities (*enkutoto*, pl. *inkutot*). Each of these spatial groupings comprised Maasai from all clans, and determined the rules of access to pasture, water, and other resources. Moreover, the sections were culturally distinguished from one another by differences of dialect, dress, ornamentation, and cultural and religious practices.[15] These complex social and spatial groupings were in part the catalyst for and product of the historical flexibility of Maasai in assimilating and incorporating other peoples.

Maasai were also characterized by virilocal residence patterns. They lived in large homesteads (*enkang'*, pl. *inkang'itie*) dispersed across the land, clustered by locality, and containing, ideally, families from more than one clan. Homesteads consisted of a thick, circular thorn fence (*esita*) that surrounded the houses, small pens for smallstock and calves, and an open central area for communal activities (in the day) and the cattle (at night). Maasai were polygynists; each wife built her own house (*enkaji*, pl. *inkajijik*) at the edge of the homestead, on the right or left hand side of her husband's cattle entrance (*enkishomi*), according to the order in which she was married (the first wife built on the right-hand side, second on the left, third on the right, and so forth). Houses were the domains of women; women controlled access to and use of their homes, even by their husbands (cf. Talle 1987, 1988, 1998).

These social and spatial divisions necessitated an array of entities and representatives to make decisions, enforce regulations, and arbitrate disputes. Women and men shared responsibility in deciding household affairs, while elder men (often in consultation with their wives and other senior women) managed the life of the homestead. Clan and inter-clan affairs and disputes (usually over marriage, bridewealth, control of children, livestock thefts, or accusations of harm or murder) were handled by meetings of elder men (*enkiguana*), who sat and listened to the disputants, witnesses (if appropriate), and each other until they reached a decision through consensus (occasionally an oath or trial by ordeal was used). Members of each male age-set met together to decide their business (such as the timing of rituals), and they also selected leaders (*olaigwenani*, pl. *ilaigwenak*) to represent their interests in other fora. Similarly, women, although not formally organized into age-sets, met together to discuss their concerns and adjudicate disputes (such as disagreements between co-wives or the mistreatment of children) and occasionally to take collective action against certain moral transgressions. Finally, elder men from the localities (and, occasionally, sections) would also meet to discuss common issues such as access to pasture and water or the location of a new homestead. Like the age-sets, each locality also had an *olaigwenani* to represent them.

The daily activities necessary to pastoralist production and the security and prosperity of the household and homestead were organized by age and gender. Young boys (*olayioni*, pl. *ilayiok*) herded smallstock and calves, older boys and sometimes *ilmurran* herded the cattle. *Ilmurran* protected the homesteads from predators and raids and served as messengers for elder men. Elder men decided where and when to water and graze the livestock, and made other "management" decisions for the herds and homestead. Young girls (*endito*, pl. *intoyie*) helped their mothers with childcare, the collection of firewood and water, cooking, and other domestic duties. In addition to these chores, adult women supervised and managed their children and other household affairs, cared for young and sick livestock, and milked their cows twice a day. Many also supported their families as traders, traveling to neighboring cultivators and markets to trade milk and hides for vegetables, flour, and other foodstuffs and household goods. All able members of the homestead therefore worked together to ensure the successful reproduction and, hopefully, expansion of their households and herds. Their relationships to one another were premised on *enkanyit*, or respect, which was expressed through appropriate greetings, forms of address, and behavior that varied according to the age, gender, and kinship relations of those involved (see examples in Merker 1910 [1904]). Although adult men and women shared common objectives, they seem to have exercised a great deal of autonomy in their pursuits and mobility, premised on such mutual respect (see discussion in Hodgson 2001a: 27–35).

Women and men not only shared responsibilities for livestock, but had both distinct and shared rights to certain livestock and livestock products. Women controlled the production and distribution of milk, the primary food staple, deciding when to give milk, and how much, to themselves, their children, husband, other immediate kin, visitors, and strangers. Women also controlled livestock hides, which they either processed for use as clothing, bedding, or mats, or traded for food and other goods. Men controlled the distribution of livestock meat when an animal was slaughtered for a ritual, visitor, or feast. In addition, men and women, as husbands and wives, shared rights in specific animals, depending on the circumstances in which the animal was acquired. As such, they consulted with one another over decisions about whether to slaughter, trade, or give an animal away. Moreover, oral evidence suggests that in addition to shared rights, men and women had individual "ownership" rights to certain goats and sheep.

Beginning in the late nineteenth century, Maasai life was radically disrupted. First, a series of disasters struck the people and herds, including bovine pleuropneumonia in 1883, rinderpest in 1891 and smallpox in 1892.[16] Many Maasai and their livestock died as a result of these epidemics and the ensuing raids, wars, famines, and social dislocations. Others dispersed as far as the coast in search of food and security, took up hunting and gathering, or settled down as cultivators. Second, although European travelers, missionaries, traders and others had traversed Maasai territories since the 1860s, in 1890 their presence was secured by the signing of the Anglo-German agreement, which formalized German colonial rule. In addition to separating Maasai in Tanganyika from their relatives in Kenya, the Germans introduced Maasai to some of the procedures and practices of state rule and forcibly moved some from their land in order to encourage European settlements. Finally, World War I shifted colonial rule over Tanganyika to the British, whose ambivalent stereotypes of Maasai, fueled by the often exaggerated stories and images of earlier British travelers and missionaries and by British experiences in Kenya, shaped their administrative and "development" policies and projects for the next fifty years (Hodgson 2001a).[17]

Determined to control the "chaos" and "menace" of the seemingly meaningless wanderings and movements of Maasai, especially their dispersal and intermingling with other ethnic groups, British colonial administrators forced all Maa-speaking pastoralists to move into the newly created Masai Reserve in the 1920s (see map I.1). They compelled "Maasai" (by which they meant Maa-speaking livestock herders) to move into the reserve with threats of political disenfranchisement, loss of land rights, and restrictions on livestock movement. Although many Maasai resisted and the boundaries of the reserve were a source of constant dispute between Maasai and colonial administrators, the British were proud of their success at reconstituting "the Maasai" as an ethnic group. But they were decidedly more ambivalent about whether or not to tamper with Maasai "culture." At times, administrators tried to "protect" Maasai from "corrupting" influences, for example by limiting the number of schools built in the reserve (which soon became Masai District) as compared to other areas of Tanganyika.[18] Yet they also imple-

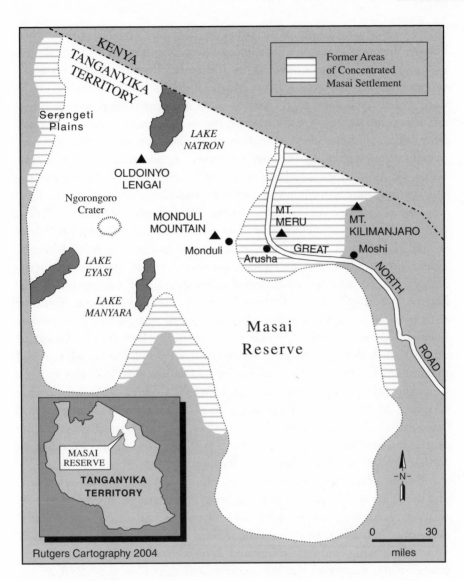

Map I.1. Masai Reserve, ca. 1920.

mented veterinary programs designed to "improve" Maasai animal husbandry, directing medicines, supplies, services, and training to Maasai men as the presumed livestock "owners" and "experts." Parallel efforts were made to monetize and commoditize the Maasai livestock economy through taxation, forced stock sales, legal restrictions on itinerant trading and bartering, and expansion of the formal infrastructure for marketing livestock and food. Meanwhile, continued land alienation of dry season grazing areas and permanent water supplies by the government and settlers made pastoralism less viable, yet most efforts by Maasai to diversify their economic base (primarily through cultivation) went unsupported by the administration. Political interventions included the formation of the Masai Native Authority (MNA), comprised initially of a council of male elders led by the *Oloiboni* as "Chief of the Masai" (and later, of just male elders). In the post–World War II period, pressure from the metropole to increase "productivity" and "modernize" accelerated the intensity of demands and the pace of interventions. After having "protected" Maasai for years from "modernization" and restricted their interaction with neighboring peoples and districts, administrators now blamed Maasai for their "cultural conservatism." They sharply intensified efforts to "develop" these seemingly intransigent people, including renewed measures to increase livestock production and offtake. In 1954, they restructured the MNA (now called the Masai Federal Council, MFC) to include educated Maasai men as representatives in order to better "control" and "modernize" their constituents.[19] Meanwhile, a resurgence of government-sanctioned land alienation and immigration of non-Maasai into Maasai areas further threatened Maasai lands and livelihoods.[20]

By the 1950s, these colonial interventions into the political, economic, and social life of Maasai had produced significant changes in Maasai gender relations.[21] Among Maasai men, the collaboration of elders with colonial authorities in the formation and running of the MNA aggravated the already tense relationships between elders and *ilmurran* (men of the "warrior" age-grade). Elder men used the deliberations and rulings of the MNA as opportunities to expand and strengthen their control over *ilmurran* and women.[22] *Ilmurran* resented the interference in their lives, and responded with increased hostility to the elders and the colonial state and a firmer embrace of their own sense of male cultural identity. Meanwhile, Maasai men who in some ways embraced aspects of "modernity" and therefore did not conform to the dominant configuration of masculinity were stigmatized and ostracized as *ormeek* (a derogatory name for "Swahilis" or non-Maasai, that is, those Africans who wore "Western" clothes, were educated, spoke

Swahili, worked in the government, or were baptized). Although politically marginal within Maasai society, *ormeek* sought and gained power in colonial (and later, postcolonial) political structures.

Despite their differences, Maasai men of all ages took advantage of their new status as livestock "owners" and "experts" to disenfranchise women from their former overlapping rights in cattle, even as women continued to perform their essential roles in livestock production (caring for calves and sick animals, managing milk production and distribution). Women's responsibilities for trading milk, hides, and smallstock for food and household supplies were supplanted as cash transactions controlled by men replaced the female-dominated barter trade. At the same time, diminishing supplies of firewood and water because of sedentarization and land alienation forced women to walk further to find and haul these domestic necessities. Women living in the poorest households took up cultivation to supplement household diets and income. Women's former freedom to travel, their economic autonomy, and their opportunities to congregate with one another were curtailed as they were relegated to the increasingly isolated and subordinate confines of the "domestic" domain. Although not all women were affected equally by these transformations, as their status, authority, and workload differed by age, fertility, marital status, and household wealth, most resented the changes (and still do). They had few options in a world where British patriarchal practices overlapped and reinforced Maasai patriarchal tendencies to exclude them not only from the emerging male-dominated domains of "the political" and "the economic," but from a sense of cultural identity that was increasingly defined by male ideologies and activities (Hodgson 1999a). As a result, the former relationships of mutual respect and autonomy between men and women were replaced by recriminations, complaints, and ridicule as men and women responded to these gendered dislocations (Hodgson 1999c; cf. Hodgson 1996).[23]

Debating the Terms

Some caveats. As numerous scholars have discussed, the notion that religion is a separate, identifiable domain of life is not necessarily the case for all societies at all historical periods. The debates about the analytic validity and conceptual boundaries of "religion" (and related concepts such as "spirituality," "conversion," "divinity," and "faith") are provocative, important, and long-standing.[24] From Durkheim (1947) to Geertz (1973) and beyond, scholars have tried to define, describe, and dispute the form and content of "religion." I will not review these discussions here, but only note that as scholars, we often have to use terms such as "religion" to clarify and deepen our analysis, even though they may not directly reflect the complicated categories, languages, or meanings of the people we are studying. To analytically distinguish "religion" as a domain for study is not to deny its articulation with other cultural, social, political, and economic domains of life, but to enable us to more clearly identify and explore the specificities of these articulations. The problem, as Landau (1999) among others notes, is when we mistake our analysis for reality and thereby reify and impose a set of analytic boundaries as empirical ones.

In the West, the emergent distinction and contrast of the "religious," "spiritual," or "sacred" spheres with the "secular" was the historical product in part of Enlightenment thought and practice. As such, the boundary between the two is historical, negotiable, and porous. Such a distinction would be valid for societies that marked a distinct, regular time or space/place for spiritual activities such as prayer, meditation, worship, or ritual. But in other societies, such as Maasai until the mid twentieth century, the sacred and secular were one and the same (see chapter 1). Maasai have no word in their own language for "religion"; instead they have adopted the Swahili word *dini* (itself originally from Arabic) to create *oldini*. I will therefore use "religion" and "religious" as analytic terms to distinguish, discuss, and analyze those beliefs, practices, and experiences that invoke or express a relationship to some other, powerful divine being(s), thing(s), or essence(s).

Second, Maasai religious beliefs and practices, like their cultural practices and social relations, are and have always been diverse, dynamic, and historical, even before colonial and/or missionary encounters (cf. Shaw 1990). Some aspects, such as their understanding of Eng'ai, their Divine presence, may have been quite stable for years, but we must still be attentive to possible differences of interpretation and perspective. Given the history of the fluidity and flux of Maasai social relations and ethnic identifications discussed above, it is likely that the cultural and religious beliefs and practices that are now identified as "Maasai" are themselves dynamic amalgams drawn from or influenced by Maasai encounters with and absorption of people from other ethnic groups. Moreover, although missionary sources provide detailed descriptions of Maasai religious beliefs and practices, like all narratives they have been filtered and shaped by missionary categories of reference and understanding (Peel 2000). Similarly, these same categories may have subtly reshaped the understandings of contemporary Maasai, especially those with significant involvement in the church. Thus, for example, spirit possession is often referred to not just as *orpeko,* but also in terms of *esetan,* or "satan."

Third, Christianity in general and Catholicism in particular are just as dynamic and historical as Maasai religion, and, despite their claims to "universality," they must be understood in their local manifestations in a given time and place. As William Christian states in his fascinating study of religious practice in sixteenth-century Spain: "The history of Catholicism in practice, both before and after the sixteenth century, is a constant process of new agents and devotions creating a community across boundaries of place and nation, and a constant adaptation and cooptation of the general agents and devotions for local purposes" (1981: 179). The centralized authority of the Pope, the Vatican leadership, and the rigid hierarchy of formal theological, canonical, and other powers vested in nuncios, cardinals, archbishops, bishops, and so forth obviously shape, but do not determine, the form and content of the local church. Local churches are very much the products of interactions among clergy, mediating figures such as catechists and teachers, and communities, set within particular historical, political-economic, social, and cultural contexts. Catholic missionary congregations themselves vary tremendously as to their charism (special mission), acceptance of and compliance with church teachings and dictates, and strategies and goals for evangelization and pastoral care. Similar divisions are often present among members of the same congregation, whether because of differences in national origin, generation, training, class, political orientation, or spiritual ideals.

Finally, I refer to the history of interactions between Spiritan missionaries and Maasai as an "encounter" (cf. Peel 2000). I recognize that "encounter" may not satisfactorily capture the dynamism, duration, and density of Spiritan-Maasai engagements and relationships that I describe in this book (cf. Peterson and Allman 1999). But I think it does index the relative agency and autonomy of both Spiritans and Maasai in shaping the terms of their connections, and thereby challenges any teleological assumptions about the content, form, or outcome of the process (cf. Peel 1995). Spiritans and Maasai shared many different kinds of encounters, in an array of settings, with a range of interpretations, meanings, and consequences. These encounters took place within political, economic, and social contexts. They were also complicated by the direct and indirect influence of other groups, including British colonizers, Tanzanian elites, neighboring ethnic groups, and diocesan priests. Perhaps most importantly, they were almost always mediated by Maasai catechists and teachers, whose dual allegiances to both Spiritans and Maasai often blurred the distinctions between the two. As such, I do not intend for my use of the term "encounter" to imply or produce a sense of these complicated historical engagements as dualistic or dialectical (cf. Comaroff and Comaroff 1991, 1997), or to reify and generalize the "culture," perspectives, and experiences of either Maasai or Spiritans (cf. Elbourne 2002: 18–19).

Overview

This book is based on mission journals, writings, and archives; interviews with missionaries, catechists, and Maasai; and ethnographic and historical data from three communities (Emairete, Mti Mmoja, and Embopong') served by Monduli Catholic mission in northern Tanzania. Fieldwork was conducted in Maasai areas for three years from 1985 through 1987, for two years from 1991 through 1993, and during shorter one- to two-month research trips in 1990, 1995, 1996–97, and 2000. My key research methods have been ongoing participant-observation of Maasai men's and women's religious beliefs and practices, including daily rituals, prayers, ceremonies, and songs; regular attendance at Catholic church services in the three communities (which have different histories of Catholic evangelization efforts); a socioeconomic census in 1992 of all households (454) and individuals (1,974) in the communities that included questions about baptism, religious beliefs, and conversion; semi-structured interviews in 1992 and 1993 with 150 Maasai men and women of different ages, which included questions about religion and evangelization and were taped and transcribed; 25 in-depth interviews with selected Maasai men and women in 2000 focused solely on Maasai religion, perspectives on Catholic teachings and practices, experiences of conversion, and views of Catholic missionaries, evangelization, and church institutions that were taped and transcribed; semi-structured interviews with the key Tanzanian catechists and American Spiritan missionaries who worked in the communities; archival research in the Tanzania National Archives in Dar es Salaam and Arusha, the Spiritan Archives in Bethel Park, Pennsylvania, the Archdiocese of Arusha Archives and Spiritan Library in Tanzania, and other smaller collections; and other interviews, including a Maasai prophet and prophetess who later converted to Catholicism.

Chapter 1 attempts to historically reconstruct Maasai religious beliefs and practices before the advent of the missionaries, with attention to the centrality of gender and power to these domains. Chapter 2 examines the origins and early history of the Spiritans in Africa, and then analyzes the similarities and differences in the lives, thoughts, and experiences of individual missionaries through detailed profiles of three American Spiritans who worked with Maasai in Monduli. Chapter 3 recounts the history of Catholic evangelization of Maasai in Tanzania, with specific attention to the gendered assumptions and outcomes of the three main evangelization approaches of the missionaries and their catechists. Chapter 4 looks at the "churches of women" that have emerged in Maasai areas by comparing the history and contemporary gender dynamics of three specific churches in Monduli: Emairete (which is now a parish headquarters), Mti Mmoja (a relatively young church), and Embopong' (which is still territory for first evangelization). Chapter 5 explores the experiences of different groups of men who participate in the church of women—Catholic Maasai, catechists, and missionaries. Chapter 6 investigates these churches further, by probing the different perspectives of Maasai men and women on conversion and the centrality of the concept of spirit (*oltau*), and related concept of spirit possession (*orpeko*), to their understandings. Chapter 7 examines the creative articulations of Maasai and Christian cultural and religious practices both within and beyond the church, with particular attention to continuities and changes in gender dynamics. In the conclusion, I review the implications of the book's findings in terms of the necessity of including gender and power as key categories of analysis in the study of missionary evangelization, spirituality, and conversion.

Although the story I tell in this book about the encounter between Spiritan missionaries and Maasai in Tanzania is a very particular one, I believe it makes several broader contributions. By demonstrating the centrality of gender to all aspects of the missionary encounter, the book challenges theories of evangelization, spirituality, conversion, and faith that presume (rather than prove) that men and women experience and express them in the same way. Moreover, by incorporating an analysis of female spiritual power into a story of gendered political and economic tensions, the book complicates dominant understandings of gender and power that ignore the moral world for the material one. Finally, the book moves beyond accounts that stress the "hegemony" and "imperialism" of missionaries to analyze the assumptions, ideas, practices, and social locations of all parties to the encounter, including how these change over time and in interaction with one another. It explores the more subtle (and sometimes not-so-subtle) interplay of agency and structure, culture and political economy, ideas and practices, on the part of both missionaries and Maasai that shaped the form and content of their continuing encounter.

"OH SHE WHO BRINGS
THE RAIN"

1

Many years ago, a Maasai woman named Kunguru lived in Monduli Juu. She was powerful and outspoken, and quickly became a leader of all women. She organized Maasai women to demand their rights and defend them. She insisted that men must share wealth and decision-making powers with women. She even argued that since women gave birth to the boys who would become men, women should therefore be the head of their families. Her demands angered the men, especially the *Oloiboni* (diviner and prophet).

One day Kunguru and a delegation of her female followers traveled to Monduli to meet with the *Oloiboni* and other male elders to discuss the need to improve the position of women. Before they reached the *Oloiboni*'s homestead, Kunguru and her retinue decided to rest, and sent three delegates ahead to inform the *Oloiboni* of their visit and request the traditional alcoholic drink for their thirst. The *Oloiboni* quickly called a meeting of male elders and leaders. After their discussion, the *Oloiboni* sent some alcohol back with the delegates. As the delegation's leader, Kunguru was the first to sip the drink, and died quickly; it was poisoned. The rest of the delegation was scared and hurried home, abandoning all thoughts of female emancipation.[1]

This mytho-historical tale of the confrontation between the powerful female leader Kunguru and the male *oloiboni* (pl. *iloibonok*) is well known among older Maasai men and women in the Monduli area. "She was a powerful woman (*kitok*)," explained "Lengare," an elder Maasai man. "She was almost like *iloibonok* even though she was a woman." Some of the oldest claimed to have known Kunguru personally, lived near her, or heard about the poisoning when it occurred. But when I asked my informants to date the story according to which age-set of men were *ilmurran* ("warriors") at the time, or the name of the *oloiboni*, I received conflicting responses. According to "Lepilall," a venerable elder from Emairete, "She was born here and her children still live here. She was a leader of women (*enkaigwenani oongoroyiok*). She was my neighbor and she died right here after being cursed by an *oloiboni* who lived here named Parit. . . . It wasn't long ago, when the

Iltareto were *ilmurran* [between 1911 and 1929]." Other elders offered different dates and facts. My concern, however, is less with the historical truth of the tale than with its greater messages and meanings. As I will discuss below, historical evidence suggests that the *iloibonok* were originally outsiders, non-Maasai men (probably Kikuyu) who insinuated themselves as prophets and diviners among Maasai sometime in the late eighteenth century. In time, they established themselves as special men with distinct spiritual powers based on their unique relationship to Eng'ai, and were adopted and incorporated as a new Maasai sub-clan, the Inkidong'i. From the beginning, they were aligned with Maasai men—as the ritual leaders of cattle raids by the *ilmurran* and the spiritual advisors of elder men. Maasai women seem to have had little involvement with *iloibonok*, preferring the customary involvements of "holy" (*osinyati*) elder men in their rituals and ceremonies. In fact, it is possible, as the story of Kunguru suggests, that women even resented the *iloibonok* for trying to use their allegedly special relationship with Eng'ai to consolidate male power and privilege and displace and mute the spiritual powers and prerogatives of women.

In other words, the story of Kunguru is a story about gender, power, and confrontation couched implicitly in terms of divine power, spiritual practice, and moral authority. It expresses the themes and tensions of fertility, birth, and death, feminine and masculine forms of action and power, individuals and collectivities. To understand it as such, however, requires explicating various elements and assumptions about Maasai economic, political, social, and cultural lifeways in historical perspective. This chapter builds on the overview of Maasai life presented in the introduction to explore the centrality of gender and power to Maasai religious beliefs, practices, and experiences in the past.

To do so, it draws on ethnographic, oral historical, archival, and missionary sources, all of which pose daunting challenges to such a historical reconstruction.[2] For example, some early commentators, such as Hollis (1905, 1910, 1943), relied primarily on just one or two key informants.[3] Others read and reported, often without direct attribution, each other's claims, making it difficult sometimes to untangle what they actually witnessed from what they merely repeated.[4] Most described Maasai religion (like other aspects of Maasai lives) in essentialist, ahistorical terms. Finally, many of the early accounts were clearly influenced by the logics, assumptions, and agendas of race, gender, imperialism, modernity, and Christianity that dominated their time.[5] Nonetheless, like all good historians, I have tried to compare, contextualize, and critically read (and read against) the available sources to tease out key aspects of Maasai belief and practice. I have also drawn on contemporary accounts provided by my informants and more recent studies of Maasai religion, including Århem (1989, 1990, 1991), Voshaar (1979, 1998a, 1998b),[6] Fosbrooke (1948), Benson (1974), Hillman (1993), Hauge (1979), and Olsson (1977, 1989). None of these is free from the problems described above,[7] but most are based on long-term observation, discussion, and participation with Maasai in Tanzania and Kenya and, as such, offer important critical and comparative material.

Gender and Power in Maasai Religion

Despite their gradual economic and political marginalization in the colonial period, as described in the introduction, Maasai women retained their involvement in the "religious" domains of everyday life. Maasai women have long been perceived, and have perceived themselves, as more spiritual and religiously observant than Maasai men. As Merker (1910 [1904]: 207) observed as early as the 1890s, while everyone prayed "in times of famine, danger, illness or other visitations" and men prayed on special occasions, women prayed throughout the day to their deity, Eng'ai.[8] Hollis (1905: 345, n.1) made a similar observation. Moreover, female principles, such as an emphasis on fertility, birth, and nurture, and a reverence for nature, were central to Maasai religious beliefs and practices.[9] But certain Maasai men, the *iloibonok*, also shared a close relationship with Eng'ai as diviners and prophets. As these brief examples suggest, issues of gender and power were expressed by and reflected in Maasai religion. This chapter explores key beliefs and practices in Maasai religion, with a focus on the gendered aspects. Although many of these beliefs and practices remain today, I use the past tense to acknowledge the dynamic circumstances of Maasai lives. In addition to change over time, there was also variation among and within Maasai sections in Tanzania and Kenya that were further exacerbated by these changes (Fosbrooke 1948). Moreover, the porousness of Maasai ethnic boundaries through adoption, assimilation, conquest, marriage, and migration produced a similar porousness of Maasai religious boundaries, as new practices and ideas were adopted or old ones were disbursed into neighboring groups such as Kikuyu, Samburu, and so forth (cf. Hobley 1911). Both the temporal and spatial variations may also account for some of the discrepancies and contradictions among the myths, stories, and exegesis reproduced by different missionaries, scholars, and Maasai informants.[10]

21

The Maasai Deity—Eng'ai

Female figures were central to Maasai religious beliefs and origin stories, beginning with the most important, their deity, Eng'ai.[11] The feminine prefix "En," Eng'ai's attributes, and many metaphorical references marked Eng'ai as a predominantly although not exclusively female deity.[12] Eng'ai was addressed by such phrases as "She of the black garment" (*Nolkila orok*), "My mother with wet clothes" (*Yieyio nashal inkilani*), and "She of the growing grasses" (*Noompees*) (Voshaar 1998a: 137). The alternate meanings of Eng'ai as "rain" and "sky" (and for some, "heaven")[13] and the metaphorical references in the above sayings—to wetness, darkness, motherhood, and growth—reinforced the association of Eng'ai with fertility—"(She) Who gives life . . . the one who is fertile and brings fertility" (Voshaar 1998a: 135)—and thus femininity. Eng'ai was therefore understood in feminine terms as the divine principle that created, supported, and nurtured life on earth (Voshaar 1998a: 130–143; Priest 1990).[14] The associations between the creative powers of Eng'ai and women were clear. As Burton (1991: 82) has argued, "Creation did not happen at once; it is instead a process, wherein the birth of any child is further evidence of a divine process that enables the world at hand to exist" (see also Broch-Due 2000).

According to most myths and proverbs, Eng'ai resided in and was one with the sky, and had a dialectical relationship of mutual dependency with *enkop*, the land or earth: *Kerisio Eng'ai o Enkop*, "the sky (or "heaven" in some translations) and the earth are equal" (cf. Mol 1996: 3). Together, Eng'ai and humans, the sky and earth, created and nurtured life; there was a necessary unity and complementarity between them. Eng'ai gave life and humans cared for life and all that Eng'ai had given.

But both humans on earth and Eng'ai in the sky had the ability to alter their relationship. According to one set of myths, this was in fact what happened in the past to distance, but not separate, Eng'ai and humans. Although the versions vary, the gist of the myth is that long ago, the sky and earth, Eng'ai and humans, lived closely together in harmony. Eng'ai offered cattle to OlMaasindat (for some, the first Maasai man); in another version, Eng'ai offered cattle to a Dorobo man (hunter gatherers related to Maasai) and OlMaasindat overheard. Eng'ai dropped a cord (or leather thong) from the sky to the earth and the cattle descended to Ol-Maasindat. The Dorobo man was jealous and unhappy and shot (or cut) the cord. Not only did Eng'ai end the flow of cattle, but She also moved further away from the earth and humans (cf. Hollis 1905: 266–269, 270–

271; Kipuri 1983: 30–31; Voshaar 1998a: 140–141).[15] In John Burton's (1991) comparative study of Nilotic origin myths, ropes often appear as the link between the world of the divine and the world of humans. He suggests that the severing of the rope "recalls the local or universal moment of birth, when two bodies of life once so closely connected, are from that moment divided and distinct entities evermore" (1991: 84). As such, the severing of the rope emphasizes the associations between Eng'ai, creation, birth, and femininity; "both individual and collective origins result from the severing of a connection; life begins through the negation of unity" (Burton 1991: 89).

Eng'ai was often described as having dual aspects: as the Black God (*Eng'ai Narok*), She was kind, helpful, and compassionate to Maasai, while as the Red God (*Eng'ai Nanyokie*), She could be harmful and vengeful.[16] Merker (1910 [1904]: 205), however, argued that although these were the correct literal translations, they "should be translated as meaning 'the divine red,' 'the divine white' [He mentioned *Eng'ai Naibor,* the 'White God'], 'the divine black,' as people do not actually see any God or likeness of God in them, nor yet anything to worship as God." Nevertheless, Hollis (1905: 264–265) reported the following myth about the two gods, a black one and a red one (note he uses masculine articles, although feminine ones are used in the original Maa text):

> There are two gods, a black one [eng-aï narok] and a red one [eng-aï nanyokye]. The black god is good, and the red god is malicious. One day the black god said to the red one: "let us give the people some water for they are dying of hunger." The red god agreed, and told the other one to turn on the water. This he did, and it rained heavily.
>
> After a time the red god told the black one to stop the water as sufficient rain had fallen. The black god was, however, of opinion [*sic*] that the people had not had enough, so he refused. Both remained silent after this, and the rain continued till the next morning, when the red god again said that enough had fallen. The black god then turned off the water.
>
> A few days later the black god proposed that they should give the people some more water as the grass was very dry. The red god, however, was recalcitrant and refused to allow the water to be turned on again. They disputed for some time, and at length the red god threatened to kill the people, whom he said the black god was spoiling. At this the black god said: "I shall not allow my people to be killed," and he has been able to protect them, for he lives near at hand, whilst the red god is above him.
>
> When one hears the thunder crashing in the heavens it is the red god who is trying to come to the earth to kill human beings; and when one hears the distant rumbling, it is the black god who is saying: "Leave them alone, do not kill them."

Although the story speaks of two gods, most evidence suggests that Eng'ai Narok and Eng'ai Nanyokie referred to aspects of Eng'ai, not separate deities.[17] Merker (1910 [1904]: 205) and others also reported that Maasai spoke of Eng'ai Naibor, "the White God."

In the Beginning . . .

Maasai origin stories, like such stories everywhere, varied by historical period and narrator. I would argue that the variation of these stories illustrates the dynamism of Maasai religion, as it changed and adapted in relation to the dispersal, intermingling, and assimilation of other groups by Maasai that was central to the very formation, and expansion, of Maasai ethnic identity (Galaty 1993a, 1993b; Hodgson 2001a). Most variations, however, featured another female figure, Naiterukop (lit. "She who begins the earth"), as the creator of the first human(s) (cf. Jacobs 1965: 198; Kipuri 1983: 27; Mol 1996: 271). Naiterukop was variously portrayed as a demi-god who gave birth to the first humans (Krapf 1854: 8–9, 1968 [1860]: 360; Fosbrooke 1948: 3), part of the first human couple who gave birth to Maasai (Benson 1974: 81), the first woman "who appeared at God's command from the bowels of the earth" to mate with the first man, Maitumbe (who came down "from heaven") (Merker 1910 [1904]: 308, 306), the first human sent down the rope by Eng'ai (Benson 1974: 81), or the wife of Maa (sometimes known as Maasindat), the first person, who gave birth to Maasai (Hodgson 2001a: 23). Krapf (1854: 17–18) reported that Naiterukop was in fact "the mediator between god and men," and Maasai directed their prayers to her (see also Johnston 1886: 418). Like Eng'ai, Naiterukop was sometimes, despite the feminine prefix "Na" and her function as a Creator, gendered male in these stories, but these seem to be a product of mistranslation or missionary and scholarly refusal to acknowledge the possibility of a female Creator (see, for example, Benson 1974: 81; Jacobs 1965: 198; Krapf 1854: 8–9, 1968 [1860]: 360). Voshaar (1998a: 65, n.3), however, argues that "I did not hear of 'her' in terms of creation or as being 'the first man' but rather as an organizing mythical female principle that is used in various ways to understand various societal institutions and organisations in Maa."[18]

Other origin stories described how people originated from a leg or knee or were dropped from the sky by Eng'ai (Benson 1974: 79–80). Coming from "above," near Eng'ai, as Benson argues, thus distinguished them from wild animals. He reports a story that attributed the creation of wild animals to Nenauner:

A legendary monster supposedly half-human, half-stone who had hair all over its body. The name is associated with *enauner*, the stick used by women to make holes in the ground, since the noise made by the monster's stone leg as it walked is similar to the thumping of the stick in the ground. He is felt to have created all the wild animals and phenomena of fear that the Maasai have. (Benson 1974: 80–81)[19]

Merker (1910 [1904]: 306, 270) claimed that Nenaunir [*sic*] ("a dragon") lived on earth and "devoured man and beast." Eng'ai had to kill it in order to begin creation. As the myth suggests, Maasai associated hair with the wild, wild animals, and liminal states. All Maasai therefore shaved or depilated their body hair, except for *ilmurran* and people in certain liminal states, such as new mothers, newly circumcised men and women, and family members in mourning (Merker 1910 [1904]: 147–148). Europeans were (and still are) often called *Loljuju*, "hairy monsters," because of their body hair (Hollis 1905: 316).

Gender, Nature, and Religious Symbolism

As pastoralists, Maasai had a close customary relationship to and dependence on the environment for their sustenance and social reproduction. Nature and its elements were understood as manifestations of Eng'ai or expressions of Her will, and were therefore central to Maasai religious beliefs and practices. The symbolic meanings of these aspects of nature were dynamic and contextual; they were shaped (and reshaped) through their use in daily and ritual practice, and, in turn, shaped the form and content of these practices. Few of these elements were explicitly gendered, although they were sometimes ascribed gender through their symbolic associations and use in practice.

First and foremost, Maasai were concerned with having sufficient grass and water to feed their livestock. Not surprisingly, then, grass and certain liquids (milk, spittle, honey, and blood) featured in their religious entreaties, practices, and ceremonies as near-sacred symbols of and gifts from Eng'ai. Grass was a sign of welcome, peace, and blessing. It was often held in the hands, tied as a sprig to one's clothing, placed in the neck of a calabash, or draped on someone's shoulders as they were being blessed.[20] Johnston (1902: 832) described how Maasai used grass to request peace or reconciliation: "When wishing to make peace or deprecate the hostility of man or god, a Maasai plucks and holds in his hand wisps of grass, or, in default of grass, green leaves." In addition, he reported that "Grass is often laid between the forks of trees as a party of warriors proceeds on an expedition, and grass is thrown after the warriors by their sweethearts. The sorcerers and 'Laibonok,' or priests, precede nearly every mystic action by the plucking of grass" (Johnston 1902: 833; cf. Johnston 1886: 417). Hollis (1905: 289) recounted even more symbolic uses of grass:

> Whenever there is a drought, the women fasten grass on to their clothes, and go and offer prayers to God. If a warrior beats a boy on the grazing ground, the boy tears up some grass, and when the warrior sees that the child has grass in his hand, he stops beating him. Again, if the Masai fight with an enemy, and wish to make peace, they hold out some grass as a sign. Whenever warriors return from a raid, and it is desired to praise those who have killed some of the enemy, a girl takes a small gourd of milk, and having covered it with green grass, sprinkles it over them. Then, if people move from one kraal to another, they tie grass on to the gourds. Should one man ask forgiveness of another with grass in his hand and his request is not attended to, it is said that the man who refuses to listen to his prayer is a Dorobo, and that he does not know about cattle.

As he remarked, "The Masai love grass very much, for they say: 'God [Engai] gave us cattle and grass, we do not separate the things which God has given us'" (Hollis 1905: 290). French-Sheldon (1892: 383) reported that Maasai women always carried a bunch of grass "which they fasten to their cowhide belts or under some of their iron rings, in order to have it at hand when an occasion arises to manifest amity."[21]

Milk, like cattle, was a gift from Eng'ai, and as a "sacred fluid" (Johnston 1886: 425), it was symbolically associated with women (who produced and processed it and controlled its distribution) and fertility (cf. Talle 1990). Women milked cows twice a day, and milk was the preferred daily staple food. It was sprinkled on the ground at the beginning of each milking, on humans from a calabash with grass in its mouth for blessing, and offered to family, visitors, and even strangers. Thomson reported that:

> Next to grass comes milk [as the most sacred thing among Maasai]. No liberties may be taken with it. The milk must be drawn in calabashes specially reserved for its reception, into which water is not allowed to enter—cleanliness being assured by woodashes. To boil it is a heinous offence. . . . It is believed that the cattle would cease to give milk. The cows, it may be remarked, are never milked, except in the dark. (Thomson 1968 [1885]: 260)

According to Hollis, both milk and grass, and the associations between women and cattle, featured in Maasai peace ceremonies:

If the Masai make peace [osotwa] with other people, whether enemies [ilman-gati] or other Masai with whom they have fought, the warriors seize two important elders, and take a cow which has a calf, and a woman who has a baby; and the enemy do the same. They then meet together at a certain spot, everybody present holding grass in his right hand, and exchange the cattle, the Masai taking the enemy's cow and the enemy the Masai's. The enemy's child is suckled at the breast of the Masai woman, and the Masai baby at the breast of the woman belonging to the enemy. After this they return to their kraals, knowing that a solemn peace has been entered into. Thus was peace restored between the Lumbwa Masai and the Masai proper, in the year of the sun [1883], at the place called the Ford of Sangaruna [on the Ruvu or Pangani river]. (Hollis 1905: 321–322)

Milk and grass were joined in many other ceremonies as well (see below), and a mixture of milk and water (enkare pus, "gray water" or "blue water") was often sprinkled on ritual participants for blessing. In our interviews, contemporary Maasai recognized the equivalence of milk and grass, explaining that cattle transformed grass into milk. As such, milk and grass were both metonymic symbols of the treasured cattle that Eng'ai had given them long ago. Thus, through their control and distribution of the sacred gift of milk, Maasai women ensured the daily reproduction of their households and forged horizontal links of friendship and exchange with neighbors, strangers, and even enemies.[22]

Spittle, a person's own liquid, was also a sign of blessing. To spit on a person (usually their head or hands) or a thing (such as a gift) was to bless them or express reverence. Newborns were spat on constantly, elders spat into the hands of juniors to bless them and wish them well, and ritual participants often spat a mixture of milk and water on whoever was being honored, prayed for, or blessed.[23] As Thomson (1968 [1885]: 166–167) reported with great glee:

With them [Maasai] it [spitting] expresses the greatest good-will and the best of wishes. . . . You spit when you meet and you do the same when leaving. You seal your bargain in a similar manner. . . . The more copiously I spat upon them, the greater was their delight; and with pride they would retail to their friends how the white medicine-man [Thomson claimed to be an oloiboni] honoured them, and would point with the greatest satisfaction to the ocular proof of the agreeable fact.

Similarly, Baumann (1894: 165) noted that "As a sign of peace, the Maasai present a bundle of grass, upon which they spit. Spitting plays a large role; I had to spit on all of the small gifts that I presented, such as glass beads, etc." Hollis (1905: 316) described how "If small children salute very old men, the latter spit on them and say: 'May God give you long life and grey hairs like mine.' " Honey beer was also often spit on people as a sign of blessing, as honey signified the sweetness of Eng'ai.

Blood, either by itself or mixed with milk, was a prized form of nourishment that all Maasai drank on occasion. It was also given to newborns, new mothers, and girls and boys after circumcision to replenish their strength and vitality (Macdonald 1899: 233). Maasai men would bleed an animal (usually any cattle except good milch cows or cows with calves) by tying a leather strap around the bottom of its neck, shooting an arrow into the bulging vein, then collecting the spouting blood in a gourd (Merker 1910 [1904]: 174; picture in Hollis 1905: 257). Maasai are also reported to have had a form of "blood-brotherhood" whereby they established peace and a formal kinship-like association with non-Maasai through cutting themselves and exchanging tastes of the blood (or meat dipped in the blood).[24] Blood was thus the symbol of life, vitality, and kinship.

Maasai also symbolically associated trees and shrubs, called *olcani* (pl. *ilkeek*), with Eng'ai. *Olcani* also meant "medicine," and the roots, bark, berries, and leaves of certain trees and shrubs were used as medicine to treat specific diseases. Hollis (1905: 335–342) listed many trees and their medicinal and other uses, including as purgatives, as fever medicines, for nerves, for problems of the spleen, and, among *ilmurran*, for bravery and strength. Usually the part of the tree being used was chewed, or it was crushed or ground, then boiled in milk, water, and/or blood and drunk. Since disease and death, like health and birth, were derived from Eng'ai, the power of *olcani* to heal and protect was understood as a divine intervention mediated through human knowledge and practice. As Hollis (1905: 334–335) reported: "When a Masai falls ill, it is said to be God's sickness [*emweiyan e'-ng-Aï*]. Some people know of medicines, which they give to sick people to cure them." Of course trees, plants, and their parts were also used to make cord, ropes, clubs, spear handles, and sticks; to fumigate milk gourds; and to provide firewood, perfumes, toothbrushes, body decoration, poison, and material for curing livestock skins (Hollis 1905: 335–342). Storrs-Fox (1930: 461) described how passing Maasai would put grass or leaves on the holes of certain old trees as a prayer "to be old like this tree."

In addition, *oreteti*, a species of parasitic fig tree, was believed to be particularly sacred.[25] The *oreteti* tree spread and grew by lodging its seeds in the cracks and crevices of other trees (fig. 1.1). As Johnston (1902: 82) described:

Fig. 1.1. Sekot and Lepayian stand in front of a sacred *oreteti* tree near Mti Mmoja. The descending vines and rising roots produce a tangled thicket that links Eng'ai and the world. Photo by author, 2000.

Little by little the fig swells and grows, and throws out long, snakish, whitish roots and branches, until by degrees it has enveloped the whole of the main trunk of its victim in glistening coils of glabrous root and branch. Gradually these enveloping tentacles meet and coalesce, until at last the whole of the trunk of the original tree is covered from sight and absorbed by the now massive fig-tree, the branches of which radiate in all directions, and sometimes in their loops and contorted forms come quite close to the ground. The green figs, which grow straight out of the trunk, are sometimes eaten by the boys and girls of the Masai, and their seniors propitiate the tree by killing a goat, bringing blood in a calabash, and pouring it out over the base of the tree-trunk, about the branches of which also they will strew grass.

Oreteti trees held water in their trunks and fissures, their sap was a reddish color, and their leaves contained a milky white substance. Maasai saw these vertical thickets as links growing from the sky and Eng'ai down to the earth and humans; they were therefore considered holy places where people could be closer to Eng'ai. Maasai men and women visited these holy trees either alone or in groups to pray, worship, and plead to Eng'ai for rain and other blessings. An *oreteti* tree viewed by Dallas (1931: 40) showed a long history of Maasai offerings:

> As evidence of the antiquity of the tradition regarding this tree may be cited the quantity of ornaments and other objects, chiefly of crude metal or wire, which, having been twisted round the young stems of the parasite growth, are now deeply embedded in the wood. This practice is still maintained, and no Masai will touch the tree without having attached some trinket to some handy portion of the trunk.

The leaves, bark, and branches of the *oreteti* tree were also used in religious ceremonies and prayers or to request blessing or forgiveness. Hollis, for example, reported that: "If one man curses another, and the curse has taken effect, the man who has been cursed calls the other and asks him to spit on him and to tie on his arm a strip of cord made from this fig-tree [*oreteti*]. The cord is first of all dipped in hot milk and then four beads are threaded on it." Dallas (1931) noted that Matapato Maasai women visited an *oreteti* tree to pray to Eng'ai for children. The ceremony was attended only by "married women young enough to bear children," and described as follows by his presumably male informants:

> The ceremony takes place in the twilight before sunrise, and all the women taking part in it are completely nude except for their ornaments. Each woman carries two long narrow gourds, that in the right hand containing milk and that in the left hand honey, each gourd being loosely stoppered with a twist of grass. The women form a ring around the tree and circle about it in a measured dance to the rhythm of a chant, in which one leads and the others sing the chorus. At a given signal all the women lift the gourds above their heads and precipitate their contents in the direction of the tree.
> The magical power of the deity prevents the ejection of the contents of the gourds held by the woman or women who are witches; even, so I was assured, if the grass stopper is removed, the witch cannot shake out the contents of her gourd in the direction of the tree. If, however, the gourd is handled by an innocent woman, the god will readily accept the offering, even if the gourd is tightly stoppered with grass. My informants professed to be ignorant of the words of the chant or incantation sung by the women as they dance round the tree. (Dallas 1931: 40–41; see also Shaffer 1985: 154–156)

This ceremony underlines the connections among women, fertility, and Eng'ai, and the use of certain natural substances such as milk, honey, and grass as sacred symbols.

Certain mountains also figured in Maasai religious cosmology and stories as the homes of Eng'ai or Her descendants. *Oldoinyo Orok,* the "Black Mountain" (Mount Meru), was recognized as holy and a home of Eng'ai. *Oldoinyo Oibor,* the "White Mountain" (snow-capped Mount Kilimanjaro), was sometimes referred to as the home of Naiterukop or Eng'ai (Johnston 1886: 417; Krapf 1854: 8–9, 13; 1968 [1860]: 360, 365), as was *Oldoinyo Oigeri,* the "Spotted Mountain" (Mount Kenya) (Johnston 1886: 418). *Oldoinyo Leng'ai,* the "Mountain of God," is an active volcano that still spouts smoke and ash in the Rift Valley. Its occasional eruptions signaled the wrath of Eng'ai (Thomson 1968 [1885]: 246; Farler 1882: 738; cf. Wakefield 1870: 306). Nonetheless, ritual delegations of barren Maasai women (*olamal,* pl. *ilamala*), led by elder men, regularly visited Oldoinyo Leng'ai to pray to Eng'ai to bless them with children.

As part of their reverence for nature as Eng'ai's creation, Maasai also treated wild and domestic animals with respect. Cattle, of course, were prized as the primary source of food, social worth, and Maasai identity. Each animal was distinguished by name, based on its colors, size, and other physical features (Merker 1910 [1904]: 175–176). Goats and sheep were also marked as individuals, although with less fanfare and prestige. Both cattle and smallstock were sacrificed and/or slaughtered during most ritual ceremonies, usually by suffocation.[26] Historically, Maasai did not hunt or eat wild animals (*olowuaru*), including the large herds of wildebeest, antelopes, buffalo, and zebra that roamed their plains (Merker 1910 [1904]: 117; Johnston 1886: 424). Junior men, however, hunted lions for protection and prestige. Snakes were usually left alone, and there was a belief that certain very prominent men returned as black pythons (Hinde and Hinde 1901: 101). Birds were never eaten, but certain species were killed so that their bodies and feathers could be used to create elaborate headdresses for newly circumcised boys. *Ilmurran* especially prized ostrich feathers for their headdresses.

Other natural phenomena, especially those concerned with the sky and weather, were also attributed to the interventions of Eng'ai and read as expressions of divine power and judgment—rain as blessing, drought as displeasure, thunder and lightning as anger, rainbows as approval, and comets as portents of bad luck (see many of the myths recounted in Hollis 1905; Baumann 1894: 163; Merker 1910 [1904]: 205–207). As Merker (1910 [1904]: 206) reported:

> The eldest of Eng'ai's children, the girl Barsai, brings the greatest of all benefits, rain, to mankind, and thereby shows that God is pleased with what is going on on earth. The eldest son, Ol gurugur, proclaims through thunder and lightning, that God is angry with mankind because of its bad behavior, and exhorts

it at the same time to improve. A rainbow is the sign that God is pleased with the deeds of the Masai, and is therefore well-disposed towards them. Winds and storms are the breaths of the angry God; hail announces the coming of rain. A thunderbolt is a sign that abundant rain will now fall and that the people will be spared ill-luck, such as cattle plagues and smallpox. A comet, on the other hand, portends bad luck, illness and death will befall man and beast. The appearance of a very bright comet in the 1880s was soon followed by the greatest cattle plague, rinderpest and pleuro-pneumonia.

The gendered dimension of this tale is also intriguing, with Eng'ai's daughter, Barsai, blessing humans with rain (and thus fertility) while her brother Ol gurugur threatens and frightens.

Other Manifestations of Eng'ai

These and other natural elements were associated with and expressed in the meaning and use of colors in Maasai religious cosmology. White (of milk, animal fat, and the white cumulus clouds that appear after a rain storm) was a sign of blessing, peace, and contentment (Benson 1974: 82–83). White chalk was often used to draw special protective designs on the face, legs, or torso of certain ritual participants; they were also sometimes anointed with animal fat (see fig. 1.2). Maasai spoke of Eng'ai Naibor, the "White God" (Merker 1910 [1904]: 205) or the "God with the white stomach." A stomach was white and content from being filled with the milk that was Eng'ai's gift to Maasai (Benson 1974: 82–83). French-Sheldon (1892: 383) described how Maasai brought a "white goat of peace" to her camp to slaughter and make "blood-brotherhood" with her. White beads also featured in Maasai beadwork.

Black (of the dark rain clouds) was a particularly auspicious color that signified holiness, respect, and "quiet gravity" (Merker 1910 [1904]: 124). Black (or dark blue) cloth was supposed to be worn by fertile women, and is still worn by people in holy or liminal states (such as new mothers, newly circumcised boys and girls, or prophets and prophetesses) to entreat Eng'ai's special protection. Eng'ai was referred to as Eng'ai Narok, the "Black God," when She was being supportive and caring. All-black animals were sacrificed in certain important ceremonies such as major age-set rituals, to entreat Eng'ai on behalf of a sick or dying person, or to beg Eng'ai's forgiveness for a grievous misdeed, such as killing a pregnant woman on a raid (Merker 1910 [1904]: 200, 210). As Merker (1910 [1904]: 207) noted:

> In cases of severe illness, a black ram or black ox is slaughtered, and part of its blood is poured on the ground of the hut as a sacrifice to Eng'ai. If the sick

Fig. 1.2. Maasai women in preparation for a ritual (which Hinde calls a "medical ceremony"), with circular white chalk markings on their faces, ca. 1900. Reproduced from Hinde and Hinde (1901: 73).

> person is an old man or old woman with numerous descendants, a cow, again black, in calf is slaughtered. The calf is left outside the village [enkang'] for Eng'ai, after the place in which it lies has been sprinkled with water from the uterus.

In addition, dark blue beads (which were categorized as black) (*emurt narok*) were worn by married men and women to mark the sanctity of their marital bonds and by other special classes of persons who were seen as having a special relationship to Eng'ai, such as *ilaunoni* (see below).

The meaning of red was somewhat contradictory. On the one hand red clothing (formerly leather rubbed with ocher, now red cloth) and skin (achieved by rubbing a mixture of ocher and cow fat) were considered distinctive markers of Maasai ethnic identity. As the color of blood, red signified kinship, life, and vitality. Hollis (1905: 323), for example, described "the ceremony of the red bead" whereby kinship was established through the exchange of a red bead (*ol-tureshi*): "When a Masai wishes to make a person his brother or sister, he gives that person a red bead, called ol-tureshi. After performing this ceremony, they call one another Patureshi, i.e., The giver and receiver of a bead, instead of by their proper names."

On the other hand, red could express anger and destruction (too much vitality, perhaps?). When the actions of Eng'ai were seen as harmful and vengeful, She was called Eng'ai Nanyokie, the "Red God." Merker claimed that red was the color of war and that the most important mark on an *ilmurran*'s shield was the red warrior mark (*osirat onyokie*) (1910 [1904]: 124, 79). Red was also associated with the relentless heat of the dry season. Red was therefore the color of power; it had the potential to be creative or destructive, or even both—destroying in order to create. The red of blood and fire best illustrate the transformative power of red. At the end of the rainy season, Maasai set fires to burn dried grasses and shrubs so that the early rains would bring tender green shoots for their cattle. The dynamic power of creation and destruction was also expressed in the red sky that marked the beginning and end of the day: "Maasai call the redness of the morning and evening sky 'ngai nanjugi [Red God]'" (Merker 1910 [1904]: 205).

These three main colors of Eng'ai—white, black, and red—were used to decorate the shields of *ilmurran,* the sites of ritual ceremonies such as female circumcision, the bodies of ritual participants, and other significant objects, places, and people.[27] Chalk was used for white, charcoal or ashes for black, and ocher for red. In addition, these and many other colors associated with nature—the blue of the sky, the green of the grass, the orange of the sun—appeared in meaningful patterns and arrangements in the elaborately beaded ornaments, jewelry, and clothing crafted by Maasai women.[28] Thus Eng'ai was sometimes referred to as *Parmuain,* "Multicolored God."

Directionality was also encoded and expressed in Maasai religious practices. As Merker (1910 [1904]: 207, n.1) explained:

> The Masai have the following names for the points of the compass (e'lubot Eng ai—the sides of God): North—kopekob, or kabekob, which also stands for the land of their origin. South—o'meroi, the battle; it is the direction in which the Masai, wandering southwards, always had to engage in battles with the old-established el meg. [used by Merker to mean "enemy"] East—engilebunoto eng olon, the sun comes up from thence. West—endiojeroto eng olon, the sun goes down there.

As a result, north and east were seen as more propitious directions than south and west (cf. Hurskainen 1990: 71). These directions determined where men and women faced when they prayed, the location of entrances to houses and homesteads, the placement of dying people and the corpses of prominent men and *iloibonok* during burial, and other practices.

Maasai also believed that certain numbers and shapes were more auspicious than others. Although Maasai counted, and every number had a corresponding hand sign, they never counted people or cattle, but just "knew" how many there were (Merker 1910 [1904]: 153–156).[29] Auspicious numbers, especially two, four, and eight, shaped many aspects of daily and ritual practice, such as the number of people in ritual delegations (*olamal*, pl. *ilamala*), cattle or smallstock collected for certain ceremonies or ritual occasions, entrances to homesteads or ritual sites, times a ritual question should be asked, timing and duration of major rituals, and composition of ritual patterns on bodies, hide, shields, and more.[30] According to Hurskainen (1990: 62–63), the number four signified completeness, good luck, and harmony, while the number eight (four doubled) meant the same thing, but gave "more weight to that which is being symbolized." Other numbers, such as nine, were believed to be inauspicious. As Hurskainen (1990: 64) noted, nine (*naudo*) had an alternative term, *enturuj*, which meant something that was forbidden, prohibited, or taboo. Forty-nine, for example, was the number of cattle that the clan of a murderer had to pay to the victim's family.

Circles were favored shapes, as evidenced by the layout of homesteads and houses, patterns of face paintings and other designs, and the common configurations of female singer-dancers and ritual participants. Circles symbolized unity and inclusion, and concentric circles (such as the houses and livestock pens within homesteads) signified the necessary parts that made up the whole. Circles also translated time into space, representing the repetitive cycles of nature and humanity, the endless rhythms of life and death that characterized the world created and nurtured by Eng'ai. One might even consider it a quintessentially female shape—of the female-controlled hearths and homes, the rounded bellies of pregnant women, the coils of iron wrapped around their arms and legs—as opposed to the phallic, linear imagery of men—in their dancing lines, spears, swords, and sticks.

Another principle of Maasai cosmology was that of symmetry, as reflected in their preference for circles and even numbers.[31] But it was also expressed in the contrast and complementarity of opposites, especially male and female. Thus, for example, the female sun (*enkolong'*) gave birth to the new day, while the male moon (*olapa*) brought it to a close (Merker 1910 [1904]: 206). Fire was obtained by drilling a hard stick ("the man") into a flat piece of wood ("his wife") (Hollis 1905: 342). Ritual delegations were often composed of an equal number of men and women. Right and left were also culturally elaborated as organizing principles of Maasai life. In addition to the alternation of co-wives on the right- and left-hand side of the cattle gates, male age-sets were divided in the "right-hand" group (which was circumcised first) and the "left-hand" group (Hollis 1905: 261–263). Finally, black and red not only distinguished contrasting aspects of Eng'ai, but also were used to name the two moieties into which all clans were organized, Odomong'i ("of the red cattle") and Orokiteng' ("of the black cattle") (Hollis 1905: 260). All of these suggest that it was complementarity, not equality, that shaped Maasai life in general and gender relations in particular. Although women were viewed as the creators and nurturers, procreation, as suggested by the description of making fire, required the joining of the different capabilities of men and women to succeed. Thus, unity, birth, and the reproduction of life were achieved only through the contrast and conjunction of opposites.

One could argue, in fact, that the complementary worlds of Eng'ai and humans, men and women, were literally and metaphorically united by the ties that linked them: the cord that was cut between Eng'ai and humans, the branches and roots of the sacred *oreteti* trees, the ties of descent, marriage, clan, and friendship that structured and organized their social world. All of these bonds were predicated on the primary bond of the umbilical cord (*osotua*) through which mothers nurtured their children, as Eng'ai nurtured Her people. These parallels were certainly clear to Maasai, for whom the word *osotua* meant not just umbilical cord, but a special friendship that was usually established by the exchange of livestock, and peace (cf. Mol 1996: 321). Moreover, because of its inherent flexibility, a cord could be both male and female: twisted to become a female circle or stretched taut to become a male line. It therefore literally tied men and women together in both social and religious terms (cf. Burton 1991). Like the lines of straight wire that women coiled around their legs and arms, or the strips of leather tied around fingers and necks as amulets, the cord as at once male and female perhaps reflected the somewhat ambiguous gender coding of Eng'ai Herself.[32]

Religious Practice

Although Maasai men and women shared a common set of beliefs about and concepts of Eng'ai, there were gendered differences in their relationship to Eng'ai, their modes of prayer and praise, and other aspects of their religious practices and beliefs. The Maasai language offered a rich vocabulary for addressing Eng'ai, including *aomon* (to pray, to beg), *asaia* (to beseech, to beg, to ask, to pray), *aserem* (to pray, to praise, to worship, to honor), *aisis* (to praise), and *aikilesh* (to pray).[33] Many prayers were made through *isin-koliotin* (sg. *osinkolio*), song-dances performed in a variety of styles according to who was performing, the occasion, and the message. The songs were usually in a call and response manner (*eoko*), with an individual leader and a group chorus.

Maasai women, as mentioned before, were responsible for daily medi-ations with Eng'ai. From the first early morning milking to their final step inside their doorway at night, women prayed constantly, incorporating the rich symbolism of grass and milk as signs of fertility, blessing, and bounty. They prayed facing either north, or toward the rising sun at dawn and the setting sun at dusk (Merker 1910 [1904]: 207).[34] According to Merker (1910 [1904]: 207):

> While praying she raises her arms towards heaven, and holds bunches of grass in both hands, or one only in the left hand, having fastened several blades of grass round her upper right arm. With each prayer a woman offers a little milk before God. She either squeezes a few drops from her own breast, of necessity the right breast, or she pours some on the ground out of a gourd. She makes the same offering at the morning and evening milking, allowing some milk to flow to the ground both from the cow's udders and from the receptacle for milk.

Their most important prayers were during the morning and evening milking of cattle when they would sprinkle some milk on the ground, thanking and entreating Eng'ai for the continued protection, preservation, expansion, and prosperity of their family and herds (Hollis 1905: 290; Merker 1910 [1904]: 207).

Women also prayed and praised Eng'ai collectively in songs when gath-ered together for chores, for an afternoon rest under a shade tree, or at ceremonies and celebrations (see fig. 1.3) (Merker 1910 [1904]: 204–211). Merker (1910 [1904]: 209) described a "festival of prayer . . . called 'Ng ai ol adjo—May God hear the word," in which married women gathered to pray to Eng'ai for children (cf. Johnston 1902: 833; Shaffer 1985: 46–47):

> The women gather in, or beside, the village as early as the morning, together with a witchdoctor (ol goiatiki) [a minor *oloiboni*] and place themselves round him in a circle. Each woman receives an amulet from him, which she hangs on the hip-knot of her leather garment. The witchdoctor then sprinkles her head and shoulders with a medicine which contains milk and honeybeer, as well as one of his secret nostrums, for which he is rewarded with several sheep.

Fig. 1.3. Maasai women singing together in a large circle at a celebration, ca. 1900. Reproduced from Merker (1910 [1904]: 57).

> The women then dance and sing throughout the day under a shady tree, and in the village all through the night until the grey dawn. In their songs they repeat the following prayer incessantly: 'Ng ai atasaia, 'j' oshiage aomon, kiamon ag' iye kiaomon en engera, en golobi en aisho—God I entreat thee always, I pray, we pray to thee alone, we pray for children, for a birth for the unfruitful wife.

As with the requests in this song for children, women's prayers and songs reflected the central concerns of their lives: thankfulness for milk, cattle, children, and health.[35]

Women also implored Eng'ai for success on raids. As Thomson (1968 [1885]: 253) recounted: "[On the day of the raid], the women of the kraal went outside before sunrise, with grass dipped in the cream of cow's milk. Then they danced and invoked Ng'ai for favorable issue to the enterprise, after which they threw the grass in the direction of the enemy." Young men were also involved; they "spent several hours at their devotions, howling out in the most ludicrous street-singer fashion, 'Aman Ngăi-ăi! Aman Mbaratien!' (We pray to God! we pray to Mbaratien! [a major *oloiboni*])."[36]

Maasai men prayed as well, just less frequently. Merker (1910 [1904]: 208) claimed that there were some married men who entreated Eng'ai:

Every morning to preserve the health of themselves and their belongings, and at the same time to give them a goodly number of wives, children and cattle. These, however, are exceptions. As a rule they [men] content themselves with saluting God in the morning when they leave their huts, by spitting several times towards the north, and sometimes towards the rising sun as well. The prayer of the old men runs: 'Ng ai pasinai, tadjabage ai nanu, njage e magilo—Oh God, protect me too, give me strength. The younger men, the warriors, pray in the morning and evening during such meals. They also pray daily on raiding expeditions, in the morning before marching off, and in the evening after arriving in camp. When praying they squat closely together, while the leader (ol aigwonai) and a benefactor (n'gamnin) walk through the group, strewing blades of grass prized as cattle food on the individuals, and utter the prayer. This runs: 'Ng ai pasinai, nja iyok n gishu, io iyok n gishu kumok, ningua iyok elolonga—God give us cattle, give us many cattle, keep us in health. When they drive the looted cattle together, they sing a song of praise, which begins: Hai narok, oho, Hai kindera iye oh—Black god, oho, we hurry hither, oh!

According to Merker, therefore, although men prayed individually and collectively, these varied in intensity, frequency, and content from the prayers of women. Moreover, both individual and collective prayers were gender-segregated; men and women prayed together only in certain ritual contexts.

For example, in addition to their daily prayers, Merker (1910 [1904]: 208) observed that Maasai men and women held regular, sometimes monthly "prayer festivals (*ologor olgeretti*)" "to pray to God to keep man and beast in health." I include the following detailed description because it illustrates many of the above points about the significance of nature and colors, and men and women, to Maasai religious practice:

A large fire of dry wood (of the ol oirien tree) is lit in the village and on it is thrown green wood with leaves (of the os segi tree), so that it makes a great deal of smoke. A powder made of the wood and bark of the ol mogongora creeper, which smells like incense, is strewn on the fire. The thick column of smoke mounts to heaven and brings the sweet scent to God. A large black ram is then led up, washed carefully with honeybeer, and strewn with powder made of the e matanguju tree. It is then suffocated, skinned, and divided up. Each participant in the feast eats a small piece of the meat, after having roasted it on the ashes. He also receives a strip of the skin from which he makes ring amulets, one for himself and the others for his family. The ring protects the wearer from every form of illness. Men wear it on the middle finger of the right hand, women wear it on their large spiral neck ornaments of iron wire. During the feast, these participants sing incessantly: "Hai narok, oho, Hai kindera iye, oh, Hai narok, oho, Hai ndogo iyok oh!": (Hai ndogo iyok—God nourish us; aidog—that the cattle may drink; ndogo iyok—give us to drink give rain).

The following day the women lay fresh cowdung on the ashes, and knead it into a puree, into which a medicine is mixed that has been prepared and brought for the purpose by an ol goatiki [minor *oloiboni*]. The making of this preparation begins the second part of the prayer fest, which is called ol ogor l on gishu, prayer feast for the cattle. While singing the same songs as before, the women apply the medicine in stripes and curves to the stock, actually to the backbone of cows and ewes, and to the right side of the abdomen of male stock, and such females as have yet not borne progeny. This brings the festival to an end. (Merker 1910 [1904]: 208–209)

Merker's description suggests that the ritual efficacy of these ceremonies was predicated on both gender complementarity and unity—both men and women participated—and the primacy of women's closer relationships to Eng'ai—women were the primary celebrants and officiators.

Finally, in times of crisis and concern, Maasai men and women held elaborate ceremonies to entreat Eng'ai for help. These usually involved prayer and praise song-dances, the ritual slaughter, roasting, and consumption of cattle, the brewing and imbibing of honey beer, and special prayers using elements of nature associated with Eng'ai such as milk, honey, grass, and water. For example, Thomson, who posed as a "white *oloiboni*," recounted how, during the disasters of the 1880s, a group of Maasai men and women he encountered prayed to Eng'ai for help: "They chanted from morn till night an incessant prayer, in the form of 'A-man Ngăiă; A-man Mbaratien' (We pray to God; we pray to Mbaratien). The women, painted in a curious fashion, with white clay on the face, danced in a ring, as they invoked Ngaĭ or Mbaratien in their own fashion" (1968 [1885]: 206–207).

Iloibonok

In addition to the constant intercessions of women, Maasai also tried to influence and understand Eng'ai's actions through their *iloibonok* (sg. *oloiboni*), male ritual leaders who had the powers of prophecy and divination.[37] Waller (1995) and Bernsten (1979a) describe the history of how *iloibonok*, who were originally not Maasai, gradually insinuated themselves, through their alliances with Maasai men in the late eighteenth century, as prophets and diviners in Maasai society.[38] Eventually they were incorporated into the Maasai kinship system as a new, separate sub-clan, Inkidong'i. Their outsider status and special spiritual powers were expressed in several Maasai myths, which claimed that *iloibonok* were direct descendants of Eng'ai, beginning with the first *oloiboni*, Kidongoi (Bernsten 1979a: 115–121). Although the versions differ, most report that Kidongoi was discovered by Maasai on or near a mountain, his special gifts were revealed, and then he was adopted into their family. He then became the apical ancestor of their sub-clan, Inkidong'i.[39] In some versions, he is described as part wild, hairy animal, and part human to characterize the unique powers and liminal status of *iloibonok*.[40] Historically, they initially lived apart from other Maasai, first in the Ngong Hills of Kenya, then later at Ngosua on the Lashaine plains, near what would become Monduli town (Bernsten 1979a: 160–171; Fosbrooke 1948: 5). Eventually, they dispersed and intermingled with other Maasai clans, but many remained around Monduli (including in Emairete and Embopong', two of the three study sites for this book), and tended to live in nucleated settlements. Nonetheless, they were always seen as "outsiders" to some extent, and their powers were viewed with an ambivalent mixture of fear and fascination, in part because they held powers to do good as well as evil and the rest of the community could do little to control them.[41]

Iloibonok were believed to have a uniquely close relationship to Eng'ai, as evidenced in their special powers: "the efficacy of the lybon [*sic*], or medicine-man, lies not in any innate ability of his own, but in his power of intercession with Ngăi, who works through him, and imparts magical virtues to various objects" (Thomson 1968 [1885]: 260; cf. Baumann 1894: 164). As a result, their roles were notoriously misunderstood by early missionaries, travelers, and colonial officers, who variously described them as "the Maasai pope" (Baumann 1894: 164), "chief-sorcerer" (Krapf 1854: 14), "king" (Farler 1882: 734), "magician" (Baumann 1894: 164), and of course "chiefs" (Johnston 1902: 830–831). But as Merker (1910 [1904]: 18) explained, "The designation 'chief' is actually not quite correct, for the ol loibon does not rule directly and exercises no real executive power. He governs only indirectly; the firm belief of his subjects in his prophetic gifts and supernatural powers of magic give him an influence over the destinies of his tribe" (cf. Fosbrooke 1948).

Iloibonok could be divided into two types.[42] The first were major *iloibonok* (*iloibonok kitok*) who had superior powers of prophesy and divination and large followings. They were called upon to appeal to Eng'ai in times of great crisis such as prolonged drought, warfare, or sickness. A few, such as Mbatian and his sons Lenana (see figs. 1.4 and 1.5) and Sendeu, were represented and treated as Maasai "chiefs" by the British in the early colonial period, but they were eventually replaced by a council of elder men as the official "native authority" (Hodgson 2001a: ch. 2; Storrs-Fox 1930: 460–461).[43] In contrast, minor *iloibonok* (sometimes called *olkuyatiki*, pl. *ilkuyatik*, with various spellings), or what Bernsten (1979a: 173), following Fosbrooke (1948: 13), calls "private practitioners," usually did not prophesy, but performed divinations

Fig. 1.4. Lenana, a famous major *oloiboni*, in his customary attire, ca. 1900. Reproduced from Hollis (1905: 326, plate XXIII).

Fig. 1.5. *Oloiboni* Lenana in jacket and hat, ca. 1900. Reproduced from Hollis (1905: 326, plate XXIII).

at the request of individual clients in their local communities to investigate more mundane, everyday problems such as the occasional ill health of people and livestock.[44] As Johnston (1902: 83) wrote, "They are skilled in the interpretation of omens, in the averting of bad luck, and the bringing of rain, and the interpretation of dreams." People consulted them according to their proximity and reputation.

The primary method of divination was to shake stones and other objects from a gourd or horn (called the *enkidong'*), then analyze them with the complex Maasai numerology of auspicious and inauspicious numbers (Hollis

1905: 324; Merker 1910 [1904]: 19; cf. Bernsten 1979a: 121–123, 178–183). A contemporary *oloiboni* interviewed by Bernsten (1979a: 179–180) offered the following explanation of how he used the stones to divine:

> When we shake the gourd, these stones come out and you count them with your hand. You can tell when it is going to rain because there is the stone of rain so that when it comes out you say, "It will rain," because it has appeared. When you prophesy that the land is bad, there are enemies in the land. The stones will see it and say, "It is bad; now the land is bad; something will happen." When the land is good, the stones say, "It is good now," because there is nothing in the land. It can also prophesy a sick person. You say, "I will consult it." You say, "The stone is bad." You can say that that man will die at that time. You try to shake it another time; you say that this person will not die. You consult it again for a woman. They bring the woman to you. You consult the gourd for this woman, to check whether or not she will bear a child. You try to consult the gourd. You see the one [stone] which gives birth, or you say that she will never give birth.

Hollis (1905: 324–330) listed three other methods of divining future events: examining the entrails of a goat, drinking honey-wine until they were intoxicated and could prophesy, and dreaming (see also Krapf 1854: 14).

Iloibonok also provided charms, amulets, and ritual medicines (*entalengoi*, pl. *intalengoi* or *emaisho*, pl. *imashon;* used interchangeably, medicines and charms) for various purposes such as to ward off sickness, promote conception, or ensure the success of a cattle raid by junior men (see Merker 1910 [1904]: 211 for a detailed list). Johnston (1902: 829) described one kind of amulet as "small pieces of metal, wood, or unclassified rubbish sewn up in skin bags, which are given to them by the 'Laibon,' or priest-doctor, and are worn round the neck on a chain or wire" (see also Mallet 1923: 279). The amulets and charms described by Merker were made of plants, bark, cowries, leather, and special secret powders. He also noted that "[the *oloiboni*] sells his wares fairly dear" (Merker 1910 [1904]: 211). Charms were prepared and provided with complicated directions for their correct use. As Whitehouse (1932/1933: 149–150) explained:

> If any one of the instructions are overlooked the charm may be rendered useless or may even work evil against its users. The Masai sometimes find that their purchases do not have the effect they desire and report the matter to the medicine man; the latter never fails to point out where an error in the method of its use occurred—and probably effects another sale!

Whitehouse's description also points to a less discussed facet of *iloibonok*—they also had the power to produce charms and ritual medicines for more sinister purposes, such as cursing other people. This evil power (*esetan*), which was usually translated by commentators as "witchcraft" (I prefer "sorcery"), could be overcome only by consulting an even more powerful *oloiboni*, who could produce a potent protective charm. This dual role of *iloibonok*—as the source of positive spiritual powers as diviners, prophets, and healers and the source of negative powers as sorcerers—helped them retain and expand their clientele: "As Maasai ruefully put it, 'If we did not have Loonkidongi [referring to the Inkidong'i clan of the *iloibonok*] we would not need Loonkidongi'" (Spencer 1991: 336). In fact, the death of any *oloiboni* was usually attributed to sorcery at the hands of another *oloiboni*.

A central factor in the rise of *iloibonok* to power was their role in guiding the raids of *ilmurran* and prophesying the outcomes:

> For instance, when the medicine man named The father of Ngupe made medicine for the warriors of Kilepo before they went on a raiding expedition, he sang:
>
> > The bulls that cannot move because they are so fat,
> > They will be beaten by Kilepo.
> > The bulls that cannot move because they are so fat,
> > Half of them have been captured.
>
> The warriors of Kilepo went on their projected raid against the people of Kahe, and captured half of their cattle. They said: 'Thus prophesied the medicine-man.' (Hollis 1905: 325)

Similarly, Thomson (1968 [1885]: 253–254) described how representatives of a group of *ilmurran* preparing for a raid visited Laibon Mbatian "to seek advice as to the time of their start, and to procure medicines to make them successful." Once they returned from their successful raid, a portion of the captured cattle were given to the Laibon "who had directed them so well, and whose medicines had been so potent" (Thomson 1968 [1885]: 255; cf. Merker 1910 [1904]: 18–19, 93–100; Fosbrooke 1948: 16–17). As Hollis (1943: 121) remarked, "In former days no war party could expect to meet with success unless he [the *oloiboni*] approved of the expedition. Of recent years the importance of the medicine man appears to have declined." Certainly the suppression of cattle raiding by colonial officials severely limited this important (and lucrative) role of *iloibonok*.

In addition to a share of the stolen cattle from raids, *iloibonok* received gifts of cattle and smallstock for consultations and charms (Fosbrooke 1948). Their spiritual powers, therefore, were a significant source of wealth, an irony not lost on other Maasai, who both admired and resented their success (cf. Bernsten 1979a: 182). They used their wealth to marry, form alliances with other men through stock partnerships and patron-client relationships, and otherwise extend their power and prestige. They also, at least in later periods, demanded that their followers provide them with increasing numbers of wives (Fosbrooke 1948: 21).

The powers exercised by *iloibonok* were inherited through the male line (Fosbrooke 1948: 14). Only some Inkidong'i men, however, chose to exercise their powers as "private practitioners." Fewer still ever developed reputations as major *iloibonok*, in part because they were supposed to come from the lineage of Mbatian. Fathers chose among their sons for their successor, and the struggles among sons of famous *iloibonok* such as Mbatian for their father's position are legendary (Bernsten 1979a: 183–200).[45] Similar struggles and jealousies occurred among the sons of minor *iloibonok* as they competed for power, prestige, and wealth (Bernsten 1979a; Waller 1995; cf. Spencer 1991). Thus, as Spencer (1991: 336) noted, "Maasai sometimes claim, 'The Loonkidongi have no brothers.'" Although the sons of Inkidong'i daughters were not supposed to inherit such gifts, there were rare exceptions (Bernsten 1979a: 209, 246). There are also reports of a few female prophet-diviners (*enkoiboni*, pl. *inkoibonok*) such as Sekenan, who lived near Magadi in Kenya (Mol 1996: 299), a young woman in Matapato, Kenya (Kipuri 1989: 167, n.9), and Ngoto Nemasi in Arusha (Parsalaw 1999: 177).

In their rise to spiritual prominence, *iloibonok* struggled among themselves and with other claimants to special powers from and relationships to Eng'ai. These included Ilkiboron, a sub-clan of the Mokesan clan who were believed to wield a powerful curse and blessing, as well as the power to bring rain through their prayers to Eng'ai (Bernsten 1979a: 114, 126–128; cf. Merker 1910 [1904]: 22, 147).[46] But they also displaced other healers and propitious individuals and lineages (Waller 1995: 31; Bernsten 1979a: 119) and claimed an expanded repertoire of spiritual powers.

Most importantly, they also seem to have, over time, disrupted the former spiritual complementarity of men and women by strengthening male power and prestige and muting the important spiritual powers and practices of women.[47] From the beginning they were aligned with Maasai men: most of their divining and prophesying was done at the behest of *ilmurran* (and to a lesser extent, elders), and they served as the ritual leaders of cattle raids for *ilmurran* (Fosbrooke 1948: 19). They also introduced new forms of gender control and inequality by severely restricting the mobility and autonomy of their wives and daughters, preventing them from even visiting the homestead of their natal families (Fosbrooke 1948: 21; Bernsten 1979a: 208–209). In addition, their production and distribution of ritual medicines marginalized the significant powers of the herbal medicines usually produced and dispensed by women (cf. Bernsten 1979a: 180–181). In response, most women seemed to have had little involvement or interest in their gifts; they continued to rely on "holy" (*osinyati*) elder men in their rituals and ceremonies.[48] Although the evidence suggests that elder men also limited the involvement of *iloibonok* in the actual age-set rituals, they did request their advice and agreement about such matters as the timing and location of the rite (Bernsten 1979a, 1979b; cf. Fosbrooke 1948). On the topic of gender, it is interesting to note how the wives of *iloibonok* contributed to the successful exercise of their husband's powers: they ground his ritual medicines, prepared honey beer to induce the drunken state necessary for his prophecies, and sang with other delegation members as the chorus to his drunken prophetic songs (*oloipirri*) (Krapf 1854: 74; Bernsten 1979a: 181, 203).

The Time of Life (and Death)

Maasai perceived life and death in terms of the circular rhythms of nature, as a regular cycle of creation then destruction, of waxing then waning. Days, marked by the rising then setting of the sun, shared the same name as the sun—*enkolong'* (pl. *inkolong'i*). Months were distinguished by the phases of the moon; both months and moon were called *olapa* (pl. *ilpaitin*). The years (*olari*, pl. *ilarin*) were marked by four seasons—the short rains, short dry season, long rains, and long dry season—whose names varied by Maasai section (see Mol 1977: 106).[49] A regular set of recurring rituals mirrored the circular cycle of nature by marking the phases of human lives, from birth to circumcision, marriage, childbirth, and death. Each ceremony signified the end of one phase (symbolic death) and the beginning of another (symbolic birth). Not surprisingly, women, as the active agents of creation, were central to these rituals of creation and transformation. As Burton (1991: 83) has argued in another context, "creation is thought of as a process by which something is brought into existence from nothing, or its negation, when some essence is transformed into a novel and unique entity."

Individuals, however, followed a linear trajectory through the circular cycle of nature and rituals. As the following myth made clear, although nature was continually reborn, Maasai had no concept of an afterlife:

One day Naiteru-kop told Le-eyo that if a child were to die he was to say when he threw away the body: "Man, die, and come back again; moon, die, and remain away." A child died soon afterwards, but it was not one of Le-eyo's, and when he was told to throw it away, he picked it up and said to himself: "This child is not mine; when I throw it away I shall say, 'Man, die, and remain away; moon, die, and return.' " He threw it away and spoke these words, after which he returned home. One of his own children died next, and when he threw it away, he said: "Man, die, and return; moon, die, and remain away." Naiteru-kop said to him: "It is of no use now, for you spoilt matters with the other child." This is how it came about that when a man dies he does not return, whilst when the moon is finished, it comes back again and is always visible to us. (Hollis 1905: 271–272)

Thus while the moon, like the sun and the seasons, disappeared only to return again, most individuals died for good, never to return. For ordinary Maasai, there was life, not afterlife (Baumann 1894: 164; Johnston 1902: 832; Thomson 1968 [1885]: 259).[50]

Given such beliefs, Maasai funeral practices were pragmatic, returning to Eng'ai, through nature, what She herself had created. Although the details varied, when someone was on the brink of death, their ornaments were removed, and their bodies were smeared with animal fat and wrapped in an animal skin. They were then left outside the homestead to die with their body positioned as follows: they were laid on their left side with their head pointing north and facing east. In addition, "the legs are pulled up to lie resting on one another. The left arm is bent until the hand rests close to and in [the] point of the head, while the right elbow is bent in a right angle, the upper arm resting on the body, the hand lying in front of it on the ground" (Merker 1910 [1904]: 200). According to Last (1883: 532), the following prayer was said: " 'Totona siddai, etung'aigi tangera'—'Sleep well, may the children you left behind fare well.' " The corpse (*olmeneng'ani*, pl. *ilmeneng'a*) was left to be eaten by vultures, hyenas, and other wild animals.[51] If the body was disposed of on the first night, this was considered a good sign. If, however, the body was found undisturbed the next morning, "the bereaved bring a black ram as a propitiatory sacrifice to an angry God" (Merker 1904 [1910]: 201). It was inauspicious for anyone to die inside the homestead, and if this occurred, or if several young people or children died within a short time, the families usually burnt the homestead and built another one in a more auspicious site nearby (Merker 1910 [1904]: 202–203). As Thomson (1968 [1885]: 259) summarized, "The Maasai believe in annihilation. To bury a corpse would, they think, be to poison the soil; it must be thrown to the wild beasts without ceremony."

Certain prominent men, including *iloibonok*, were, however, buried in graves marked by stone heaps:

> The bottom of the grave, one meter deep, is spread with an ox hide, over which fat has been poured, and the body is laid on it in the position described above [on the side, facing east with head pointed north]. A second hide, which also has fat rubbed into it, is then spread over the body. The grave of a chief [*oloiboni*], and very often those of old men of the El Kibiron [a section] as well, is crowned with a larger or a smaller pile of stones. Passing Maasai in [the] future throw a few bunches of grass on the grave as a sign of respect for the dead man, or instead they pour some milk as an offering from time to time, on the grave of the chief, which is regarded as holy. (Merker 1910 [1904]: 202)

Moreover, it was believed that some of these men returned to earth in the shape of snakes (Johnston 1902: 832; Merker 1910 [1904]: 210). As Hollis (1905: 307–308) described:

> When a man is on the point of death, people say that he is about to cut his heart [*oltau*]; and when he dies and is eaten (by hyenas), his soul [*oltau*] dies with him. It is believed that all is over as with the cattle, and that the soul does not come to life again. But when a medicine man [*oloiboni*] or a rich person [*olkarsis*] dies and is buried, his soul turns into a snake as soon as his body rots; and the snake goes to his children's kraal to look after them. The Masai in consequence do not kill their sacred snakes, and if a woman sees one in her hut, she pours some milk on the ground for it to lick, after which it will go away. There is a black snake, which is sacred to the Aiser [Laiser] clan; and if a person of another clan were to strike the snake whilst the owners were present, they would tell him to desist as it belongs to them. . . . The other clans and families have their sacred snakes as well.

Thus a person's *oltau* (soul, heart, spirit) did not live on, although Hollis (1905: 307–308) claimed that "It is believed that the souls of some big people like Mbatian go to heaven [eng-aï] after death and burial." Johnston (1902: 828) reported that a year after the burial of these important men, "the eldest son or the appointed successor of the chief carefully removes the skull of the deceased, making at the same time a sacrifice and a libation with the blood of a goat, some milk, and some honey. The skull is then carefully secreted by the son, whose possession of it is understood to confirm him in power, and to impart to him some of the wisdom of his predecessor." Interestingly, Leakey (1930: 205) reported that older women were also buried—the procedure was the same as that for older men, except that women were placed on their left side in the grave and men on their right side.

In terms of mourning practices, the reported evidence suggests that the gender and age of the deceased shaped the appropriate response. Hollis (1905: 306–307), for example, wrote:

> When a father of a family dies, the whole family mourns for him. His widows lay aside their earrings, necklaces, and beads; his daughters leave off their

chains, beads, armlets, and anklets; and his warrior sons and boys shave their heads. His wives wait for a whole year before they put on their ornaments again. If any other person dies, the women of the family leave off their small neck ornaments but not the iron rings or the ear-rings, and the men shave their heads. The mourning lasts for one month. If a baby dies, its mother only lays aside her ornaments.[52]

Merker (1910 [1904]: 201–202) added that in addition to taking off all of their ornaments, during the mourning period all of the bereaved (of an adult man) shaved their heads, did not participate in feasts or dances, and were unable to marry. In addition, "on the death of a warrior [*olmurrani*], his comrades, members of his company, and his brothers and half-brothers mourn him by shaving their heads and laying aside their ornaments" (Merker 1910 [1904]: 202). These different practices perhaps suggested a different status between men and women, but one cannot also assume that they measured the relative grief felt at the death of a given person.

Between life and death, however, Maasai individuals participated in a series of rituals that marked significant events, rites of passage, and transitions in their lives. Although there are far too many to discuss here, I do want to briefly describe the following ceremonies, with particular attention to the forms of involvement of men and women: childbirth, naming, circumcision, age-grade promotions, and marriage. Here I challenge other scholars, such as Århem (1990), who insist on classifying these into "important, large scale rituals" and "lesser, family rituals" according to the extent of attendance and participation by people (men, really) from outside the homestead and the type of livestock (cattle or smallstock) that was sacrificed. To focus only on the "important" rituals Århem discusses, all of which are part of male age-set promotions, is to further the androcentric bias of most studies of pastoralists, which presume that something is important only if it focuses on men and, conversely, that if some area or ritual is important, men must be the focus (and of course the opposite, that if women are the focus it is not important). The so-called family rituals that Århem lists—birth, marriage, and female circumcision—celebrated femininity and fertility, and were just as crucial to Maasai life-stage transitions as the male age-set rituals. Moreover, in contrast to his timeless, ahistorical prescripts, many women (and sometimes men) from outside the homestead participated and cattle were occasionally sacrificed. And finally, the difference between the "public" and "private" nature of some of these rituals did not necessarily mark a status distinction of public over private—perhaps women-centered rituals were more private to protect men from their greater sacredness, intimacy with

Eng'ai, and thus spiritual power and presence. Except for childbirth, the timing of these other rituals was decided by elder men and women according to the phases of the moon (with a preference for a full moon) and the seasons (preferring to celebrate in the post–long rains time of plenty) (Merker 1910 [1904]: 208). My discussion focuses on the normative or generic elements of the rituals, not on the variations and complexities of specific performances, in order to describe how the ceremonies drew on and produced the rich symbolic repertoire of nature, colors, shapes, directions, and so forth. Moreover, the descriptions highlight the role of gender in these rituals, in terms of the roles and participation of men and women, the deployment of gendered symbols and associations, and the use of gendered spaces and sites.

The birth of a new child prompted the celebration of a series of rituals that thanked Eng'ai and celebrated the fertility and procreative power of women.[53] Childbirth was the time of women, and it took place in the female-controlled space of the home. It was therefore a deeply religious time that brought women even closer to Eng'ai: *asaisai,* the word for giving birth, was derived from *asai,* "to pray, to beseech, to beg." As the birth was taking place, female relatives and neighbors brought milk and other foods and gathered in front of the house, while men, including the father, stayed far away. Once a healthy child was born (usually with the help of a female midwife), the women sang and danced to thank Eng'ai for the successful birth. The new father rewarded them with an ox, which was promptly slaughtered, roasted, and eaten. Often another ox was slaughtered the next day as well. Women visited with the mother, held and marveled at the new child, and spit and chanted their blessings and gratitude. The newborn child and mother were fed a mixture of blood and milk to restore their energy (Macdonald 1899: 233).

The main ceremony, however, was *orkiteng' lentomono* ("the bull of the child"), where the child was given its first name by her or his mother (previously the child was called by a nickname).[54] Male and female relatives attended the feast. Honey beer was served, and a black bullock was slaughtered in the doorway of the child's house, then roasted and eaten. The details of the ceremony varied by section, but Merker (1910 [1904]: 56–59) described the following: in the late afternoon, the participants seated themselves in a circle under a shady tree, with all the men on one side and women on the other. The infant sat on his mother's lap while she conferred with other women about an appropriate name. The other women suggested joking names such as "the short one." Eventually the mother's oldest brother stood and asked what the child was to be called. The mother replied with the given name, and everyone cheered.[55] She then hung a string of large and small beads around the child's neck. Everyone rose, proceeded in single file to the entrance of the homestead, and then danced around the thorn bushes that were used to seal the gate at night. As they danced, they sang a prayer asking Eng'ai to bless and watch over the child. Afterward, the festivities continued, as men drank and women danced and sang songs of praise and thanksgiving to Eng'ai. The ceremony took place in the same way for boys and girls (see also Hollis 1905: 293–294; Leakey 1930: 186–187).[56]

The next set of major rituals was the circumcision (*emurata*) of young men and women, which differed significantly by gender.[57] Male circumcision was a highly public affair, and more than one boy could be circumcised at the same time.[58] Young men were circumcised during a certain "open" period of several years, after obtaining the permission of the *oloiboni* and their elders.[59] After some preparatory rituals,[60] the boy's head was shaved and his body hair (except for his eyelashes) was removed and thrown under his bed in his mother's house (Bagge 1904: 168; cf. Storrs-Fox 1930: 448). He took off his skin cape and ornaments, and dressed in a long black leather garment prepared by his mother. (At this point Hollis said that the boy went out to cut an *elaitin* tree, which was then carried by girls and planted at the door of his mother's house.) The next day, the boy woke before dawn, went outside the homestead, and washed himself with cold water to help numb his body. After sunrise, his mother opened the homestead gate and put a leather hide on the ground by the right-hand gatepost. The boy then sat, naked, on his leather garment, with his legs wide apart. One man held the boy from behind while the circumciser (usually a Dorobo man) performed the procedure. According to Bagge (1904: 168), before the operation, all the participants were smeared with a stripe of white clay on their forehead and nose, and a white line was drawn to mark the place on the boy's penis where the circumcision was to be performed. Afterward, milk was poured on the cut, and then the boy picked up the leather garment (on which was the milk and his blood), and walked backward into his mother's house, where he poured the liquids on the ground or in his bed. The gathered men and women then feasted on meat and honey beer.

After the ceremony, the young men stayed in their mothers' homes for several days, where their wounds were cared for and they were well fed on milk, meat, and blood. Once their wounds were somewhat healed, they donned long blackened feminine garments and women's earrings (*surutya*), used white chalk to paint patterns on their faces, and joined other newly circumcised boys (*esipolio,* pl. *isipolio*—note that this is a feminine noun) in roving bands with bows and arrows. According to Merker (1910 [1904]: 65), on their first day out, the boys slaughtered a white male goat in the plains, then roasted and ate it, throwing the gnawed bones into the fire (this meal was called *olkine lombenek*). Hollis (1905: 298) observed that the boys spent their time shooting at young girls with arrows (the tips were blocked with pieces of honeycomb) (perhaps to foreshadow their emergent legitimate sexual relationships with the girls?) (see also Storrs-Fox 1930: 449). The *isipolio* also collected ostrich feathers and shot small birds to make wreaths that they wore around their heads like crowns (see fig. 1.6) (Bagge 1904: 169; Leakey 1930: 190). According to Storrs Fox (1930: 449), the *isipolio* had to observe the following rules:

They must enter the village before the cattle every evening

Must not drink blood or cut meat or touch it with the hand

Must not wash

Must not have sexual intercourse with girls (this is not strictly kept)

Must not fight or be struck by anyone. Anyone who strikes a novice must put milk on his head.

Must not go out in the day time without the head-dress of stuffed birds.

As Leakey (1930: 191) characterized it, "during the period of the novitiate the boys . . . are free to go anywhere 'like women.'" Thus, after roaming the plains during the day, the *isipolio* returned to their mothers' huts at night (after sunset according to Hollis). Once they were fully healed, their heads were shaved again by their mothers, they discarded the feminine garments, and they put on the ornaments and dress appropriate for *ilmurran*. Each young man was then presented, by his father, with a spear, sword, and stick, "the insignia of his new status as a warrior" (Leakey 1930: 191). They were called *ilbarnoti* ("the shaved ones") until their hair grew long enough to plait, and then they were called *ilmurran*.

According to Richard Reusch (n.d.: 7), a Lutheran missionary who claimed to have worked with Maasai for over thirty years, to have witnessed a male circumcision ceremony in 1924/1925 (possibly an early initiation of the Ilterito age-group), and to have spoken with elder men about the history of the practice, there was also a later ceremony celebrating the new sexual freedoms of the *isipolio*:

Fig. 1.6. Three recently circumcised Maasai boys (*isipolio*), ca. 1900. They are dressed in black, feminine garments with feather headdresses and have white chalk circles on their faces. Each holds a bow and arrow. Reproduced from Merker (1910 [1904]: 64).

> After the wounds are healed, the circumcised are assembled at certain holy places. . . . There they stand in a circle. Around them in a wider circle stand the women and circumcised girls of the clan. A Medicine Man [*oloiboni*] or Elder calls for a circumcised one who has never had any sexual relations with a woman. One or two usually step out. A hole, resembling the female organ, is made in the ground and the young man or men . . . have to fecundate the earth through this hole. The women and girls greet this act with shrill loud cries. . . . As soon as the act is finished, a shrill cry gives the sign that every warrior may catch the running women and girls. It is believed that they are possessed by the spirit of the God of fertility and act in his name and on his behalf. If a woman gets pregnant, there is no shame on her. Not every woman is obliged to attend this ceremony or orgy. Those who come do it by their own free will. Usually younger women, who have had no children until then, take part in such an orgy.

He also described a "period of liberty" that followed the above ceremony, during which time:

> Warriors can use every woman or girl whom they can catch, except their own mothers and sisters. They can steal secretly during the night into the house of another man and use his wife. During the period of liberty they are not punished for it, for "they are possessed by the spirit of the God of fertility." Many young wives of elderly men lure in those days the young warriors into their homes, especially those who had not yet any children from their elderly husbands. After the period of liberty is over, the black phallic stone is buried [by the *oloiboni*] and the normal laws are again followed. (Reusch n.d.: 8)

Although I have found no evidence to corroborate these practices (including the black phallic stone that the *oloiboni* supposedly unearthed to open the circumcision period and buried to close it), they are useful in emphasizing the symbolic meanings associated with male circumcision (as recognizing male sexual potency and bestowing legitimate sexual access to certain women) and the centrality of Eng'ai and Maasai women to the production of this stage of adult masculinity.

Moreover, in addition to the obvious ritual significance of the timing, spatial location, elements used, and so forth of the circumcision ceremony and its aftermath, there were several other aspects that are important to note. First, the reputation of the boy's parents, especially his mother, depended on his performance during the actual cutting—he was supposed to be silent and not flinch, as a sign that he had the "hardiness and self-control" to be a "warrior." If he groaned, cried out, or even winced during the operation, his mother (Merker says both parents) was beaten, his parents were humiliated, and he was taunted as a coward (*ebirio*) for a long time. Second, as Merker (1910 [1904]: 62) observed:

A great many women attend these feasts, and especially all those women who have been barren until then. Some of the former are there as mothers of the celebrating boys and some as companions of the barren women. The latter, on the other hand, come in order that they may be pelted with fresh cow-dung by the boys—a proceeding which, according to a universal conviction among the Masai, will make them fruitful.

Thus, in addition to the symbolic acknowledgments of the strong ties between mothers and their sons, male circumcision was also a time and site to celebrate and cultivate the fertility of women and the potency of men, and the necessity for men and women to join together for procreation to occur. Young men were seen as possessing a powerful sexual potency, especially during this ritual moment when they were transformed and blessed by Eng'ai.

Female circumcision (*emurata*) was a more private, woman-centered affair. There was no open or closed period for female circumcision; girls were circumcised at any time after (or shortly before) they began menstruating and before they were married. As with the boys, it was only performed after a series of other required rituals and could include one or more girls (perhaps sisters). Girls prepared for their circumcision in similar ways to boys: they shaved their heads and the hair was thrown under the bed in their mother's house. In addition, they took off all of their ornaments and clothing, and dressed in a long leather garment that their mother had prepared (*orkilani*). A sheep or bullock was also slaughtered, called *Oloitupukunieki* ("the [animal] which has caused her to be taken out [from amongst the girls]") (Hollis 1905: 299). The site of the actual circumcision differed, however: while boys were circumcised outside the house, girls were circumcised inside, in the doorway. Merker (1910 [1904]: 66–67) described the ceremony as follows (see also Hollis 1905: 299):

> The mother takes care to benumb the necessary parts with cold water, while encouraging her little daughter, who sits on the ground with beating heart. The operation [by an old woman who is an experienced circumciser] is a simple cutting off of the clitoris, and is carried out with a sharp piece of iron (ol moronya) of the same kind as is used for shaving heads. The small wound is afterwards washed with milk, which, with the blood that has flowed, sinks into the ground. Nothing is used to stop the bleeding in this operation either.

A girl could cry or wince; there was no test of bravery. Moreover, she was circumcised in her mother's presence and only women could witness the actual cutting. Bagge (1904: 169) in fact claimed that it was usually the girl's mother who circumcised her. Once the operation was completed, "the women of the village prepare a feast amongst themselves on the circumcision day, to which the girl's father contributes an ox, and the mother brings honeybeer" (Merker 1910 [1904]: 67; cf. Bagge 1904: 169).

Afterward, the girls (like the boys) recovered in their mother's home, were called *isipolio* (sg. *esipolio*), and wore special clothing to mark their liminal status. Instead of the ostrich feather/bird crowns, however, girls wore "a plaited circlet of grass (*ol marisian*) on their foreheads, in the front of which they stick an ostrich feather" (Merker 1910 [1904]: 67).[61] They also smeared special designs of white clay on their faces. Unlike the male *isipolio,* they stayed close to home and did not roam the plains during the day. Once a girl was completely recovered, her marriage arrangements were completed and she soon became a wife.

Circumcision, therefore, marked the transformation of children into adults: boys became men and girls became women. The transformation was about sexuality and gender. As *ilayiok,* uncircumcised boys were not supposed to engage in sexual play or intercourse with anyone, not even young girls. But as *ilmurran,* they had a tremendous amount of sexual freedom in both their legitimate relationships with girls and their illicit (but pervasive) affairs with married women. In contrast, although uncircumcised girls were sexually active (although not necessarily engaging in intercourse), once they were circumcised, their sexuality was linked to fertility and channeled, through marriage, into procreation. Girls, in other words, became not just women, but potential mothers, while boys became sexually active (and potent) men. Only later, once men became junior elders and married, would they become potential fathers and have their sexuality linked to procreation.

Thus while the circumcision ceremonies of boys and girls had certain parallels, they also had striking differences. These differences worked to encode and express normative gender differences, such as associating women with the more intimate sphere of the household and home and men with the more public space of the outdoors (Århem 1991; Talle 1998; but see Hodgson 1999a). Moreover, in terms of emotions, boys were supposed to suppress any expression of pain or emotion, while girls could cry or flinch. Despite these differences, however, it is important to note that adult women were central to both ceremonies, while adult men were involved only with the male circumcision. As mothers, women shaved their children's hair, prepared the special leather garment that would drape and support them during the ceremony, supervised the timing and logistics of the event, and cared for their healing. In the case of her daughter, the mother was present and in control throughout the ceremony (as compared to the girl's father, whose only job was to contribute an animal for the celebration feast). In the case of her son, her responsibilities included opening the homestead gate to connect the homestead and the wild (marking the liminal status of *ilmurran* as part domesticated, part wild), invite Eng'ai's presence, and signal that it was time for the actual procedure to occur. She did not, however, witness the actual cutting (the sources contradict one another as to whether a boy's father witnessed the procedure). But, as the parent most responsible for the upbringing of her son, she had the most to lose or gain by the "success" of the procedure. If her son showed any pain, she was beaten and disparaged. If he was brave and silent, however, and became an *olmurrani*, she gained new respect (and power) as his mother, a status she marked by wearing special ornaments. Moreover, women prayed quietly during the procedure, then trilled their praise and thanksgiving to tell Eng'ai that it was successfully completed. Circumcision, therefore, whether male or female, recognized the procreative and creative powers of women, who, like Eng'ai, gave birth to and nurtured both men and women. The gendered aspects of the ceremonies symbolically marked the distinct but complementary gender roles and responsibilities of the young boys and girls, their mothers and fathers, and the other adult men and women who were present.

Once circumcised, men then participated, over the years, in a series of rituals to mark their promotion from *ilmurran* to elders (Fosbrooke 1948: 26–33). The performance and timing of these rituals varied somewhat by territorial section, and some sections had additional rituals. The two most important were called Eunoto and Olong'esherr. The purpose of Eunoto (from the verb *aun*, "to plant") was to promote *ilmurran* from "junior warriorhood" to "senior warriorhood" and to choose a ritual leader, the *olaunoni* (also from *aun*, thus "the planter").[62] Both Merker and Hollis focused their discussion on the selection of the *olaunoni*, with little description of the actual Eunoto ceremonies. According to them, a delegation of *ilmurran*, in consultation with the *oloiboni*, secretly selected one of their own to be the *olaunoni*, based on his qualities of "holiness" (*osinyat*) as determined by moral purity and physical perfection: "They choose a man whose parents are still living, who owns cattle and has never killed anybody, whose parents are not blind, and who himself has not a discolored eye" (Hollis 1905: 299). He must be "a distinguished man in physical beauty, perfect build, strength and health" (Merker 1910 [1904]: 73). The chosen man was not told about his fate, because it was believed that he would run away, hide, or kill someone to avoid being forced to quit being an *ilmurran* before his time and to be elevated above his peers (Hollis 1905: 300). Instead, he was seized during the ritual, forced into a special ceremonial hut (*osingira*), and pushed onto a wooden stool in the center of the hut:

> Others put a string of circular blue beads (ngonongo) round his neck, fasten the spiral ear ornaments of brass wire (insurutia) which old men and women wear, in the lobes of his ears, take off the short leather warrior cape putting on him instead the long garment worn by married people. Finally all those present cheer the new olaunoni and shout "tadarawa ie iyok engishon," i.e., remain poor, bring us good fortune. (Merker 1910 [1904]: 74; cf. Hollis 1905: 300; Lewis Deposit, ca. 1915: 80)[63]

The *olaunoni* was supposed to remain poor, depending for his sustenance on gifts of livestock and milk from his age-mates, and be humble and gentle in his ways (in contrast to the masculine ideals of bravado, aggression, and autonomy that characterized *ilmurran*). In exchange, he exercised a certain political authority over his age-mates, working to prevent conflicts and arbitrate disputes (Fosbrooke 1948: 39–40). Anyone who disobeyed him was beaten (Merker 1910 [1904]: 73–74; Hollis 1905: 299, n.1). Moreover, according to Bernsten (1979a: 81), his age-mates collected the bridewealth for his first wife; thereafter "the ritual leader and his first wife were considered the 'father' and 'mother' of the age-set; age-mates visiting their kraal never stayed in her house [and thus did not have sexual relations with her]." Finally, as the first of their age group to undergo each transition ritual, they "brav[ed] the danger of transformation in advance of their peers and act[ed] as lightning rods for possible supernatural danger" (Galaty 1983: 370).

The first possibly dangerous stage of ritual transition occurred during Eunoto, when the sexual and dietary rules followed by *ilmurran* began to shift. In addition to the selection of the *olaunoni*, the Eunoto ceremony entailed the blessing of the age-set, the end of prohibitions on sexual relationships between *ilmurran* and circumcised women, the granting of permission to marry, and the first step toward the end of certain dietary restrictions.[64] During the ceremony, all *ilmurran* were blessed by their *ilpiron* ("fire-stick elders," comprising men from the age-set that was two cycles senior), who circled them, "drinking honey wine and spraying it out of their mouths as a blessing" (Storrs-Fox 1930: 452). In addition, *ilmurran* who had not had sexual relations with circumcised women were allowed to enter the *osingira* hut with their families for special recognition and blessing (Storrs-Fox 1930: 452; Galaty 1983: 375). The hut itself, according to Galaty (1983: 374–375), was built only by " 'good' and 'holy' mother, defined as those who had not had sexual relations with members of their sons' age-set." These women also built what he called the "sacrificial sanctuary" for the slaughter of the sacred ox, taking turns sinking the short posts in a circle around the ox according to the ritual and political prominence of their sons (skins were then attached to screen the sanctuary from outside view) (Galaty 1983: 374).

Other elements of the ceremony involved the slaughter, roasting, and presentation of the sacred ox by the *ilpiron* to the *ilmurran*, much dancing and singing by *ilmurran*, prayer dances by women, and several blessing ceremonies (Bagge 1904; Galaty 1983; "Maasai Initiation Ceremonies" 1949–1950; Whitehouse 1932/1933). Among Maasai from Naivasha, male and female participants smeared a mixture of ocher and fat on their bodies in "fantastic designs" (Bagge 1904: 167). *Ilmurran* who had killed a man in warfare, however, were smeared with ocher mixed with water (not fat) on the left-side of their body and "on their right half they paint En-Doroto (white mud) and water. Both sides of their bodies are covered with a simple design made by drawing the nails of four fingers in any given direction in a wavy manner" (Bagge 1904: 168). According to Galaty (1983: 373), "The final two days of Eunoto are anticipated by a week of dancing, dance days being named after the red ocher (*enkipaata nanyokie*) and then the white chalk (*enkipaata naibor*) used to adorn the participating moran." At the final blessing ceremony: "They were each presented with a ring of skin (*olkerreti*) carved from the ox-hide, which they placed over their fingers. Then the elders blessed them by smearing them with a mixture of chalk, milk and water, up their right legs and across their foreheads. The age-set was then given a new and formal name" (Galaty 1983: 375; cf. Margetts 1963). The next morning, their mothers (or other close female relatives) shaved the long hair of the *ilmurran*, thereby marking their promotion to the first stage of elderhood by physically transforming them into elders.[65]

After Eunoto, the men held smaller feasts to mark their progressive transformation into elders. One was called Olgeten Lolbaa, which entailed the slaughtering of an ox for a neighborhood feast and mock warfare between the *ilmurran* and women and girls over the meat (Merker 1910 [1904]: 104). Another was the milk-drinking ceremony, whereby the prohibition against an *olmurrani* drinking milk alone was removed. According to Storrs-Fox (1930: 453): "This ceremony is performed by each warrior individually. He is given milk by an elder in his mother's house, and drinks it by himself. He shaves his head [more likely his mother shaves it] and does not grow a pigtail again."

The last major age-set ceremony was Olong'esherr, in which the men were released from the prohibition against eating meat touched by a woman. The two hands of the age-set were also formally united as one, given a new, unifying name, and promoted to elderhood (Merker 1910 [1904]: 74).[66] The key moment of the ritual involved wives feeding their husbands meat to overturn the prohibition. According to one commentator, a wife could not, however, present meat to her husband if she had had sexual intercourse with any other *ilmurran* or uncircumcised boy since her marriage.[67] In addition, men received the "signs of elderhood: wooden stools, tobacco containers, herding sticks, and their own branding irons, all indicating that they were adult males, independent to their fathers, and free to establish their own kraals of cattle and wives" (Bernsten 1979a: 68). Historically, the Kisongo section performed the first, usually at Edoinyo e Moruak ("hill of the elder men"), a small hill in the Sanya plains between Mount Kilimanjaro and Mount Meru (Bernsten 1979a: 68).

Finally, the culmination of the marriage process between a man and woman was celebrated by a major wedding ceremony.[68] Betrothal itself could take many forms, depending in part on the age of the prospective bride and groom. Usually it involved gifts of tobacco and honey from the groom (or his family) to the parents of the bride (Macdonald 1899: 233). Merker (1910 [1904]: 44) and Hollis (1905: 302) agreed that if the woman was a young child, the gifts went to her father. If she was older, however, Merker (1910 [1904]: 44) stated that the father of the groom asked permission from the girl's mother: "After which the bridegroom assures himself of the girl's consent. As soon as the mother has obtained her husband's agreement to the match, the bride's head is smeared with butter or beef fat as a sign that a betrothal has taken place and the girl is now engaged. She is then known as *atesera*." Before the wedding ceremony, the groom brought bridewealth gifts (usually livestock; the amount and kinds vary by accounts) to the bride's father and mother, accompanied by a female relative (such as his mother, his sister, or one of his senior wives) carrying honey. He gave the bride's father a cow, after which the two men called each other *Pakiteng'* ("the giver and receiver of a cow"), and the bride's mother a ewe, after which they called one another *Pakerr* ("the giver and receiver of a sheep") (Merker 1910 [1904]: 44–45; Hollis 1905: 302). Merker (1910 [1904]: 45) noted that "cattle paid as dowry money [*sic*] must be uniformly black or white." Livestock and other gifts were also exchanged between and among various family members on both sides, especially from any co-wives or children of the groom to the new bride (Merker 1910 [1904]: 45). In addition, "in the early days after the wedding the mother-in-law receives several more pots of honey from her son-in-law, also hides for clothing and iron wire from which to make arm and leg ornaments" (Merker 1910 [1904]: 45).

Early historical accounts of the actual wedding feast vary. Hollis (1905: 303) described the journey of the bride to her new home in her husband's homestead:

> After the bride's wedding-garments have been oiled, she puts them on, and is given a gourd which has been ornamented with cowries. This is put on her back, and she is taken by her husband, who is accompanied by two of his friends and two of the old women from his bride's kraal, to her future home. She does not hurry but walks very slowly until she reaches her husband's kraal, where a child is given her to feed.

Merker (1910 [1904]: 47–48) said nothing about the journey, but described the wedding feast. Family, friends, and neighbors brought gifts of food or drink and gathered under a shady tree in the morning. An animal was slaughtered, and the upper bodies of the bride and groom were decorated with a paste of beef fat and red earth. Then everyone formed a circle, with the groom and men on one side, and the bride, women, and children on the other, with the bride and groom facing one another. The bridal couple just sat without eating, while everyone else ate, drank, and shared advice and good wishes with them. A dance closed the feast late in the evening. The next morning, there was more dancing and two sheep were killed (one from the groom, the other from his father-in-law). Women and girls rubbed their bodies and leather garments with the fat from these animals. After the feast the wedding couple went to their new house. The groom's mother brought a small child, which the husband sat on his wife's lap so that she could feed it a small gourd of milk. "The ceremony," according to Merker's interpretation, "not only emphasizes the hope of many descendants, but they also believe it has the miraculous power of bringing this to pass."

Thus, in addition to the daily rituals and prayers of women, Maasai men and women also participated in a series of rituals to mark the phases of their lives. There was no distinction between the secular realm of the everyday and the sacred realm of ritual; rather, both were saturated with the sacred as Maasai invoked, beseeched, and praised Eng'ai. The ritual and ceremonies described above merely condensed and concentrated sacred power and practices to achieve some significant transformation or goal (cf. Asad 1988). Moreover, the gender differences and complementarity so evident in the tasks of daily life were expressed and reinforced by these ritual happenings. And finally, in contrast to statements by Jacobs and others about "the rather slight role which women possess in the ritual life of the Maasai generally" (Jacobs 1965: 185), women were central to the enactment of these rituals, especially those related to male age-sets. As Kipuri (1989: 97) has argued, "not only are [Maasai] women *not* mere spectators, but [they are] essential actors."

Monitoring and Maintaining the Moral Order

Since Maasai had no concept of the afterlife, they focused on leading good and holy (*sinyati*) lives in the present so that Eng'ai would be pleased and bless them with good health, children, and cattle. The focus of their religious beliefs and practices was thus on maintaining the complementarity between Eng'ai and humans, between the sky and the earth, and correcting—through daily prayers and ceremonies of reconciliation and forgiveness—any transgressions or disturbances that occurred to this relationship. These transgressions ranged from the relatively minor (lies or insults) to the fairly common (cattle theft from other Maasai) to the major (sexual intercourse between a man and a pregnant woman, or murder), and were dealt with accordingly. Moreover, as the primary mediators with Eng'ai, women were central to monitoring and maintaining the moral order, especially when the transgressions involved challenges to their creative and procreative powers.

Maasai had a range of ways to express contempt, dislike, or anger at inappropriate behavior or objectionable people by invoking the wrath of Eng'ai. One way was to spit on the ground in front of or at another person, thereby inverting the normative meaning of spitting as an act of blessing (Hollis 1905: 315–316; Merker 1910 [1904]: 122). Insults and angry curses (*oldeket*, pl. *ildeketa*) were also quite common. These included:

Mikinjirie Eng'ai! (May Eng'ai trouble you!)

Tananga naisula! (Die with those who have been conquered!)

Mikinosa olowaru! (May a wild animal devour you!)

Es suti! (Dirt, dust, that is, may you be swept out of the hut like rubbish!)

Todoroi! (Die when the sun sets!) (Merker 1910 [1904]: 109–110; Hollis 1905: 344)

Merker (1910 [1904]: 110) also listed a series of sexually explicit insults that young men and boys used to tease one another (such as "Fuck your mother!"), or that *intoyie* and *ilmurran* called one another ("Hi, asshole!"

"You clitoris!"). He claimed, however, that if a husband insulted his wife with one of these sexually explicit terms, it was sufficient cause for a woman to return to her natal home and return her bridewealth. Hollis (1905: 344) observed that Maasai did not curse their children with very bad names, calling them instead *Esoit!* ("Stone!") or *Engumoto!* ("Pit!"). Mothers, however, had a particularly potent way of cursing their disobedient sons: "If her son refuses to obey her, she strikes her stomach and says, 'You were born in this': whereupon the son is said to sicken, and can only recover when his mother makes a rope of fibre which she hangs round his neck" (Hollis 1910: 478; cf. Bianco 2000).

Maasai also had several phrases or oaths to assert their honesty or the truthfulness of a particular claim. According to Merker (1910 [1904]: 219), these included *'aisha 'Ngai inkishu* ("In truth as God may give me cattle"), *maoa Eng'ai* ("May God kill me if I lie"), and *maoa en abere* ("May a spear kill me if I lie"). Another oath involved "biting some blades of grass with the words *'madaduarigi kuna n godjet ten eledjer ata 'Ngai'* ('May this grass poison me if I lie in the sight of God')" (see also Macdonald 1899: 233). In more casual circumstances, a male Maasai would attest to the truth by adding "by my sister's garment," while a woman would add "by my father's garment" (Hollis 1905: 344–345).

Although they seem to have had no concept of evil spirits, Maasai did believe that other people, both Maasai and non-Maasai, were capable of intentionally evil actions, including using charms and curses to bring misfortune, sickness, or even death on other people (Merker 1910 [1904]: 210–211; cf. Krapf 1854: 18). Merker (1910 [1904]: 210) claimed that the practitioner of *esetan* (which he translated as "witchcraft")[69] "obtain[ed] his results by the power of his charm only, which power is the outcome of the composition of the concoction, and of repeating of a definite formula, and of the making of particular gestures." Another form of *esetan* was to smear the magic medicine under the fingernail of the index finger, point at the person concerned, and murmur a spell (Merker 1910 [1904]: 156). Thus Maasai never pointed with their fingers at other people, and the index finger was called "the magician" (*sakutushoi* or *olasakutoni*).

People accused of such malevolent actions were forced to take an oath or submit to an ordeal to prove their innocence. According to Krapf (1854: 27), "When the accused Mkuafi is to take an oath (múmăke) the Ol-ibon boils some roots which he mixes with meat and puts into the mouth of the oath-taking person. In case of guiltiness the meat will in the Wakuafi opinion, stick to the man's throat and move neither backward nor forward, so that he must die." There was also the ordeal of blood (*olmomai losarge*) that required the accused to say, "If I have done this deed, may God kill me," then drink blood (or a mixture of milk and blood) (Merker 1910 [1904]: 219–220; Hollis 1905: 345). Another was the ordeal of the dry wood (*olmomai enjerta natoijo*), in which the accused was given a dry twig and a green twig: "In accepting these, he invites the punishment of God to fall on him if he is guilty. He will then either die like the dry stick, or he may remain fresh and alive like the green one" (Merker 1910 [1904]: 219–220). Others were the ordeal of the bow, the ordeal of the earthen stool, and, for non-Maasai, the ordeal of the goat (Merker 1910 [1904]: 220). According to Merker (1910 [1904]: 220), "The majority of those assembled [to hear an accusation] decide when an ordeal is to be used, and which one. The accused, and he alone, must submit to the ordeal, he cannot appoint a substitute. . . . If the accused has come to no harm within ten to fourteen days after the ordeal, he is regarded as entirely free from suspicion."

Maasai also believed in "the evil eye," which could sicken both humans and cattle. According to Merker (1910 [1904]: 211), "One who is afflicted with the evil eye (erta gonjek) may not show himself in the vicinity of a village. Everyone shuns him fearfully, so he builds himself a separate village in which he lives alone with his family. If he ventures to enter a strange village, he must be prepared to be beaten to death."

To protect themselves from curses and the "evil eye," men, women, and children wore protective amulets and charms that they made or obtained from *iloibonok* (see list in Merker 1910 [1904]: 210–211). In addition, Merker (1910 [1904]: 210) noted that "women, who go amongst strange tribes in the neighboring districts to buy vegetables, protect themselves more particularly against their spells. They smear their foreheads and cheeks with cowdung, or wear a cord round their necks on which is a row of small split wands."

Another egregious moral transgression was the murder (*loikop*) of another Maasai.[70] Most Maasai sections distinguished unintentional killing from premeditated murder, and there were differences in the penalties for murder according to the gender, age, marital status, and parental status of the killer and victim. If an adult man was murdered by another man, there were two alternatives: "blood revenge," whereby the brothers or other male family members of the murdered man would seek to kill the murderer, or the payment of "blood money" (*oloikapani*) by clan and section members of the murderer to the family of the deceased. Merker (1910 [1904]: 214) estimated the amount as two to three hundred cattle, but noted that it was often less. Moreover, Hollis (1905: 311–312) added that blood money was not usually paid until two years had elapsed, "for they say that the dead man's head is still fresh." A murderer could seek sanctuary from blood revenge in the homestead of the *oloiboni*, but was still responsible for paying the blood money. In contrast, if a married man murdered a girl or woman, there was no blood revenge, only the payment of a fine in cattle (Merker 1910 [1904]: 215).

Lesser transgressions included the failure of an *olmurrani* to live up to the code of dietary and sexual restrictions (*enturuj*) that regulated their behavior, especially those prohibiting sexual intercourse with married women. Despite the ban, however, illicit relationships between married women and *ilmurran* seem to have been pervasive. If the transgressors were caught, they were beaten, and the man had to pay a fine to the woman's husband. Sex between a married man and his daughter or classificatory daughter (that is, a daughter of one of his age mates) was, in contrast, considered a very serious crime, punishable by beatings and the destruction of his house and cattle (Hollis 1905: 313). Although Hollis claimed that elder men enforced the "incest" sanctions, evidence of *olkishiroto*, discussed below, suggests that it might have been elder women.

Women had several collective forms of ritual attack to handle serious moral affronts to their fertility and procreative powers. One was *olkishiroto*, which Hollis (1910: 480) described: "In the event of a man having intercourse with a pregnant woman, and thereby causing her to abort, he must submit to a punishment which is called *ol-kishuroto*. All the women of the neighbourhood collect together and, having stripped, seize the guilty person and flog him, after which they slaughter as many of his cattle as they can, strangling and suffocating the animals with their garments" (see also Spencer 1988: 205). In another form, called *oloirishi*, women collectively attacked men who prevented their wives from participating in their collective fertility gatherings (Spencer 1988: 201).[71]

Some transgressions to the moral order were more unintentional, such as accidentally killing a pregnant woman in a raid. Often these actions were interpreted as transgressions only in retrospect, as family members experiencing a series of unusual illnesses or deaths reflected on the possible reasons that Eng'ai was punishing them (Merker 1910 [1904]: 210). Anyone who thought he or she might be guilty of a possible offense then sought forgiveness from Eng'ai through ritual sacrifice and prayer. In the case of the accidental killing of a pregnant woman, Merker (1910 [1904]: 210) described how the guilty man sacrifices a pregnant black sheep to God, in the actual place where he previously committed the deed. Before killing the animal, he prays to God, states the object of the sacrifice, and begs for remission. He throws the blood and uterine water (en gepa) as well as the fetus and uterus, both cut in pieces, on to the place of his crime, in order to make atonement. He takes neither the meat nor hide of the beast he has slaughtered with him, but leaves it all there, when he returns to his village at the completion of the sacrifice.

Through such sacrifices and prayers, Maasai tried to rectify and maintain their relations with Eng'ai to ensure Her continued blessing on their families and homesteads.

As the above discussion suggests, Maasai recognized a range of moral transgressions, from the very minor to the severely egregious, and a range of appropriate punishments, from fines to beatings to blood revenge. Since the crimes themselves were judged in moral terms as affronts to Eng'ai, the purpose of the punishments was to seek redress and try to restore the moral order.

Conclusion

Women's religious and ritual activities reflected and expressed their sense of identity as Maasai and as pastoralists, and their centrality to the reproduction of Maasai life. Like Eng'ai, women were the creators of life, responsible for nurturing and protecting their children. While elder men conferred with one another about where to graze and water livestock or move their homesteads, women served as daily intermediaries with Eng'ai to ensure the survival and reproduction of their herds and families. Women also played key roles in the numerous ceremonies and rituals that marked significant events and life-stage transitions in Maasai life. As mothers and wives, they were crucial to the progressive age-grade transformations of their sons and husbands from *ilayiok* (uncircumcised boys) to *ilmurran* to elders. Men moved to the next age-grade status in part through the symbolic actions of women. Finally, as evidenced by many of their prayer songs and their ritual attacks, women also used their spiritual authority as a platform to assert their moral authority and critique immoral activities, especially those perpetrated by men.

Yet, as the stories of the poisoning of Kunguru and the rise of the *iloibonok* suggest, spiritual power was also a dynamic site of gendered struggle that was intimately linked with other domains of power and authority. The incorporation of the *iloibonok* into Maasai society and their claims to special powers from Eng'ai challenged the centrality and significance of women's spiritual roles as intermediaries with Eng'ai, and thus the gendered complementarity upon which Maasai social relations were based. The economic and political marginalization experienced by Maasai women in the colonial period only further politicized the realm of the spiritual, by producing the gradual separation of the sacred from the secular, of the moral from the material, and gendering these domains as female and male, respectively. As we shall see, Maasai women, in turn, tried, like Kunguru, to assert their moral authority to critique what they perceived as the increasingly immoral practices of men. At the same time, they worked to enhance their spiritual power by joining forces with the new healers in their midst, Spiritan missionaries.

MEN OF THE CHURCH

2

The people of Africa will not be converted by the work of clever and capable missionaries, but through the holiness and sacrifices of their priests.
—*Father François Libermann, 11th General Superior of the Spiritans* *(Koren 1983: 260)*

Although Catholic Spiritan missionaries[1] waited until the 1950s to begin systematic evangelization of Maasai in Tanzania, they had a long history of missionary endeavors throughout the world, especially in Africa. This chapter investigates the origins, history, and agendas of Spiritan missionaries, focusing on their establishment and expansion in East Africa. My purpose in this chapter, in part, is to consider these men as human beings, to provide glimpses of their motivations, assumptions, expectations, and experiences in a manner that seeks understanding, not immediate condemnation. Like some of the best current work in colonial studies and critical development studies (for example, Cooper and Stoler 1997; Pels 1997), I try to move beyond simplistic morality plays of good and evil to expose and analyze the nuances, ambivalences, and tensions that informed, shaped, and were produced by the encounters between these men of the church and Maasai men and women. My task is made easier by my longstanding personal and work relationships with many Spiritans, as described in the preface (cf. Beidelman 1982). The missionary encounter was not just a matter of the interplay of the "religion" of the missionaries and the "culture" of Maasai, but of the cultural, religious, political, economic, social, and gendered beliefs, interests, and practices of all involved. It is therefore essential to excavate and understand as much about the "culture," background, social status, gendered assumptions, and practices of Spiritans in general and individual missionaries in particular as it is to do the same for Maasai men and women.

Moreover, given the often solitary nature of their work and the tremen-

dous impact of their individual personalities and practices on their relationships with Maasai, I seek to understand and distinguish Spiritans as much
as possible as individuals—like all of us, imperfect, fallible, and products of
their place, time, and training. Spiritans share a common vision and mission,
as exemplified in their constitution and rules of order and instilled in their
seminary training and socialization.[2] At the same time, however, they are
divided by personal, political, theological, and generational differences. Thus
the second part of the chapter compares the lives, thoughts, and experiences
of three American Spiritans from different generations who were central to
Maasai evangelization efforts in the Monduli area at different periods: Father
Eugene Hillman, the first Spiritan to begin systematic evangelization of
Maasai in the 1950s; Father Girard Kohler, who served as head of the Monduli parish from 1985 to 1993; and Father William Christy, one of the latest
(and, it seems, last) generation of American Spiritans to work in Maasai
areas. Although many Spiritans, primarily from the United States but also
from other countries, have been involved in evangelization work with Maasai, I have selected these three men because they exemplify three different
generations of missionaries and three distinct approaches to and experiences
of mission and Maasai.

The Early History of the Spiritans[3]

Founding and Charism

The Congrégation du Saint-Esprit (the "Congregation of the Holy
Spirit," or the "Spiritans") was founded by Claude-François Poullart des
Places[4] in 1703 in France as a seminary and religious society to train impoverished students for the priesthood so that they could serve poor and
marginalized peoples in France and overseas. In 1848, the Congregation
merged with an explicitly missionary society, the Societé de Sainte-Coeur de
Marie (the "Society of the Holy Heart of Mary"), to become the Congrégation du Saint-Esprit et de la Sainte-Coeur de Marie. Father François
Libermann,[5] the founder of the Societé, was elected the first superior general
of the newly formed Congregation (he was the eleventh superior of the
Congregation). He is perceived by the Spiritans as their second "founder"
because of his revitalization of the organization and the continuing salience
of his missiological teachings (e.g., Libermann 1962–1964; cf. Kohler 2002).
Father Libermann was the son of an Orthodox Jewish rabbi, and his experience as the member of a disparaged religious minority in heavily Christian

Alsace informed his ideas about evangelization (Kieran 1969a: 344). He argued that missionaries should never force anyone to convert to Christianity, should concentrate on the long-term establishment of the Church rather than the rapid conversion of as many people as possible, should train and install native clergy as soon as possible, and should mold Catholic teachings and practice to the "customs . . . taste and manners" of the societies in which they were working (Koren 1983: 247–64; Kieran 1969a). As he wrote to his priests in Africa:

> [The missionaries] must pay particular attention to which customs and habits are characteristic of the people and the land. They must carefully avoid disturbing these customs (unless they are against God's laws) and modifying them in a European fashion. They will simply try to make [the people] more perfect in their own way of life and in accord with their own customs. (Quoted in Koren 1983: 260)

Moreover, he recognized the importance of laypeople working as catechists to help missionaries "spread the word." In short, Libermann's vision was "to establish a local Church with a local clergy and a local laity capable of carrying on without outside help" (Koren 1983: 278).

Libermann's teachings were echoed by several pronouncements from Rome. *In Supremo Apostolatus,* an apostolic letter written in 1839, denounced slavery and the slave trade and "declared that the black people were not, as some people alleged, by nature morally degraded and intellectually inferior" (Kieran 1969a: 344). Similarly, *Neminem Profecto,* an instruction issued by Pope Gregory XVI in 1845, informed missionaries that their primary goal was to establish strong local churches run by native clergy; therefore, "an education of high quality must be given to fit people in missionary lands to occupy the highest positions in the Church" (Kieran 1969a: 344–45). Moreover, "the instruction reminded missionaries that their work was spiritual and that they must not become involved in political and purely secular affairs" (Kieran 1969a: 345). *Cor unum et anima una,* "one heart and one soul," became the motto of the Spiritans.

After the merger, the Spiritans quickly expanded their missionary activities and worked to internationalize their membership by founding provinces in Ireland, Germany, Portugal, and the United States (Koren 1983: 278–96). Since American Spiritans eventually led the evangelization efforts among Maasai, a brief history of the founding and expansion of the United States Province is pertinent. During the same period that they were beginning to work in Africa, Spiritans from France moved to the United States to serve the increasing Catholic immigrant population, founded the first province in the United States in 1874, and opened the first seminary in 1874.[6] They established many parishes and schools, and soon chose as their special apostolate to work with African American (and later Hispanic) communities. In 1878 they founded the College of the Holy Ghost (which became Duquesne University in 1911) in downtown Pittsburgh to offer education to poor immigrants. They established a junior seminary in Ann Arbor, Michigan, in 1949, a brothers' novitiate in Richmond, Michigan, in 1958, and in 1960 a collegiate seminary at Bethel Park, Pennsylvania, from which students could take classes at Duquesne. As a result of the geographic expansion of the Spiritans through the United States, the USA Province was divided into USA Eastern and Western Provinces in 1964, and the Diocese of Arusha, which encompassed most Maasai areas, was confided to the USA Eastern Province.

Missionary training during the end of the nineteenth century took several years. A typical sequence for Spiritan priests was to spend at least one year as a postulant studying philosophy at junior seminary; then, if they were at least sixteen years old, they joined the Spiritans as novices. During their year of novitiate, they studied the rules and constitution of the Congregation, and were challenged to develop spiritually and to assess and affirm their religious vocation. After the novitiate, they were professed and took the vows of poverty, chastity, and obedience. They then entered senior seminary to study theology, complete their other studies, and take special courses on missionary life. Their training ended with their consecration as priests (Kieran 1966: 83).

Despite the many years of philosophical and theological training, however, there seems to have been little if any practical training to prepare these young priests for their future hardships and challenges as missionaries. Joseph Chanel, an early French explorer who visited the Spiritan mission at Kilema on Mount Kilimanjaro in 1894, raved about the lack of instruction in practical matters of survival, such as food preparation and medical care (1900: 109–12). He blamed the matter on the priests who directed the novitiates and seminaries, who either had never experienced the daily trials of missionary life in new mission outposts themselves, or had conveniently forgotten their experiences by the time they returned to France to assume their teaching posts. Nonetheless, he was appalled by the deadly toll of such negligence, reporting that since 1884, twenty-one out of forty-eight missionaries sent to East Africa had died, thirteen of them during their first five years (Chanel 1900: 111). He compared the missionaries to young soldiers and martyrs, who left France full of enthusiasm and energy to carry the word of God to "savage" peoples in distant lands, with only secondary thought to the deprivations they would encounter. "In sum," he complained, "we can say that although these young missionaries leave well prepared from a moral point of view, it is entirely a different matter from a material point of view" (Chanel 1900: 111).

Early Spiritans in Africa

An accidental landing in Mauritania in 1778 by some Spiritan priests led to the establishment of the first Spiritan missions in Africa. Initially, most of their work occurred in French territories and colonies such as Senegal and Madagascar. But in 1858 the bishop of the Spiritan mission in Reunion sent his vicar general to Zanzibar to explore the possibilities for future missionary work. The first Catholic mission station in East Africa was then established on Zanzibar in 1860 and transferred to the Spiritans in 1862. A few years later in 1868, the Spiritans opened their first mission on the mainland of present day Tanzania at Bagamoyo (Koren 1983: 272). The Prefecture of Zanguebar, as it was called at the time, was established in 1860 and officially confided by Propaganda Fide to the Spiritans in 1863. (During this period, Propaganda Fide in Rome assigned, or "confided," geographic areas to specific Catholic missionary congregations, in part to minimize conflicts among congregations.)[7]

The Catholics were, however, not the first Christian missionaries in East Africa. They were preceded by missionaries supported by the Church Missionary Society (C.M.S.) who tried to establish a mission base in Mombasa, Kenya, including Johann Krapf in 1844, Johann Rebmann in 1846, and J. J. Erhardt in 1849 (Oliver 1965: 6). The first Lutheran missionary, Johann Greiner, arrived to work in Dar es Salaam in 1887 (Sahlberg 1986: 60). Oliver, like many scholars, attributes the "missionary invasion of East Africa" to the travels and accounts of David Livingstone, who promoted East Africa as a land ripe for "commerce and Christianity" (Oliver 1965: 9–11). Moreover, he argues that the sensationalist accounts of Livingstone's death in 1873 changed prevailing images of Africans among missionary groups from "perishing heathen" to "suffering and neglected" potential converts (Oliver 1965: 34).[8]

The early Spiritan missions were primarily staffed by bilingual fathers from the Alsace region of France and lay brothers from Germany. Because of their rural origins, they were more interested in strengthening rural areas and "improving" agricultural practices than in developing educated elites (Kieran 1969b: 51). They built hospitals and orphanages; taught the cate-chism, basic literacy, and agriculture in their schools; ran trade schools and technical training workshops; and established large plantations near their mission stations for teaching, experimentation, food, and income (Kieran 1969b: 52).[9] Their main constituency was freed slaves, mostly children— both captured slaves sent to them by the British and slaves they "ransomed," or paid to redeem (Bennett 1963; Kieran 1966; Oliver 1965). These first stations in turn were the bases for the establishment of inland missions in Tanzania and Kenya in subsequent years (Bennett 1963; Kieran 1966; Koren 1983; Oliver 1965; Walker 1933).

In this early period, the main evangelization strategy was the formation of Christian communities. They produced these by supervising the marriages of their ransomed slave converts (most of whom were children that the Spiritans had supported and educated), then moving them into self-contained "Christian villages" surrounding the mission stations on the main-land (Kieran 1966: 119–43; 1971; Koren 1994: 22; Oliver 1965: 23). Fam-ilies in these villages lived in homes on streets, with a common chapel and store, and small plots of land for their personal use. They worked for the mission, usually on the plantations, for five days a week in exchange for weekly allotments of food and clothing. Missionaries set strict rules to con-trol their labor, mobility, and public and private behavior. By 1896 the num-ber of Christian villages run by Spiritans in East Africa had risen from five in 1885 to fifty-two (Kieran 1966: 127) and the practice was praised by travelers and members of the church hierarchy (Oliver 1965: 24). Spiritans believed that these villages would attract potential converts by serving as examples of the moral and material benefits of Christian life. They also hoped that subsequent generations of children borne to these initial converts would become the nucleus for African clergy (Kieran 1966: 49–62; 1971).

The Spiritans, like all Catholic missionary congregations at the time, were financially dependent on several key sources. These included two or-ganizations in France—the Societé pour la Propagation de la Foi ("Society for the Propagation of the Faith") and the Oeuvre de la Sainte-Enfance ("Holy Childhood"),[10] financial aid from the French government, support from their missionary congregations, and whatever food and funds each mis-sion could raise from its plantation's projects and other economic ventures (Kieran 1966: 394–416). These sources could be precarious and even fickle, depending on the priorities and agendas of outside agencies and states with multiple commitments, and the vagaries of climate and labor on the mission station and plantation. In 1886, for example, the French government turned down a new request from the Spiritans for financial aid "with the statement that there were many other French missions in the world who had not received as much support as that already given to the Holy Ghost Mission in East Africa" (Bennett 1963: 69). Moreover, both the Society for the Propagation of the Faith and Holy Childhood demanded annual reports from the missionaries that they supported, and published missionary accounts in their respective publications.[11] Later, each vicariate and prefecture received an annual stipend from the Society for the Propagation of the Faith (Oliver 1965: 24) and small contributions from local African Catholics.

The Vicariate of Kilimanjaro

Initially the Spiritans were restricted to the coastal areas of East Africa, but in 1881 they received permission from Rome to move inland. As clearly seen in the map of the Vicariate of Kilimanjaro (see map 2.1), the Spiritans avoided the hot, dusty plains that made up much of their assigned territory by gradually moving up the mountain ranges to establish new mission stations in first the Usambara mountains and then the slopes of Mount Kilimanjaro[12] and Mount Meru.[13] Their route of expansion also overlapped conveniently with the new railroad, which extended inland from Tanga on the coast, through Moshi to Arusha (Kieran 1966: 367).[14]

The first Spiritans reached Kilimanjaro in 1890. Traveling from Mombasa, Bishop John Marie deCourmont, Father August Commenginger, and Father Alexandre LeRoy (who later became superior general) arrived on the slopes of Mount Kilimanjaro on August 14, 1890 (LeRoy 1914: 225).[15] They soon established the first mission at Kilema in 1891, from which they started many new mission stations in the Tanga and Moshi areas. In recognition of the success of this expansion, Rome created the Vicariate of Kilimanjaro in 1910 to cover much of northern Tanganyika (Tanga Province and Northern Province).

By this time, the standard missionary practice for Spiritans had changed from the sponsorship and spread of Christian villages to the establishment and running of schools for African children. There were several reasons for this change. Debates among the Spiritan leadership had begun to question the effectiveness of the Christian communities in producing permanent converts and potential clergy. There were also reports of dissatisfaction and restlessness among villagers themselves at the strict regulations and requirements imposed on their lives and livelihoods by missionary dictates. Their demands

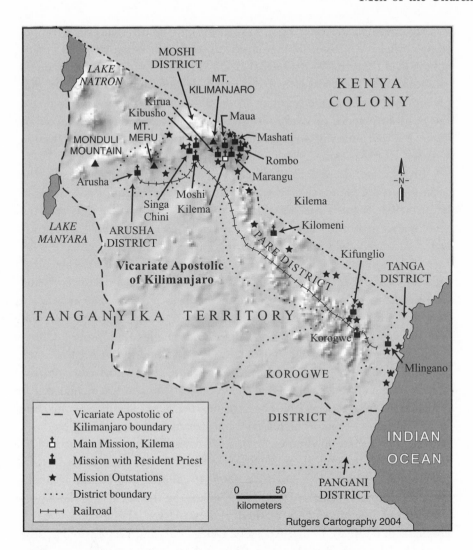

Map 2.1. Relief Map of Vicariate Apostolic of Kilimanjaro, ca. 1945.
Note how the Catholic missions follow the mountains and the railway
through northern Tanganyika, clustering around Mount Kilimanjaro.
Based on map obtained from Bethel Park archives (24C-22-01).

included payment for their labor, individual rights to own land, and freedom to open their own stores. Some refused to work, others ran away, and many complained (Kieran 1966: 49–65, 121–22; 1971). In addition, the supply of ransomed and freed slaves had drastically declined. The British had quit giving freed slaves to the Spiritans in the 1880s as accusations surfaced that the Spiritan practice of ransoming slaves actually contributed to slavery by making it that much more profitable. Slavery was subsequently outlawed in German East Africa in 1891.

In response, the Spiritans agreed with Father LeRoy's argument at the 1884 General Chapter that "it was not the least use waiting for Africans to be attracted to the Christian villages and that it was imperative that the missionaries go out to them. Hospitals to heal the sick and schools to instruct were considered the best way to win them over. . . . [They] decided the future of the mission would rest on the training of boys and girls as catechists" (Kieran 1966: 62).[16] Although there were some later efforts to teach and baptize adults, the conversion of children was primary. Missionaries believed that unlike their parents, children were still relatively unshaped by their culture and customs, and could be socialized and taught to be "proper" Christians. Standard schools, built near the mission station, offered a basic curriculum of reading, writing, math, science, and religion. In addition, the Spiritans opened "bush schools" at mission outstations to teach children rudimentary literacy and math. The missionaries visited regularly, employing local Africans to teach the children, and catechists to teach religion, with minimal compensation. The German administration, especially District Officer Johannes, assisted the mission in the expansion of the schools in Kilimanjaro by insisting that parents send their children and providing books and other supplies (Kieran 1966: 191).[17] Thus, by the late 1920s the school had become "*the* missionary method of East Africa" (Donovan 1978: 17, emphasis in original), so that Apostolic Delegate Arthur Hinsely told a gathering of bishops in East Africa in 1928: "where it is impossible for you to carry on both the immediate task of evangelization and your educational work, neglect your churches in order to protect your schools" (Listowel 1965: 102, cited in Donovan 1978: 7).

The shift to schools as the primary evangelization strategy provoked a new set of debates among Spiritans about the best way to expand the local church: Should scarce mission resources be used to train catechists or future clergy? For some Spiritans, the ultimate goal was still to recruit and train African men to be ordained as priests: "Roman Catholic missions, stiffened by injunctions from the Propaganda, aspired from the first to nothing less than a celibate African clergy, versed in Latin, and armed with a theological learning comparable to that which was imparted in the seminaries of Europe. Such requirements could only be fulfilled by the total adoption and prolonged education of young boys" (Oliver 1965: 216). But training clergy required tremendous resources to construct and support junior and senior seminaries and seminarians. Other Spiritans, such as Father Aloyse Munsch, the first vicar general of the Vicariate of Kilimanjaro (1910–1922), preferred to expand the system of bush schools to provide basic education for everyone and promote the training of catechists, rather than concentrate mission resources on the education of an elite African clergy (Kieran 1966: 65).

Like all Christian missionary orders working at the time, the Spiritans were deeply dependent on African catechists for their evangelization efforts. Catechists played a prominent and expanding role in evangelization from the early twentieth century onward. As Father Gogarty wrote in 1927, catechists "are the great helpers of the missionaries: they teach Christian doctrine along with secular knowledge to hundreds of catechumens, before they are passed into the hands of the priests" (1927: 66). In Kilimanjaro, for example, the number of catechists grew rapidly from 50 in 1905, to 117 in 1911, to 183 in 1913 (Kieran 1966: 215). Catechists were recruited from mission schools and orphanages and trained by the missionaries in the basic tenets of Catholic faith. They were selected because of their literacy and moral standing, and were encouraged to marry and live full-time in the communities in which they worked. Their minimal training was supplemented by occasional refresher courses, apprenticeships with more experienced catechists, and, ideally, regular meetings and discussions with the missionaries. Catechists worked as translators for the missionaries and were responsible for instructing and monitoring prospective converts in the schools, communities, and outstations and serving as Christian models and mentors for other Africans. They also led morning and evening prayers in the villages, and presided over weekly services when the priest was absent (Kieran 1966: 208–20; Gogarty 1927: 66). As the key intermediary between local people and the missionaries, catechists therefore had enormous power in shaping the terms and outcomes of the missionary encounter in particular communities, as well as the contours and content of the relationship between individual missionaries and their parishioners.[18] Despite their crucial roles, however, they were paid only minimal salaries. Their growing numbers meant that these salaries represented significant parts of mission budgets, but these were not even half the wages available for working on plantations (Koren 1983: 459–60).

In contrast to other areas, Spiritans were tremendously successful in evangelizing local people in Kilimanjaro. Attendance in their schools soared from over 3,000 students in 22 schools in 1901 to over 16,000 students in 150 schools by 1914 (Kieran 1969b: 61; Gogarty 1927: 39). As Oliver (1965: 195) notes, "Thirteen years after the foundation of the first station at Kilema [in 1891] it was reported that the neighbourhood was 'virtually Christian.' " Despite a difficult period during the First World War, by the late 1930s, the Vicariate of Kilimanjaro contained 4 fathers, 11 brothers, 87 sisters, 241 teachers, and 46,000 Catholics (including catechumens) out of a population of 650,000 (Koren 1994: 240).[19] As Father Gogarty, who served as Vicar Apostolic of Kilimanjaro from 1924 to 1931, bragged, thirty years after the Spiritans first arrived at Kilimanjaro: "The Wachaga grew peaceful, gave up fighting, adopted Christianity in great numbers and are now settling down to become planters of coffee, which, they understand, the civilized people of overseas use in great quantities" (1927: 63). Clearly this statement glossed over many divisions, disputes, and disagreements among and between Spiritans and the people living on Kilimanjaro, who had now come to be called "Chagga," yet it also reflected a certain truth: the Spiritans had been extraordinarily successful in attracting Chagga people to Catholicism. Much of the successful expansion of the vicariate took place under the leadership of Father LeRoy, who served as superior general of the Spiritans from 1896 to 1926, and was financed by the tremendous success of the Spiritan coffee plantations on Kilimanjaro (cf. Kieran 1969b).

Initially, there was a significant gender bias to their success; young men were the majority of early converts. The first woman requested baptism at Mandera mission in 1897, and girls were first baptized in Kilema and Bura in 1899 and 1902, respectively (Kieran 1966: 72). Parents were reluctant to let their girls attend school and catechism classes, despite the insistence of the missionaries. After the Spiritans began a catechism class for women and another for girls in Kibosho in 1898, the chief, Mlelia, complained. Merker, the district officer, intervened, and the Spiritans agreed to close the class for women if allowed to continue the class for girls (Kieran 1966: 206).

Father Munsch also recognized the importance of educating African girls in order to produce "Christian families." He therefore welcomed the Sisters of the Precious Blood, a primarily German order, into the vicariate. In addition to educating girls, they worked in local hospitals and dispensaries (Kieran 1966: 73–74).[20] The increasing presence of Catholic sisters helped assuage the concerns of parents, as did the creation of local dispensaries, which served the needs of mothers and their children. As a result, there was a dramatic change in female education: although by the late 1890s there were only about 400 girls in all of the mission and bush schools in the Kilimanjaro area, by 1903 there were 2,160 girls in the Kibosho schools alone (Kieran 1966: 207). According to Kieran (1966: 207), "Nuns were then put into the chief mission stations. The Vicars Apostolic agreed that for the education of girls they were indispensable, and Kilema and Rombo declared that, since their arrival, conversion figures had risen and that their former pupils, when married, made the best mothers of families." Nonetheless, some girls did not want to attend, and a number of parents continued to object.

An important moment in the history of the vicariate occurred in the aftermath of the First World War, when German missionaries withdrew, Propaganda Fide reassigned the vicariate to the Irish Province of the Spiritans, and Father Henry Gogarty, an Irish Spiritan, was appointed vicar apostolic in 1924 (Walker 1933: 169). (The vicariates of Bagamoyo and Zanzibar were also assigned to the Irish Province during the same period.) Although the Irish Province had been sending men to the missions since 1860, it was formalized as a province only in 1911. In contrast to his predecessors, Father Gogarty was eager to train African clergy, and quickly founded St. James seminary at Kilema in 1925. Enrollment soon grew from twenty-three seminarians in 1927 to eighty-two in 1933 (Walker 1933: 171–72). He also supported the provision of advanced education to Africans and the improved training of African teachers; he founded St. Patrick's Teachers' Training School at Singa Chini in 1925 (Kelly n.d.; Koren 1994: 243; Walker 1933: 175).

Eventually, the huge burden of working in so many areas forced the Irish Province to withdraw from several vicariates, including Kilimanjaro. The Vicariate of Kilimanjaro was then transferred to the American Province in 1933, and Father Joseph Byrne, an Irishman who had become an American citizen, was appointed vicar apostolic. Father Byrne was also a great supporter of expanding the educational infrastructure of the vicariate. Shortly after his appointment, he reportedly claimed: "It is my intention . . . to direct all of my efforts to the question of schools: to develop training schools for catechist teachers, so as to multiply through them the number of Catholic schools. I am convinced that the school question is of prime importance, not alone because of the education given in the school, but above all because the Catholic school is the foundation of a country's Catholic life" (Walker 1933: 184).

Not surprisingly, with the transfer of the vicariate to the American Province, there was a huge influx of American Spiritans. Although the first three

American Spiritans to work in East Africa sailed together in October 1923,[21] by 1927 almost all new Spiritans arriving in East Africa to work in the vicariate were Americans (Koren 1994; LeClair 1993: 59–62). In 1953, the vicariate became a diocese, and Father Byrne was installed as the bishop of the new Diocese of Moshi, where he continued to serve until 1959. In the meantime, Kondoa, Tanga, and Mbulu had been excised from the vicariate to become dioceses in their own right.

The Diocese of Arusha

The Diocese of Arusha was established in 1963, and Father Dennis V. Durning, an American Spiritan, was appointed bishop. The new diocese was over 27,000 square miles, encompassing the now thriving commercial town of Arusha, the verdant slopes of Mount Meru, and the highland plains on which Maasai lived (see map 2.2). The diocesan headquarters were in Arusha, where the first mission station had been founded in 1907 after early attempts to found a mission were rebuffed in 1896 (Gogarty 1927: 38). By 1922, when Father Gogarty visited, it was still a relatively small town on the slopes of Mount Meru, with a small Catholic church under construction, a few Catholics from Goa, India, working as traders and storekeepers, and many Arusha living in and around town (Gogarty 1927: 69; cf. Peligal 1999). Although the somewhat controversial relationship between Arusha and Maasai will be discussed in subsequent chapters, it is important to note here that Arusha spoke Maa and followed many of the cultural and social practices of Maasai, but preferred to farm rather than rely primarily or even solely on livestock for their subsistence.[22] The Arusha accompanied Spiritans such as Father Hillman as translators and catechists in the early days of Maasai evangelization.

Spiritans in the Diocese of Arusha were part of three supervisory structures: the bishop, their "sending" province (the U.S. East Province), and their "local" Spiritan administration, which at this point was called the District of Kilimanjaro (Spiritans in the District of Kilimanjaro also served in the Diocese of Moshi and the Same Prefecture) (LeClair 1993: 133). Spiritans were supervised by their principal superior, the elected head of the District of Kilimanjaro, who discussed their postings and other personnel matters with the bishop of each diocese.[23] The district and its American Spiritan members were in turn supervised by and cared for by the provincial superior, the elected head of the U.S. East Province, and his officers. As the number of African Spiritans slowly grew, they began to demand their own

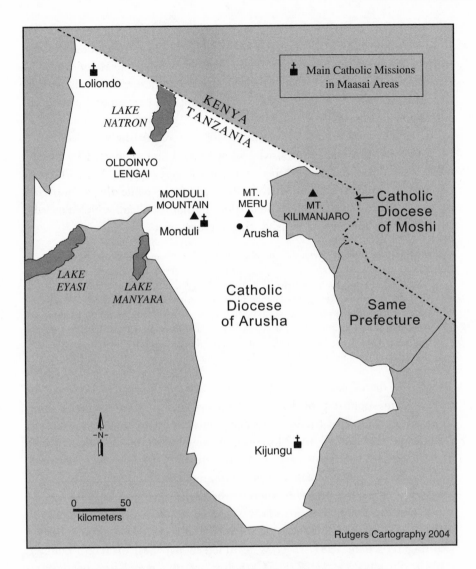

Map 2.2. Catholic Diocese of Arusha, ca. 1960. The three main Catholic missions serving Maasai areas at the time, Loliondo, Monduli, and Kijungu, have huge territories for first evangelization and pastoral work.

congregational structure. In 1989, with the formation of the new East African Province (which had initially been called the East Africa Foundation), many Spiritans working in East Africa were put under its supervision. The Americans, however, retained financial and other ties with the U.S. East Province, and the U.S. provincial superior continued to supervise their assignments and duties.

In addition to the missionaries, the Diocese of Arusha was also staffed by Tanzanian diocesan priests, who were trained and supported by the diocese and committed to working in it for the rest of their lives. Spiritans received a monthly allowance from their province, while the bishop paid diocesan priests a monthly stipend that Father LeClair, a Spiritan who worked in the Diocese of Arusha, characterized as a

> mere pittance. It is certainly not enough for the Priest to live on. Sure the Parish should take care of the clergy stationed there; but in some cases the Parish is so poor that no help is available. They simply can not and do not support the local clergy. If the Bishop feels he is unable to provide the necessary funds, the consequences can be quite alarming. . . . This lack of support often results in the local Diocesan priests having to take up some sort of business. It might be something like a small farm, a transportation service, or almost anything which will help the Priest make ends meet. (LeClair 1993: 293–94)

As will be discussed in chapter 3, the structural differences between the training and support provided to missionary and to diocesan priests was sometimes a source of friction, especially when most missionaries were still Americans and Europeans. Moreover, it contributed to the reluctance of many diocesan priests to work in Maasai mission stations, most of which were located in remote areas with poor congregations and minimal economic opportunities for the priests to support themselves.

When the Diocese of Arusha was created in 1963, there were only five parishes and around 8,000 Catholics in the diocese. By the time Bishop Durning retired in 1989, there were nineteen parishes, over one hundred mission outstations, and 47,000 Catholics out of a population of approximately 600,000 (Kelly 1999: 2). Bishop Durning was succeeded by Bishop Fortunatus Lukanima, who was replaced by Bishop Josephat Lebulu in January 1999. A few months later, the Diocese of Arusha was elevated to become one of only five archdioceses in Tanzania, and Bishop Lebulu became an archbishop. In an ironic historic reversal, the new archdiocese now contained within its boundaries the dioceses of Moshi, Same, and Mbulu. As noted in the Spiritan newsletter at the time, "Historically, Moshi is the success story of the Church in northern Tanzania, with half a million Christians, hundreds of priests from there and even more religious. However, in recent years Arusha has become the more important city politically, and internationally, and is now the archdiocese—still with more Maasai cattle than people, more tourist hotels than churches."[24]

Spiritans and the Changing Colonial Regimes

From the beginning of their work in East Africa, the Spiritans maintained a formal policy of political neutrality to minimize conflicts with the changing colonial regimes and maintain the trust of local peoples. Initially, besides ongoing relationships with the French government, their main political relationships were with the British and the Sultan of Zanzibar. Although the sultan readily agreed to requests to found a new mission, the British were suspicious at first as to whether the mission was a sign of French imperial interests in Zanzibar (Bennett 1963: 56–57). Once the issue was resolved, however, the Spiritan mission managed to avoid any major political entanglements, except over ongoing British concerns about their practice of ransoming of slaves (Bennett 1963).[25]

The political calculus changed substantially for the Spiritans once the Anglo-German Agreement was signed on July 1, 1890, and the political boundaries of German East Africa were fixed. Although, according to Bennett (1963), the Spiritans would have preferred British rule, they tried to get along with the Germans. The fact that many Spiritans, as mentioned above, were from Alsace, now a German territory since the Franco-Prussian War, did not help matters. Nonetheless, the Spiritans tried to maintain their strict policy of political neutrality, refusing even to help as translators during some boundary disputes (Bennett 1963: 68).[26] But the French character and roots of the Spiritan missions troubled the Germans, who tried to force all missions in their territory to teach German, even if the missionaries were not German. The Germans even appealed, unsuccessfully, to Rome in 1887 to replace the Spiritans with a German Catholic congregation from Bavaria. Despite sometimes tense negotiations, including the Spiritan authorities' invocation of the freedom of religion clause in the 1885 Berlin Act, the matter was somewhat defused in 1886 when laws prohibiting Catholic orders in Germany were modified and the Spiritans were able to begin recruiting and training missionaries from Germany (Bennett 1963: 69). Finally, an 1878 decree divided East Africa so that the Spiritans maintained their current missions and the remainder was given to a "purely German missionary society" (Bennett 1963: 70; cf. Oliver 1965: 163). Meanwhile, despite the disagreement, Spiritans maintained good relationships with most Germans in East Africa, who continued to admire and praise their work (Bennett 1963: 70). And once German members were slowly integrated into their work, "all frictions came to an end" (Bennett 1963: 75).

Two decades later, the political calculus changed again with the advent of the First World War. Once war broke out, all German Spiritan brothers were mobilized for military service, most for local defense troops in German East Africa. Many of the French Spiritan fathers and brothers also served their country in the war. After Germany's defeat in East Africa, almost all German Spiritan fathers and brothers were interned as "enemy aliens" or deported and imprisoned as "prisoners of war" for several years in Egypt or India. Many were not allowed to return. Six fathers and thirteen brothers from the Vicariate of Kilimanjaro were deported, of whom only five were allowed to return to East Africa after the war (Koren 1994: 116; see also Walker 1933: 168–69). The Lutheran church suffered perhaps even greater dislocation, as the many German missionary societies, including the Leipzig society working in Kilimanjaro, were banned from working in Tanganyika.

Once the British took over Tanganyika from the Germans in the post–World War I period, the Spiritans tried to ensure amicable relations with the new colonial regime by making several important changes in the composition of their missionaries working in Tanganyika. They quickly appointed several Irish Spiritans as vicars apostolic, and reassigned the vicariates to non-French Spiritan provinces. The Vicariate of Kilimanjaro was reassigned to the Irish Province, and Father Henry Gogarty was appointed vicar apostolic in 1924. By the 1930s, all of the vicariates in Tanzania were confided to the Irish, Dutch, or Americans. As discussed in detail below, these changes in the nationality of Spiritan missionaries not only influenced their relationships with the British colonial administration, but also had significant effects on their missionary outlook, practices, and priorities.

The Spiritans seemed to have had cordial, if ambivalent, relationships with British administrators. The British advocated and instituted several changes that affected missionary groups. They immediately instituted a "sphere of influence" policy, based on a similar policy they had implemented in Kenya, that required Catholics and Protestants to build their mission stations at least ten miles apart in order to minimize friction among competing denominations (Kieran 1966: 282).[27] They also encouraged the Spiritans and other missionaries to revise their curricula to minimize their training in agriculture and focus more on literary education (Kieran 1969b: 67). British administrators depended on the schools run by Spiritans and other missionaries to produce educated Africans for clerical, administrative, and service positions within the colonial apparatus. Yet, since most of the British were Anglican, they were wary of promoting the expansion and influence of the Catholic Church.[28]

During World War II, the Spiritans were allowed to work and move about freely in Tanganyika, but new missionaries were prohibited from joining them. As a result, much of their work stagnated, as they tried to cover their commitments with minimal personnel. After the war, British policies toward Catholics and other missionary groups remained much the same. But Britain's postwar "development" programs put new pressures on missionaries to improve and standardize the quality of their schools and medical facilities and expand their involvement in other "development" efforts (Hodgson 2001a). These demands, as described in chapter 3, made it even more difficult for missionaries to do their "religious" work of evangelization, religious instruction, and pastoral care.

Spiritan Missionary Portraits

As the preceding historical overview suggests, the nature of missionaries and their work changed over time, shaped by their successes and failures, their interactions with local communities, and the shifting political, economic, and social contexts within which they were trained and worked. But missionaries themselves also varied—in attitudes, assumptions, and approaches. These differences could profoundly shape their relationship with local churches, and thus their experiences as missionaries. In the following section, I present portraits of three American Spiritan missionaries who worked from Monduli mission with Maasai at very different periods. Each of these men was clearly a product of his time and training, shaped by dominant missionary paradigms and structures. One of the most significant structural changes was the innovative decrees that emerged from the Second Vatican Council (commonly referred to as "Vatican II"), which met from 1962 to 1965. These directives, as described in more detail in chapter 3, sanctioned respect for other religions, the use of local languages in services, and other liturgical innovations. Vatican II therefore had a profound impact on the nature of mission. But each missionary also underwent personal transformations in his ideas and practices as a result of his missionary experiences with Maasai. Comparing the similarities and differences in their lives offers insights into the relationship between the ideas and actions of individual missionaries and the lofty goals of their collective mission, between practices and principles. It also reveals the sometimes tremendous influence that Maasai men and women had on the missionaries, and thus the dialectical nature of the missionary encounter. Finally, the portraits offer glimpses into how their ideas about gender (and race and ethnicity) shaped their assumptions, attitudes, practices, and experiences.

"Dangerous Ideas": Father Eugene Hillman

I had heard stories about Father Hillman ever since I first arrived in Tanzania in 1985. His confreres spoke of his brilliance and his impatience with lesser minds. They also praised his groundbreaking work as the first Spiritan missionary to begin full-time evangelization of Maasai, and his widely read and controversial books based, in part, on his experience with Maasai, including *The Church as Mission* (1966), *The Wider Ecumenism: Anonymous Christianity and the Church* (1968), *Polygamy Reconsidered: African Plural Marriages and the Christian Churches* (1975), and *Inculturation Applied: Toward an African Christianity* (1993). But he had left Tanzania many years before, and I had never had the opportunity to meet him. As I drove up to interview him in the Spiritan retirement home in Sarasota, Florida, therefore, I was more than a little apprehensive about finally meeting this almost mythical man. We had exchanged letters and then emails and phone calls, and he had welcomed my request to meet with him, but I was still nervous: What would he think of me, a woman who had worked for the Spiritans for three years in the Catholic Diocese of Arusha as a teacher and development worker, but who was not Catholic herself, had since divorced and remarried, and was now an anthropologist? Would these issues influence our interview, and if so, how?

Fortunately, I found little to be scared of in the slightly bent, older man who met me at the door of his small one-bedroom apartment. He was gracious and kind, happy to talk about his life and help me with my research, but clearly a smart, articulate thinker given to constant critical and, especially, self-critical reflection and analysis. We spoke for several hours, had a simple sandwich lunch, looked at his pictures, and then visited a nearby photography store so that I could copy some of his pictures on a scanner. By the time I left, I was sorry that it had taken me so long to meet "Gene" (as his friends called him) and somewhat surprised by the similarities in our views on Maasai life, the Catholic Church, and the future of both. We have since maintained occasional contact by email and phone, and I have sent him copies of my work on Maasai.

Father Hillman was born in 1924 in Boston, Massachusetts, moving to the nearby suburbs of Norwood when he was in the fifth grade. He decided in high school that he wanted to be a missionary, in part because "being a missionary was a heroic figure . . . in the subculture that I lived in."[29] And he specifically wanted to work in Africa, perhaps because of "some romanticism or other." After writing to several missionary organizations, he decided to approach the Spiritans, because he "liked [their] literature." As he elaborated in a short, published autobiographical sketch, "Faithful to the vision of their founders, they emphasized commitment to the least, the lost, and the left-out populations of our planetary village" (Hillman 1994a: 162). He attended Cornwells, the Spiritan junior seminary in Bensalem, Pennsylvania, from 1942 to 1944, a year of novitiate in Ridgefield, Connecticut, and then, after his profession as a priest in 1945, senior seminary at St. Mary's in Ferndale, Connecticut. He was ordained on September 15, 1950, and sent to work in the Vicariate of Kilimanjaro in 1951.

Father Richard LeClair, a fellow Spiritan who studied at the same time as Father Hillman, offers some additional insights in his memoir into the tenor of missionary training at the time (LeClair 1993). According to Father LeClair, many of the young men who attended Cornwells did not continue to study for the priesthood. Those who did continue spent the year in novitiate studying the Spiritan rules and constitution in a quiet, secluded setting under the direction of a novice master, a senior Spiritan priest who guided their reflections and study through individual meetings and group retreats. Many prospective Spiritans left at this stage, some only a few days after beginning the novitiate. Those who survived this "time of testing" (LeClair 1993: 14) were professed on August 15 of the following year, the Feast of the Assumption.[30] Profession involved making temporary vows of chastity, poverty, and obedience for a three-year period (with the possibility of renewal for another three-year period). In senior seminary, they studied philosophy and theology, but very little about missiology (theories and methods of evangelization), the history and culture of Africa (or any other missionary site), or practical matters such as language, first aid, and proper food preparation. As Father LeClair wrote in his memoir, "in Seminary, we were taught nothing of the customs of the African people. At that time, language was not a problem either; for we never had to learn it. Later we would learn or attempt to learn and to speak Swahili. But on that first day in Mombasa, my companion and I were not able even to say 'Jambo. . . . Hello.' So much for being prepared for a very special work in the Church" (1993: 36).

Father Hillman echoed these concerns, noting that "after a standard seminary training that was oriented toward the pastoral ministry in American suburbia, I was hardly prepared for cross-cultural ministry in Africa" (Hillman 1994a: 162). To make up for this lack of formal missionary training, he read widely on "whatever I could find on the meaning and methods of missionary activity. The writings of Yves Congar, Henri de Lubac, Pierre Charles, Jean Daniélou, and Anscar Vonier were my best sources, together with some encyclical letters by two popes dealing explicitly with the meaning and methods of missionary ministry in the Catholic tradition" (1994a: 162). But "the most exciting aspect of this self-education was the discovery of anthropology and the rich meanings of the word 'culture' " (1994a: 162). He attended some anthropology lectures at Fordham University in 1951, did some preliminary readings, and years later was "carried along enthusiastically by such writers as Monica Wilson, Victor Turner, and Clifford Geertz. These were complemented by the anthropologists I met in Africa doing their original field research: Alan Jacobs among the Masai, and Robert Gray among the Batem" (1994a: 162).

Father Hillman's first assignment was to teach theology in the Catholic senior seminary in Kibosho. But he lasted only a year because of pedagogical disagreements with Bishop Byrne. As he explains in retrospect:

Against the prevailing pedagogy of the seminary, I had argued that the students should be encouraged to read contemporary books and journals and should be discouraged from memorizing their Latin textbooks. Moreover, I had raised questions about the morality of colonialism and the Christian acquiescence in evil. I had even wondered aloud about such topics as the relevance of a Latin liturgy in Africa, the exclusive use of foreign forms of prayer and music in the churches, and the imposition of Jewish and European names at baptism. Nor did my history course avoid mentioning the institutional church's seamy side. Worse still, my interest in African cultures had led me into intensive discussions about the colonial attitudes and ethnocentric methods of missionaries who, when not condemning local cultures, generally ignored them.

The Christian Gospel was being presented to African peoples as though they had no cultures of their own. They had only to memorize the catechism and keep all the rules made by the dead, white European males, while culti-vating all the post-Reformation animosities of separated Western Christians. In schools and churches the people were being resocialized systematically into all the culturally conditioned and historically dated confessional practices and pieties developed through the various Euro-American experiences and inter-pretations of Christianity. Indigenous languages were bypassed in parts of Tan-zania and Kenya. Christian communication was mainly through Swahili, even among peoples for whom this Bantu language was as foreign as Greek. (Hillman 1994a: 163)

In response to these "dangerous ideas" (Hillman 1994a: 163; quotes in original), Bishop Byrne "sent me to Arusha, far away from the seminary. It's the bad influence I had on the seminarians; I've always had a bad influence on seminarians ever since!" At the time, Arusha mission encompassed all of what would later become the Diocese of Arusha, but was mainly just St. Theresa's, a town parish serving "Chaggas who happened to live in Arusha. They ignored the Meru tribe, they ignored the Arusha tribe, the Maasai, they didn't even know there was a tribe called Sonjo." But the superior of Arusha Mission, Father Egbert Durkin, an English Spiritan, welcomed Father Hillman and encouraged him to begin some work with Maasai.

As described in more detail in the following chapter, after a slow start, Father Hillman spent the next sixteen years working with Maasai. He opened the first Maasai mission in Monduli, which was the administrative headquarters of Masai District (later Monduli District). Visitors in 1960 described Father Hillman and the Monduli mission as follows:

> The mission house at Monduli . . . has character: a superb crucifix, carved by an African convert, and a gentle African Madonna look down on the library of a man who loves Africa and the intellectual Catholic writings. His desk is chaotic, piled with manuscripts, photographs, lists. Broadbladed Masai spears are propped casually beneath the crucifix, a warrior's painted shield stands in a corner beside a hunting rifle, a camp-bed, chop-boxes. Father HILLMAN, Boston-born Holy Ghost father who runs the mission, looks like a romantic's picture of the "White Hunter"—bronzed, strong, Khaki-clad. Naked Masai 'moran' saunter in and out, three teenage Masai boys, wearing only a short orange calico cloak knotted over one shoulder, are the cooks, "houseboys," guides and good friends of the priest. (Moss and Moss 1960: 1)

From this deeply masculine base, Father Hillman spent much of his energy building, supervising, and supporting schools and a few dispensaries in Maasai areas. Despite the exhausting nature of his work, he made time to reflect on and write about his experiences. Father Girard Kohler recalled how, in 1966 when he lived with Father Hillman, Father Ralph Poirier, and Father Thomas Tunney in Monduli, Father Hillman would spend most afternoons in his bedroom reading and writing. He would emerge at 5 P.M. for "sundowners" (drinks) and "start talking. Everybody else had to sort of be there to be the sounding board, to respond. . . . He [would] say something, and we [would] agree with it, or challenge it, or bring up another point of view . . . and that was valuable to him" (GK/21).[31] Among Father Hillman's readings at the time were key works in the field of critical theology, especially the writing of Protestant and Anglican theologians and missiologists such as Robinson, Barth, Tillich, and, perhaps most importantly, Roland Allen (Hillman 1994a: 163; EH/18).

Another significant influence on Father Hillman's ideas was his interactions with neighboring Lutheran clergy. The Lutheran church had reinvigorated its Maasai evangelization work in the 1950s, after a hiatus produced by the expulsion of its German missionaries following World War I. As Father Hillman (1994a: 163) recounts, "eventually, my activities [in Maasai areas] caught the attention of the Lutheran leadership, and they assigned a couple of zealous American missionaries to the area." Father Hillman was rebuffed in his initial efforts to encourage dialogue with these early Lutheran pastors: "I said [to a Lutheran pastor], 'We should be talking to each other, we have common interests.' He said, 'You people shame the Bible, how could I be talking with you?' So it was the old, middle ages attitude." But eventually, in the early 1960s, another Spiritan, Father Vince Donovan, became acquainted with several Lutheran pastors teaching at Makumira, the Lutheran seminary near Arusha. He initiated regular meetings between interested Lutheran and Catholic clergy to discuss the differences and similarities in their perspectives and practices on such issues as baptism. As Father Kohler recalls, "They just took it into their heads that this would be a nice thing on a very sort of theoretical level to sit down, half a dozen people or so, and talk theology. And let's see where this thing goes. Talk about it. Not any practical fights, territory and all this. Just talk about it. Your theology of sacraments, your theology of grace, your theology of salvation, whatever it is." Father Hillman participated in their meetings, presented several papers to the group, and was clearly stimulated by the ecumenical nature of the discussions. Ironically, it was Lutheran missionaries who introduced Father Hillman, Father Donovan, and the other Catholic priests to the work of Roland Allen and some of the other theologians who would force them to radically rethink their missionary methods (GK/9–10).

Father Hillman's readings, experiences, deepening knowledge of Maasai religious practices and beliefs, and debates and discussions with his Catholic confreres, Lutheran colleagues, catechists, and Maasai friends led him toward "the broader ecumenical vision articulated, with increasing insistence, in my own writings: *The Church as Mission* (1965), *The Wider Ecumenism* (1968), and *Many Paths* (1989)" (Hillman 1994a: 163). A critical catalyst for his advocacy of a "wider ecumenism of interreligious dialogue" that would include "non-Christian" religions was his growing support of the controversial idea that God's grace was universally available to all religions, instead of limited to Catholics or Christians:[32] "Is the church's mission compromised by God's magnanimous proffering of grace to all nations through the religious systems available to them in their own cultural worlds, not only before but also after the arrival of missionaries from Europe and North America? Is the Creator's saving love for a people constrained by the late arrival among them of lisping and bickering preachers?" (Hillman 1994a: 163). These questions were clearly shaped by his time with Maasai: "My confidence in the ubiquity of saving faith was enhanced by the general behavior of my numerous pre-Christian friends, still immersed fully in their own cultural world. Nakudana ole Sunkuiya and Kamonduli ole Ngari [both Maasai], like the rest of us, appeared consistently to be both 'saints and sinners at the same time' (Luther), or 'saints always in need of purification' (Vatican II)" (Hillman 1994a: 163). Of course, his characterization of them as "pre-Christian" (as opposed to, say, "non-Christian") implies a temporal hierarchy and underlying hope that they would, eventually, become Christian.

Over time, Father Hillman became very "optimistic" about Maasai religion; he saw it as a "very positive religious experience." In particular, "I was always impressed by the attitude manifest by people when they were praying," especially in contrast to the "bloodless abstractions found in the Roman Missal" (Hillman 1993: 16). When asked whether he saw any difference in "how Maasai men and women engage with their religion," he responded that "you see more of it with women than men." He noted the "intensity" of Maasai women's praying, especially their fertility prayers; they were "very reverent, very energetic. And everybody took them seriously. When a group of women arrive[d] at a Maasai boma and request[ed] gifts of cattle or money, or whatever they wanted, they got them." He recalled a fertility ceremony that he had witnessed in the mid 1960s on top of Lolkisale mountain, where there were some "very big, very ancient trees" (it is unclear if these were *oreteti* trees):

> I remember seeing women there, it was actually Easter Sunday one year, but they didn't connect it with Easter. . . . And they were parading around this great tree and spilling milk on the tree and chanting, asking God for children. '*Eng'ai aomon inkerra*' [God I beg you for children]. With plumps of grass in one hand and kibuyus of milk in the other. . . . There was grass, or maybe they used the grass to sprinkle the milk. And there were a couple of men dressed like women.

When asked how many women were there, he replied "hundreds." "They came from a lot of places, there were women who were not Maasai as well. And these women who were not Maasai all said, 'These ceremonies are the greatest. Any of us who pray here with these Maasai, we all have children. We know we will conceive.'" As the Maasai women explained to him, "You see, this big tree that we go around and put milk on, we're praying here. That's not God, but this is where our mothers and their mothers and their mothers all came and prayed. And that's why we're all here." In sum, according to Father Hillman, "that's what their religious thing is, celebrating life."

Building on these ideas, Father Hillman eventually proposed some even more radical changes in church practice. Most notably, in 1967 he presented a paper to a conference of seventy African bishops in which he argued that the Catholic Church should consider a "more tolerant attitude toward the good-faith polygamous marriages of people who subsequently wished to participate fully in the sacramental life of the Christian community" (Hillman 1994a: 163–64). Official church practice at the time mandated that, in order to be baptized, a polygamous man could retain only one wife and must abandon the others. In contrast, Father Hillman suggested that the Church baptize all members of a polygamous family with the proviso that the husband could not marry any additional wives. He believed that polygamy would eventually fade of its own accord with modernization and education.[33] Although his paper on the "polygamy problem" had been requested by Archbishop Del Mestri, who was the apostolic nuncio to East Africa at the time, the new apostolic nuncio, Archbishop Satorelli, "took exception" to the paper, and maneuvered to prevent Father Hillman from continuing to work in Tanzania. As Father Hillman summarized the episode: "'Dangerous ideas' again" (Hillman 1994a: 163–64).[34]

His critical engagement with and reflections on his Maasai work clearly transformed him from a zealous missionary eager to save Maasai souls to what some might call a "missionary basher" (cf. Kirby 1994b: 138). He describes the change as

aa gradual process of coming to respect them. And I remember raising questions at different times, "What are we doing here for these people?" Because when I got to know individuals and I was very fond of a lot of people there and knew them. I said, "They are as good as any people I ever knew, what are we adding to their lives?" So, I raised those questions. And I did a lot of study, and I wrote to theologians and wondered "what's the real rationale for missionary work?" They have a religion of their own that works. And I found that they prayed more than any Christians I knew. So, that's how I got interested in theology. When I was a seminarian, I published a paper ... in *Theological Studies*, which gave me a lot of self-confidence. I said, "My God, I can get published in *Theological Studies*," which is the most prestigious journal in English. And so I had enough self-confidence to keep writing and searching things, and trying to articulate a viewpoint. And I was always amazed at how few people bothered to refute whatever I was saying. I said, "Maybe it's frightening!"

Nonetheless, several of his ideas informed the discussions at Vatican II, and "some of my proposals and sentences found their way into the conciliar decree on the missions" (Hillman 1994a: 163).

After his departure from Tanzania in 1968, Father Hillman earned a masters, then a doctoral, degree, worked as the Africa director of the Christian Children's Fund, based in Nairobi, and then held a series of missionary, research, and teaching positions in Kenya and the United States, including many years teaching social ethics at Salve Regina University in Newport, Rhode Island. Most importantly, he kept reading, thinking, and writing, publishing his views in an array of books and articles. Among other things, "I learned to speak of sinful social structures in the secular terms of modernity, and to appreciate the relevance of liberation theology worldwide" (Hillman 1994a: 164). Throughout his work, he continued to call for a critical reevaluation of missionary assumptions, methods, and practices that would recognize their "chronic ethnocentrisms" (Hillman 1994a: 164) and respect local religions, cultures, and societies:

> We must have an "incarnational" method for inserting the Gospel, as a leaven, into the cultural worlds of other peoples. We must recognize their traditional symbol systems and social structures as instruments capable of serving God's good purposes. History provides no evidence that the Holy Spirit works more efficaciously through Western systems and structures than through the other cultures that have always served the vast majority of humankind.
>
> The Christian mission should not contribute to the destruction of the cultural worlds of other peoples and promote among them foreign ways of being human and religious—ways borrowed uncritically from the historico-cultural experiences of Western peoples. The incarnational principle tells us that the Word of God should be expressed not only through the linguistic symbol systems of each people but also through all their other cultural forms and structures, including their traditional religions, which are, like languages, culturally and historically constructed symbol systems of meaningful communication. (Hillman 1994a: 165–66)

In other words, "Is it perhaps time now to rethink the meaning of the Christian mission in terms of a mutually enriching dialogue with the other cultures and their respective religious components, allowing the Holy Spirit to speak to us through them, even as we expect the Spirit to speak to them through us?" (Hillman 1994a: 166).

Ambivalent Aims: Father Girard Kohler

Father Girard Kohler began his missionary work in Tanzania in 1964, over a decade later than Father Hillman. This tumultuous decade saw radical changes in Africa (including the independence of Tanzania in 1961), the United States (the beginning of the Vietnam War and subsequent radical political and social protests), and the Catholic Church (most notably the Second Vatican Council). The Diocese of Arusha was established in 1963 in the midst of these sweeping transformations. While Father Hillman experienced these events as transitions that reshaped aspects of his missionary experience, they were already established by the time Father Kohler arrived in Tanzania. Nonetheless, the bulk of Father Kohler's formation and training occurred before Vatican II, so he experienced some dissonance between his pre–Vatican II training and post–Vatican II missionary practice.

I met Father Kohler ("Gerry" to his friends) soon after I arrived in Tanzania in 1985. At the time, he had just taken over Monduli mission, where he worked until he moved to Kikatiti, a non-Maasai mission, in 1992. During my first year, we met socially at gatherings of Spiritans, Spiritan Associates (lay people like myself working for the church with the financial sponsorship of the Spiritans), diocesan clergy, and Catholic laity. We also spoke professionally, in my capacity as the project proposal writer for the new Arusha Diocesan Development Office (ADDO), which was started by the Diocese of Arusha in 1985 in the aftermath of the 1983–1984 drought to assist local communities in their transition from food relief efforts to development projects of their own choosing. Our initial four-member team also assisted priests working in the diocese to design, fund, implement, and supervise development projects in their parishes and missions. By 1986, ADDO had expanded to more than twenty employees (mostly Tanzanian, including several Maasai); the bishop had selected me to replace Father Edward Hearn, a Spiritan priest, as coordinator of ADDO after his resignation; and ADDO was actively engaged in an array of projects (including food security, development education, water development, women's development) in predominantly Maasai areas. Now Father Kohler and I met more often, as he was deeply involved in building a large church in Emairete, for which we were helping him seek funds.

Father Kohler was still running Monduli mission when I returned to Tanzania in the summer of 1990 and then again in 1991 through 1993 to conduct research for my dissertation. With the church in Emairete completed, he was now busy building a large church in Monduli town. He helped me get situated in Emairete, my primary research community, and offered advice and assistance with the other two communities, especially Mti Mmoja, which was one of his active outstations. I met him regularly when he conducted church services in Emairete and Mti Mmoja, and occasionally stopped by Monduli mission to chat. I formally interviewed him twice, in April and May of 1992, and took extensive pictures of an Easter baptism service that he conducted at Mti Mmoja in 1992. We have continued to stay in touch, including an intense exchange of letters after he read my early article on how gender shaped the history of Spiritan evangelization efforts among Maasai, "Engendered Encounters" (Hodgson 1999d), and disagreed with some of my interpretations and findings. Throughout the years, Father Kohler has been a helpful, critical, and sometimes wry and humorous commentator on my work, his own missionary experiences, and Spiritan and Maasai life.

Father Kohler was born in 1937 in St. Paul, Minnesota. He attended the Spiritan junior seminaries in Ann Arbor and Bensalem, made his temporary vows after a year of the Spiritan novitiate in Ridgefield, studied philosophy and theology at Ferndale, and was ordained on September 22, 1963 (Koren 1994: 592). In 1964, he was assigned to the Diocese of Arusha, where he was posted to Loliondo mission after being sent to the Maasai school and mission in Simanjiro to learn Swahili with just a "dictionary and a grammar" (GK/21). Initially, he worked with Sonjo people near Loliondo, but in 1966 he began to help Father Vince Donovan with the direct evangelization of Maasai in the Loliondo area. He moved around several times, including a two-year stint in the United States as vocations coordinator for the Spiritans, before he took over Monduli mission in 1985, where he initially led a team of five Spiritan priests and one Spiritan brother.

While Father Hillman could perhaps be characterized as "the thinker," Father Kohler may be thought of as "the builder." He was responsible for building a number of churches, schools, and dispensaries throughout the Diocese of Arusha, including Maasai areas. As a result of his efforts, which included a large church in the town of Monduli, the diocese expanded and improved its institutional infrastructure. Ironically, Father Kohler, at least by the time I met him near the end of his missionary career, was much more comfortable building new churches than peopling them. His perspective on his many years of work in the diocese of Arusha, with Maasai, Arusha, and other people, was decidedly ambivalent. He supported the idea of evangelization and mission, but seemed more comfortable in the role of parish priest serving established churches. In part I am sure that this was a result of his age at the time that we met, and a clear understanding, based on experience, of the physical toll and emotional frustrations of first-evangelization work, especially in Maasai areas. But I also sensed something deeper, a reluctance to create new communities of Catholics that suggested a wariness about the mission enterprise in general and Maasai evangelization in particular. At several points in our interviews, he noted that he was hesitant to baptize Maasai communities. He often thought that they were not "ready," because either they had not learned enough or they did not demonstrate sufficient Christian practice and community. Moreover, he recognized that baptism created a "huge responsibility" for him as a priest and for the church as an institution: "I mean [baptism] is good, that's the goal, but I just don't do it, I don't feel right. My feeling is that it is a horrible responsibility. . . . I'm responsible before God for having baptized these people." He also worried that the church itself was not well prepared to assume responsibility for these newly baptized people, given its history of erratic evangelization and pastoral care, which often meant that baptized communities were abandoned for years. He described a recent case in a community near Loliondo, where Spiritan missionaries had instructed and baptized Maasai many years ago, and then subsequent priests had not followed up:

> All these people who were just abandoned for umpteen years and the Lutherans are taking them now and re-baptizing them and we're all shocked that they didn't accept the Catholic baptism. But they were just abandoned. They were baptized, and some people did something, but whatever it did it wasn't enough. And the priests that came along subsequently didn't take on the responsibility, no transport, we weren't interested at all in Maasai . . . whatever the reasons were.

Too often, he explained, missionaries worked with certain communities as "pet projects," and their successors found new communities to work with rather than continue with the old. As a result, "I am shy and nervous about baptizing."

Nonetheless, when we spoke in 1992, Father Kohler was excited about a community of Arusha who had approached him recently and requested instruction: "It's a very encouraging group. I'm tickled with it. I had it in the back of my head for a long time. As a matter of fact I traveled around there two or three times in the course of the years, but never started anything. Until, suddenly, they started something." By this time, he felt strongly that this was the process that missionaries, especially expatriate missionaries, should follow: waiting for communities to invite them in, to take the initiative themselves to seek instruction and to establish a church.

The fact, however, that the community that approached Father Kohler was predominantly Arusha highlighted an ongoing set of tensions within the Diocese of Arusha about ethnicity. Although there were several missions that served the needs of Arusha people, including the churches based in the town of Arusha, some Spiritans were reluctant to work with Arusha who lived interspersed with Maasai in rural areas; "even now, people are more concerned about Maasai per se. . . . It was a kind of Maasai-itis thing. . . . The Maasai were so special, so unique." Conversely, the predominantly non-Maasai who attended services in the towns, including Monduli town, were annoyed that their pastors spent resources and time evangelizing Maasai. In Monduli, a district headquarters filled with people of diverse ethnic backgrounds from all over northern Tanzania, including many Chagga, "they have mass. Daily mass for [goodness] sakes. And the priests are here, and they get as probably as good an attention as they have any right to. But they would like more attention."

Father Kohler himself seems to have an ambivalent regard for and relationship to Maasai: "I'm not afflicted, I hope, with Maasai-itis. As a matter of fact, sometimes I think I can't stand them." His published articles on the "Apostolate to the Maasai" referred in several places to Maasai in terms that marked them as not only different, but as inferior or backward in certain ways. For example, he claimed that they were "essentially unreflective," and that a certain method of extension education was perhaps "too [ambitious] . . . for the level of sophistication of the individuals being trained" (Kohler 1977a: 412). Similar attitudes were reflected in many of his interactions with Maasai. Although Father Kohler is the first to acknowledge that at times he has a "phlegmatic personality," his irascibility and temper flared in several encounters that I witnessed between him and Maasai men and women, even during church services. He had little patience with extraneous noise during services (such as children crying or women whispering) and movement (people arriving late or leaving to go to the restroom). As I recounted in my field notes from an Easter baptism service at Mti Mmoja in 1992: "Gerry was preaching at this point with Edward translating. . . . Children were crying, at one point Gerry turned to a crying child behind him and angrily said 'Nyamaza!' ['Shut up!'] The mother tried to quiet the child, then took it outside." He also became frustrated if women did not remember the words to prayers or songs, or if they otherwise diverted from his liturgical script.

In addition, during the service he sometimes embarrassed Maasai men and women who had erred from proper Christian (but not Maasai) practice in some way. In one case, Father Kohler refused in front of the congregation to baptize the son of a Maasai widow who had conceived the child long after her husband's death unless the widow publicly named the biological father (in Maasai custom, widows are encouraged to keep having children after their husband's death, and all these children are considered the offspring of her deceased husband). In another, he commented to a man and woman who had been married in customary terms for several years and now wanted to have their marriage blessed in the church: "I'll do this quickly since it really isn't a wedding, I mean this couple already has kids and all!" Finally, a Maasai friend of mine reported that when Father Kohler had asked the baptismal candidates in Mti Mmoja what baptismal names they had selected, one responded "Teresia." Father Kohler got angry and told everyone present that there was no point in Maasai choosing "mzungu" (Swahili for "white, European") names. He then kicked everyone out of the church and stormed away. A group of elder men were then called upon to console him and convince him to return and continue the service.

Although my evidence is only anecdotal, my sense was that Father Kohler treated Maasai women with greater disdain than he did Maasai men, at least educated Maasai men. As will become clear in subsequent chapters, gender was an abiding concern of Father Kohler's and a source of enduring frustration. Despite his best efforts to interest and instruct Maasai men, Maasai women dominated his classes and church services. He attributed this in part to what he characterized as women's oppression by men: "the men treat them as children, still. I think they probably feel it is good for them." Yet in many ways, as the above examples suggest and chapters 3 and 4 will make clear, Father Kohler had himself adopted a similar attitude toward Maasai women.

Father Kohler has since retired from active missionary work in Tanzania for health reasons. He has held a series of administrative and fund-raising jobs for the U.S. East Province of the Spiritans. He has traveled throughout the United States doing "mission collections," that is, giving sermons at local churches about his missionary work in order to collect offerings for the Spiritans. But he has also reflected on his work and experiences in Tanzania, sometimes in print, and has achieved a peace of sorts with his own human foibles and fallibilities. As he wrote in an essay about the enduring influence of Father Libermann's teachings and life, Father Libermann's exhortation to seek a

"practical union with God" works itself out daily, for us, in the apostolate, in our fidelity to the Gospel imperative to proclaim the Good News quite literally to the ends of the earth. Ours is not the spirituality of the cloister, of the monastic charism, of the clerical *per se,* nor necessarily of their particular practices. Apostolic activity is the font and the forum of our spiritual lives. Our holiness flows from our ministries, specifically to the most abandoned and impoverished of peoples—"the most wretched," in Libermann's apostolic vision, which dared go beyond the conventional wisdom of his era. (Kohler 2002: 2)

Yet, Father Kohler continued, "following that perspective, experience has taught me the wisdom of Libermann's insistence that flexibility is vital for our lives and for our apostolate, being responsive to what is happening to us, and around us. My own major frustrations, and failures, in Africa have been due to lack of adaptability to the realities of life" (Kohler 2002: 2–3).

Post–Vatican II Practice: Father William Christy

Father William Christy differs from Father Kohler and Father Hillman in a very important way; "[The difference between] Kohler and myself is that I am a totally post–Vatican II production."[35] As such, and as a relatively new missionary when I met and interviewed him, he had little of the self-criticism of Father Hillman or the ambivalence of Father Kohler reflected in his work or words. Instead, he was eager, engaged, and energetic about evangelization. He equated the changes produced by Vatican II in missionaries to the process and experience of conversion, "think of the turmoil that they went through, the uncertainty, but then the commitment they made." "Which," he added, "I think . . . may have made them better missionaries than myself." As one of the latest generation of Spiritans to work with Maasai, he has also learned tremendously from the lessons, experiences, experiments, and mistakes of his predecessors: "I get to stand on the shoulders of giants, really, when you think of Jackson, and Donovan and Hillman and Kane and all those men who went before. Ned [Father Marchessault] standing out there in Endulen is kind of the last touchstone of that era. We'll have to build a little shrine up there so that we can remember . . . the heady days. And the stories. The stories. We had so many characters."

We first met briefly in 1990, when he was doing his overseas training and I was spending the summer in Tanzania doing preliminary research for my dissertation. We did not meet again for ten years, until the summer of 2000, when I returned for further research on the missionary encounter to discover that Father Christy ("Bill") was now in charge of Monduli Juu parish, which encompassed my three primary research communities, Emairete, Mti Mmoja, and Embopong'. (That we did not meet during my research trips in the intervening decade is one indication of the vast size of the diocese and the scattered nature of the missions within it.) I found him friendly, kind, and eager to talk to me and help me with my research. I attended his church services in all three communities, spoke to him informally about his work on numerous occasions, and interviewed him in July 2000 at the fathers' house in Monduli town, just as he was preparing to finally move up the mountain to the fathers' house at Monduli Juu (his move had been delayed for over a year because of various personnel issues).

Father Christy was born in 1963, and raised in Levittown, Pennsylvania. After graduating from Cornwells in 1982, he enlisted in the Marine Corps, where he chose to become a Reservist and continue his education. During his two years at Indiana University of Pennsylvania, he began to reflect more substantially on his life and future: "I was in a pre-law program, my superiors in the Marine Corps were open to the idea that I could go on to a law degree and become a Judge Advocate in the Marine Corps, and everything was just too programmed, you know. What I was going to do for the next twenty years was already mapped out and then I just rebelled against it." So he started writing letters to different seminaries. Although he was familiar with the Spiritans from his high school experience, he initially rejected joining them "because I didn't want to make an emotional decision." But he eventually changed his mind and chose the Spiritans:

> In the end, the Spiritans were involved both overseas and in North America [and] they were doing parish ministry, education ministry, missionary work. . . . So at the time I didn't know what I wanted to do for ministry. So it seemed like a good idea to join the Spiritans because then the options were left open. Whereas, if I had joined the Maryknolls, then it is exclusively a missionary congregation, or [if] I joined the Diocese, it would have been exclusively in the parish or maybe education.

He transferred to Duquesne in 1984, attended Catholic Theological Union (CTU) in Chicago for his graduate work in theology, spent a year in Farnham, Quebec, for his novitiate, and was professed in 1988.

In contrast to Father Hillman and Father Kohler, Father Christy did take courses at CTU in missiology, with an emphasis on cross-cultural ministry. In response to Vatican II and other changes in the Catholic Church, CTU and other major seminaries in North America had revised their curriculum to explore the history, theories, and methods of mission. Nonetheless, Father Christy was "disappointed" because the definition of "mission" was so expansive that "anything then was mission": "So an . . . Irish-American nun working in a Polish-American parish in Chicago was saying

'I'm doing cross-cultural ministry!' " In response, he distinguished "cross-cultural mission" (working with minority communities in the United States, all of whom have had at least minimal "exposure to Christianity" and understanding of " 'Western' civilization") from what he called "cross-civilizational mission" (working overseas with communities that lacked exposure to Christianity and Western civilization). "So," he continued, "anyone in the North American context, whether they are working in a Latino community or a Native American or Black American [community], there will be a connection point on their basic Western civilizational level. Whereas [at the] 'cross-civilizational' level you don't have that. And so you must start at a base, a more basic level of interconnectiveness." In other words, with "first evangelization [you are] coming to an area that has no tradition of the Christian faith; they have no concept of what you are about to present to them, so you are starting at a much different level."

A few courses at CTU, however, were useful for his future work, because they examined how "different cultures would look at things." "I remember one course in particular, on Eucharist. And so we were exploring how all of these different cultures would look at Eucharist, so that kind of was a good primer, saying that you have to be able to place yourself in the mindset or to appreciate the mindset of different civilizations as they approach the Eucharist."

"These were," I interjected, "kind of anthropology courses in some way?"

"Yes," he replied. "We also did that with initiation, different types of initiation, looked at . . . what would that mean in Papua New Guinea? What would that mean in Japan? What would that mean in South America amongst traditional people or indigenous people? So that way it was a general [introduction]. But no one ever said 'This is how you do first evangelization.' "

Instead, his training in first evangelization was "on the job" through discussions, observations, and practice with experienced Spiritans. From 1989 to 1991 he lived in Tanzania doing his Overseas Training Program (OTP). OTP was a recent innovation by Spiritans to introduce seminarians to the work of mission. In Tanzania at the time, it entailed about six months of language and cross-cultural training, and then an eighteen-month apprenticeship in a mission station (cf. LeClair 1993: 50). Father Christy did his OTP at Kikatiti mission on the slopes of Mount Kilimanjaro in the Diocese of Arusha, which was a "very mixed ministry." Kikatiti served a diverse range of congregations and needs, from pastoral work with established communities of Chagga Catholics to evangelization work with Maasai and other groups living near the shores of a large lake called Nyumba ya Mungu. After Father Christy returned to the States and was ordained in 1992, he went back to Tanzania. He served briefly in Kikatiti, and then moved to Mto wa Mbu, where he stayed for about five and a half years. Initially he worked with a French Spiritan, Father Michel Robert, and then he became pastor of the mission once Father Robert left. Mto wa Mbu was a large town on the main tourist route from Arusha to Ngorongoro Crater and the Serengeti plains. The town had a diverse ethnic community of traders, shopkeepers, mechanics, curio vendors, and more.[36] In addition to this large, primarily Swahili-speaking community, the Spiritans at Mto wa Mbu served two Swahili-speaking outstations and ten Maasai-speaking outstations. The Maasai work consisted of "first evangelization and accompanying newly baptized communities." During his time at the mission, they led three groups of Maasai in different villages through "first contact, first teaching [for] two years, two and a half years of catechumenate, and then baptism."[37]

After two years of work at the Spiritan East African Provincialate headquarters in Arusha, Father Christy was assigned to Monduli Juu parish in 1999. The negotiations between the archbishop (the Diocese of Arusha became an archdiocese in 1999) and the Spiritan leadership over his assignment reflected the sometimes conflicting needs and concerns of both:

> There was some pushing and pulling about my assignment. The Archbishop wanted me to go to Loliondo and was willing to send two Diocesan priests, newly ordained, with me. . . . However, my superiors wouldn't agree to it, that a Spiritan [would live] so isolated, so far from community. The Bishop was looking for the Spiritans to take on another work in Maasailand from what we were already doing. So Monduli Juu became a good compromise. . . . In terms of religious life, my community is here in Monduli and my ministry would be in Monduli Juu.

Because of the leaves and sabbaticals of some other Spiritans, and a general shortage of personnel, it still took another year for him to actually move into the fathers' residence in Emairete, which is the village in Monduli Juu where the large church is located. In the meantime, he had to cover three "missions": Monduli town parish, the large military stations and camps on the outskirts of Monduli, and Monduli Juu parish. His work included monthly visits to each of the twenty-six often remote outstations encompassed by the parishes of Monduli town and Monduli Juu. By July 2000, an African Spiritan returned from sabbatical to Monduli parish, and Father Christy was able to work exclusively in Monduli Juu parish. As he wrote in the Spiritan newsletter, "I saw Monduli Juu in those busy days as a refuge, a place of peace. I saw it as a place where I could do the ministry I most love—first evangelization and community development. Mostly, I wanted time to know people, to sit in the homesteads and drink tea, to teach the catechumens, to become part of the fabric of life in the villages that I served" (Christy 2001: 3). Nonetheless, a number of his sermons that I heard during the summer of 2000 were about his simultaneous excitement, anticipation, and trepidation at moving to Emairete and taking over the work of Monduli Juu parish on a full-time basis.

Of course, once he arrived in Monduli Juu, he was just as busy, according to his own reports. Perhaps most importantly, since no one had lived in the fathers' house for several years, he had to "set up house": "there was no electric power, no water. . . . The solar lighting has been rehabilitated, water tanks have been patched and filled, an outhouse has been dug, firewood has been cut and now I am turning over a small garden. My house is small, a cabin really, but it is well built and snug" (Christy 2001: 3). Despite these tasks, he was able to baptize two new groups of catechumens, teach three other groups of catechumens, serve twelve communities of baptized Christians, begin a series of lessons for his catechists, and even take the time to visit and stop for a "cup of tea" (Christy 2001: 3). Yet none of this would be possible, he acknowledged, "without the catechists" (Christy 2001: 3).

Whether because of his training, the accumulated insights of his predecessors, his relatively short time as a missionary, or his personality, Father Christy had a much less ambivalent, less angst-ridden understanding of baptism than Father Kohler. After a discussion of his evangelization methods (see next chapter), I asked him how he determined when a group of Maasai who had participated in his instruction classes was ready for baptism. He replied:

> There is both the individual and collective sense. You have to . . . gauge the kind of commitment. How are they committed to coming to the teaching times? And what not. You look for real evidence of faith. Personal prayer life. When people are sharing about the teaching and what not. How much they absorb not only on an intellectual but on a daily basis into their lives. And also, very important, when they start asking for baptism. When they start saying "And us? When will we be baptized?"

He interpreted such requests as evidence of a "faith commitment" on the part of the group, and responded by devoting usually another year of instruction to help them prepare for baptism. When I asked if there were certain formal elements that his catechumens were required to know for baptism, he said that it varied a lot:

As I tell my catechists, and I try to follow it myself, we fill whatever container is brought. So if somebody comes to you with a *kopo* [Swahili, "a tin can"], fill the *kopo*. If they come with a Sadolin [a larger container], fill the Sadolin. If they come with a *debe* [Swahili, "an 18 liter tin"], fill the *debe*. So we teach to the capacity of each person. You know, sometimes you get an old *koko* [Swahili, "an old woman," literally "a grandmother"] who comes and you spend two years and . . . the gospel is transforming her life and relationships with other people, but she can't remember the sign of the cross. So . . . you know?! There is no criteria in that way, that this person should be baptized because they know the Our Father, the Hail Mary, the Gloria and what not.

He was however, more "regimented" and "demanding" with children, especially those who were preparing for First Communion and confirmation.

Father Christy's flexibility was also clearly evident in his attempts to blend Maasai and Catholic cultural and religious symbolism, practices, and beliefs. He was a strong advocate of "inculturation," a concept developed fully after Vatican II that referred to efforts to adapt Christianity to local cultures, to promote "a continuous dialogue between Faith and culture" (Shorter 1988: 11) because of a recognition that both are constantly evolving processes with diverse manifestations in different places and times. Father Christy actively sought to learn as much as he could about Maasai beliefs and practices, and to weave Maasai symbolism, ritual forms, and religious stories into his liturgies, sermons, weddings, burials, and other religious occasions. He also attended Maasai rituals such as male and female initiations and age-set promotions to bless the participants, if they were Christians. This is the arena in which Father Christy perhaps learned the most from earlier generations of Spiritans, whether the theological discussions of Father Hillman or the practical lessons of Father Donovan, Father Kane, and Father Robert. In contrast to Father Hillman, when Father Christy was beginning his Maasai evangelization work in the early 1990s, he had a large repertoire of evangelization methods, liturgical practices, and missiological models to draw on.

In addition to his interest in first evangelization, Father Christy was also eager to devise income-generating projects to make Monduli Juu parish and its mission outstations more financially self-reliant. One of the projects he implemented was the cultivation of safflower, an oil-seed thistle plant full of sharp thorns to protect the berries from animals. Two mission outstations each planted two acres of safflower, with the hopes of investing the money until each outstation had ten acres of safflower, for a projected annual income of $1,000. "By that time," according to an article written by Father Joseph Kelly in the "Mission Diary" section of the *USA Eastern Province Newsletter,* "the people will have seen the value of the exercise and will have their own plots of safflower dotting the countryside that was once the domain of only the wild beasts, but is gradually becoming the home of self-reliant Christians" (Kelly 2000: 3).

Cor Unum et Anima Una

As the history of Spiritans and the three brief Spiritan profiles suggest, although the Spiritans shared, according to their motto, *cor unum et anima una,* or "one heart and one spirit," among themselves and with the people they served, they were also divided by generation, nationality, training, theological perspective, cultural assumptions, and more. Moreover, the experience of evangelization, and of other countries, peoples, and ways of life, was itself often a transformative process, challenging and reshaping prior assumptions, beliefs, and practices on the part of the missionaries. Such transformations occurred at the collective level as well, as Spiritans built up a cumulative store of knowledge, insights, and practice for the benefit of subsequent generations. Father Christy and Father LeRoy, separated by one hundred years, confronted very different realities in their missionary situations, and had very different tools and technologies available to facilitate their work.

The portraits also reveal some of the disjunctures between what Father Christy calls "the community of theologians" and "the community of practitioners." While theologians of mission might debate whether to baptize polygamists with reference to church law, missionary practitioners struggle with the real implications for people's lives. "We are responding," explained Father Christy, "to a real life situation on the ground." This dissonance between the ideals and the realities of the missionary enterprise also seemed to be a source of Father Kohler's ambivalence and frustration after decades of work in Tanzania. Ideally, of course, there is communication, learning, and even overlap between the two communities. Father Hillman clearly viewed himself as both a theologian and a practitioner, and his practice radically transformed his theology. In many ways Vatican II was both a response to the input and experiences of missionaries like Father Hillman and a catalyst for further changes and debates, as seen in the work of Father Kohler and Father Christy.

EVANGELIZING "THE MAASAI"

3

Will it be possible one day—we hope soon—to build on this strange foundation a religious structure that God has revealed to us? To reestablish aspects that have been forgotten or deformed? To fill in the existing gaps? To baptize these extraordinary people whom few Europeans have yet studied, where no missions have been established? Why not? No doubt it will require a lot of energy, patience, tact, prudence, sweat, and maybe even some blood. It will require living their nomadic life, learning their strange customs. But none of these is beneath the power of a missionary who remembers his mandate from the Catholic Church and who is under the grace of God. Like the apostles! Are there still any in Christian countries? Apostles ready for anything and pleased with everything, for our admirable bandits in Maasai lands!
  —*Father Alexandre LeRoy, C.S.Sp. 1914,*
  Au Kilima-ndjaro, *pp. 432–33*[1]

Building on the history and biographies presented in the previous chapter, this chapter describes the history of the encounter between Spiritan missionaries and Maasai in Tanzania since the Spiritans opened the first mission station in Masai District in the 1950s. It examines the three successive evangelization strategies of the missionaries—the "school" approach, the "*boma*" approach (or "direct evangelization"), and the "individual" approach—in the context of their perspectives and assumptions about Maasai (especially Maasai gender ideologies and relations), their intentions and outcomes, and changes in the wider political-economic context of the Tanzanian state and Catholic Church (especially the impact of Vatican II). Each approach was the product of a particular historical and cultural conjuncture, and each provided different obstacles and opportunities for Maasai men and women to negotiate and renegotiate gendered relations of power among themselves and with the missionaries. Although significant differences existed between the approaches' objectives and practical implementation, all three shared certain implied gendered concerns, such as the formation of male leadership, a reluctance to challenge the authority of male elders, and an unwillingness to consider seriously the interests and talents of women.

To analyze these processes and tensions, I address the strategies on two scales. On the one hand, I discuss the implementation, assumptions, and shifts in approaches at the broad level of the Diocese of Arusha. Not only were all Spiritans responsible to their bishop and to diocesan leadership for policy directives and spiritual guidance, but they also met together in formal and informal gatherings to share ideas and experiences and discuss their practices. A key institution for such discussions was (and still is) the Maasai Deanery, a formal gathering of all missionary and diocesan clergy working in Maasai areas that met regularly (all other members of the diocese met in the Arusha Deanery).[2] On the other hand, in order to examine in greater detail the actual implementation and experience of these approaches, especially the centrality of gender and power to the encounter, in both this and the following chapters I draw on ethnographic and historical data from three Maasai communities—Emairete, Mti Mmoja, Embopong'—served by Monduli mission, but with very different histories of evangelization. As described in more detail in chapter 5, Emairete has the longest and most intense history of interaction with the Catholic Church, and is now an established headquarters for the parish of Monduli Juu; Mti Mmoja has had a more sporadic and recent involvement with the Catholic Church, but has a small, stable church; and Embopong' is still the site of ongoing "first evangelization" efforts ("first evangelization" refers to the outreach, teaching, and baptism of people from areas with little or no prior interaction with Christianity). These comparative case studies offer insights into the micropractices and micropolitics that shaped the evangelization efforts and experiences of Spiritans and Maasai alike.

Early Encounters

Spiritan missionaries began to live and to work full-time in Masai District in the 1950s. Although Spiritans had been officially responsible for the evangelization of Maasai in Tanzania for over one hundred years, they were dissuaded, in part, by enduring stereotypes of Maasai as tall, proud, "noble savages" defiantly persisting in their outmoded traditions despite the rapidly "modernizing" world around them.[3] As Father Kohler wrote about these earlier encounters:

> Other more progressive and responsive groups of people claimed their prior attention. As has been the pattern elsewhere as well, settled peoples living in

farms and villages were more amenable to the Church's structures and discipline. Moreover, the Masai have long been looked upon as intransigent, dangerous, and amoral, in keeping with their romantic image of cattlemen and warriors in the wild. (Kohler 1977a: 410)

Father Hillman agreed: "As far as Catholic missionaries were concerned it was a waste of time, [Maasai] were just unredeemable savages. They had that popular image of being hopeless." A series of three articles published in 1953 by Father Thomas Dolan, C.S.Sp., in *Mission News*, a Spiritan periodical, reiterated these images (Dolan 1953a, 1953b, 1953c). As the title—"Cowboys of Tanganyika: The Masai"—suggested, Maasai were "cattlemen who hold off from both civilization and Christianity" (Dolan 1953a: 3), in marked contrast to "the Wa Arusha and tribes of the Bantu race" who "even as pagans . . . follow high moral standards and make the steps toward Christianity with docility" (Dolan 1953a: 3). Moreover, Father Dolan's gender and age prejudices were clear: "Masai women and children are often dirty, slovenly and stupid; the old men, with their skinny, weak bodies, give no indication of what they once were physically. The young men, from seventeen to thirty, represent the ideal of the savage warrior because of their magnificent physiques, most of them more than six feet tall and perfectly proportioned" (Dolan 1953a: 3). These enduring stereotypes began years before, in the early accounts of missionaries and explorers such as Thomson (1968 [1885]) and Johnston (1886), who drew on the exaggerated tales of Swahili travelers to characterize Maasai as fierce savages (cf. Hodgson 2001a: 25–26).[4]

Despite these stories and stereotypes, Father Alexandre LeRoy, one of the first Spiritans to encounter Maasai, was quite taken with these "famous pirates of the desert" when he met them in 1890 (LeRoy 1914: 153). In contrast to the many warnings he received about their ferocity and violence, he found that, with the possible exception of the *ilmurran*, Maasai were "civil" and "very peaceful" (LeRoy 1914: 153). In two long chapters of his book *Au Kilima-ndjaro*, he described his observations of the work of men, women, and children, daily life in the homestead, women's trading expeditions, material life, dress and ornaments, political system, and religious practices and beliefs. The familiar trope of the Maasai as noble savage (or in his words, "authentic savage" [LeRoy 1914: 408]) shaped his narrative and observations, but it also informed his wistful hopes:

They are truly the representatives of the race that Thomson, quite rightly, called the most beautiful, the most extraordinary of Africa. They are, without a doubt, the terror of the surrounding tribes. But, after seeing their superb figures, their academic bearing, their pride, their distinctiveness, their manners, one recalls the words of Saint Gregory the Great: "What a shame that these men are not Christians!" (LeRoy 1914: 408–11)

Although he regarded the "moral freedom" of the *ilmurran* as "the most serious obstacle to the penetration of Christianity among them," he acknowledged that Maasai had ideas of good and bad and therefore a moral system. Moreover, they had a basic religious foundation: a belief in a God who was concerned for their welfare, in the concept of a soul, of life after death, sacrifice, atonement, and prayer (LeRoy 1914: 422–27, 432). And so he wondered, and hoped, whether it would be possible someday to evangelize them (LeRoy 1914: 432–33).

Father LeRoy's hopes for the sustained evangelization of Maasai, however, took sixty years to be realized. In addition to the continuing resonance of the stereotypes noted by Father Kohler, Spiritans were also dissuaded by the prospects of learning Maa, the distinct and difficult language spoken by Maasai, as opposed to the easier "Bantu" languages, and the complicated logistics of working with a mobile population (Kieran 1966: 223). As Father Gogarty wrote in 1927, when he was the vicar apostolic of Kilimanjaro: Maasai "are the wildest tribe in the Vicariate. To evangelize them is a problem for they are nomads" (1927: 68). Like colonial administrators, missionaries found it far easier to work with settled farmers rather than seminomadic pastoralists.

There were, however, a few early Maasai converts, primarily children who had been given by their parents to Kilema mission during the 1893 rinderpest epidemic that devastated their herds and lives (Chanel 1900: 84–87; Kieran 1966: 224; LeRoy 1914: 464).[5] Other children were given to the missionaries by the Germans, who captured them on punitive expeditions against Maasai cattle raiders (Chanel 1900: 85–86). According to Joseph Chanel (1900: 84–87), a French explorer who visited Kilema in 1894, the mission cared for about forty-five Maasai children, including seventeen young girls. These children worked on the mission banana plantations to support themselves, attended school, and pursued religious instruction. One Maasai girl, called Tchacoula (presumably for *chakula*, the Swahili word for food), cooked for the missionaries (Chanel 1990: 109). Chanel published two pictures of them: the first of ten Maasai girls ranging in age from about six to sixteen accompanied by the "old Christian woman" who supervised them, and a second picture of thirty-four young Maasai boys from about five to ten years of age. All the children had shaved heads and were wrapped in one (for the boys) or two (for the girls) pieces of plain cotton cloth. At least three Maasai families also settled on mission land and promised to accept instruction (Chanel 1900: 84; Kieran 1966: 224). Ironically, given the radical differences in missionary "success" among Maasai and Chagga and ongoing ethnic rivalries between the two groups, these Maasai orphans later became some of the first catechists working with Spiritans to build new mission stations and evangelize Chagga peoples at Kibosho and Rombo, among other places in Kilimanjaro (Kieran 1966: 224; EH/5).

Moreover, as Father Kohler suggests, the tremendous success of evangelization efforts in the Moshi area of the Vicariate of Kilimanjaro, and its relatively comfortable climate and living circumstances, seduced missionaries into complacency. According to Father Hillman, the focus on Chaggas as opposed to other groups that lived in the Vicariate was also a "fixation of the Bishop [Byrne]," who advocated a "quantification" theory of mission: "They thought the more people, . . . greater numbers is progress. . . . And the Chagga people were very responsive in a way that non-Bantus weren't." Competition with the Lutheran church was also a factor. As Father Hillman noted, "the Meru could have been just as responsive [to the Catholics] but the Lutherans were very intensively engaged with the Meru people." Therefore, "it was always a struggle with the new Bishop to get any new person out for [Maasai areas]. Everything was going to Chaggaland." In time, especially after Bishop Byrne was replaced by Bishop Joseph Kilasara,[6] a Chagga Spiritan, rivalries and stereotypes among Africans within the vicariate also influenced the situation, as Chagga priests and laypeople dominated decision making about the allocation of resources and missionaries: "They didn't see any point in doing anything except serving Chaggas" (EH/8; cf. MMJ/18 Jan. 1962).

From Assimilation to Inculturation: Shifting Approaches

In 1958, during the waning years of British colonial rule in Tanganyika, at a time of acute generational turmoil and gendered tension for Maasai, Father Eugene Hillman and several other American Spiritans began to live full-time at their new mission station in Monduli, the district headquarters of Masai District (MMJ/3 July 1958).[7] Spiritans had been visiting Monduli since 1949 to say monthly mass at the government primary school, prompted by the Catholic teachers at the school, who had begun to teach religion to the children.[8] But lack of adequate transportation, the high cost of fuel and equipment, and already substantial pastoral commitments prevented priests working in Arusha from sustained work in Maasai areas (LMJ/Background). In 1951, two Spiritans began weekly visits, and brought the children to Arusha for feast days (Anon. 1970: 1). In 1953 they built a small chapel, and finally they built a fathers' residence in 1957 after a long delay in receiving permission from the British colonial administration to obtain land in Monduli town.[9] The sudden appeal of working with Maasai, after decades of avoidance, was due in part to the personal initiatives of Father Hillman, who for the past few years had been traveling weekly from Arusha to various Maasai homesteads "in order to influence the traditional leaders of the various sub-clans and age grades to be friendly towards the church" (Kohler 1977a: 410). Father Hillman received reluctant permission from his pastor to visit Maasai areas during the weekdays, but "the rule was he had to be back for ministry on Saturdays, confessions, and Sunday mass" (GK/1). As Father Hillman himself proudly wrote, "I became the first Catholic missionary sent to evangelize the Masai people in Tanzania" (Hillman 1994a: 163).

Other American Spiritans shared Father Hillman's attraction to the perceived "exoticness" of "the Maasai," the rigors of safari work, and the adventures of bush life. Bored with the easy rote and routine of parish work among Chagga people in Moshi and the townspeople of Arusha, these Americans yearned for a challenge. Few Spiritans from other countries shared these interests, and they were happy when most of the Americans joined the Diocese of Arusha when it was created from the Diocese of Moshi in 1963, with Father Dennis Durning,[10] an American Spiritan, as bishop: "In a sense, they sent all the troublemakers and people they didn't want in Moshi over to this side to get rid of them, as it were. A good riddance sort of thing" (GK/1–2). But the very characteristics of "rugged individualism" (GK/2) which made the Americans "troublemakers" within the structures and discipline of Moshi Diocese enabled these "creative maverick-type people" (GK/2) to overcome the logistical difficulties of working in Maasai areas (see also Naas 1971: 56).[11] A few, however, "didn't fit in too well," and shifted to pastoral work in parishes in Arusha town and more settled, non-Maasai areas (GK/2).

As the commercial, administrative, and geographical center of Masai District, Monduli was a convenient site from which to launch expanded evangelization activities with Maasai. Set on the slopes of Monduli mountain (see map 3.1), it enjoyed seasonable weather, permanent water supplies, and fertile land. It was connected to Arusha by passable roads and a functional telephone system, and had a government hospital, government school, post

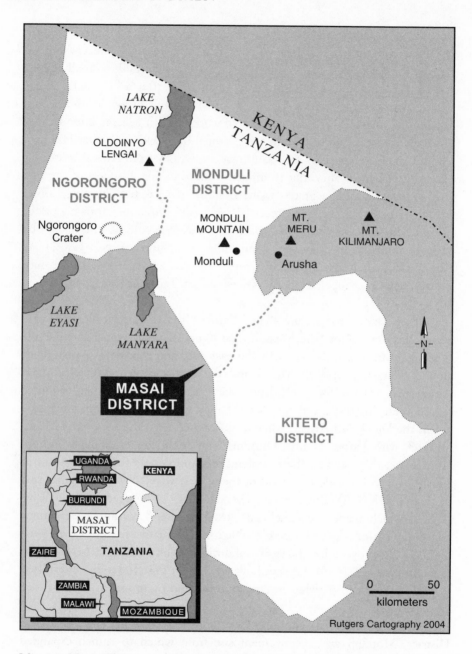

Map 3.1. Masai District, ca. 1950. The map also shows the later divisions of Mason District into Ngorongoro District, Monduli District, and Kiteto District.

office, courthouse, thriving marketplace, and array of small shops and res-
taurants. Several British citizens lived in Monduli, including colonial officers
and personnel, and a few settlers on surrounding coffee plantations and
farms. Many educated Africans from other areas of Tanganyika lived there
as well, working as clerks, dressers, nurses, teachers, and functionaries for
the district and native authority (Hodgson 2001a; GK/25–27). The Olkiama
(later renamed the Masai Council), a council of male elders representing all
the Maasai localities, met regularly in Monduli, as did the native authority
(Hodgson 2001a). Monduli remained the headquarters of Monduli District
in 1974 when Masai District was split into Monduli and Kiteto Districts,
and in 1979 when Ngorongoro District was created from part of Monduli
District.

In the late 1950s, Masai District encompassed more than 24,000 square
miles and had a population of approximately 100,000 (see map 3.1).[12] Its
boundaries approximated those of the former Masai Reserve, into which
Maasai herders had been forced, coerced, and cajoled to move after its creation in 1922 (Hodgson 2001a: 51–59).[13] As is clear from its name, Maasai
were the predominant ethnic population, although Arusha had been moving
into communities surrounding Monduli town for many years and members
of other ethnic groups lived in the towns. Some Arusha were resettled in
Masai District by colonial officials to reduce the problems of overcrowding
and resource scarcity caused by their high population density on and around
Mount Meru.[14] Other Arusha moved of their own accord, exchanging cattle,
daughters, and gifts with Maasai for access to land. Maasai were increasingly
marrying Arusha women as second and subsequent wives to farm for their
households and homesteads (Hodgson 2001a: 58–59, 95–96, 103, 135). Simultaneously, the colonial government also alienated much of the most fertile
land that served as dry-season grazing lands and drought reserves to sell to
more "productive" European settlers or to delineate as forest reserves (with
subsequent restrictions on use and access) (Hodgson 2001a: ch. 2). They
also took over or sold the rights to key permanent water sources such as
Lemisigie, a mountain stream that flowed from Monduli mountain and was
the main water source for the plains below (Hodgson 2001a: 52–53).

Establishing Presence

Initially, the Spiritans' work with Maasai was based on the theory of
"preevangelization": a "theory constructed by theologians, according to which
it is stated that not all peoples are ready for the gospel, and somehow must

be made ready for it" (Donovan 1978: 55). The theory of preevangelization was itself predicated on the dominant theology of mission at the time, a theology of salvation. According to Father Donovan:

> The theology of salvation was the theory on which all mission activity was based, out of which the activity flowed. The mission compound with its many necessary buildings was the symbol of that theory and theology. The compound stood for the church, the ark and haven of salvation, the repository of grace, and, indeed, of God. Outside that compound lay the vast area of tribal life and pagan culture empty of all worth and goodness and holiness and salvation. The missionary process was a movement away from tribal and human life and culture to the church where salvation resided. It was a process of salvation from this world and from human life. (Donovan 1978: v–vi)

Spiritans believed that, unlike Chagga or other African groups, Maasai faced an overwhelming obstacle to "salvation"—their culture. Maasai were perceived as "not fit for Christianity" because of "their whole lifestyle . . . polygamy was a big thing, the stealing, the marauding around. That really these people wouldn't accept the gospel, or couldn't accept the gospel" (GK/6). Most missionaries agreed that it was "impossible to preach the gospel directly to the Masai" (Donovan 1978: 55). "[Masai] are primitive, in the extreme, and have no interest in religion," wrote one Spiritan (LMJ/27 Dec. 1957).

As Father Hillman recounted years later, these stereotypes were the product of "ignorance" on the part of the missionaries in understanding Maasai, who "projected such a foreign image. They weren't wearing clothes like civilized people would and all that kind of thing. So it was the ethnocentrism, the culture-bound character of the missionaries themselves." In contrast, "I found it intellectually very stimulating to be among the Maasai, discovering things. And I was playing anthropologist as well." Father Hillman's early strategy was to meet people, learn about Maasai life, and establish his presence.[15] Since he did not speak the language, he first used educated Arusha boys to translate for him on his trips into Maasai areas. He subsequently sought educated Maasai boys to help him as translators, guides, and, eventually, catechists. He visited the government school in Monduli, where some children had become Catholics under the influence of their Catholic Maasai teachers (who were originally from Kenya), obtained a list of these young men, then searched for them throughout Maasailand. He also sought the educated sons of former Maasai orphans who had been raised at Kilema mission. Eventually, "we gathered little groups here and there and some were willing to become catechists." His work was greatly facilitated by the eventual purchase of a second-hand Land Rover, which, according to one of his Spiritan peers, "hardy and versatile vehicle that it is . . . [enabled them] to go anywhere in Masai-land with impunity and the knowledge that they could get through in any type of weather and roads. Thus you might say, that it is not sufficient to merely have zeal to convert the Masai, but also a suitable and tough vehicle is also needed" (LMJ/Background).[16]

The School Approach

Once there was a group of educated Maasai to serve as catechists and teachers, Father Hillman and other Spiritans began to focus their efforts on teaching and converting Maasai children who they believed were not fully socialized and enculturated into the sins of their parents. Thus, from the mid 1950s to 1970, following the standard missionary approach of the time, Spiritans spent most of their time building, repairing, supervising, and provisioning the church's primary schools in Masai District. As Father Hillman recalls:

> My aim everywhere was to build schools, to establish schools. That was . . . the dominant missionary method of the time. . . . And it was on the assumption . . . that the cultures were undergoing change anyway, and the future . . . culture will be shaped by the school, and the people who went to school. . . . We could measure the results . . . with the number of kids that [went] through and graduate[d]. . . . [The schools] functioned as factories for producing Christians, Lutherans or Catholics depending on what school they went to.

Thus the mission journal for these years is replete with entries detailing journeys to collect students and take them to school, drive them home, search for missing students, transport teachers, drive sick students to and from the hospital, and purchase and transport food and supplies to the schools.[17] By 1958, the priests of Monduli mission were supervising six lower primary schools, and in 1962 they requested and received permission from the district education committee to start seven more, including one in Emairete (MMJ/ 6 Nov. 1958; 10 Jan. 1959; 10 Mar. 1959; 28 May 1962). Their transport and administrative burden was further expanded in 1963 when the priests started and supervised a food program at the schools (MMJ/4 June 1962; 4 Nov. 1962; 6 Feb. 1969). When not traveling, the priests spent time attending various district level committee meetings on education, Maasai development, and, in occasional years, famine relief (Anon. 1970).

Successful students could continue their studies through a network of Catholic schools, teacher training colleges, and seminaries. Maasai students

Fig. 3.1. Father Eugene
Hillman speaking to two
Maasai boys on the porch of
his house at Simanjiro
School, ca. 1960.
Reproduced courtesy of
Father Hillman.

could go on to study at the Catholic middle school at Simanjiro, supervised
by a full-time priest-in-residence.[18] Graduates of Simanjiro, depending on
their exam results, could then continue their education at the Catholic
Umbwe secondary school in Moshi, the Catholic Teacher's Training College
at Singa Chini, or, for those young men considering the priesthood, the
small Catholic seminary at Burka (which was moved and enlarged in 1966
to become Oldonyo Sambu Junior Seminary).

The schools (and some dispensaries[19]) helped the Catholic Church to
establish a "physical presence" in their sometimes fierce competition with
the Lutherans for territory in Maasai areas (cf. Anon. 1970: 1). As Father
Kohler described relationships with the Lutheran church in the period, "[it
was] dreadful, dreadful. Fighting all the time. Getting schools . . . they'd get
one school, we'd get a school; they'd get one school, we'd get a school. It
was really territorial" (cf. Donovan 1978: 7). The Lutherans were the first
to build schools in Maasailand, opening three in the early 1930s. After almost twenty years of very low attendance and Maasai resistance, there was
a "revival of Lutheran Mission activity" in 1948, and agreements were
reached whereby the Lutherans opened new bush schools and dispensaries.[20]

The fervent territorial battles were kindled by the longstanding colonial policy of delimiting denominational "spheres of influence" to control the "spirit
of jealous rivalry" between the churches.[21] As late as 1951, a request to obtain
land in Monduli town on which to build a Catholic chapel "was refused on
the grounds that one religion among the Masai, the Lutheran, was enough
and the introduction of another denomination would only confuse the Masai
and lead to a 'holy war'" (Anon. 1970: 1). But a change in district com-
missioners in 1952 led to a change in policy, and a half acre of land was
finally granted.[22]

Spiritans also built schools for "humanitarian" reasons as part of their
campaign to assist in Maasai development. They were, in part, fuelled by
perceptions that Maasai were the victims of "negative development" policies
by first the British, and later the "Swahilis," who dominated the post-
independence government. Some missionaries saw their duty as overcoming
years of intentional "underdevelopment" through preferential, even at times
exclusive, "development" projects and programs for Maasai (cf. MMJ/9 Jan.
1961). As Father Kohler explained, "If you don't have people who can read
and write and [are] somehow educated, they'd get lost, absolutely smothered
by the Swahilis." Father Hillman claimed that every school he started was
"illegal," because "the colonial government did not want all the Maasai to
get so much education. . . . The government policy as far as I could ascertain
was to keep Maasailand as primal as they could, because the Maasai would
be insufficiently sophisticated to protect their land. And the government
would steal their land and give it to colonial settlers, which they did regularly" (cf. Hodgson 2001a: chs. 2 and 3).[23] "I always thought," he mused,
"that [the Catholic Church] should be engaged in development as much as
in evangelism. . . . Authentic development can be a form of evangelical witness too." Thus, in addition to his work running the schools, serving on the
Masai Education Committee, and working with non-governmental organizations (NGOs) such as Oxfam, Misereor, and Catholic Relief Services to
institute school feeding and famine relief programs (Kohler 1977a: 410),
Father Hillman spent many years trying to build an animal husbandry school
for Maasai. Although he began his efforts in 1960 and continued until he
left in 1969, administrative reluctance and interference prevented him from
building the school.[24]

But most importantly, the schools were central to the evangelization
objectives of the Spiritans and the diocese. The intention was to teach religion, to attract converts, and to prepare young boys to be influential *Catholic*
leaders of their communities in the future (Anon. 1970: 1; Kohler 1977a:

410; cf. Labode 1993: 131). As Mwalimu Daniel Lolgolie, the long-time Catholic catechist and head teacher of the Catholic primary school in Emair-ete for nine years said: "The priests emphasized that the purpose is to teach the youth, to prepare the youth so that when they become adults, they will be the people who will help us to explain religion in Maasailand. . . . We can slowly teach the children in the schools so that the church can spread through those children."[25] The basic premise, according to Father Donovan, was obvious: "If children entered a mission school, they would not emerge from that school without being Christians" (Donovan 1978: 7). And the premise, he added, "was essentially correct" (Donovan 1978: 7). The future of the Catholic Church among the Maasai depended on these "parents of tomorrow" (Donovan 1978: 6).

Spiritans were evidently much more interested in educating future fa-thers than mothers, however—almost all of the students in their schools were boys. Although they shared the government's aim of educating Maasai boys so that they could become teachers and clerk-dressers, they also wanted boys qualified to work as catechists and eventually priests for the church. According to the gender ideologies of the missionaries and the doctrines of the Catholic Church (especially the pre–Vatican II church) positions of formal leadership in the Catholic Church—as priests, catechists, lay lead-ers—were, by definition, male positions. The duties of catechists—to teach religion (sometimes alone, sometimes with a priest) and to perform the non-sacramental, pastoral duties of a priest in the priest's absence—were, in their similarities to the work of priests, implicitly viewed by most missionaries as "male" tasks: "[The catechist] was usually a dedicated and good-living man, not young, and not trained" (Donovan 1978: 6).[26] Even the Catholic com-munity leaders they hoped to train were, necessarily, male leaders, for who among them could imagine female leaders if female catechists were not pos-sible—much less, female priests? In contrast, positions of servitude—as sis-ters, members of altar committees—were primarily female. The Spiritan vi-sion of a future Catholic Church in Maasai areas mirrored this power hierarchy—requiring men trained and qualified to fill these leadership positions.[27]

Religion was therefore a core course in all of the schools, even the gov-ernment school, beginning with the first year of primary school (MMJ/2 Feb. 1959; EH/10; DL1/6). "The aim of the church," explained Mwalimu Daniel, "was to teach religion. We had to teach a regular syllabus, but the main purpose was to teach religion." Both Catholics and Lutherans taught at the government school, and in each other's schools if there were children

Fig. 3.2. Maasai students in the first classroom built at Simanjiro School, ca. 1960. The child slumped on the desk is a young girl. Reproduced courtesy of Father Hillman.

from their congregation and willing catechists.[28] "During these sessions," recalled "Steven," a Maasai student who attended the government school in Monduli, "these priests [and catechists] came to convince us, to tell us how good it is to join their church. And we were saying, 'What is this now?'"

The children were courted in other ways as well. As Steven recalled, "[The catechists and Catholic teachers] took us to the Catholic mission on Sunday to see the church, to attend mass, and to meet with the priests. . . . The most interesting bit was the meeting of the priests, because it was there we got a very good lunch, sweets, socks . . . we had shoes, we had shirts." Other religious groups in Monduli, including Muslims, also courted the boys at the government school. Some children took advantage of the competition for their attention and visited, ate at, and received gifts from all of the denominations. According to Steven, "[before we were baptized], we moved, you know. When resources dried up in the Catholic Church we went to the Lutherans . . . for parties, and we became Lutherans. And sometimes to the

Fig. 3.3. Father Eugene Hillman meeting in his office at Monduli
mission with Roimen (*seated*), the great grandson of Oloiboni Parit, and
Clement Njui (*standing*), the son of an *oloiboni* from Ngorongoro, who
later became a catechist and teacher, ca. 1960. Reproduced courtesy of
Father Hillman.

Anglicans. To the Pentecostals."[29] "Some boys," remarked one Spiritan,
"jump back and forth from one dini [religion] to another" (LMJ/11 Mar.
1958).

As with earlier evangelization methods, catechists were central to the
success (or failure) of the school approach and thus the broader missionary
enterprise, since the work of running the network of schools left most missionaries little time for pastoral duties or religious instruction. A 1960 survey
of East Africa showed that ninety percent of all religious instruction was

being given by catechists, not priests (Donovan 1978: 6). As one Maasai man stated, the catechists "played a greater role than the priests themselves" in influencing and instructing the children. Many Maasai that I interviewed spoke of how individual catechists or Catholic teachers, *not* Catholic priests, convinced them to become Catholics. Steven explicitly remembered the influence of Mwalimu Daniel and his brother: "They convinced us. . . . They were a very quiet, nice people . . . poor as well, [although] not today." Even Father Hillman acknowledged the importance of "the zeal of the local catechist" in encouraging, teaching, and nurturing children. African teachers were also instrumental in courting children. As Father Hillman explained, "If the teachers said 'Well, the Catholics are better than the Lutherans,' then the kids would listen to the Catholic teachers. And Lutheran teachers would say the opposite." But some Lutheran teachers in the government and native authority schools were a bit overzealous (and presumably some Catholics were as well); these Lutheran teachers were repeatedly accused by the Spiritans and other Catholics of bullying and coercing students to follow Lutheran instruction (e.g., LMJ/12 Nov. 1957, 26 Jan. 1960). By 1962, in addition to the catechists teaching at the schools, Monduli mission had established nine "catechetical centers" with resident catechists in Maasai areas (Anon. 1970: 2).

The children were given time to reflect about the decision to be baptized. Initially, most baptisms took place during Standard 4 or 5 at the Simanjiro Middle School.[30] Later, "it was shifted to Standard 8 . . . [so that] they could have a better sense of what they were doing" (EH/10). In the beginning, the priests did not ask for parental permission, "because the parents didn't know. They would say, 'Well, whatever you people do in school, it's OK, do what you do.' And so it was very superficial. The surprising thing is that in some cases it stuck" (EH/10). In addition to the influence of certain catechists and teachers, the reasons some former students gave for deciding to be baptized ranged from just "follow[ing] what other [students] were doing," to a desire to continue their education with the support of the church, to an understanding of "Jesus Christ" and a sense that "it was good." But a few resisted using their new "Christian" name, despite pressure from the missionaries.

The approach and objectives of Spiritan missionaries confronted Maasai gender relations and ideologies of the 1950s, set within the eclipse of colonial control. By channeling their religious instruction to young boys through schools, in alliance with the colonial regime's coercive and unpopular education policy, the missionaries raised the suspicions of adult Maasai, especially men. Initially, Maasai elders were unsure about the purpose or value of formal education and wary of the motives of the colonial officers and missionaries. They were therefore unwilling to allow schools to be built, and sent their sons to school only under threat of sanctions, including fines and prison. When Father Hillman and another Spiritan first visited Emairete in 1962 to discuss building a primary school, the male elders told them that they were not pleased with the idea. Eventually, a compromise was reached whereby the priests could run the school for one year, at which time community members would meet again to decide whether the school should be allowed to continue (MMJ/26 Sept. 1962). Many educated men claim they were selected by their fathers to go to school as part of the community quota system because they were the least favorite son. Others were chosen because they were the youngest and most dispensable in terms of labor needs. Roving headmen tracked and caught the young sons of still-resistant fathers. Boys were warned to run away and hide if they saw a stranger wearing a red hat (the headmen wore a red cap with a black tassel to mark their position), but not all could run fast enough or far enough (DL1/5).[31]

Although by the 1960s Maasai elders were more tolerant of education, they were deeply troubled by the idea of baptism and religious conversion. When parents were asked for permission to baptize their sons, most refused. According to Mwalimu Daniel, they were concerned that their sons

> would be separated from their parents, they would wear white clothes, . . . that is they would change, they would become different people. But if they only learn things like how to read and write, a regular education, but are not baptized, *basi,* when they come home, they will be normal people like other Maasai. But once he is baptized, he will have a different faith. He will separate from us completely.

These men asserted that their religious belief was integral to their cultural identity, so that religious conversion was as much a matter of culture as faith (cf. Kirby 1994a). The baptism of boys threatened the increasingly rigid parameters of normative masculinity: a man could not be both a Christian and a Maasai. The few Maasai men who were active adherents to Christianity were disparaged as *ormeek,* a pejorative term for Maasai who had adopted European clothes and ways, including education and Christianity (Hodgson 1999b). As a result, although some boys were baptized in the schools, few remained active Catholics once their education was completed.

Moreover, since most of the schools had very few girls, if any, the instruction and baptism of Maasai girls and women was not a pressing issue.

They could learn about the missionaries and their teachings only through their brothers and sons. But this was due only in part to the priorities of the Spiritans and the constraints of Catholic doctrine, as discussed above. Maasai elders were pleased that missionaries did not force them to educate young girls. Their simple objection—"If they go there, they'll never marry" (DL1/6)—betrayed their fears about the potential threat posed by education to their control of women and the unquestioned cultural expectations that all women would marry the suitor of their parents' choice. If a Maasai girl did not marry, there would be no bridewealth or new alliances with other families, and her father and later her brothers would probably have to support her throughout her life. Father Hillman claimed that Spiritans tried to get girls in the school as well, "but it was a very hard struggle getting boys even; most people were reluctant." He thought Maasai girls were "very sheltered," recalling how the girls at the Simanjiro school would come to meet with him only in groups of two or three, "never one alone." (He interpreted this as a sign of their fear of men, rather than the appropriate respect behavior [*enkanyit*] for an older man.) According to Father Hillman, some Maasai parents told him that once girls had attended school, "they would not do what they were told." In particular, "they wouldn't marry the person the family decided they should marry." And then they would "drift off to the towns and become prostitutes." In time, "they did open up a little bit on this. We used to get more girls to school. But, you know, for ten boys we'd probably get three or four girls." Many of these girls were the daughters of the *jumbes*, local government officials who had been to school themselves, "spoke Swahili and knew the world was bigger than Maasailand." But even these girls "never went on in school." He estimated that of the three hundred students boarding at the Simanjiro middle school (Standards 6 through 8), only about ten were girls (see also Moss and Moss 1960: 6).

When, for example, the Catholic Church opened a small school for girls in 1959 in another area of Masai District, only eight girls attended (MMJ/31 Mar. 1959; 16 April 1959). The priests feared reprisals from parents, so they kept the girls at school during the first long-term break in May: "We decided it would be too dangerous to let the girls go home so soon again" (MMJ/ 28 May 1959). During the long break in 1960, their fears were confirmed when a school girl was circumcised in order to marry her off and prevent her from returning to school. But the plan failed. The priest met with the male elders of her community, and together they decided that her father would be fined, she would return to school, and her smaller sister would

begin school in January (MMJ/28 July 1960). The possibility that their educated daughters might be sources of wealth through employment or through
marriage to educated, employed men was rarely considered. In fact, many of
the educated Maasai men who became teachers, catechists, and professionals
chose to marry these educated young women (cf. GK/22).

Although, as discussed below, the schools were much less successful than
the missionaries hoped in terms of producing large numbers of active male
converts, some of the Maasai men they educated did become influential
political leaders, teachers, development workers, and, of course, catechists
and priests. One of the most important was Edward Sokoine, who served
as a member of Parliament and eventually prime minister of Tanzania. Sokoine was born and raised in Emairete, and attended school in Monduli. As
I discuss elsewhere (Hodgson 2001a: 196–201), Sokoine was a mythic figure
for Maasai, especially for those in Emairete and the surrounding Monduli
area. Many men followed his example and went to school, trained as teachers, and entered local politics. Ironically, however, according to Father Hillman, although Sokoine was "extremely bright," he was initially "hostile to
education." He missed most of Standard 8, but Father Hillman convinced
him to take the exam for further studies, which he passed. Father Hillman
arranged for him to attend a Catholic secondary school in Moshi. Although
Sokoine ran away several times, Father Hillman "chased after him." Shortly
after he was circumcised and selected to be an age-set leader (*olaigwenani*)
for his group, Sokoine was baptized a Catholic by Father Hillman. In time,
as he became both a traditional Maasai leader and a leader in national politics, he served as one of the most adamant advocates of education for Maasai, cajoling, lecturing, and berating them to send their children to school.
He argued for certain other changes to Maasai cultural and social practices,
but supported polygamy. As a polygamist himself, he fathered eleven children
with his two wives. Toward the end of his life, according to Father Hillman,
Sokoine "got religion in a big way" and "became very church going." He
was killed in a controversial car "accident" in 1984 in the midst of leading
a national anti-corruption campaign focused on government officials.

For the future of the Catholic Church, however, the pool of educated
men who could serve as catechists, teachers, and priests was even more important than such famous figures as Sokoine. The school approach itself was
predicated on the availability of such men, who in turn produced more catechists and teachers like themselves.

The Boma Approach

In the mid 1960s, frustrated by the "failure" of the school approach to produce long-term male converts, Father Vincent Donovan, an American Spiritan who had worked for a time with the schools, proposed a radical new approach to evangelization in Maasai areas: the direct evangelization of adult Maasai in their *bomas* (the Swahili word used by missionaries and others to describe Maasai homesteads [*enkang'*, pl. *inkang'itie*]).[32] As Father Donovan complained in a 1966 letter to his bishop: "The best way to describe realistically the state of this Christian mission is the number zero. As of this month, in the seventh year of this mission's existence, there are no adult Masai practicing Christians from Loliondo mission. . . . That zero is a real number, because up until this date no Catholic child, on leaving school, has continued to practice his religion, and there is no indication that any of the present students will do so" (Donovan 1978: 15).[33] Therefore, he continued:

> I would propose cutting myself off from the schools and the hospital, as far as these people are concerned—as well as socializing with them—and just go and talk to them about God and the Christian message. . . . I want to go to the Masai on daily safaris—unencumbered with the burden of selling them our school system, or begging for their children for our schools, or carrying their sick, or giving them medicine. Outside of this, I have no theory, no plan, no strategy, no gimmicks—no idea of what will come. I feel rather naked. I will begin as soon as possible. (Donovan 1978: 15–16)

Working in the Loliondo area of northern Masai District, he began to visit selected Maasai *bomas* to teach adult residents of the *boma* as a group, with hopes of baptizing them as a "natural" "community" whose members would support each other and work to teach and evangelize other *bomas* (Donovan 1978: 84–91; Friedman 1980: 18; Kohler 1977a: 412). As Father Donovan explained after a "community" of thirty-one Maasai were baptized in 1966:

> The people baptized are to be given immediate responsibility in running their own Church. They will be responsible for further evangelization in their own and surrounding sections. They will be responsible for any building which they see must be done. They will be responsible for finances, answerable only to themselves. In short all of the work of the church will be theirs, except for conferring of the sacraments—for which we European priests will be responsible until they get their own Masai priests. (LMJ/26 Dec. 1966)

In sum, "our work of evangelization is finished with these Masai of the Loliondo valley. They are on their own" (LMJ/26 Dec. 1966).

According to Father Donovan (1978: v–viii), earlier missionary approaches such as the Christian villages and schools were predicated on a "theology of salvation" (see above) that sought to save as many "pagan" souls as possible by converting them not only to Christianity but to Western forms of modernity, civilization, and religion. This theology presumed the superiority of not just Christian religion but Western culture. In contrast, the *boma* approach was premised on a "theology of creation." "Evangelization," he wrote, "is a process of bringing the gospel to people where they are, not where you would like them to be" (Donovan 1978: vi). Missionaries must therefore "respect the culture of a people, not destroy it. The incarnation of the gospel, the flesh and blood which must grow on the gospel is up to the people of a culture" (Donovan 1978: 30). In other words:

> The way people might celebrate the central truths of Christianity; the way they would distribute the goods of the earth and live out their daily lives; their spiritual, ascetical expression of Christianity if they should accept it; their way of working out the Christian responsibility of the social implications of the gospel—all these things, that is: liturgy, morality, dogmatic theology, spirituality, and social action would be a cultural response to a central, unchanging, supracultural, uninterpreted gospel. (Donovan 1978: 30–31)

The two theologies were therefore premised on radically different assumptions about culture, the form and content of the Christian message, and the meaning and purpose of missionary work. Nonetheless, despite its respect for their history, culture, religion, and society, the theology of creation still presumed a need for the work of Christian evangelization among "pagan" peoples.

Father Donovan's "radical departure" was greatly influenced by the writings of the Anglican theologian Roland Allen, especially *Missionary Methods: St. Paul's or Ours?* (1962 [1912]) (Donovan 1978: 32–37; Kane 1995: 7; GK/ 9–10; Naas 1971: 63–65). In his widely influential book, Allen, who served as an Anglican missionary in China from 1895 to 1903, compared the missionary methods of St. Paul with those of contemporary missionaries. St. Paul evangelized people quickly without the help of catechists, baptized converts after minimal instruction, advocated financial self-support for missionaries and their congregations, taught only the most basic elements of Christianity, and encouraged local churches to take responsibility for discipline and authority. In contrast, missionaries in the nineteenth and twentieth centuries, according to Allen, spent large amounts of money and time evangelizing and instructing people, taught not just the gospel, but "Law and Customs" (Allen 1962 [1912]: 6), relied heavily on the help of catechists, and seemed reluctant to allow local churches to assume financial and spiritual responsibility for themselves. Allen therefore proposed a set of principles, based on St. Paul's methods, to restructure contemporary missionary practice so that it would be based on a "spirit of faith" in the ability of local churches to grow, manage their own affairs, and shape the Christian message according to their needs. He urged missionaries to "plant churches," not just "establish missions" and "convert individuals" (Allen 1962 [1912]: 81–83). As Father Donovan wrote in 1967, following Allen: "A missionary's job is to preach the gospel, establish the Church among a few and then leave" (1967: 206).

Father Donovan's new approach was also facilitated by broader changes in Catholic doctrine. The debates and decrees of the Second Vatican Council, which met from 1962 to 1965, spurred many missionaries into critical reflection about their ideas, assumptions, and methods. The Second Vatican Council was the first council to include indigenous bishops from Africa and Asia, and "every theologian in Rome during the first session was struck with the force and newness of this experience" (Foreword to Hillman 1968: 8; Donovan 1989: 6). As part of the "new vitality" and "wider vision" that emerged from discussion of the "needs and hopes of the young churches" (Foreword to Hillman 1968: 8), Vatican II's directives on the role of the church in evangelization recognized the validity of other religions and therefore their legitimacy for believers, acknowledged the importance of respecting cultural diversity, and called for ongoing dialogue and collaboration with followers of other faiths (*Ad Gentes* nos. 11, 12, 20, 26; *Nostra Aetate* no. 2; reprinted in Abbott and Gallagher 1966). As stated in *Ad Gentes* no. 20: "If in certain regions, groups of men are to be found who are kept away from embracing the Catholic faith because they cannot adapt themselves to the peculiar form which the Church has taken on there, it is the desire of this Council that such a condition be provided for in a special way, until such time as all the Christians concerned can gather together in one community" (reprinted in Abbott and Gallagher 1966; cf. Kohler 1977a: 410). As both responses to and catalysts for changes in missionary ideas and practices, such radical pronouncements created an atmosphere of feverish excitement among missionaries, infusing them with new zeal for their work.

Vatican II coincided with the establishment of the Diocese of Arusha in 1963, which "took as its founding spirit that of the Council" (Kohler 1977a: 411). The separation from the Diocese of Moshi enabled the Spiritans in Arusha to set their own priorities, which were to concentrate their resources and energies on Maasai evangelization, and develop the necessary

127

structures and practices to further their efforts. As one of four priests elected to the first official Senate in June 1967 to consult with the bishop on diocesan policy and problems, Father Hillman was able to influence these decisions (MMJ/27 June 1967). The diocese started Oldonyo Sambu Junior Seminary in 1966 to train "boys from the four tribes of the Diocese" (MMJ/19 Sept. 1966), that is, "indigenous people" (MMJ/18 Oct. 1966), not "Swahilis." Although accusations of discrimination soon forced the bishop to open the school to all Africans in the diocese, Oldonyo Sambu was for many years one of the only secondary schools to welcome Maasai boys (MMJ/15 Jan. 1967).[34] At the same time, the diocese also revised and expanded its training programs for catechists, especially those working in Maasai areas. A catechetical training center was opened near Arusha, and formal courses, materials, and programs were developed to train catechists in a more systematic manner.

Finally, the political context of the missionary enterprise changed radically during this time as well (cf. Ludwig 1999). Tanzania gained independence in 1961, and Julius Nyerere, a Catholic and former schoolteacher, was elected president. Some Spiritans believed, with good reason, that the new national government treated Maasai even worse than the colonial administration had. Many African government officials regarded Maasai with contempt and were eager to take their remaining fertile land (EH/38–39). As I have written elsewhere:

> At Independence, development became the legitimating project of the post-colonial nation-state in Tanzania; the African elites who took power embraced the modernist narrative and its agenda of progress. For them, "the Maasai" represented all they had tried to leave behind, persistent icons of "the primitive," "the savage," "the past." . . . Elite Africans, who were intent on integrating the people of Tanzania into a socialist nation by forging links of language, infrastructure, and a sense of national identity translated the former racialized distinctiveness of Maasai into a heightened sense of ethnic difference marked by pronounced cultural and visual signifiers. (Hodgson 2001a: 148)

As part of President Nyerere's policy of overcoming ethnic distinctions in favor of creating a nation, the government launched a series of measures to modernize "the Maasai." These included campaigns to force Maasai to replace their leather capes, blankets, cotton cloths, and ocher body rubs with "modern" attire; to enforce the teaching and use of Swahili; and to coerce them to adopt more "productive" methods of livestock husbandry. At the same time, Maasai lands were alienated by legal, illegal, and extralegal means for game parks, commercial farms, and the personal estates and farms of government workers (Hodgson 2001a: chs. 4 and 5; Hodgson and Schroeder 2002). In general, Maasai were treated as second-class citizens and suffered increased economic and political disenfranchisement.

The Spiritans responded to all of these changes with a series of long discussions about the problems and future of their work among Maasai and the "renewal" of the Spiritans (e.g., MMJ/22 May 1965; 27 Aug. 1965; 27 July 1967). They interpreted Vatican II's decrees espousing cultural relativity to mean that Maasai culture was no longer an obstacle to evangelization, and that previously "unchristian" practices such as polygyny could be ignored.[35] Adult Maasai were now "fit" for Christianity:

> As far as the Masai were concerned, we had to overthrow the assumption that they were not yet ready for the gospel. We had to believe that the gospel, the message of Christianity, the revelation of God to man, is for everyone, for the entire human race, for every people in every segment of that human race—as they are, where they are, now. (Donovan 1978: 56)

Where Maasai culture had resisted adaptation to Catholicism, Catholicism would now relent and adapt itself to the contours of Maasai culture. A Maasai translation of the Mass was prepared, and controlled "experimentation" with alternative approaches to evangelization, culturally sensitive liturgies, the use of "indigenous" baptism names, and modified confession and communion practices began.[36] As a creative response to the "failures" of the school approach, Father Donovan's "*boma* approach" was a product of this time of reflection, inquiry, and change.

Despite Father Donovan's reputed success,[37] extensive implementation of the approach did not begin until 1970, however, when the government nationalized the schools and hired Catholic catechists as teachers.[38] With no schools and few trained catechists, the missionaries were compelled to involve themselves in direct evangelization of Maasai whether they wished to do so or not. By this time, the *boma* approach had developed from the naive, romantic ideas of one missionary into a more formal approach (Naas 1971). First, initial contact was made with the elder man of a homestead to ask his permission to talk to the entire homestead (DL1/9; cf. Donovan 1978: 22). At the first few meetings with homestead members, the missionary asked those present to share their ideas and stories about Eng'ai, creation, death, and other religious concepts (DL1/9; cf. Donovan 1978: 45). In time, he began to discuss Christian ideas about God and those same concepts. He communicated only the *kerygma*, the core ideas and beliefs of the Christian message, "unencumbered with extraneous cultural and historical baggage"

(Kohler 1977a: 412; cf. GK/10). Parables were revised in accordance with Maasai symbols and scenarios to stimulate discussion and dialogue about the similarities and differences between Maasai religious beliefs and the Christian message (DL1/9; cf. Donovan 1978: 41). For example, the story of the Good Samaritan became the story of the Good *Ormeek* (Maa for stranger, Swahili, non-Maasai), while the Prodigal Son was forgiven by his father through the act of spitting (Donovan 1978: 79–80). Finally, at the end of the teaching period, each *boma* that accepted Christianity was baptized together as a "community" (DL1/9).

According to Father Naas, who used the *boma* approach when he was stationed at Monduli mission in the early 1970s, catechists were still central to this approach:

> We work in teams consisting of a missionary priest or layman and one or two Masai catechists, some of whom have had a formal training of two years. Together we prepare our work thoroughly; the catechists do most of the actual teaching in the kraals, for the simple reason that none of the expatriate missionaries involved has enough knowledge of the extremely difficult Masai language. (Naas 1971: 58)

Meetings were held about twice a week with each *boma*, preferably in the morning between 8 A.M. and 11 A.M. (Naas 1971: 58):

> The style of meetings is quite similar to that of their own meetings: after an opening prayer, often a communal song, the theme of the meeting is presented, and then evolved along the lines of the audience's own reflections and traditional belief, and of our own prepared "lesson." There are times when we meet in the early hours of the night, between seven and ten p.m., in a more informal way; then we talk in smaller groups: sometimes a family, sometimes the kraal's members of one agegroup. These latter meetings are usually lively dialogues, with little "instruction" from our side. Then we usually share the group's food, and stay with them overnight. (Naas 1971: 58–59)

As Father Naas warned later in the same article:

> Certainly the missionary ought to be cautious; he always runs the risk of preaching laws and traditions, habits and conventions, instead of preaching the Word of God, i.e., preaching Jesus Christ. By doing this he not only dislocates the vocation and duties of his own church, but at the same time he seriously damages hope and life in those who trust him for the Word from the Lord. (Naas 1971: 62)

The greatest challenge was how to develop methods to teach adults who were predominantly illiterate, as opposed to literate school children. The missionaries necessarily had to rely on some combination of the spoken word and visual images. In addition to using pictures, stories, and songs, they developed several tools to facilitate their teaching (Kohler 1977a: 412–13). The most renowned and widely used was a small plastic disk with five stick figure pictures on each side developed by Father Ralph Poirier, another American Spiritan who worked in Maasai evangelization from 1963 to 1981 (see fig. 3.4).[39] According to a legend provided in an issue of the *Spiritan Missionary News* (vol. 20, no. 3, August 1996, p. 11), the ten figures represent the following biblical stories, passages, and lessons:

1. * Mary carries Jesus, the light and the truth, on her back. (Luke 2)
   * The eye sees because it is in the light of truth.

2. * Jesus raises Lazarus from the dead. (John 11)
   * Jesus stretches out his hands to us and says, "I wish to raise my friends. Do you wish to be my friend?"

3. * The forgiving father and the returning son. (Luke 15)
   * Two members of the church welcome a repentant sinner who is holding grass as a symbol of his sorrow. "Whoever you forgive, you are forgiven." (Matthew 16)

4. * A half-dead person lies on the ground. Two Maasai come along, see their tribesman and pass by.
   * An outsider from the enemy tribe sees the helpless Maasai lying there, approaches and takes care of him.
   * A person is hitting another on the face. "Turn the other cheek—don't hate the oppressor—love him." (Matthew 5)

5. * A dish holding bread. A gourd holding wine.
   * The sacred meal of the baptized to which believers are invited. They surround the table of the Lord. (Matthew 26, Mark 14, Luke 22)

6. * A cross.
   * The friend of Jesus carries a cross. (Matthew 26–27, Mark 14–15, Luke 22–23, John 18–19)

7. * Jesus rises on the third day, overcoming death. We have the same life in us that raised Jesus from the dead. He raised us up. (Matthew 28, Mark 16, Luke 24, John 20)

8. * The rain cloud reminds us of prayer which Jesus taught his people.

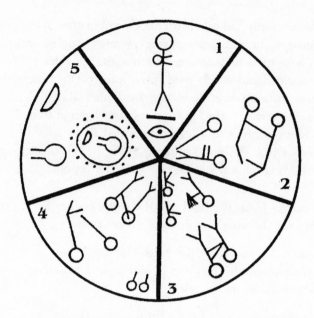

Fig. 3.4a. The front side of the plastic disk designed by Father Poirier as a teaching tool for Maasai evangelization.

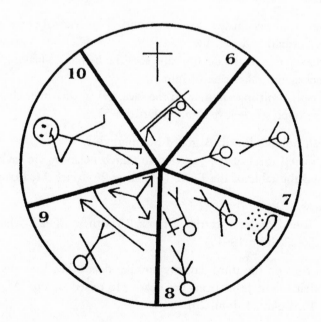

Fig. 3.4b. The back side of the disk.

* The person pointing downwards shows us the good things he has received and thanks God for them.

* Person pointing to self and heaven: we are God's children and so we ask our Father for what we need. (Matthew 6)

9. * Jesus is going to God to prepare a place for us. He points heavenward and with his other hand he points earthward: "I will not leave you orphans. I will send you the Holy Spirit." (John 14)

10. * We are the body of Christ on earth: many members, one body.

* Do you wish to be a member of Christ's body?

These then were the key lessons, the kerygma, that many Spiritans taught Maasai. Father Poirier selected them according to what he called their "gut-value criterion": "Each lesson must be so constructed that when it is finished the people want what it has to offer. Each lesson must be a pearl of great price. Each lesson, to be effective, must draw a response similar to 'Wow! Look what I am being offered that I didn't have before. Hey, I want that!' " (Poirier 1984: 12).

Father Poirier drew them as stick figures intentionally, to minimize the distracting details of other visual aids: "During one teaching session I witnessed a teacher using very large drawings of biblical characters dressed in the time of Jesus. While the teaching was going on people kept asking each other questions about or commenting on the funny headdresses, the ugly beards and the heritage of the people in the drawings. The distractions were more important to the Maasai than the teaching itself" (Poirier 1984: 16–17). In response to these and other experiences:

> I came to some conclusions about the criteria for judging visual aids. They should be small, for each individual, not involved, free, durable, with the meaning pictured in, having the possibility of people copying them themselves. I quickly reduced all my paraphernalia to one little circle of stick figures. They actually learned easier with them. There was no distraction. The very simplicity helped their minds to remember longer with greater clarity. (Poirier 1984: 18)

Each student was given a disk to serve as a mnemonic to remember the lessons and as a tool to teach others. For at least one illiterate Maasai woman, the disk was invaluable: "As I was teaching one day," wrote Father Poirier, "a young lady who was studying her little copy of the Circle suddenly stood up clutching the little piece of cardboard to herself and gushed out, 'Hey everybody, I can understand this, it is written in our language!' " (Poirier

1984: 19). But not all the Spiritans, catechists, or Maasai found the disk as useful or easy to interpret. As Steven, a former catechist recalled, it was a "difficult tool to use . . . very difficult to understand . . . not clear . . . people cannot relate to it" (cf. GK/19).[40] Even Father Poirier had mixed success; he held his first baptism in one area after almost five years of instruction (KMJ/3 Nov. 1979).

With such tools in hand, a guiding principle of the *boma* approach was to address, teach, and baptize adult Maasai not as individuals, but as a community, *boma* by *boma*. As Father Kohler summarized, "the people were approached as a community (the kraal, the 'boma'), were taught as a community, and faith was elicited from the community" (1977a: 412; Naas 1971: 58). Critical of "individualism" as a Western obsession that had shaped missionary practice, Father Donovan claimed that "community" was the more important social unit in African societies. "Because of the structures of life in Africa," he argued, people must be approached not as individuals, but on the level of community, "that is, on the level of the homogenous group of people that considers itself a living, social organism distinct from other social groups" (Donovan 1978: 84). In the case of Maasai, he was adamant about the power of community to control the actions of its individual members: "I am quite certain no individual adult Masai would have agreed to participate in a lengthy, ordered dialogue and discussion between the Masai culture and the Christian message. He agreed to take this step only within the framework of his community, with his community, bringing his relations and relationships along with him" (Donovan 1978: 84). And so, "finding a real community among the Masai," Father Donovan claimed that he was able "to teach them as a unit, to dialogue with them as a group, because there was a similarity of feeling and reaction among them" (Donovan 1978: 86). Guided by these ideas, Father Donovan would baptize all members of a *boma* "community," even those who frequently missed instruction classes or did not understand their lessons (Donovan 1978: 92).

Despite the rhetoric of "communities," actual implementation of the *boma* approach reflected the gendered assumptions and concerns of the missionaries. Although both men and women as members of *boma* "communities" were taught and baptized, the energies and interests of most missionaries were primarily directed toward converting male members of the community and developing male lay leadership. The preference for male converts and leaders was made explicit in several ways: the first step of the *boma* approach was to meet with the elder men of the homestead, and the homesteads of the *ilaigwenak*, or influential male leaders, were targeted as the first *bomas* to be taught (GK/8; Donovan 1978: 22). Missionaries hoped to replicate the extended patriarchal families of *bomas* as church communities, with men as "leaders" and women and children as submissive "followers." The very categories by which missionaries referred to men and women in their journals betrayed their own gendered perceptions of proper roles: women were occasionally distinguished by marital status (either "women" or "wives"), while men were distinguished by age, and, implicitly, authority ("men," "elders," or "murran," never "husbands").

The presence and participation of men was therefore mandatory, while the presence of women, when noticed, was tolerated, and their active participation was occasionally encouraged (e.g., Donovan 1978: 111–12). The history of evangelization efforts in one homestead in Mti Mmoja illustrates this argument. Father Robert Butts, a Spiritan, tried to meet with a certain homestead once a week for four months. Out of nine attempted meetings, only four were "successful" in that a satisfactory number of men showed up and a lesson was taught. Once it rained and he was late arriving, so the elders left, thinking he was not coming; twice "no one" showed up at all; twice everyone was "drunk" (once to welcome guests, another time for mourning); once a circumcision ceremony was taking place; and twice only one male elder showed up (MMJ/"Transcription from Rev. Butts' Notebook, 1975"). Father Butts's accounts of his attempted meetings are representative of other accounts in the journal: meetings were seen to succeed or fail based on the presence or absence of the elder men, while the attendance of women was rarely tallied or mentioned. It seems clear, in fact, that entries claiming that "no one" was present should be understood to mean no *men* were present. Father Mort Kane, who replaced Father Butts at Monduli mission in 1975, at least acknowledged the presence of women at lessons, but his greater concern for the attendance of men is quite evident. Continuing instruction at the same homestead, he arrived one day to find only three women and news that the male elder was traveling. Although annoyed, "[w]e taught a lesson anyway" (MMJ/16 Aug. 1976). But his frustration with the absence of men at his lessons grew, until a few weeks later he informed the homestead that they would hold a meeting about "their future . . . as the *mzee* (Swahili for 'elder man') has not shown up at any lessons for 6 weeks" (MMJ/6 Sept. 1976). When the delinquent elder missed the scheduled meeting, Father Kane and his catechist decided that "we would not go there again until [the elder] petitions for our presence and can guarantee his presence at every lesson" (MMJ/13 Sept. 1976). A month later, in another homestead where usually a dozen women and three or four men had been attending instruction, he refused to teach one day when the men were absent "on the principle that unless the leaders are present we do not teach" (MMJ/15 Aug. 1976; 19 Aug. 1976; 14 Oct. 1976). Implicit preference for instructing men was now explicit principle.

The *boma* approach posed a new set of cultural, spatial, and institutional constraints and opportunities for Maasai men and women to negotiate their gendered relations of power. The radical change in the pedagogical style and content of instruction made Catholic teachings linguistically and culturally accessible to interested Maasai women (and men). Formal text-based instruction and teacher-led drills in Swahili and English on the catechism were replaced by dialogue and discussion in Maa (often with the assistance of a translator) about core religious concepts, with an emphasis on mutual understanding, translatability, and respect for Maasai beliefs and practices.

Furthermore, shifting the site of religious instruction from schools to homesteads had radical implications since each space had very different gender associations. Schools were foreign, linked to the state apparatus and colonial modernization programs, and explicitly male-dominated. In contrast, homesteads were female-dominated domains at the center of Maasai society, beyond the reaches of the state. Since Maasai protocols of hospitality precluded forbidding the missionaries from visiting, adult female residents of the targeted homesteads now had direct access to missionary instruction, and adult men were forced into direct engagement with missionaries. Since few men were interested in instruction and baptism, however, they used, as the above accounts indicate, a range of tactics to directly and indirectly communicate their disinterest: polite avoidance, conflicting engagements, sudden "travel" plans, ceremonial obligations, frequent absences, and other more "pressing" responsibilities. Some male elders even refused to let missionaries enter and teach in their homesteads. Others complained to the bishop (e.g., MMJ/1 Feb. 1967; 16 Feb. 1967).[41] Of course some of these excuses, such as observing mourning periods, were legitimate. The overwhelming frequency of excuses and absences, however, suggests that men made sustained efforts to avoid attending instruction classes or that attendance held a very low priority in their lives.[42]

In contrast, Maasai women took advantage of the opportunity provided by the *boma* approach to meet with missionaries, hear the Christian "message," and convert to Catholicism. Journal entries such as those written by Father Butts and Father Kane, when they bother to mention women, suggest that Maasai women attended instruction more regularly and in far greater numbers than Maasai men. The reports of other Spiritans, catechists, and

Fig. 3.5. Father Kelly shaking hands with an *olmurrani* in Emairete, ca. 1960. Reproduced courtesy of Father Hillman.

Maasai men and women confirm this finding. Despite the evident disinterest of most missionaries in instructing *just* women, women were an insistent presence at *boma* instruction, communicating their interest through their regular attendance and active participation. It was mostly "women . . . who came to the teachings," recalled Steven, a former catechist. "Men did not have the patience at all. . . . [But] women were very dedicated listeners. They were interested. They wanted to follow this . . . and then singing as well. . . . They were singing a lot. Maasai songs." Although women had fewer reasons to leave the *boma*, uninterested women could always busy themselves with childcare, cooking, water hauling, and other domestic tasks.

Even confirmation instruction was better attended by women. For example, the first meeting "to prepare elders for confirmation" (MMJ/30 Dec. 1976) in Emairete was described as "poorly attended but good interest shown by women" (MMJ/4 Jan. 1977). Attendance at the next week's meeting required special comment: "the men were as numerous as the women" (MMJ/11 Jan. 1977). But when the bishop visited a few weeks later for confirmation services, only twelve candidates attended, mostly women (MMJ/2 Feb. 1977). A later investigation of the small attendance revealed that "[the male elder of the homestead] was off looking for food and so lamentably missed confirmation. Half the women in his *boma* did not come because of fear. They did not want to be absent from the *boma* when the *mzee* arrived back from safari" (MMJ/24 Feb. 1977). But half of the women, despite possible repercussions if they were perceived as disobeying his authority, did attend.

In their enthusiasm to participate in instruction, some women challenged established gender roles. Father Donovan describes how one young mother was "the first woman of all to speak out in public in our meetings with the Masai" (Donovan 1978: 110). While the elder men were at first upset, they began to accept her involvement as she continued to ask questions and make comments in session after session. In time, she taught herself to read and write, and eventually she began to teach neighboring homesteads, challenging both the missionaries' and Maasai notions of appropriate gender roles (Donovan 1978: 112). The Monduli mission journal offers rare glimpses of other women who served as translators and teachers (MMJ/13 Jan. 1977; 17 Nov. 1976).

The Spiritans were discouraged by their failure to convert men. Some, like Father Kohler, blamed the "weaknesses of community" among Maasai:

> The Masai are nomads, they wander—some more, some less. The "boma," in which people are instructed, baptized, and experience the Church, tend to break up and move, and are re-formed—usually with different members. Even nuclear families are disjoined for various social needs. While theoretically giving rise to constant opportunity for individual missionary effort and a spontaneous expansion of the Church, this scattering of communities because of the peripatetic nature of Masai society has raised havoc with a sense of Church community. (Kohler 1977a: 413)

In effect, he concluded, "the 2,000 baptized Maasai are still leading largely individual and private Christian lives of sorts" (Kohler 1977a: 413). Spiritan disillusionment with the *boma* approach was also fueled by a growing recognition that the rhetoric of Vatican II—with its promise of permanent deacons, respect for other cultures, and innovation in missionary methodologies—had not been effected in reality (cf. Hastings 1991). Many missionaries had hoped to train and install community leaders as permanent deacons to serve the pastoral needs of newly evangelized communities, helping to defy the "choke law," whereby "the pastoral work needed for new and many Christians begins to choke out the possibility of further evangelization"

(Donovan 1978: 99; cf. Hastings 1976: 33–35; Hillman 1966: 29). Few indigenous African and Asian bishops wanted innovation and radical change in the practices and powers of priests, however, and some were far more conservative than their missionary counterparts. Despite earlier pressures from Rome to train permanent deacons, for example, other Tanzanian bishops prevented Bishop Durning from ordaining the half dozen men who had been trained in the Diocese of Arusha. Among other problems, the bishops feared such practices would lead to married clergy (GK/9). Finally, with the expansion of its missions and mission stations the local church "was feeling the need to consolidate itself and exert more centralized authority" (Kohler 1977a: 412). The era of experimentation was ending.

The Individual Approach

As missionaries searched for a more effective approach, forced sedentarization in the 1970s imposed a new social/economic/political/spatial structure on Maasai: the village. Under Operation Imparnati, the 1974–75 villagization scheme introduced by President Nyerere, large, interlinked territories of Maasai were divided into "villages," Maasai living in the villages became "residents," and a village "government" was appointed (Hodgson 2001a: ch. 4). The immediate pretext for forcing Maasai to live in permanent, concentrated settlements was to help them "develop" by easing the provision of services such as schools and dispensaries. Villagization made the missionaries aware of a new possibility for "community," the village. Now they could instruct interested individuals, regardless of their school attendance or homestead residence, by designating meeting places convenient to numerous homesteads. As Father Kohler remarked at the time, "[t]he Government is moving the entire population into socialized villages; the Church can flourish in these new settlements" (Kohler 1977a: 412; see also Kohler 1977b).

Adoption of the individual approach, that is, the instruction of interested village residents at some common meeting place, did not occur as a general shift in methods throughout Maasai areas, but on a village by village and missionary by missionary basis.[43] One context for the application of the individual approach was in areas such as Emairete where the transition from first evangelization to pastoral care of the people had occurred. In this context, the individual approach was a sign of the "success" of previous evangelization efforts in the area; as more and more people in an area were baptized, they required ongoing pastoral care, and fewer people remained who had not yet heard the "good news." The individual approach was the most efficient way to instruct the remaining non-baptized people who lived scattered in different homesteads. The second context was in communities such as Embopong' that were considered areas for first evangelization. Here the approach represented an important modification of one of the key objectives of the *boma* approach; it de-emphasized the importance of the "natural," "homogenous" community of the *boma* in favor of the autonomy of individuals, regardless of their *boma* affiliation, to attend instruction. Despite the change in form, however, instructional content and methodology could remain much the same, including the willingness to adapt Christianity to Maasai cultural forms.

Such an "individual" approach appealed to aging missionaries tired of trekking through the bush from homestead to homestead. They were also searching for ways to accommodate themselves to the constraints on their time and resources produced by the "choke law." Few young replacements were arriving, and only a small number of the growing cadre of Tanzanian diocesan priests, including Maasai priests, were interested in working in Maasai areas.[44] In 1996, for example, there were only six diocesan priests and eleven Spiritans working in Maasai Deanery parishes. Of these, some worked in education, the Flying Medical Service, building, and pastoral ministry as opposed to being "directly involved" in "preaching the gospel to Maasai."[45] Most diocesan priests preferred assignments in parishes closer to Arusha so that they had more opportunities for generating additional income to supplement the minimal diocesan funds they received to support themselves and their work. "First evangelization," wrote two Spiritans, "is a very expensive apostolate [in the Diocese of Arusha]. We have large areas to cover with little or no income. The Bishop does not support us and never has. The US-East Province gives a very helpful $500 a month to its members in Maasailand and some support to some East African Province members working in Maasailand. . . . Where there is not outside support the priest spends most of his time in business projects or working on his farm."[46]

And the church did flourish, but not in the form the missionaries desired. With the transition to the individual approach, the gender difference in interest, as evident from baptismal registers and survey responses from the three communities, became vividly apparent. Now that anyone was free to attend religious instruction, regardless of school enrollment or *boma* residence, women flocked to the classes. In contrast, few men attended these classes; they no longer had to make excuses and had more important matters than meetings attended mainly by women. In Emairete, Mti Mmoja, and

Embopong', as in most other Maasai communities, adult women greatly outnumbered men in attendance at instruction classes, participation in the rite of baptism, and active involvement in the Catholic Church (see chapter 4). Because of the marked discrepancy in the interest of Maasai men and women, the Catholic Church in Maasai communities soon became known as the "church of women." Since the individual approach was the dominant approach in the diocese during my research, it is described in greater detail in chapter 4.

Inculturation in Practice: Continuities and Contradictions

Clearly, the *boma* approach and individual approach were changes not just in the form of evangelization, but in the content and process as well. As discussed briefly in chapter 2, for many Spiritans, this meant adopting a mode of instruction premised on dialogue rather than monologue (Mtaita 1998: 129–35), the incorporation of Maasai religious concepts, symbolism, and practice into Catholic teaching, rituals, and practice, and Catholic acceptance (even encouragement) of many Maasai rituals, ceremonies, and cultural practices. The work of Father Hillman, Father Donovan, Father Poirier, and other Spiritans and their catechists was part of an emerging trend in the Catholic Church called "inculturation," that is, the adaptation of the central concepts of Christianity (the kerygma) to the cultural milieu of different peoples.[47] This section briefly examines some contemporary examples of inculturation among Maasai in order to explore its assumptions about Maasai culture, religion, and gender and provide a sense of how the Catholic Church currently operates in Maasai areas. Maasai understandings of and perspectives on these practices will be explored in chapter 6.

The idea of inculturation actually has a very long history in the Catholic Church, since at least a 1659 decree by Rome that told missionaries to bring their religion but not their culture to other lands and to allow converts to participate in indigenous rituals and customs "unless they were contrary to Christian faith and morals" (Kieran 1969a: 343). This "method of adaptation," as Kieran calls it, led to charges of syncretism and the "dilution of Christian doctrine," so that by the time the Spiritans arrived in Africa in the late 1800s, such methods were out of favor (Kieran 1969a: 343). Yet in 1884, the Provincial Council of the Vicariate of Zanguebar agreed that they should study local customs and rituals in order to decide which ones could be tolerated and which should be condemned as superstitious or immoral (Kieran 1969a: 351–52). The call for more knowledge and further study has been repeated throughout the years, especially on the prevalent and controversial practices of initiation rites and polygyny.[48] Moreover, even before Vatican II, some Spiritans contemplated the development of "paraliturgical ceremonies," such as, for example, a ceremony "to promote, enhance and put a religious significance on [the] custom of [Maasai] circumcisions" (LMJ/Jan. 1957). "Of course," the writer cautioned, "this ceremony could not compromise the church and should not compromise the Masai" (LMJ/Jan. 1957).

Over the past two decades, I have witnessed a range of inculturation practices by Spiritans, from a Portuguese Spiritan's idiosyncratic choice to dress only in the red cloths and beaded ornaments of *ilmurran* (except for his socks and shoes, thick-framed glasses, and skullcap) to a complex liturgy for a marriage ceremony that elegantly interwove elements of Maasai and Christian belief and practice. Most Spiritans worked in what might be called the midrange, incorporating Maasai symbols (especially grass and milk), sacred colors (black and white), artifacts (calabashes, shields, leather capes, animal skins, stools), and ornaments (especially beadwork) into their vestments, sanctuary, altar, vessels, and liturgies. They drew on and elaborated Maasai myths and stories in their instruction and sermons, conducted instruction and liturgies in Maa (through a translator, usually a catechist), used Maa translations of the Bible and prayers, promoted the development and performance of Maasai Christian songs, encouraged baptized Maasai to take Maasai names, and accepted Maasai who wore their customary dress, ornaments, ocher, and so forth. Despite these changes in content, however, the key elements of these services—including the offering of the peace, New and Old Testament readings, and recitation of the creed and "Our Father"— as well as their order, followed standard practice.

Although some Lutheran pastors, especially those who were American missionaries, practiced similar modes of inculturation, the Lutheran church was generally regarded by Maasai and Catholics alike as far less tolerant of Maasai cultural and social practices. In an informal conversation one day, "Thomas," a Catholic Maasai who I have known for many years, offered a vivid critique of the practice by some Lutherans of prohibiting Maasai converts from wearing their customary dress and ornaments. He pointed to my small silver dangling earrings. "Why are your earrings OK to wear, but my Maasai ones aren't?" He grabbed my silver bangle bracelet. "And who is to say that your bracelet is fine, but my beaded one (shaking his wrist) is not? Surely Jesus didn't care about such things!"[49]

Inculturation raises a series of important questions about the relationship among culture, religion, knowledge, and gender that I would like to briefly review here. First, how can culture be distinguished from religion, especially in the case of Maasai where, as discussed in chapter 1, historically the two were never distinct domains of belief and practice? Can any religion, even Christianity, ever be expressed, explained, practiced, believed, or questioned in a cultureless form or with cultureless content? Second, the objectives of inculturation required learning as much as possible about Maasai "religion" and "culture." These missionaries therefore confronted theoretical, epistemological, and methodological questions familiar to anthropologists and other ethnographers: How does one learn about religion and culture? Through key informants (such as catechists or indigenous clergy), other Spiritans (including apprenticeships), secondary sources (including the books by Father Donovan and Father Hillman), casual discussions? How does one's fluency in the local language and length of stay shape what is understood and learned, even who is spoken to? If conflicting accounts of cultural or religious practice are received, whose version counts? Moreover, as with many earlier anthropologists, the issue of gender is central. Despite the large number of female participants, Spiritans relied primarily on Maasai men (especially catechists, but also elder men, and *ilaigwenak*) for information. Moreover, almost all of their encounters with Maasai women (who, until recently, did not speak much Swahili) were mediated by men (usually male catechists) serving as translators and go-betweens. Therefore, like British colonial officers and other Europeans and Americans before them, they tended to receive and replicate very androcentric understandings of Maasai life. Their concepts of Maasai culture and religion were also deeply ahistorical and essentialist, conveying little sense of the historicity, dynamism, and diversity of Maasai beliefs and practices.

These issues raise questions about understanding, translation, and reception of both the content and the form of cultural knowledge. If missionaries ever had only partial understandings of Maasai ideas and practices, how did their reiteration of these in their teaching and preaching shape and re-shape Maasai beliefs? How did missionaries select from their growing knowledge of Maasai language and "culture" to choose the best words and concepts to translate and convey their message? How did these linguistic choices affect Maasai understanding and reception? How was this cultural knowledge re-worked and perhaps even resignified as it was shaped into Catholic forms of music, performance, liturgy, and instruction?[50]

Finally, despite its seeming respect for Maasai cultural and religious practices and beliefs, the underlying message of inculturation was that these were not good enough; Maasai still needed to hear the "Good News" of the New

Testament. But why? If the rationale was no longer one of "salvation," that is, of saving their souls from eternal damnation (see earlier discussion), what was its replacement? The issue posed a fundamental personal and theological challenge to Spiritans. As Father Poirier wondered, "What is the Good News of Christ? Why is it good? What drives me to become a missionary? What is so good about our faith that I am driven to come to Africa to share it with others?" (Poirier 1984: 12). In response, he and other Spiritans posited a range of rationales to justify their ongoing evangelization work among Maasai (and other "pagan" peoples). Most centered on the fact that Maasai did not believe in the afterlife, and therefore lived their lives afraid of death (at least according to the missionaries). As Father Poirier wrote:

> The Maasai see a dead body and have no hope. The very limits of their existence are defined by the fact of death. "We are not like the grass," they say, "that dies in the dry season and comes afresh every rain, or the moon which dies and resurrects on the third day. We are like cows waiting to be slaughtered not by men but by God, for God's pleasure. God gives life and God takes it away." (Poirier 1984: 6)

As a result, according to Father Poirier, their lives were ruled by fear: fear of each other, fear of Eng'ai's anger and retribution, fear of death, fear of the unknown (1984). The ten lessons of the disk, therefore, taught the fundamental lessons of the New Testament, which he believed would bring revelation and therefore hope to Maasai, including light, resurrection, forgiveness, love, thanksgiving, and everlasting life (Poirer 1974, 1984).

Father Christy voiced similar ideas: "The Maasai God is arbitrary; the Maasai God can bless today and curse tomorrow. The Maasai concept of God is to be respected and feared and keep your head down. You don't want to be too close to God, because God can be either very generous or very unforgiving with his favorites." Although he acknowledged that Maasai ideas of the afterlife had changed, "the concept of communion with God in the afterlife is not strong, if at all present. Death is death and death is the end." Eng'ai is the "Old Testament God" who "does not ask for personal choice."

Inculturation therefore raises many questions as both a theology and a practice. But these questions and debates were not limited to missionaries alone. The approach has clearly influenced the ideas, attitudes, and practices of Maasai men and women—catechists, parishioners, and non-Catholics—as they have come to learn about and understand (and, for some, practice) the Catholic faith.

THE CHURCH OF WOMEN

4

So what do these contemporary "churches of women" look like? How do these churches differ among the three communities, given their different histories and "stages" of evangelization? Who are the members of the church of women? How do they see themselves and their participation in the Catholic Church? Why have Maasai women been so eager to create a church of women, despite the resistance and reluctance of Maasai men and Spiritan missionaries? How do women, men, catechists, and missionaries participate in and understand the particular form the Catholic Church has taken among Maasai? How have the ideas and practices of both Maasai and missionaries worked together to shape the content and form of current liturgies, catechism, and practices in the Catholic Church, especially given Spiritan ideas of inculturation?

This chapter compares how the contemporary "church of women" operates in three communities—Emairete, Mti Mmoja, Embopong'—with different histories of evangelization and explores how some of the Maasai women who participate in it understand the "church of women." The following chapter probes the perspectives of Maasai men, male catechists, and Spiritan missionaries. Although they may differ in some regards from other Maasai Catholic congregations in Tanzania, a comparative study of these three congregations does suggest some common themes and patterns by providing insights into the gender, culture, and power dynamics of the churches; the idiosyncratic relationships between individual priests and church members; the centrality of catechists to daily life in the church; and the mutual agency of all involved in influencing the content and form of the contemporary church of women.

Emairete

Emairete has the longest and most intense history of interaction with the Catholic Church, in part because it is located on top of Monduli mountain, near the district headquarters of Monduli town (see map 4.1). The community lives in and around a large caldera: most homesteads are on the slopes of the caldera, circling the plains that are used for livestock grazing. Every family has at least one small farm in the valleys or on top of the ridges. Because of its rich, fertile land, it is, by Maasai standards, a densely populated community. Moreover, as more and more Arusha have moved to, married into, or been resettled in the community, it has become very ethnically mixed, with 26.7 percent (n = 132) of adult women and 13.1 percent of adult men (n = 65) identifying themselves as Arusha in 1992, from a total adult population of 291 women and 204 men (Maasai Census, 1992). A notable feature is that many of the Maasai residents belong to the Inkidong'i clan, the clan of *iloibonok* (diviners and prophets). They moved to the area after they were evicted in the 1970s from their settlements on the Lashaine plains south of Monduli town to make room for a military training camp.

After Father Hillman started a school for boys in Emairete in 1961, Spiritans visited the school and community regularly. Mwalimu Daniel Lolgolie, an Arusha man, was the school's first teacher, and became and remained (until the present) the main catechist for the community. He taught religious education in the school, and continued religion classes when the school was nationalized in 1970. Father Poirier began intensive direct evangelization of adults, using the *boma* approach, in 1970,[1] but it lasted only five years, since "in a short time we got so many people" (DL1/11). After that, "people searched us out themselves" (DL1/9). By 1975, after villagization, enough Maasai and Arusha had been baptized, and interest in the church was so strong, that the missionaries could successfully switch to the individual approach. Instruction was first held in convenient homesteads, then near a trailer that the priests set up, and, finally, in the grand church built in 1988 (see fig. 4.1) (DL1/9). More formalized lesson plans were designed and followed, with formal syllabi covering the Old and New Testaments, and memorization of certain prayers and creeds. Catechumens were baptized only after successfully completing a two-year course of instruction (DL1/10).[2]

Spiritan involvement in the community, however, has not been as constant or consistent as the above historical sketch suggests. Priests visited the

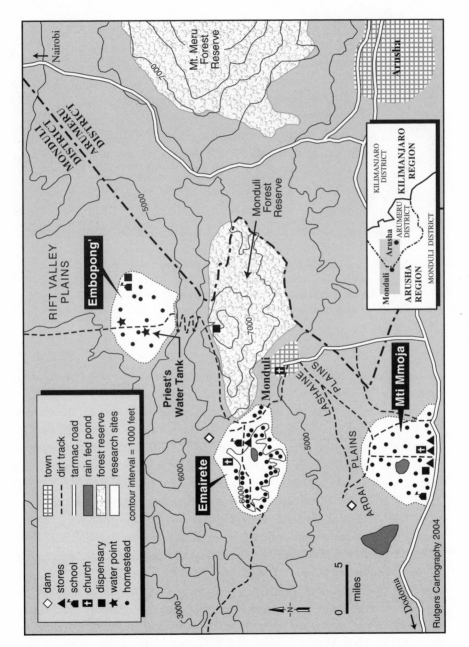

Map 4.1. Research communities: Emairete, Mti Mmoja, and Embopong', ca. 2000.

Fig. 4.1. The grand church that was built in Emairete in 1988. On the left-hand side is the main entrance and vestibule. The circular building in the center is the sanctuary, and the classroom/meeting room is to the right. Groups of women are circulating in front before services. Photo by author, 1992.

community and occasionally spent the night, but most were not regularly present in the community, even after construction of the fathers' residence was completed in 1988. Religious instruction and most pastoral duties were left to the catechist, Mwalimu Daniel, for almost thirty years (GK/29–31).

Several schoolboys were baptized prior to 1970, but the first *boma* baptisms were held by Father Poirier in 1972 with three *bomas* comprising fifteen adult women, six adult men, and eighteen children (MMBR/12 June 1968, 29 Mar. 1970). Initially, baptisms held throughout the *boma* approach years had an almost even number of males and females, but soon females (adults and children) outnumbered males almost two to one (EBR/17 May 1973, 11 Oct. 1973, 5 July 1974). Once the individual approach began, adult women outnumbered men at least two to one at each baptism, but more often by three to one or a greater proportion.[3] With rare exceptions, the men who were baptized were junior elders, between twenty-five and thirty-five years of age, and many were Arusha, not Maasai. In 1992, 58.4 percent (n = 87) of adult Maasai women in Emairete reported being baptized or in instruction, as compared to 31.1 percent (n = 42) of adult Maasai males (Maasai Census, 1992).

Despite the flurry of baptisms in the early 1970s, few of the new Christians regularly attended church. Monthly masses held by Father Butts in 1975 were attended by "basically school children and teachers" (MMJ/1975—"Transcription from Rev. Butts' notebook"). Even in 1977, Father Kane and Mwalimu Daniel were considering "an ongoing syllabus for teaching the newly baptized or those baptized in '74 and '75 but seemingly 'unengaged' " (MMJ/21 Mar. 1977). Concerns about these baptized but "unengaged" Christians prompted further reflections on "the state of Emairete Christians." Father Kane and Mwalimu Daniel concluded that "some are stuck in their *mila* [Swahili for customs, beliefs, culture] and when it comes to choosing or sacrificing something for the sake of their Christian Commitment, it's the mila that prevails" (MMJ/7–9 Sept. 1977). An incoming priest delayed confirmation services in 1985 "until the Christians there can be evaluated" (MMJ/17 Apr. 1985). With the completion of the new church in 1988, however, attendance at the instruction classes and church services swelled. Services I attended in 1991–1993, 1995, 1996–1997, and 2000 averaged about two hundred women and forty men (most often Arusha). But even in 1992, Father Kohler said that the current priest had "serious doubts about the depths of their [the residents of Emairete] Christian response, what they know."

The church was built near the edge of a prominent hill on the side of the caldera, close to the shops, school, and market. It was designed to combine certain key elements of Maasai spatial aesthetics in the shape of the Christian cross. At the "bottom" of the cross is the vestibule, a long entrance corridor with the vestry and catechists' office to each side and a font of holy water in the center. The vestibule leads to a large, circular sanctuary with two entrances on either side. To the left is the rectangular priests' house (including a sitting room, two bedrooms, a small kitchen, and a bathroom), and to the right a large rectangular room used for meetings, instruction, and choir practice. Above the church, at the "top" of the cross, is a large bell tower. All of the buildings are painted the deep red color of ocher preferred by Maasai. Into the early 1990s, the church served the community of Emairete (including the non-Maasai schoolteachers and other government workers) as well as the surrounding communities of Eluwai and Enguiki, all of which had at one time been part of the village of Monduli Juu. A few women even walked the fifteen kilometers from Embopong' to attend services. As discussed by Father Christy in chapter 2, in 1999 the church became the headquarters for the new parish of Monduli Juu, encompassing not just the communities on the mountain, but over twenty outstations, including Embopong' and Mti Mmoja.

Since 1991, when I first began living in Emairete, I had attended many church services. I participated in standard services, major religious celebrations such as Easter and Christmas, and baptisms and marriages, and witnessed the performances of several priests, including Father Kohler and other American Spiritans and Father Simon Lobon, a Kenyan Spiritan. Generally, these services followed a standard liturgy, with the priests speaking or reading in Swahili and a catechist translating into Maa. The Emairete church also had a formal choir, comprising about twenty younger men and women.

I was therefore curious to see how Father Christy structured his liturgy when I returned in 2000. A few weeks before, while Father Christy was still on leave, I had attended a First Communion service in Emairete supervised by a diocesan priest and Father John Laiser, a newly ordained Tanzanian Spiritan from Lashaine whom I had taught fifteen years before at the Oldonyo Sambu Junior Seminary. I was delighted to see him, and we quickly caught up on each other's news. A gentle, soft-spoken young man, he was elated about his upcoming assignment to Zimbabwe. A wedding of one of Sokoine's sons had been scheduled to take place during the service as well, but was delayed because of some family issues. That day, in part because of the First Communion and wedding, over three hundred people (about forty of them men) attended church, many in their finery. The thirty girls and ten boys who were going to receive First Communion were very dressed up. Some girls wore shiny white polyester dresses, white lace gloves, and small white hats. Others wore Maasai outfits, including elaborate beaded necklaces and headdresses. The boys all wore pants and shirts.

The service was fairly standard, with the catechists doing much of the work, including giving the sermon. All the readings and sermon were delivered in Swahili first, then Maa, with the prayers and Creed in Swahili. The choir, led by "Maria," a young Maasai woman dressed in a bright blue cloth and stunning beadwork, sang most songs in Swahili, with only occasional Maasai songs. Maria was an elegant and poised conductor, and the ten young men (all in pants and shirts) and ten young women (most in Maasai dress) in the choir carefully followed her directions. The presentation of the gifts (the offerings, wafers, and wine) was made by representatives from the first communicants: four boys and four girls (all of whom wore white dresses, not Maasai dress). After communion, the women applauded and ululated, and many of the children received bright plastic garlands. A Lutheran pastor

Fig. 4.2. Girls bringing gifts for the priests after receiving First Communion in Emairete. Some wear white dresses and hats, others wear blue cloths covered by khanga wraps. Accessories include elaborate bead necklaces, earrings, and bracelets and plastic garlands. Toward the back a few girls wear the complicated beaded head covering that marks them as almost of marriageable age. Photo by author, 1992.

who was visiting the service was invited to say a few words, the children brought gifts for the priest to the altar, and then the service was over.

A few weeks later, on the first Saturday (in Emairete, Mass is held on Saturdays to accommodate the priests' other obligations and the market schedule) of Father Christy's return, much seemed familiar to me. Large groups of women sat outside the church chatting and laughing; a few men hovered on the steps and in the entrance to the vestibule. Father Christy, dressed in a white alb, greeted and talked with everyone, enjoying the light teasing and repartee that is central to most Maasai social interactions. When the church bell rang promptly at 10:30 A.M., everyone rushed into the church to be seated. There were a total of about 240 people (approximately 170 women, 15 men, and 50 or more children) present. The women and children sat on the left and center aisles, facing the altar, while about 15 adult men (mostly Arusha) sat on a few pews in the front right side. Mzee Ngoilenya, the chairperson of the church, sat alone in a chair in front of the right-hand pillar near the altar. The altar was covered with a red and white–checked cloth, and a hairy piece of animal hide was draped over the priest's chair.

Once everyone was settled, the choir processed in singing, followed by Father Christy and three catechists, Mwalimu Daniel, Mwalimu "Francis," and Mwalimu "Mateo." Father Christy had draped a beaded leather cape around his shoulders as his chasuble; each of the stick figures from Father Poirier's disk had been sewn onto the cape in beads. After greeting everyone in Maa, Father Christy spoke Swahili, with Mwalimu Daniel as his translator. The service proceeded much as before, in Swahili with Maa translations. Unlike the previous service, however, where a female schoolteacher had read one of the readings, all the readers were men. With a constant smile on his face and no notes in his hands, Father Christy preached an animated sermon that Mwalimu Mateo translated in just as animated a fashion. As I summarized in my field notes:

> In the past, the Maasai believed that God had two faces, a black face and a red face. God was described as red-faced when it was dry, during the drought, when the sunset was bright red against the sky. The black-faced God was so-called because of the black rain clouds. The red-faced God was an angry God, while the black-faced God was generous and giving. But the God of the Bible is not an angry God, we have seen that He is a generous and giving God. Yet you may wonder why such a good God would let things like drought, hunger, and death happen. . . . When I left for the United States, the weather was warm, and it had been raining—we even got stuck in the mud going to Father John's ordination!! But now I have returned and it is cold and very dry . . . so dry that people from everywhere are bringing their cattle up to Emairete for water and grass. It is dry here, but in other parts of Tanzania people have lots of rain and food—is this because they are blessed and we are damned? Why does God let these things happen? Why did Jesus choose to resurrect the one little girl, yet let so many other people die [the Gospel reading was Mark 5: 21–43, where Jesus brings a young girl back to life]? This is an example of what lies in store for all of us in the kingdom of God. But we can't just lie about and wait for it to happen, we have to confront our problems and trials as an example to others and to God of what we can do. Does God just want us to cover our heads with a cloth and lie on the ground, resting until the drought and hunger are over? No, He wants us to work together to combat the hunger and drought, to share our resources, to serve as an example to ourselves and others.

Most people paid attention to the homily, in great part because both Father Christy and Mwalimu Mateo were gifted, engaging presenters.

At the end of the service the church secretary, an Arusha man, announced that the catechists had decided that the church should sponsor a feast for people being confirmed in August. They therefore asked every person who was to be confirmed to donate one thousand shillings, and all other church members to give five hundred shillings to pay for the party and small gifts. Mwalimu Mateo chimed in, reiterating the request and reminding everyone that families always contributed livestock and gifts for circumcision ceremonies, and this was a similar occasion and demand. Finally, Father Christy stood up. "Fine," he said, "but I have something to add. No one is forced to pay this money. Everyone who has been attending instruction for confirmation will be confirmed, whether or not they pay for the party. Sacraments are not bought!"

The next week, however, there was a drastic decline in attendance—only about forty women with their children and five or six men. No one mentioned the demands made for money the previous week; instead, they attributed the small attendance to the drought conditions, which forced women to work even harder to ensure the basic survival of their households. But it was clear that many were embarrassed to attend because they had nothing at the moment to give for the regular offering, much less the special offerings—not even a few *sentis* (Swahili for "cents," equivalent to less than a penny). Everyone was adamant that the shrinking numbers had nothing to do with Father Christy, whom they liked and respected. As discussed below, I witnessed a similar decline in attendance at Mti Mmoja that summer.

"Sarah," as I shall call her, was an active member of the Emairete church. She and I quickly became friends when I first moved to Emairete in 1991, in part because she had been educated through Form 2 (equivalent to junior high school) and thus spoke fluent Swahili (which was a relief for me as I struggled with my Maa in those early months). At that time, she was in her early twenties, married to an *olmurran* of the Landiss age-set, and the mother of two children. Her father was one of the wealthiest men in the area, with huge herds of cattle at his homesteads in Emairete and Embopong'. He, and therefore she, were members of the Inkidong'i clan, the clan of the *iloibonok*. Her husband, "Lengogo," was from a poor family, had studied in school through Standard 7, and had worked for Sarah's father for several years as a herder to earn the right, through his brideservice, to marry her. Sarah was beautiful, with a gentle, kind way about her. She was also very smart, and an acute observer of the everyday twists and tangles of social life and relations in Emairete.

Sarah was instructed by Father Benedict Nangoro (a Maasai diocesan priest) and Mwalimu Daniel, baptized in 1988 by Father Thomas Tunney (an American Spiritan who was then the pastor of the Emairete church), and later confirmed. In the early 1990s, when Sarah and her family still lived in her father's homestead, she attended church regularly. In 2000, however, I saw her at services only occasionally, in part because in 1996 she and her husband had moved several miles away to establish their own homestead (she was still his only wife). (A Greek farmer who once owned a large farm in the area had left, and the village had allocated the land to residents.) One day, Morani and I trekked over the mountain to interview her in her new homestead. She was home with her husband, one of his friends, and her small children. While Sarah prepared and served us tea, Morani and I chatted with Lengogo and his friend. Sarah soon joined us, lying on the grass and chatting with me as the men continued to talk. She and her husband seemed remarkably comfortable and free with one another, performing little of the customary respect behavior common in other marriages. Her husband sat quietly in her house when we interviewed her, listening carefully and respectfully to our discussion. As Morani and I walked back, I asked him if he thought that Sarah would have answered any questions differently if Lengogo had not been in the house. "No," he replied. "They are not afraid of each other."

During our interview, she told me that all of her children had been baptized, but her husband had no interest in the church. "Why," I asked, "did you decide to seek instruction and join the church?"

"I needed the church," she replied, "which is why I went." She continued: "The benefits that I get from going to church are that I know that Eng'ai will help me a lot, because I know that Eng'ai is there at all times. . . . Eng'ai helps people, especially if you open your *oltau* (heart, spirit) for Her. I pray to Eng'ai because I know that She has power over everything—children, cattle, and your life as well."

"But has your involvement in the church prevented you from participating in Maasai life and rituals in any way?" I asked. "No," she replied:

> Some churches follow Maasai customs . . . but the Lutherans and Pentecostals don't accept Maasai customs, they hassle Maasai in big ways. The problem is that if you join the Pentecostals, you are forbidden from participating in all the aspects of Maasai culture that I have described [the life-cycle ceremonies], so that when you enter the Pentecostal church you can't slaughter a sheep for your child, and you can't do all the things as part of being a new parent, so you don't do any of the ceremonies involved with having and raising a child that I described. So we think that it is only the Catholic Church that accepts Maasai culture and customs—even a Catholic wedding incorporates Maasai culture. . . . You can [even] join the Catholic Church without marrying [in the church], and the church will still let you join.

When I probed further as to her ideas about the relationship between Maasai religious practices and beliefs and those of the Catholic Church, she responded that although she thought "the Maasai God and the Christian God were the same," there were some differences in Maasai and Christian rituals: "Maasai follow practices that are part of their culture, while Christians follow practices that are part of the church." Maasai who did not attend church "know nothing about Jesus and why we follow him." "Some Maasai just don't know the importance [of church]; others have attended instruction but then are prevented from coming by satan, and some don't go because their *oltau* won't let them." As for men, "I think men don't want to go to church, especially *ilmurran* . . . because they follow Maasai customs."

Earlier in the interview, Sarah had described in great detail the various life-cycle ceremonies that marked birth, naming, initiation, marriage, age-set promotion, death, and other transitions in Maasai men's and women's lives. From her accounts and those of other men and women (confirmed by my own extensive participant observation), it seemed that these rituals had not changed significantly from the accounts of the early 1900s, at least in terms of formal practices. Meanings were another matter. Sarah and her husband ensured that all of the relevant ceremonies were carried out for their children so that they were seen, and saw themselves as, fully Maasai. In addition, however, Sarah and her children also attended church and participated in new rituals such as baptism, communion, and weekly church services. She saw these as a complement to, rather than a contradiction of, Maasai customs and rituals. Her only criticism of the church was about Mwalimu Daniel: "The priests should get rid of him because he has destroyed the unity of the church. He is a big reason that some people no longer go to church. A lot happens in church that shouldn't." She refused to elaborate, but her sentiments were shared by some of the other men and women I interviewed.

Sarah's mother, whom I shall call "Koko Nayieu," was also a baptized Catholic, but she had a very different background than Sarah and therefore a different relation to and understanding of the Catholic Church. In contrast to Sarah, Koko Nayieu was illiterate and spoke very little Swahili. She was one of seven wives, had ten children, and despite being married to a very wealthy man (of the Seuri age-set), she still had to work—to carry water and firewood with a child on her back, to care for and feed her children and household. "My job was to have kids." She was taught by Mwalimu Daniel, then baptized and confirmed on the same day. She joined the Catholic Church because "it was said that we should go to church because the church followed the words of Eng'ai and the church could get rid of this thing called satan." Before being baptized, Koko Nayieu suffered from *orpeko*, or spirit possession. As she explained, "I go to church to get rid of this illness that makes me crazy, to get rid of this illness that I can't get rid of myself, even with the prayers that I sing." But she found that her illiteracy and lack of fluency in Swahili made the Catholic liturgy difficult to understand; "It is hard for a person who hasn't been to school to go and listen to things of the paper (*impala*) which they have never seen before, especially when you are used to one language." "Until today," she concluded, "I don't understand the things of the church."

For Koko Nayieu, as for most illiterate women whom I interviewed, the church provided yet another place to pray to Eng'ai: "When I go to church I pray in the same way that I pray at home. I mean, the prayers of the church are the same as these that we have inside here. The prayers are the same thing. When you stay inside your house you pray to Eng'ai, you say 'My God, take this milk. Please blow good things on me for my cattle and children. Rid the world of disease'." She told us that she prayed to Eng'ai throughout the day:

> When you walk you spill milk for Eng'ai: "My Eng'ai please bless me with cattle and children, guard me and give me your good things, boys and girls." And when you stay inside you pray to Eng'ai. When the cattle leave after milking, you pray until they return in the evening—it is like a year. In the night when you sleep you pray to Eng'ai. That's the reason that when you awake you ask people how they are doing, it's like another year. So that's what I do, I pray all the time every day.

As for the relationship between Maasai religion and Christianity, "I don't think the church has brought any changes to Maasai customs, because this church follows the ways of the Maasai, it really follows Maasai ways." She believed that Eng'ai was at once the Mother (*ngotonye oltungani*) and the Father (*menye oltungani*) of people and the world. Like Sarah, she recited all of the details of the various Maasai life-cycle ceremonies and participated in them regularly. Although married to a wealthy Inkidong'i man, Koko Nayieu did not think that *iloibonok* had any special relationship to Eng'ai: "They are just like me." Moreover, she added, "it is not like Eng'ai gave them the power to make rain." She did, however, regret that "the prayers [in church] are divided between those of the Maasai and those of the priests, because the Maasai prayers don't go forward [to Eng'ai] like those of the priests."

Finally, there is the story of elderly "Koko Naomon," who was probably in her nineties when I interviewed her in 2000 (as an *ndito* she had danced for *ilmurran* of the Tareto age-set) in Emairete. Koko Naomon was barren, but in keeping with Maasai custom, she had been given a daughter by another co-wife. Koko Naomon's adopted daughter married a very wealthy man, who allowed Koko Naomon to live in his homestead in Embopong' since she had no sons to take care of her. Although frail and failing in her health (she was almost blind), Koko Naomon was full of stories and commentaries about Maasai customs, the Catholic Church, and the changes she had experienced in her life. Like Koko Nayieu, she suffered from *orpeko*, and subsequently sought to join the Catholic Church. "I went to instruction because satan came inside me, it came inside me even though I was this old. . . . People found me just lying here, I couldn't even eat. All I could do was drink water, I lost a lot of weight." She was instructed by a catechist named Mwalimu Peter in 1992. "What were you taught?" I asked. She replied:

> I was asked if I had renounced satan. "Go away satan!" Don't use the name of God in vain, don't deny people food, don't distinguish among your children, if someone comes and hits you, kneel because Eng'ai will rescue you. Stop doing bad things, stop being mean, stop witchcraft, stop all these bad things. Give up all of these things and accept Jesus. At the time I accepted and truly now I don't do these things anymore.

Once she was baptized and confirmed by Father Nangoro, she never suffered from *orpeko* again. Although she rarely goes to church these days because of her blindness and other infirmities, when she lived in Embopong' she would visit Emairete for about three weeks at a time so that she could go to church.

Unlike Sarah, Koko Naomon believed that certain Maasai rituals and ceremonies had changed over time. "All these ceremonies I've told you about are from the past," she warned. "There are even homesteads [these days] that don't cut *elaitin* [special trees cut as part of circumcision ceremonies]!" She remembered wearing skins instead of cloth as clothes, and described some of the ornaments, such as the thick curled metal earrings, that had disappeared.

Koko Naomon also thought that "the ways of worshipping these days have become modern ways." Although the Catholic Church "respects all things to do with the Maasai past," it had nonetheless, she believed, brought many changes. For her, one of the most troubling was the use of Swahili as the primary language of prayer, ritual, and song in the Emairete church: "so if you go there and you don't know Swahili, what have you gone there to do?" "The only meaningful thing," she said, "is the sacraments. You get them

157

in your mouth and you leave." Moreover, unlike Sarah and Koko Nayieu, Koko Naomon thought that Eng'ai and "the God of the church" were distinct, so that "you don't pray to two gods. You pray to the God of the church and give up the other God." "Eng'ai and the Christian God are not the same. The God I know was the one who gave birth to me. They are telling us to forget that God and take up with the new one. The Maasai God is no longer here." Finally, she has fond memories of the *boma* approach. "Now they baptize in churches, before they baptized in homesteads. The Christians would fill the homestead and there would be a big celebration. I wish they would go back to baptizing in the bush. I wish they were more like the first priests."

Mti Mmoja

Mti Mmoja, the second community, has a shorter and more erratic history of Catholic presence and involvement. Mti Mmoja means "one tree" in Swahili, referring to the one large tree growing near the stores and dispensary on the tarmac road that connects the regional headquarters of Arusha with the famous game parks of Ngorongoro, Tarangire, and the Serengeti. Like Emairete, a mix of Arusha and Maasai live in the community, which actually comprises sections of two "official" government villages, Lendikenya and Arkatan, set on the rolling Ardai plains. Many Arusha were resettled in the area in the 1970s and 1980s. Of the 222 adults surveyed in 1992, 16.7 percent of the women (n = 37) and 9.5 percent of the men (n = 21) identified themselves as Arusha (Maasai Census, 1992). The high elevation (between 1,320 and 1,480 meters), geographical location (southwest of Monduli mountain), and fairly consistent rainfall make the land suitable for cultivation and animal husbandry (see map 4.1). Homesteads are spread across the plains, with farm plots clustered together at regular intervals. A large rain-fed pond provides water for domestic and livestock use during the long rains; at other times the community relies on a nearby dam. Fuel wood is scarce, however, since all the trees were cut as part of the ill-conceived Northern Province Wheat Scheme in the late colonial period (Hodgson 2001a), so every few days women must make a day-long trek to the slopes of Monduli mountain to cut and gather wood.

As discussed in chapter 3, the initial *boma* classes held by Spiritans in 1975 to 1976 were quite unsuccessful, resulting in no baptisms despite numerous classes. Only a few schoolboys were baptized at this time. Another American Spiritan taught in the area from 1982 to 1983, encountering some competition from the Lutherans. They arrived one day in the village, showed a movie, promised a grinding machine, brought some adults and children to sing and hold a service, and installed a catechist in the homestead the Spiritan was working from. But, having recently conceded to the Anglicans in a similar situation in a nearby area, the Spiritan accepted "the advice of the Bishop and a few Christian Maasai leaders of the area" and "decided to stay and fight": "I made it clear to the Masai people of the area that they had to choose between the Lutheran approach and the Catholic approach." He explained that "we are both Christians" and "believe basically the same thing, but there are minor things we disagree on. I also refused to teach just women—I would not divide the family." If only a few people wanted to become Catholics, he advised them to join the Lutheran church "because I didn't see the value of a little division in the group." The people chose the Catholics, and the competition with the Lutherans invigorated them; "the attendance, interest, and spirit of the people have improved." But worries about the Lutheran methods remained: "It seems to me the Lutherans are trying to build the church on fear of the devil taking possession of women" (MMJ/Jan. 1982–June 1983). Nonetheless, he never baptized people in the community. But the Lutherans returned, baptized a large group of women after minimal instruction, and left.

A Maasai diocesan priest taught people with the individual approach for two years (1985–1987), and baptized a group of people, mainly women (MMJ/23 Apr. 1987). A few months later he was transferred, replaced by an African Spiritan who continued individual instruction, baptizing twenty-three adults—all women—during Easter 1990, and fifteen women and one man during Easter 1991 (MMBR/14 Apr. 1990, 30 Mar. 1991). He helped the women build a modest church in 1990, and a small school in 1991 (see fig. 4.3) (GK/37–38). Peter Kierie, an African Spiritan deacon from Kenya, instructed the next group, and Father Kohler did the baptisms: nineteen adult women, one adult man (an Arusha), and forty-eight girls and boys (MMBR/20 Apr. 1992). In 1992, 51.6 percent (n = 48) of all adult Maasai women residing in Mti Mmoja reported being baptized or in instruction, compared to 15.4 percent (n = 10) of adult men (Maasai Census, 1992).

I attended the Easter baptism service led by Father Kohler at Mti Mmoja in 1992. Since Father Kohler had told me that it would begin at noon, I arrived at 11:30 A.M. About thirty women were seated outside the small wooden church, and Peter, the deacon, was hovering around in a suit with a piece of paper in his hands, trying to organize people. People slowly trickled in, many walking two to three miles from their scattered homesteads.

159

Fig. 4.3. Congregants wait for the Easter baptismal services to begin at
Mti Mmoja Catholic Church. Photo by author, 1992.

At one point, Peter pulled all of the benches outside of the church and asked
the baptismal candidates to sit on the benches according to the order of their
names on his list. No such luck: most people ignored him, others wanted to
sit on the benches, all were talking among themselves. Peter spoke Swahili
to everyone, and Mwalimu Edward, the catechist, translated into Maa,
which only added to the confusion, since few of the women spoke much
Swahili. More people trickled in. The mood seemed pretty sedate. The
women, almost all dressed in their best customary dress and favorite ornaments, sat in front of the church, chatting quietly among themselves. The
few men present, all dressed in pants and shirts and some with jackets, stood
talking in a small group on the side. At one point, Peter badgered the women
to search for larger pieces of wood, since they had brought only tiny ones
for the Easter fire. Reluctantly, some women got up and looked half-
heartedly around the church (which had few trees) for some wood, then sat
down, empty-handed. Through their body language and mutterings among
themselves, they made it very clear that they did not feel obliged to listen
to Peter or to follow his orders.

As I moved about, talking to both the women and the men, one man asked if I had a camera in my bag. I said yes, that I wanted to ask Father Kohler for permission to take pictures during the service. "There is no reason to ask Kola [as they called him], but you should ask the *mwenyekiti* [Swahili for chairperson] of the church, that woman over there."

"Certainly," I replied, "but I still need to ask Father Kohler, since he might get upset." They carefully eyed one another. "Yes," said one man, as the others nodded in agreement, "he can be hard-headed." I walked over to talk to Esta, the *mwenyekiti*, who happily agreed to my request to take photos.

Finally, at about 1:30 P.M., some women spotted Father Kohler's car approaching the church. The women all stood up and began to sing, clapping their hands. But their performance seemed dispirited and forced—they were not singing together, or loudly, or dancing and swaying. As soon as Father Kohler stopped his car, they quit singing and sat down or milled around. The roof of Father Kohler's car was loaded with benches, and he seemed harried and tired. The men walked over and greeted him, and then he conferred with Peter and Mwalimu Edward for a while. The ensuing preparations (including moving the benches back into the church) and planning took another hour or so.

Eventually, everything was almost ready. People sat on the benches along the inner wall of the church and on the floor, or stood outside the church looking in through the windows. There were about eighty women, forty children, and eight men present, with only one older man wearing customary Maasai dress. A woven mat was spread on the floor with the gifts, a Bible and a liturgy book on it. Father Kohler was still talking to Peter about the order of the ceremony—should they bless the fire, candle, and water outside first, then do the readings and the baptism, or . . . ? Finally they agreed on a plan. Father Kohler walked over to the mat, took off his shirt (he had a sleeveless undershirt underneath) and put on his white alb and green stole.

Throughout the service, Father Kohler spoke in Swahili and Mwalimu Edward translated into Maa. After a welcome to everyone, there was a prayer and then the readings. Father Kohler read them first in Swahili, sitting on the edge of the mat, and then several men took turns reading the Maa versions. They read slowly and poorly, and no one seemed to pay much attention. The women sang Christian songs in Maa, but with little enthusiasm. Children cried, women walked in and out, and everyone seemed pretty disinterested. In his sermon, Father Kohler discussed death and the meaning of baptism, especially the afterlife. He concluded by turning in a circle and

Fig. 4.4. Father Kohler preparing the gifts at his altar on the floor of the Mti Mmoja Catholic Church. Photo by author, 1992.

jabbing his fingers at everyone, telling them that "God's work is every-where—there, and there, and there!"

Everyone left the church to prepare for the baptisms. As the women sang, the congregation circled the fire as Father Kohler blessed it and the Easter candle. But it was too windy for the candle to stay lit, so Father Kohler gave up and just dunked the candle in a clay pot filled with water to bless the water. He told the already baptized Christians to go inside the church and the candidates to stand outside. The first candidate to be baptized was the only adult man in the group (Moses Lengaa, who would become the primary catechist for the area). As Father Kohler stood in the doorway, the man walked up and his sponsor put his hand on his shoulder. Peter asked him his name and checked it against a list. Father Kohler read the baptismal candidate's name from a yellow Post-it that had been stuck to his shirt, poured water from a cup over his forehead, and pronounced him baptized. As he walked into the church, the women inside and out ululated briefly. And so it continued for the remaining women and children in line to be baptized. Many of them received colorful plastic garlands to wear around their necks from their sponsors or families.

Fig. 4.5. Father Kohler baptizing a female catechumen on Easter Sunday at the entrance to the Mti Mmoja Catholic Church. The woman is held by her sponsor as Father Kohler pours holy water on her from a metal cup. Mwalimu Edward stands to the right of her sponsor. Photo by author, 1992.

Fig. 4.6. Anna (*third from the left*) surrounded by her friends who have come to celebrate her baptism in Mti Mmoja. They are standing outside her husband's rectangular house. Photo by author, 1992.

Once the baptisms were complete, the candidates stood in a semicircle in the church while Father Kohler anointed their foreheads with holy oil. "Now," Father Kohler said, "it is time for Holy Communion, to feed these new Christians with holy bread and water." He asked everyone who was going to take communion to raise their hands so that he could count the wafers. While he prepared the communion, everyone sang another song, and then took a rather chaotic collection of mostly small coins, with a few fifty- and hundred-shilling notes thrown in.[4] Men gave their offerings first, followed by the women. During the giving of the peace, the men stood in a row while the women and children walked by, usually with a bowed head in the customary form of respect greeting. Most greeted Father Kohler and Mwalimu Edward in a similar fashion. The men then shook hands among themselves and with Father Kohler, and the women shook hands among themselves as well. Men took communion first, then the women. After Mwalimu Edward showed the newly baptized man and women how to cup their hands and dip the wafer in the wine to receive communion, Peter administered it to them. After blessing two marriages among the newly baptized, Father Kohler reminded the new Christians to take a piece of wood home from the Easter fire to light their home fires. With a final song, the service was over.

After driving some people home, I joined a party of women at the home of "Anna," a newly baptized woman who was the wife of the village secretary. As we walked up, the women stopped just outside the compound gate and began singing and dancing. Anna stood in her doorway with her children as the women sang Maasai Christian songs and praise songs for Anna. When they stopped, I was led, with two of my companions (Koko Naserian and her daughter-in-law), to the husband's house while the other women joined Anna in her home. We drank sodas and then joined the other women for a meal of rice and potatoes. As we ate, I listened to the women gossip about Father Kohler. (We had seen Father Kohler's car enter a nearby homestead for a similar celebration.)

The Mti Mmoja church was still going in 2000, when I returned for a service led by Father Christy. He had told me that although the time was officially 11 A.M., the service would not begin until around noon. When I arrived at 11:30 A.M., eight women were sitting in front of the church, and three men, including Mwalimu Moses Lengaa, the current catechist, were standing to the side, talking among themselves. Father Christy was already there, chatting with the men and women. Mwalimu Moses was very concerned about the small turnout, but soon a few more women walked up,

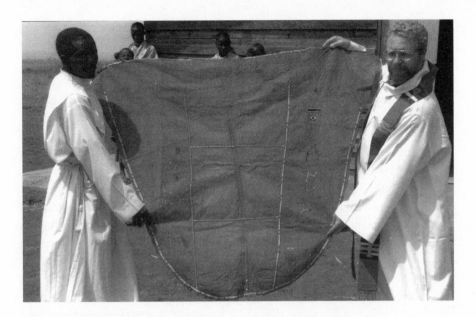

Fig. 4.7. Father Christy and Mwalimu Moses display Father Christy's beaded leather cape outside the Mti Mmoja Catholic Church. The figures on the cape represent each of the pictures from Father Poirier's disk (see fig. 3.4a,b). Photo by author, 2000.

including his wife and Esta, the founder of the church. Father Christy encouraged everyone to go into the church, but they sat outside. After he and Mwalimu Moses had dressed in their vestments, he asked everyone to go inside again, but there was still no movement. Frustrated, Father Christy said, "Fine, we'll go in and get started and you can decide if you want to join us." So the fifteen women, three men, and several children went in.

Father Christy wore the same beaded sheepskin cape, decorated with the pictures from Father Poirier's disk, that he had worn during the Emairete service (fig. 4.7). As he explained to me later, "an elder wears such skins to give blessings, usually with some decoration on it. His senior wife makes it and receives a sheep from him in return. The wife of one of my catechists made this for me, and I gave her a sheep." Twelve benches now lined the church, facing the altar, which was a wooden table covered with a white cloth. Father Christy greeted everyone in Maa, most of the prayers were in Maa, and all of the songs were in Maa. One woman led the singing, with men and women singing together, in a call and response format. Occasionally Father Christy or Mwalimu Moses would tell them which song or kind of

165

song (such as a song of thanks) to sing. In his sermon, Father Christy spoke about how to be a good Christian. As an example, he described the virtues of women waiting patiently in line for water rather than jumping ahead. After a basket was passed around for the offering, several women, including Esta, spoke during the intercessional prayers. During the announcements at the end of the service, Joseph, the church secretary, reminded everyone about the upcoming confirmation celebration in Emairete and asked the women to stay after church and harvest the few beans that had grown in the church garden. Mwalimu Moses then stood up and admonished everyone about using the church for meetings: "It is a place of prayer and worship!!" It was difficult to hear him, however, because two women had left the church and were sitting in the doorway talking. "Go away! (*Enchom!*)," Mwalimu Moses yelled at them. "Take your meeting elsewhere!" After the services, nine women went to harvest beans in the church garden.

By the end of the service there were only about twenty-five women in attendance. Mwalimu Moses and Esta said that attendance was unusually low and attributed it to the drought: "Everyone is searching for food and water!" According to Father Christy, the drought had also reduced their ambitious plans for the confirmation celebration. "All of my parishes had asked for the celebration to be held in August, when they would have harvested and had plenty of food and money to buy gowns and so forth. But now they have cut back their plans dramatically to just a bowl of rice and a soda." "Which," he added, "is fine by me."

One day in 2000, Mwalimu Moses and I interviewed Esta, the self-proclaimed founder of the Mti Mmoja church, and Sinyati, head of a small Christian community, outside their homes (a third woman sat quietly and just listened to our discussion). As another woman prepared some ginger tea for us, we chatted about the weather, the upcoming local elections, and other matters. An older man, possibly of the Seuri age-set, walked by and wanted to join us, but the women told him to leave: "These were women's affairs." He teased them, but finally left. An *olmurrani* was also present and very reluctant to leave, but they chased him away as well. We spoke with Esta first, then Sinyati. Esta, an older but still energetic woman, was very self-composed. She thought quietly about each question before answering.

Esta first told us how she had started the Mti Mmoja church:

> At the time, there was no church in the area, so I went to Moita [a nearby village] for instruction for three months. I returned [to Mti Mmoja], then went back to Moita to get baptized. When I returned, we started the church near the tree over there. Only two of us were baptized, me and Nembarbal. But

when we started the church it was full of people. This church was started by only two people. But all of my homestead followed us and were baptized, even my husband is baptized!

She joined the church because "my *oltau* wanted to go to church, and so I went and was baptized." As she explained, "Before, we had our eyes closed, we were blind then. Then we came to see the light of truth, we came to understand Eng'ai's ways. We were in instruction until we were baptized." The main thing that she learned about in instruction and in church was love (*enyorrata*); "Before, you either loved or didn't love a person. Now, you love them as you love yourself. . . . The big thing that we have learned in church is love." Because of her "love of Eng'ai," and her new ability to express that love every Sunday in church, she had received many blessings, especially in the form of children. "Eng'ai has helped me in many ways. When I entered the church I was a young wife with two children and now I have had many more and I have come to be an old woman (*entasat moruo*). So I think that Eng'ai has helped me with many things." As she concluded, "Every day I pray to Eng'ai for life, children, and cattle."

Although her answers might have been influenced by the presence of Mwalimu Moses (which I think unlikely, since she was clearly more senior, and therefore more powerful and respected by the community, than he was), Esta had only positive things to say about the Catholic Church. "There is nothing bad about the church. . . . It has only brought changes for the better. The church has helped us in many ways." Moreover, she preferred the Catholic Church "because I can follow my customs. . . . The only thing that we have been told to stop is sorcery (*esetan*). Otherwise Maasai customs are fine. You just follow the customs as in the past." She (correctly) recalled the names of all of the priests who had served the Mti Mmoja church. "They are all good people, I saw nothing bad in any of them." Finally, in response to a question about why there were more women than men in the church, she replied, "Maasai customs (*oregie*) have been difficult (*egol*) for a long time. It is women who were able to see that there was light (*ewangan*), and we tried to persuade the men. But the men got stuck, so therefore there are only a few these days."

Sinyati, who was somewhat younger than Esta (perhaps in her forties), spoke very softly at first, using elegant hand motions to elaborate her descriptions of the roles and responsibilities of men and women in different rituals. She became very animated, however, in response to our direct questions about her faith and involvement with the Catholic Church. Like Esta, she joined the church "because my *oltau* wanted to (*oltau lai otaiyieu*)." She was instructed and baptized by Father Nangoro, and still attended church regularly. "I was taught to love everyone so that we could live together." Moreover, her commitment to the Catholic Church posed no problems for her as a Maasai; "I follow Maasai customs as usual." As for the difference between men's and women's participation, "women have seen that the church is good." When I asked Sinyati if she was a "leader" in the church, she said no. "I am not a leader. But I am the chair of our small Christian community" (using the Swahili word *jumuiya*).

"And what does the *jumuiya* do?" I asked.

"We pray together every time we get together."

I interviewed "Koko Naserian" a few weeks later. Koko Naserian was the mother of one of my dear friends whom I had worked with at ADDO in the mid-1980s. When I first met Koko Naserian in 1985, her husband was still alive, an ancient, shriveled man who spent his days cloaked in a thick blanket in the warm sun or huddled by his wife's fireplace, with a thick black cattle-hair whisk in his hand and a tobacco container through his ear. Although we could not communicate very well at the time, Koko Naserian welcomed me warmly to her homestead with a frothy cup of milk tea. Through the years, as I visited regularly and often stayed in her homestead (with the wife of my friend), I watched Koko Naserian grow in power and respect. Once her husband died, the homestead formally passed to the management of her elder son, but the reality was that Koko Naserian supervised and controlled life in the homestead. She advised her sons, directed the labor and lives of her daughters and daughters-in-law, disciplined (and played with) her grandchildren, and commanded the respect of everyone with her wise words and calm countenance. And she always made me feel welcome after I had greeted her with my head bowed for her hand in blessing, in proper recognition of her age and status.

When I interviewed her in 2000, her homestead was smaller but still vibrant. Her eldest son had moved his wives and children to start a new homestead nearby. My friend, who still worked in Arusha, had built a large cement block house with electricity, running water, and a driveway for his truck on one side of the homestead. He tried to visit every weekend, and his new wife often spent several days at a time living in the house with their children. Koko Naserian's other sons came and went as they attended school, moved the livestock, or pursued various enterprises such as mining to earn money. As before, while the men came and went, Koko Naserian managed the homestead and the women and children within it.

Although most of her daughters and several of her sons were Catholics, Koko Naserian had been baptized by a Lutheran pastor in 1991. At the time, it was easier and faster to attend instruction by the Lutheran pastor, and Koko Naserian saw little difference between the teachings of the Lutheran and Catholic churches. "I went to instruction because it was about praying to Eng'ai and I like to pray to Eng'ai since I pray all the time. And so we gather together in church to pray." As she explained later:

> I started going to church because of the changes that have occurred. In the past, Maasai only prayed to Eng'ai and people worshipped at the *oreteti* trees. They prayed when children were born, at circumcision ceremonies, and at all times that they needed Eng'ai. But now things have changed—people say they are going to church to pray to Eng'ai. . . . I don't care where people go to pray, whether Maasai places or the church, I like to pray in all places at all times.

Although the church had brought changes such as "books to pray from" and "circles that show things [Father Ralph's disk]," all were prayers to Eng'ai, who is "the Father and Mother." "Maasai have no books, disks, or bread. But they pray when they prepare food, when they slaughter cattle and goats, and when they drink milk." As for the gender difference in participation, "Women accept Eng'ai. In the past, women prayed to Eng'ai more often [than men]. They said '*namoni aiyia*' [I pray to you], but men didn't say it."

Despite being baptized as a Lutheran, Koko Naserian was ecumenical in her practices. In the past, she often attended Catholic services in the company of her daughters and daughters-in-law, in part because the church was close to her home. She also sought help and healing wherever it was available. For example, in 1992 when one of her grandsons was very ill, she attended a prayer service of Pentecostals in the health clinic (organized by the doctor) to pray for him. Although by 2000 she no longer went to church because of the long, difficult walk, she still prayed at home, "and Eng'ai listens."

Koko Naserian did not just stay at home, however. Several months after my friend's wife had a new baby, Koko Naserian appeared on their doorstep one evening with a delegation of older women to perform the critical naming ceremony. Under the light of the full moon, they coached the mother in the details of the ritual, and then Koko Naserian came up with the child's name after the teasing names had been bantered about. A feast and celebration followed.[5]

169

Embopong'

Embopong', the third community, is the only one of the three communities still considered as territory for first evangelization. The name, which is Maa for a type of candelabra tree that grows in the area, refers to one of four Maasai localities that make up the formal government village called Mfereji. Mfereji lies to the north of Monduli mountain, on the floor of the Rift Valley, connected to Emairete by fifteen kilometers of a very rough dirt road (see map 4.1). The lower elevation (about 1,200 meters) and dry, dusty conditions made cultivation impossible (although, desperate for food, some people tried), but served as ideal conditions for smallstock browsers. Only a few Arusha lived in Embopong', mainly Arusha women who married Maasai men and cultivated small farms on the slopes of Monduli mountain to support their families. In Embopong' 10.1 percent (n = 19) of the women and 2.6 percent (n = 5) of the men surveyed in 1992 identified themselves as Arusha, from a total population of 189 adults (Maasai Census 1992). Its difficult and remote location has severely limited both governmental and non-governmental involvement in the area. Nevertheless, a small school and dispensary were built by the government in the 1970s and continued to operate intermittently, despite a constant lack of personnel and supplies. In addition, with the recent expansion of private hunting in Tanzania, a foreign hunting company has bought exclusive "rights" to hunt on the land by paying an annual fee to the village for "development" projects and hiring *ilmurran* as trackers.

In part because of the desolate location and difficult logistics of Embopong', Spiritan missionaries have had only sporadic and inconsistent interactions with the community. Father Poirier made a few exploratory visits to the government school in the early 1970s, but the road was too rough for his bad neck, and his ongoing *boma* work in Emairete was both successful and time-consuming (DL1/11). In 1984, another American Spiritan baptized sixteen schoolboys and two schoolgirls, after instruction, but he was soon moved to another position (MMBR/9 Feb. 1984). His replacement visited the area several times, but decided that despite being "well received," "this wasn't worth the effort. There were so few people, so scattered. The infrastructure, or the possibilities, the sense of what would have to be done was such that he decided no" (MMJ/13 June 1985; GK/35).

Pentecostals also made rare visits to the area, especially during times of hunger. World Vision drove through in 1992 with a truckload of dried maize, demanding that anyone who wanted the food had to be "saved" there and then. Many women, desperate to feed their families, reluctantly complied. Later, they dismissed the incident as meaningless, laughing at the potent disrespect of World Vision's silly demands.

Only in 1991 did Father Simon Lobon, a recently ordained Spiritan from Kenya, return to the area and begin instruction classes for interested individuals once a week under a shade tree near a common water tank. A year later, on a lush February day in 1992, I accompanied Father Lobon to his weekly instruction class in Embopong'. After slipping along the jagged switchbacks on the road from Emairete down Monduli mountain and across the jutted track of the Rift Valley to Embopong', Father Lobon and I met a small group of women gathered under an acacia tree near the water tank (known by this time as the "priests' tank"). We parked the car, and our two other passengers, who ran the diocesan outreach program for handicapped people, walked to another set of trees to meet some of their patients. I accompanied Father Lobon to a nearby homestead to return a calabash that he had been given, full of milk, by a woman at the last class. As we entered the homestead, several women greeted us, especially once they recognized Father Lobon. One woman took the calabash into her hut and quickly returned with another one full of milk. We left to return to the water tank, with several women promising to join us. As we walked, we passed two *ilmurran* sitting on the ground. "*Ilmurran* never come to instruction," Father Lobon told me. "And if they do, they just sit or sleep on the side and don't pay attention."

"So no men ever attend?" I asked.

"The men told me that instruction was a matter for women and children, not them," he replied. "They said that they would help me if I needed it, but they were not interested in what I had to say."

When we returned, about twelve women, ranging in age from newly married *isangiki* (about fifteen or sixteen years old) to elderly *koko* ("grandmothers"), were seated on stones in a circle. Father Lobon exchanged routine greetings with everyone, and then chatted with the women about community news since his last trip. He then crossed himself and recited, "In the name of the Father, the Son, and the Holy Spirit" in Maa, and the women joined him. He led them in several prayers in Maa, including the "Hail Mary," then everyone crossed themselves again in unison. Father Lobon asked them to sing a song, so while one woman sang the lead, the other women clapped and sang the chorus (a common format for Maasai singing). They practiced several new prayers, with the women repeating each line after Father Lobon.

Some women concentrated hard while others just mumbled along. When he asked them to take turns saying the Angelus, some women giggled and refused, a few recited it almost perfectly, and the others repeated it only after substantial prodding. Father Lobon knew the names of all the women in the class, and teased and encouraged them through the prayer. The women themselves got along well, laughed a lot, and seemed very comfortable as a group with Father Lobon. After some more work on the prayer, they sang another Christian song together in Maa, and then Father Lobon told them a story. When some women teased him about his pronunciation, he asked "Nanyore," a young married woman, to serve as his translator (as a Samburu, he spoke a dialect of Maa, but some Kisongo Maasai found his accent difficult to understand).

The story was an elaborate tale about jealousy and mischief between two co-wives. Briefly, the older wife, who was jealous of the attention her husband was giving to the younger wife, destroyed some of her husband's possessions. She framed the damage so that the younger wife was blamed and was soon sent home for her alleged misdeeds. But then the older wife suffered several mishaps of her own, which she interpreted as punishment for her tricks on the younger wife. The older wife admitted her guilt to her husband and apologized to the younger wife. The younger wife returned home, and they all lived happily ever after. Once he was finished, Father Lobon asked the women what lessons they had learned from the story. At first, the women stared at each other and the ground in an awkward, uncomfortable silence. Eventually, a few women replied, saying that the story had taught them to be nice to one another and not do mean things. After a pause, Father Lobon explained that the lesson of the story was that everyone was equal before God and therefore should not be jealous of one another. Another song followed, then the recitation in Maa of the "Our Father," and then a final song.

After class, a woman approached Father Lobon and asked if it would be possible for him to bring some maize flour from town on his next trip. He politely demurred (Maasai consider it rude to directly refuse a request). We then walked to another homestead, escorted by a group of women, to greet a woman who had just given birth. Nanyore, who was the youngest wife of the elder man whose homestead we were walking to, pestered Father Lobon about when he would baptize the group. "As soon as you know the prayers and the stories of Jesus," he replied. He told me that he had taught them the cross, the Our Father, the Hail Mary, and the Angelus, but still had to teach them the Creed, which would take at least a month. "I won't baptize them until I see the fruits of faith," he explained. After visiting the new mother, giving her a bar of soap as a gift, and drinking some tea in her house, we returned to the car and drove home.

Everyone in Father Lobon's class looked forward to their upcoming baptism during Easter 1992, a year after their instruction had started. In the weeks preceding Easter, they were preoccupied with plans for a celebration, requests for baptism sponsors (one woman asked me!), worries about appropriate clothes (many wanted to wear white dresses), and other concerns. But three weeks before Easter, Father Lobon visited all of his students in Embopong' to tell them that he was delaying their baptism for another year because he had decided that they were not ready. Furthermore, he was canceling instruction classes until after Easter. Before he could resume classes, however, he was transferred to another mission. His replacement did not continue the instruction in Embopong'. Abandoned, the women remained partly instructed, but never baptized until Father Christy resumed classes in 1999 and baptized the first group in 2000.

In 2000, I visited Embopong' with Father Christy, his catechist Mwalimu Francis, and my assistant Morani for the first Mass Father Christy had held since he had baptized twenty-eight women and one man in late April of that year. We drove to the "priests' tank" where Father Lobon had held catechism classes. Because of the late rains, the Rift Valley was parched and dusty and the Embopong' tank was dry. Mass was supposed to start at 11 A.M., but Father Christy said we would wait until about noon so that people would have a chance to come once they had heard the car. Two older women were sitting talking to a man near the tank when we arrived. Father Christy had brought a blue plastic box in which he had all his Mass gear, including his beaded leather cape, and a folding camp chair.

While Father Christy and Mwalimu Francis waited for people to arrive at the tank, Morani and I decided to drive to a nearby homestead where we had often stayed. We discovered that since our last visit, the homestead had split in two over accusations by "Leyio," a junior elder, that the wives and mother of "Leng'ai," his age-mate, had cursed him. As soon as Leyio, who is slightly crippled from polio, saw me, he asked me for a lift back to the tank to church. "I was the only man baptized by Bill in April," he told us. "My wives and children were also baptized, and I am now the head of the church." When I asked why he had decided to be baptized, he replied "because I wanted to." (Although Leyio had received many months of treatment and therapy for his polio from the Catholic Church's handicapped project, he never mentioned this as a reason for his participation.)

Leng'ai's elderly mother, "Koko Nasisi," also greeted us in her new homestead. She had been a regular participant in Father Lobon's catechism classes and was delighted to see us. She told us that she had finally been baptized and went to church, but not the Catholic Church. "I wanted to be in the Embopong' church, but it just fell apart—no priests came and nothing happened. So I joined the Lutheran church [in a nearby community] because I really wanted to be baptized."

"Do you go to services regularly?" we asked.

"Yes, I do," she replied. She said she liked the new priest [Father Christy] though; he chewed tobacco like Maasai, and offered it around. Moreover, the Catholics were respectful of Maasai culture and customs.

"Does the Lutheran pastor chew tobacco?" I asked.

"No way!!" she replied. "And he won't let us chew. He tells us it is a bad thing, as are many of our customs and ceremonies. But if we don't do the ceremonies, then we are not Maasai anymore, so what are we supposed to do?"

Koko Nasisi decided to go to church with us, but changed her mind when "Nashioki," her daughter-in-law, wanted to attend, and Leng'ai told them that someone had to stay in the homestead. So Morani and I, Leyio, Leyio's new wife, "Nashioki" (who brought several leather drums and drum-sticks from her house), and another woman piled into the car and drove to the water tank, with the women drumming and singing Christian songs during the ride. When we arrived, Father Christy had shifted under some trees, and about ten women were sitting on rocks facing him, talking together. Once our group settled in, he opened his box to get organized. First he pulled out six plastic beaded rosaries and gave them to Mwalimu Francis. "Since we don't have enough for everyone," he told Mwalimu Francis, "do what we did the other day with the kids, have a competition." So while Father Christy put on his vestments and made an altar by wrapping his plastic box with the beaded leather cape, Mwalimu Francis explained to the women that they had to say three different prayers to get a rosary: the Our Father, the Hail Mary, and the Angelus. Nashioki went first, said all the prayers with occasional prompting from Mwalimu Francis, and received one of the plastic rosaries. Nanyore followed, succeeding only after substantial prompting. Most of the women, however, hid their faces in their hands and refused to participate. Another woman tried, but she recited the prayers in such a faint voice that we could barely hear her. She only knew two of the prayers, however, so Mwalimu Francis refused to give her a rosary. This upset Leyio, who told him to quit playing games and just give the women the rosaries, but Mwalimu Francis refused. He told the women they had to earn them; they were not decorations, but were designed to help them in their prayers.

Soon, Father Christy started the service. He noted (in Swahili, with Mwalimu Francis translating into Maa) that it was the first Mass since their baptism, and even though they were very few, they would work together. Moreover, he hoped that once the problems of water and food were settled, others would join. He wanted to work with them, so he planned to visit them on the first and third Tuesday of each month. The service was somewhat abbreviated, with only a Gospel reading by Father Christy. The women did not seem to know many songs, or at least the songs that Father Christy and Mwalimu Francis wanted them to sing. Father Christy and Mwalimu Francis prompted them, often singing themselves so that the women could learn the tune and words. The women tried, with Nashioki playing the drums, but they needed a lot of work. (Mwalimu Francis told me later that some choir members from Emairete had visited several times to teach them songs, but they just could not remember them.) During intercessionary prayers, Father Christy asked Mwalimu Francis to start. Leyio then said a prayer, but the women stayed silent. Father Christy urged them to pray, and finally a very old woman said a prayer. Father Christy tried to encourage the women to pray by telling them the following story: "Maasai have a ritual they perform when the rain is nearby, but still hasn't come down. They take two young, uncircumcised girls (*intoyie*) and dress them in black, as well as a black sheep, and they make them walk around and around the rain pond so that Eng'ai will see them and it will rain. Thus as you see, it is very important that we hear your voices and your prayers as women."[6]

In his sermon, Father Christy compared attending church with men going to *olpul*. "No man is forced to go," he explained, "but he chooses to go. He encourages his friends, but he doesn't force them. The *olpul* is not just about eating meat, but about praying to Eng'ai; everyone comes with his prayers. It is also a time for community and sharing. Everyone brings their own unique, special gifts to *olpul*—one man is talented at making the soup, another at collecting the necessary medicines, another at roasting meat. At *olpul*, everyone works together; although they never do it at home, men collect wood and water and do other necessary tasks. Also, when a man attends *olpul*, he gets a special ring. He can then visit another *olpul* and show his ring. 'Ah, you are part of another *olpul*, *karibu!*'"

In a similar way, he argued, Maasai, who move around a lot, can visit another church. "Are you baptized?" the church will ask.

"Yes," s/he will reply.

"Welcome!!"

During communion, he dipped the host in the wine and gave it to each person as they slowly walked up, saying "The Body and Blood of Christ" (*osesen esarge te Yesu*). He saved the peace (*osotua*) for the end of the service, because of the dust. After asking for announcements (there were none), he asked the women if they preferred to meet at the school next time, so that they could bring their water containers and gather water after church, thus saving them time and energy. Leyio, claiming his rights as the church leader, stood up to reply. "No way," he replied. "We should keep meeting here because this is the place where we have always met." After explaining that he had been in another village for a while tending a sick child, he started castigating the women: "Did any of you do what I asked when I left? I asked you to begin building the church, but nothing has been done. You have to take responsibility. Why aren't more people present? Church is not a game, but a commitment!" Father Christy interjected that he was glad Leyio had mentioned it, as Father Laiser had come down for services a few weeks before and no one showed up. "As the leader of the church," Leyio continued, "I am responsible for showing you children [he used the Maa word *inkerra* to refer to the women] the right path. We have to work together as believers to build and expand our church." He went on and on, haranguing the women, with Morani translating into Swahili for Father Christy. (During the service, Leyio complained to Morani about Mwalimu Francis, accusing Mwalimu Francis of destroying "Simon's church," referring to Father Simon Lobon.) Father Christy finally interrupted to silence Leyio, saying they could meet after the service if necessary.

After the service, Father Christy was barraged with questions from the women. Nashioki wanted to know if he would come pick them up for the confirmation service in Emairete. "But I don't have a car, only a motorcycle," he replied. "But how do you expect us to walk all that way carrying our small children?" she asked. She hectored him about it, but he said he really could not help. (Later, on the way back, he joked to me about riding his motorcycle down, picking someone up, taking them to Monduli Juu, returning for another passenger, and so forth until he had transported them one by one up the mountain.) Mwalimu Francis reminded everyone about the requested contributions for confirmation, which were one thousand shillings and a goat. Nashioki exploded in anger: "We don't trust you with our money; show us the papers that describe how much you've already received and where it is now!" She asked Father Christy to replace Mwalimu Francis with a full-time catechist who would live and work only in Embopong'.

"But where they would live and how they would live?" he inquired.

"We'll take care of them," she replied.

"We'll talk about it at the next service," said Father Christy.

"Nasidai" was among the group of catechumens that Father Lobon taught in the early 1990s. She was a tiny, birdlike woman who quickly and eagerly welcomed me into her home and life. After the first instruction class that I attended in 1992, she invited Morani and me to visit her and spend the night in her homestead. We agreed, and made plans to meet her one son, "Loserian," an *olmurran* of the Landiss age-set, a few days later so that he could guide us to their home. After a long, arduous drive, we arrived at her homestead deep in the Rift Valley, several miles from the dirt track that cut across the plains. About five hundred yards away stood a much larger homestead, which I later learned comprised several families from different clans.[7]

Nasidai's homestead was surrounded by a tall, thick thorn fence. The entrance led into a small cattle kraal, surrounded by a smaller thorn fence and three thatched houses. After we parked the car outside the homestead, there was a flurry of introductions and greetings to her husband and two co-wives in the midst of yipping dogs and crying children. "Saning'o," her husband, was kind and gracious, but old and infirm. Although he was a member of the Inkidong'i clan, he was not a practicing *oloiboni*. As he retired to the house of his third and youngest wife, Nasidai invited us into her house. Like most Maasai homes, it had an outer vestibule for more formal guests to sit, then a large interior room with two leather beds set on stick frames, a small pen for young animals, and fire set among three large cooking stones. In addition, Nasidai had carefully crafted two sets of shelves from mud and cattle dung in the wall of her house to house her *kariboi* (a make-shift kerosene lantern created from a bottle with some kerosene inside and a cotton wick), *sufuria* (aluminum pots), metal spoons, and plastic cups and bowls. After exchanging greetings and news, she welcomed us with some milk "tea" (comprised of *olchani*, dried herbs, not tea leaves), and then a platter of cooked beans.

As we ate, she reached under her bed and pulled out a small metal trunk where she kept her most precious personal items. When she opened it, we saw several pieces of carefully folded official-looking papers, beaded jewelry, cloth, a light blue plastic rosary, and Father Poirier's disk. She proudly showed us the disk and told us what she knew about each of the diagrams. "This is Mary carrying baby Jesus," she explained, pointing to diagram one. As for diagram two of Jesus raising Lazarus from the dead, "These people are holding hands." And so on. Once she was finished, she took a container

Fig. 4.8. Two female Maasai catechumens from Embopong'. Nasidai stands at the right with bare shoulders. Photo by author, 1992.

of tobacco out of the trunk, refilled the container she wore around her neck, then returned the tobacco and disk to the trunk, closed it, and pushed it back under the bed. After I had set up my small blue igloo tent, to much heckling and teasing from her co-wives and some of the children ("Look at her tiny round house [*enkaji inkininyi*]!"), and carefully driven my car through the thorn gates into the cattle kraal at the insistence of her husband ("It won't be safe outside the homestead. If you are staying in my homestead, I am responsible for your safety and the safety of your belongings."), I returned to Nasidai's house. We spoke late into the night about her history, life in the United States, the differences between my husband and her husband, and more. Loserian had quickly disappeared upon our arrival, but late in the night he and an age-mate climbed over the thorn fence near my tent, whispering greetings as they passed by.

I visited and stayed with Nasidai many times over the next two years, and she occasionally visited me in my home, a room that I rented in a widow's house in Emairete, when she came up the mountain to work on a small farm that she had been given by a relative. Unlike some other women whom I befriended in Embopong', Nasidai never asked me for anything, but she was always grateful for my small gifts of sugar, tea, beans, and rice. As is common for women, we exchanged small metal rings as a sign of our friendship.

Nasidai was eager to learn about and convert to Catholicism. She always turned up for instruction classes, practiced her prayers and songs, and tried, with great difficulty, to remember all that she had been taught. "Oh, Teresia (as she called me), there are so many names and stories, it is so confusing! All I want is the love of Eng'ai and to be baptized in the church. My *oltau* is desperate for baptism."

"What about your husband?" I asked. "Is he interested in becoming a Catholic?"

"Oh no," she replied. "My husband is not in the church, he is completely a Maasai (*Metii kanisa, olmaasindat tukul*)." Her son Loserian teased her gently about her involvement with the church; taunting her with the gossip that Father Lobon had a "special" relationship with some of the younger women. "Perhaps," she replied. "But even if the rumors are true, I will still go to instruction—what else can I do?"

As the time for the planned Easter baptism neared, she struggled to earn enough money to buy the white dress that she dreamed of wearing at the service and to purchase food for the celebration she was planning at her home. One of her income-earning ventures was to pick the edible wild greens (*mchicha*) that grew in Embopong' in the rainy season and sell them at the weekly market in Monduli town. To do so, she had to walk about twenty kilometers from her home in Embopong', across the Rift Valley, up Monduli mountain, through Emairete, then down the mountain into Monduli town. She and a friend passed by my room in Emairete for tea late one afternoon on their way home after market day. "Were you successful selling the *mchicha*?" I asked. "The price was so low that it was like selling the *mchicha* for free!" she responded, with a sad, disgusted look on her face. Desolately, she reached under her top wrap, pulled out the empty sack that had contained the *mchicha,* and threw it on the ground. She then reached in for her money purse, untied it to show me that it was also empty, and threw it on the ground. "It is useless," she muttered, "very bad." My offer of a ride home to Embopong' the next day cheered her up a bit, but she was still distraught.

Given the tremendous effort and energy that Nasidai had expended to prepare for her impending baptism, she was deeply distressed when Father Lobon abruptly decided to postpone the ceremony. "Why, Teresia, why?" she demanded. "We tried to learn everything, but we are not people of school." I tried to calm her down and assure her that one day she would be baptized, if that was what she wanted. "But we are ready to be baptized now! Why did he cancel the celebration at the last minute and so suddenly?!" She raised the issue every time that we met over the next few months, desperately searching for answers to a situation that she did not understand. When I left Tanzania in late 1993, after two years of research, she presented me with a beautiful beaded cross that she had sewn as a parting gift. And seven years later, in 2000, she was finally baptized by Father Christy.

Comparative Perspectives

This history of Spiritan engagement with the three communities and the profiles of some of their female congregants offer several important insights. First, they provide detailed evidence to support the argument made in the previous chapter about the gender dynamics and outcomes of the different evangelization approaches. With the shift from schools to homesteads to individuals, Maasai women joined the church in increasing numbers, while Maasai men generally avoided the church. The enthusiasm of Maasai women for the Catholic Church was all the more surprising given the erratic and intermittent nature of religious instruction, administration of the sacraments, and pastoral care. Although these irregular interactions were partly due to the size and logistics of Maasai areas, they also varied, as the histories suggest, by individual priests according to their interests and commitment, the structures shaping their work, and the complexities of their relationship with the communities.

Second, although Spiritan accounts attribute most of the initiative behind the founding of these churches to the missionaries themselves, we see glimpses of the role of women (and a few men) in starting and continuing the churches. People in Mti Mmoja tell a very different story about how their church began, based on the efforts of one Maasai woman, Esta. Similarly, it was a small group of women who kept the church going for many years in Embopong' after Father Lobon's departure. As Father Christy acknowledged, "I really credit those three women who went and requested baptism from the Lutheran church. They . . . kept the nucleus of the community together, just praying in the *bomas* and things like that. Mostly it was the women. And I was very impressed at the level they had retained over that period." These stories, like others I heard, underlined the importance of the agency and interest of women and men in forming and supporting new churches. Without the efforts, energy, and commitment of these early adherents, there would be no church. Although, as discussed in chapter 5, people were attracted to the Catholic Church for different reasons, no one was coerced or forced to participate. If anything, the first Maasai Catholics faced teasing, ridicule, and even harassment from their family and friends. Yet, despite these obstacles, women such as Esta and a few men felt moved to learn about and eventually join the Catholic Church. The fledgling church of Embopong' is in itself a testament to the drive and perseverance of a small but very committed group of women.

The profiles suggest that the churches comprised women of different ages, wealth, educational backgrounds, religious experiences, and other distinctions. Despite these differences, most of these women have come to recognize, perceive, and accept themselves as members of a shared collective enterprise. What they had in common was a desire to join the church, a yearning that many attributed to their *oltau*, their heart and soul, the site of their most direct link to Eng'ai. Some women, such as Esta, led, and many women followed, creating vibrant spaces of fellowship, community, prayer, and worship. Despite their collective enthusiasm, persistence, and patience, however, the mood and morale of their churches was strongly influenced by the different dispositions, styles, and commitments of individual missionaries. Father Christy's youthful eagerness contrasted markedly with Father Kohler's tired surliness, and the women responded accordingly.

Thus the contemporary churches of women are the products of dynamic, interactive processes of give and take among Maasai, missionaries, and catechists, set within the shifting political, economic, and social contexts of the time. This is clearly evident in the form, content, and modes of involvement of the three churches. Drawing on the premises of inculturation, Spiritans taught, preached, and blended a mix of Maasai and Catholic theology, beliefs, and practices in both Maa and Swahili. Stories of the Black God (Eng'ai Narok) and Red God (Eng'ai Nanyokie), conniving co-wives, and men's *olpul* featured in Catholic lessons about sharing, forgiveness, and sacred gifts. Spiritans used Maasai symbols, colors, and artifacts in their services, liturgies, and vestments. At the same time, Maasai men and women incorporated Christian imagery, phrases, and symbols into their ritual and aesthetic repertoire (especially their ornaments). Maasai women such as Maria, the choir leader in Emairete, were in fact responsible for much of the innovation and adaptation in producing Maasai Christian songs.[8] Similarly, Maasai women quickly adopted Christian images and symbols, especially the crucifix, into their beaded ornaments, especially their necklaces.

Despite the familiar language, stories, and symbols of the Catholic services to Maasai, the description of the Mti Mmoja and Embopong' services and interviews with church members suggest that most Maasai needed a long period of learning and socialization to become familiar with the liturgical format and order of service. In Embopong', the newly baptized participants required significant coaching to complete even the abbreviated service led by Father Christy. They were confused about which prayers to say when, when to stand or sit, and how to behave "properly" during the service. The congregation in Mti Mmoja was more comfortable with the rites and routine, but still needed some coaxing to remember the correct order of prayers, readings, and songs. In contrast, services in Emairete, which were the most complicated and elaborate in terms of liturgical elements, language, and choreography (of the offerings, the peace, and communion), went much more smoothly, in part because there were always enough long-time participants to lead and direct newcomers (and those who were confused could sit quietly and remain unnoticed). The catechumenate differed for these three churches as well, ranging from one year of instruction in Embopong' to two years in Mti Mmoja and Emairete.

Moreover, the three churches were dynamic institutions; participation and attitudes waxed and waned depending on what parishioners thought of the priests and catechists, as well as other demands on their life (such as the difficulties feeding their families during the drought of the summer of 2000). Several Catholics that I interviewed in Emairete in 2000 thought that their church had been on the decline, but was improving dramatically now that Father Christy was there. "Before Bill came," said "Lemenye," a young Catholic man, "the church was about to fall apart, he has helped to pull it back together so that many faithful have returned to church. So Bill came and reinvigorated our church." They attributed the problems to the inconsistent (and sometimes inconsiderate) presence of the priests, which had alienated the parishioners, and laziness and bickering on the part of parishioners themselves. As "Lepilall," a venerable elder and the former chair of the church in Emairete noted, "The church is great, but we ourselves are destroying it because we don't go to pray. If all of us who were baptized went to church, we couldn't fit in the building!" Similarly, there was clearly a difference between Father Kohler's and Father Christy's missionary styles and relationships with parishioners in Mti Mmoja, as reflected in the tenor and tone of the services.

The accounts of the services also suggest that the churches were as much social spaces as religious places. The "church of women" provided frequent opportunities on a regular basis for women to meet as a group, talk to one another, sing, and pray. In addition to the class or service, women gathered before to chat in small, circulating groups, and often remained long afterward to talk (see fig. 4.9).

As described in the accounts, the few men (mostly non-Maasai) who attended services mingled quietly together on the outskirts of the women, and left quickly once services were finished. The joy of women in such gatherings was vividly evident after one Easter baptism service that I attended in Emairete in 1992, when they danced and walked together in a large group from homestead to homestead, laughing, talking, and singing Christian songs (see figs. 4.10 and 4.11). The women whose homesteads were visited would offer the group tea, food, and, later in the afternoon, alcohol. The men stayed far away while the women celebrated together from midday until late evening. The churches in Emairete and Mti Mmoja also had active chapters of the Catholic women's organization WAWATA (Wanawake Wakatoliki wa Tanzania), which provided further opportunities to meet and discuss both social and religious matters.

In addition to providing opportunities for women to come together collectively, the churches provided both formal and informal leadership opportunities for women. Although men were usually elected or appointed to the

Fig. 4.9. Maasai women singing and dancing Christian praise songs after the Easter baptism service in Emairete. Photo by author, 1992.

formal positions such as "chairperson" and "secretary" (which required literacy skills and proficiency in Swahili), women seemed to dismiss, ignore, or at best put up with the presumed authority of these men. Even in situations as in Embopong' or Mti Mmoja, as described above, where they were berated by these male leaders, the women sat quietly (or talked loudly), stared at the ground in assumed postures of "respect" (*enkanyit*), and proceeded to ignore the men's demands. Once in the privacy of their homes and female companionship, the women mocked and gossiped about the men. As a result, the male church leaders (many of whom were *not* respected elders) were made to seem silly with their posturing, pleas, paper, and pens. Moreover, despite the formal titles, men and women often acknowledged women's roles as the legitimate leaders of the church. In Mti Mmoja, men filled the position of "chairperson" and "secretary," while women filled the "shadow" positions of "assistant to the church head," and "assistant to the church secretary." Yet in my interaction with one of the male parishioners at Mti Mmoja about permission to take pictures with my camera, he was more concerned that I ask Esta, the "assistant to the chairperson" (although he called her the "chairperson" [*mwenyekiti*]), than the male chairperson or even

Fig. 4.10. Maasai women walking through the Emairete crater after the Easter baptism service. In the course of the day and evening they visited the homesteads of many of the newly baptized women to eat, drink, dance, sing, and celebrate. Men stayed far away. Photo by author, 1992.

Fig. 4.11. A group of Maasai women singing Christian songs to praise their host, a newly baptized woman, at a homestead in Emairete. The woman's husband stands in the distant background near a group of other men seated in the shade, warily watching the proceedings. Photo by author, 1992.

Father Kohler himself. In Emairete, half of the positions on the church council were reserved for women, and an educated Maasai widow served as the parish representative to the diocesan lay council in Arusha. "Since they are the majority of the church," explained Mwalimu Daniel, "we want to encourage them in leadership." Women also served as the leaders of WA-WATA, the Emairete choir, and other church groups.

Perhaps the most accessible leadership opportunities for women were in the "small Christian communities" (called *jumuiya* in Swahili) active in Emairete and Mti Mmoja. "Naoyeyio," an elderly Maasai Catholic woman, described the activities of her *jumuiya* in Emairete, which met every Thursday evening: "[Our *jumuiya*] discusses all the good words of Eng'ai that were talked about in church. . . . When we meet we have a service. Often we take a collection to help sick people or the family of someone who has died, or we go to help work on the farm of someone who is sick or the family of someone who has died." She said that her *jumuiya* had many members, including all of her neighbors who had been instructed. In addition to their regular prayer meetings, the *jumuiya* also took turns cleaning the church. Many of the *jumuiyas,* like Naoyeyio's, were organized and led by women.

Finally, some Maasai women were even, finally, becoming catechists, with the encouragement of the archdiocese. One of the most remarkable of these women was Mwalimu Lea, who I met at Mwalimu Moses' homestead one day when I was interviewing him. She was an extremely dignified, soft-spoken woman with gentle mannerisms. She had studied in primary school until Standard 7, when she was circumcised and married. But her husband died when she was very young and still pregnant with their first child. She had had another three children since his death, but had refused, under considerable pressure, to remarry. She lived with her father and brothers, who helped to care for her, but only minimally. She was initially drawn to the Catholic Church because she (and others) believed that it had helped two barren women from a nearby village have children. In addition, she liked what she learned in instruction, especially about the rights of widows, "so when [a widow] asks for something, she should be listened to. And Eng'ai will help her; She is with her every hour. And once I heard this I realized that I no longer had to get remarried to help myself, since Eng'ai can help me and loves me even more than I love myself." When I asked why she was interested in becoming a catechist, she replied:

> What attracts me [to becoming a catechist] is that I will be able to help my friends, to teach them how to pray. I am very happy that I will be able to teach

them. There was a woman who taught us, and it was clear that she had a voice. I told her that I very much wanted to help her, especially since she had just given birth. I wanted to be a teacher, and she gave me permission. So I have volunteered to be a catechist. I teach everyone in the neighborhood to have the grace of God and to be filled with the Holy Spirit.

She was studying with Mwalimu Moses, who was eager to teach her, and she had begun attending diocesan training seminars. "At [the recent] synod," Mwalimu Moses explained, "we asked for female catechists to teach other women how to be saved. . . . Women are great witnesses of faith . . . indeed they were the first."

In many ways, therefore, the Catholic Church has enabled Maasai women to create an alternative female community beyond the control of Maasai men. Although Maasai men occupied positions of formal power within the church, especially as catechists and lay leaders, women found their presumptions of bureaucratic power irrelevant if not laughable. Women were much more interested in coming together to learn, to pray to Eng'ai, and to talk to one another than in the formal hierarchies and obligations of church bureaucracy. It was the spirit, not the structure, of the church that appealed to them.

BEING A MAN IN THE
CHURCH OF WOMEN

5

So how do we understand the participation of Maasai men—as members, catechists, and leaders—in the "church of women"? Have these men become feminized in some way through their involvement with the church? Why have so few men chosen the church, and so many avoided it? How do Spiritan missionaries engage and understand these churches of women?

Different Paths

As discussed in chapter 3, some Maasai men have been involved with the church since its beginnings. They usually came from one of three groups: younger Maasai men who attended Catholic schools, very old Maasai men who became Catholics before their death, or Maasai men who lacked social standing and respect. Men from the first group became the teachers, catechists, and role models that the missionaries relied on to evangelize subsequent Maasai. Many served the church with tremendous energy and enthusiasm, despite the minimal compensation they received in return. A few Maasai men even became diocesan priests—the first, Father Fred Oloshiro, was ordained in 1976, and others in ensuing years. Other men participated in the church when they were in school, but became inactive once they left school, either because of disinterest on their part or because there was no mission station near their home. And some remained active Catholics despite the difficulties and even the disdain of their families and peers.[1]

One early and active male adherent was Edward Mbarnoti, whose father, Boniface, was one of the Maasai orphans raised by the Catholic mission at Kilema, near Moshi, after the disasters of the 1880s. According to Father Hillman, Boniface had been baptized and married a Maasai woman "in the church" who was also an orphan. Boniface worked as a catechist for Chagga near Kilema, before moving back to Masai District and marrying four more wives (EH/5). Edward, the son of one of those wives, had been educated, and was just posted to teach in Kibaya when Father Hillman contacted him in the late 1950s about working as a catechist. Father Hillman recalled that "Edward was very enthusiastic about doing something. And he had already, on his own initiative, gathered a few Maasai kids." Edward introduced Father Hillman to the local *jumbe* (colonial government representative), who agreed to allow more formal instruction. Over time, Edward was very supportive of the evangelization work of the church, teaching religion himself in the schools and mission outstations and helping Father Hillman identify other prospective teachers, catechists, and catechumens. He also convinced Edward Sokoine to return to secondary school, and gave him his first political job as secretary of the Masai Council (EH/13).

Father Hillman and the other Spiritans were therefore thrilled when Edward Mbarnoti was appointed "Chief of the Masai" by the British in the waning days of colonial rule. As chief, he was in charge of the Masai Council (formerly called the Masai Native Authority, usually referred to as the Olkiama by Maasai), the hierarchical system of male African representatives and elders that mediated, implemented, and enforced colonial dictates (Hodgson 2001a). Bishop Durning, Father Hillman, and other Spiritans attended his installation ceremony on August 27, 1959, which included a speech by Governor Richard Turnbull, followed by meat eating and a celebration.[2] For the next few years, Father Hillman and Chief Mbarnoti worked closely together, pleading with the district commissioner for more schools, famine relief, and medical services in Maasai areas.[3] When opportunities such as health postings or new schools presented themselves, Chief Mbarnoti used his leverage to try to channel these to the Catholics.[4] He even pleaded with the U.S. Eastern Province to send more missionaries to work with Maasai, in a letter that outlined his perspectives on Father Hillman and Catholic evangelization:

> When I was a young boy in a government school, I wanted to write a letter to the Bishop of Moshi Diocese, to ask why there were no missionaries working for the people of my tribe. The teachers told me that school boys should not write letters to Bishops. When I became a government school teacher myself some years later, I decided to write to the missionaries at Arusha mission and ask them to help my people. Although they already had too much work, Fr. Hillman came to see me 250 miles away from Arusha mission. Many things have been done since then for my people. The Catholic Faith is taught in all the government schools now.
>
> The fathers have 3 mission schools and six dispensaries. There is a mission with 2 fathers in Monduli; and a mission with two fathers in Loliondo. Fr.

Hillman is so loved by our people in every part of our vast country that he has been made an elder of the Masai tribe. I am very happy because of all this progress in that past seven and a half years. But I must still ask for more missionaries. There is so much to do, because the Masai are very war-like people and they are nomads. Only a few hundred are Catholics. And this faith we must have. Also some protestant missionaries are working very hard to convert our people to their mistaken faith. We Catholics must hurry, because things are changing fast in Africa. . . .

I want to make everything clear to you because this is my most important duty as a Catholic Chief of between 60 and 70 thousand people of the Masai Tribe in Tanganyika. I worry about all these people because very few have even heard the name of Jesus.

Please help us to give the Faith to the Masai people.

Edward ole Mbarato
Chief of all the Masai[5]

The letter conveys Chief Mbarnoti's appreciation and zeal for Catholic evangelization and assistance, his internalization of the dominant colonial and missionary stereotypes of Maasai as "war-like," and his antipathy toward Protestantism as a "mistaken faith." I suspect, but cannot confirm, that Father Hillman had a role in drafting this letter, if only to encourage Chief Mbarnoti to write it in hopes of dislodging more resources and missionaries for Masai District. I found a similar testimonial by another Maasai, Victor Kimesara, from the same period that seems to have been circulated to potential donors. It included a short note at the bottom from Father Joseph Brennan, the procurator of the Vicariate of Kilimanjaro at the time, asking for money to build three medical dispensaries in "Masai Land."[6]

After independence, Chief Mbarnoti became a member of Parliament representing Masai District. But he lost reelection in 1965 to a landslide victory by Edward Sokoine, his former protégé, who had mobilized Maasai elders, men, and women with his activist defense of their rights (Hodgson 2001a: 199). Edward Mbarnoti stayed in politics for many years, becoming an active member (and eventual chair) of the local branch of TANU and head of the Masai District Council (MMJ/26 Mar. 1967). Eventually, he returned to teaching in Monduli, and was fondly remembered by many of his former students. Throughout the years he remained a strong ally of the Spiritans and the Catholic Church.

But what of the men of Emairete, Mti Mmoja, and Embopong'? One day, as we sipped warm Cokes in the cool shade of his modest general store, "Joseph," a young Maasai man who was the church secretary in Mti Mmoja, described how and why he became involved in the Catholic Church:

"I started religious instruction when I was an *olmorani* attending Simanjiro [Animal Husbandry School, which was run by the Catholic Diocese of Arusha]. There was a lot of religion in the area; the school itself was religious. The day I was baptized [in 1986], my parents didn't attend, but I was confirmed that day as well. I decided [to be baptized and confirmed by] myself; my parents weren't Christians then."

"How did your parents react?" I asked.

"When I returned home I told them that I had to pray. They were shocked because usually in Maasailand *ilmurran* are not able to go to church and receive the sacraments. In Maasailand, they are mocked, especially by other *ilmurran*, who think that you [a Christian] don't eat meat and sleep with women.... They think I am a strange person.... They said I was confused."

Joseph was taught and baptized by two very active Maasai diocesan priests stationed at Simanjiro mission at the time, Father Moses Sangale and Father Fred Oloshiro. He claimed that he went to church every Sunday and had served as church secretary for three years. "Going to church," he explained, "is one way to talk to Eng'ai, to ask forgiveness for your sins, to see my friends." Moreover, "we Christians come together every Sunday to worship Eng'ai, because if everyone just worshipped by themselves at home it would have no meaning."

Similarly, "Letani," a young *ilmurran* who was baptized by Father Christy in 2000, said that he started attending instruction classes and going to church in Emairete because he "heard that they talked about Eng'ai there and that Eng'ai was present in that place.... And when we went there, we were taught many good things." He was baptized "because we were taught that a person who wasn't baptized wouldn't be born a second time, just like Jesus was baptized." Now he was preparing to be confirmed in August 2000. He was an active member of the Emairete choir, which he "joined to praise Jesus Christ." But he was teased by other *ilmurran* for his Catholic beliefs, especially when they contradicted certain customary obligations between *ilmurran* and *iloibonok*. "We are still required to do things with the *oloiboni*," he explained. "In every meeting [of *ilmurran*] we are threatened, and the other *ilmurran* demand that we give money to go and see the *oloiboni*. But we [Catholic *ilmurran*] try to tell them that we won't collect money to go to the *oloiboni*. We will contribute money to build unity [among *ilmurran*], but not for the *oloiboni*." Other young men who were baptized while they were still *ilmurran* also reported being teased and taunted by their peers. As "Lemenye," an educated member of the Inkidong'i clan in Emairete who was baptized while he was still an *olmurrani,* said, "Those *ilmurran* whose spirits (*iltauja*) haven't been taken, they tease me, all those pagans!" "For example," he continued, "if an *olmurrani* from your age-set visits you and you pray before the meal he laughs and says, 'What, don't you think that Eng'ai knows you are alive?' Every time you pray they laugh and go ahead and eat their food without praying."

Lemenye decided to be baptized several years after he completed Standard 7 at the Emairete primary school. "I went to instruction," he told us, "because I had many ideas in my head about things that were happening in Maasailand that weren't good, like moranhood. Moranhood has become useless, it doesn't help anything in my life. It is a childish thing in which you hang around with people here and there." He felt strongly that "the church should just get rid of moranhood." As we drank tea in the house that he shared with his second wife (after praying, of course), he voiced several other strong opinions about the past and future of the church and Maasai. He was very critical of the *ilmurran* and others who drank alcohol, especially certain catechists "who drink but teach that you shouldn't drink." (He mistakenly believed that the Catholic Church forbade the consumption of alcohol.) One source of his vehemence against alcohol might have been that his late father was renowned for sponsoring costly, multi-day drinking bouts for his fellow elders. While these sessions garnered his father prestige and respect among his peers, they also decimated one of the largest cattle herds in the area, which would have been Lemenye's inheritance. Lemenye considered himself a very devout Catholic who had benefited greatly from his involvement in the church; "Eng'ai has helped me a lot. I agreed in my spirit (*oltau*) to go, and She has given me life."

Similarly, Steven, the former catechist who was raised in Mti Mmoja, described how he was a "very, very dedicated Catholic" as a young man:

> Every Sunday I would go to mass, every Sunday, every Sunday. I would even organize my own group at home [in Mti Mmoja] to pray or go to Monduli. I had to go every weekend. On Saturday, I would leave my village to go to Monduli and stay with friends there overnight. Early in the morning I would go to church, which would finish at around eleven, twelve. I would go around in the town of Monduli, the market day, and go back home, 10 kilometers. . . . And that was my life, you know.

Since we had once worked together, I knew a great deal about Steven's fervent embrace of Catholicism. I recall a day in the mid 1980s when I gently teased him about the small picture of Jesus that hung with a rosary and beaded cross in his car. "Is this what you think Jesus looked like?" I asked. "A pale *mzungu* (white) with long, straight hair?" "Of course," Steven replied. "That is what we were taught in church!"

These men—Joseph, Lemenye, Letani, and Steven—were all considered *ormeek* by other Maasai because of their education, alternative employment (except Lemenye and Letani), fluency in Swahili, possession of and comfort with "Western" clothes, and eventually their conversion to Catholicism. *Ormeek*, as I have analyzed in detail elsewhere (Hodgson 1999b, 2001a), is a Maa word that originally meant strangers, Swahili, non-Maasai, and for some, enemies—that is, people who did not speak Maa and follow Maasai cultural, social, and pastoral ideals. By the 1930s, the term was used to mark and mock Maasai men who were educated or worked in the colonial administration as headmen or clerks. These men were viewed as profoundly "other"—not-pastoralists and therefore not-Maasai. Over time, however, the term has lost most of its negative connotations, as more and more younger men have gone to school, learned Swahili, worn "Western" clothes with ease, and pursued jobs in the government, development, farming, mining, commerce, and other sectors. Nonetheless, as Letani and others mentioned, the tensions for male Catholics were most acute when they were *ilmurran*, and subject to strong pressure to conform to the ideals and practices of their peers, including important cultural and social proscriptions and ritual obligations.

The second group of male converts, senior and venerable elders, has a long history of participation. Koko Naserian's father, a famous Maasai *olaigwenani* in Ngorongoro known as Oltimbau, was baptized a Catholic shortly before his death in 1959 (EH/5).[7] Even a few famous *iloibonok* are reported to have become Catholics in their old age (EH/27). For these men, the waning years of their lives were the time of their greatest wisdom and spirituality. Their spiritual closeness to Eng'ai was manifested, in part, in the tremendous efficacy of their blessings and curses during this period. Moreover, these men had usually proved themselves as worthy of *enkanyit* through their actions and accomplishments, including, most importantly, their wealth in cattle, wives, and children. Few people would therefore dare to tease or mock their participation in the church.

One such man was "Lepilall," a venerable elder (Ilterito age-set) who was baptized in 1988 in Emairete, and later confirmed. He served as the chair of the church for many years. Most of his wives and children were also baptized, and one of his sons attended Oldonyo Sambu Junior Seminary. He joined the church, he explained, "because I decided myself, not because of any illness." What he liked most about the church was that it "gathered

Fig. 5.1. Scurry, a Catholic young man who works as a medical aid for the Catholic Diocese of Arusha. His *ilmurran* peers, who stand on either side of him, consider him an *ormeek*. Photo by author, 1986.

everyone together, young and old, to cooperate together." He was actively involved in supervising the building of the church, and blessing it once it was finished: "I donated a cow and sheep and prepared a small calabash, following the customary ways." Although he no longer attended services because of his age (he could barely walk), he still kept up with the news and gossip. He liked Father Christy because "he is kind and he knows how to teach people. His *oltau* is very nice (*sidai oltau tukul*)."

The final group comprised men such as Leyio, the chairperson of the Embopong' church. Men in this group had usually "failed" somehow as pastoralists, often by losing their livestock through mismanagement or mishap. When I first met Leyio in 1992, he was completely drunk and his wife and newborn child were clearly very hungry and living in wretched conditions. When Leyio started yelling at his wife to quiet her crying child, Leng'ai and his wives publicly berated him for spending whatever money he had on alcohol rather than food for his family. It was therefore no surprise to discover, when we visited in 2000, that the age-mates had decided to split up their homestead. Lacking social prestige and *enkanyit* among other men, men such as Leyio had little to lose by seeking alternative sources of recognition, resources, and power in the church as chairpersons, secretaries, and such.

As these stories suggest, the few Maasai men who became and remained active Catholics did so for a range of complicated and interconnected reasons. Most described their desire to join the church as a matter of faith and spiritual attraction. Yet some clearly had aspirations as well to exercise authority and power through the formal leadership positions available to them in the church bureaucracy as chairs, secretaries, treasurers, and parish council members. The reactions of other men to their decisions varied according to the age and status of the converts. Men such as Joseph and Letani, who joined the church while they were still *ilmurran,* suffered the ridicule and taunts of their male peers. In contrast, the involvement of respected elders such as Lepilall met with muted (if uncomprehending) acceptance by other men.

Female congregants of all ages seemed to accept male church members as fellow congregants, but ignored and ridiculed men who tried to exercise and assert authority over them in their capacity as church leaders. In general, men and women followed the customary protocols of *enkanyit* in their public interactions, based on their respective gender, age, and kinship relationships. Before services, women gathered together in small groups to talk among themselves. As other women arrived, they greeted the groups they walked by, stopped to greet individual women and exchange the news, and then settled in with some of their friends. A few women flitted between groups, especially younger women trying to formally greet various older kinswomen.

Men who passed by greeted the women as a group (usually, *"Entakwenya naoyeyio"* ["Greetings, respected women"], to which the women replied, in unison, *"Iko"*). Sometimes an older woman would greet a man by name (usually because of an exchange or kinship relation that they might have established, such as "Pakerr" [of the sheep that you gave me]), or a man would greet an individual woman with whom he had a specific relationship, such as a neighbor, clan-sister, or the wife of an age-mate. The man usually approached a group of men, greeted them as a group or individually, then huddled together with them near the church entrance, talking among themselves. As they talked, children and young women (such as their classificatory daughters) who owed them respect silently approached them, heads bowed, waiting for the men to put a hand on their heads and greet them. The children and women then quickly moved away as the men resumed their conversation.

Maasai gender protocols were also evident inside the church and during the services. Men sat on the right side of the church, facing the altar, while women and small children sat on the left-hand side. The priests and catechists greeted the men first during the peace, and men came forward before the women for the offering and for communion. After services were concluded, the men left quickly, while most women took their time, often clustering with their friends outside for more news and conversation.

One notable exception to these socio-spatial patterns was a Maasai woman I will call "Mary," a wealthy, educated widow who served on the parish council. She often arrived late, sat with the men, and was one of the first people to make an offering or receive communion. If anything, her seemingly anomalous actions confirmed rather than disrupted Maasai gender protocols. She had refused the levirate (living with her husband's brother after her husband's death), was economically independent and self-supporting, and therefore was recognized by everyone in the community as the head of her household and homestead. She was, in other words, a Maasai man in many ways, and reinforced her claims to a certain status and respect by asserting her right to follow certain male practices and privileges.[8]

Maasai women were much less amenable when some men, especially junior men, tried to exercise or assert their authority over the women by virtue of their leadership positions in the church. As chair of the church council, or secretary or treasurer, these men would make announcements, present reports, demand contributions for celebrations, or order the women to do something such as stand, sit, move, or sing. Most women ignored the announcements and reports, talking quietly—and sometimes not so quietly—among themselves, or just leaving the sanctuary. Women's responses to direct demands depended on their relationship to the man in terms of age, status, and kinship, *not* on the assumed power of his church office. Following Maasai gender-age protocols, they quietly did whatever respected elder men requested. Younger men, especially those perceived as disrespectful in manner or tone, had a tougher time. Most women ignored their directives, some quietly complied, and a few older women would occasional berate the young man as impudent and rude.

In private conversations in their homes, away from the eyes and ears of men, some women mocked the church officers (and even some of the catechists), young and old, as silly and pompous, more concerned with their papers and pens than their prayers and spiritual relationship to God. Even supposedly respected men such as Mwalimu Daniel did not escape ridicule. I heard several conversations in which women gossiped about his many (alleged) "women friends," imitated in sometimes hilarious charades his occa-

196

sional displays of public drunkenness, and scoffed at what they saw as his pretensions to power. Women also "voted with their feet"; if they knew in advance that only Mwalimu Daniel was leading the service instead of a priest, few bothered to attend. At one Saturday Mass Mwalimu Daniel presided over in August 1992, only twelve people showed up for services.

In sum, Maasai women accepted Maasai men as fellow congregants, but ignored, if not disparaged, men who tried to exercise power over them because of their formal leadership roles in the church, rather than because of customary age-gender-kinship protocols. In general, women were more interested in the church as a social, sacred place of collective prayer and worship than a bureaucratic edifice of petty powers.

"Without Catechists, There Would Be No Church"

What, then, of the primarily male catechists who taught and served in the churches? What did they think about these "churches of women" that they helped to build? How did they understand, contribute to, and mediate the peculiar gender dynamics of the churches? The Spiritans, like all missionary orders, were deeply dependent on African catechists for their evangelization efforts. If anything, their dependence on catechists only grew over the years, as the number of missions and mission stations increased beyond the capacity of the few missionary and diocesan priests to provide ongoing instruction and pastoral care. In the course of my research, I interviewed and observed many of the catechists who worked in Emairete, Mti Mmoja, and Embopong'. Their stories demonstrate their centrality to Spiritan evangelization efforts, probe their roles as intermediaries or "middle figures" (Hunt 1999) between the missionaries and churches, and thereby complicate and enhance the history of Maasai evangelization presented above. Perhaps most importantly, the endless energetic work of these men to teach, build, maintain, and expand the Catholic Church among Maasai disrupts any easy binary between "Maasai" on one side and "missionaries" on the other, for the catechists were both.

Mwalimu Daniel Lolgolie, the first catechist in Emairete, began working for Father Hillman as a translator in the late 1950s. I interviewed Mwalimu Daniel twice, in 1992 and 2000, in the large rectangular building in his homestead that served as his office, place for meeting with visitors, and even bedroom when he did not sleep with one of his wives. In accordance with Maasai custom, each of his four wives had her own home on his compound, and his mother lived nearby as well. Mwalimu Daniel had attended the government primary school in Monduli town, where he was baptized in 1956, without the knowledge of his parents, when he was in Standard 4. He lived with Father Hillman for at least a year at the Monduli Mission station, so that his parents began to call him the "priest's child." With the support of Father Hillman, Mwalimu Daniel wanted to continue studying for the priesthood, but the church had a rule at the time that the only son of a family could not become a priest. Instead, he studied at the Catholic Teacher's Training College for one and a half years, until Father Hillman opened the boarding school for boys in Emairete and asked Mwalimu Daniel to teach. Eventually the school hired some other teachers, and Mwalimu Daniel taught there for nineteen years until it was nationalized in 1970. Mwalimu Daniel then took some courses at an extension seminary for catechists, and returned to Emairete as a full-time catechist to teach religion in the government school and catechism, First Communion, and confirmation classes in the church.

Mwalimu Daniel was proud of his many years of work for the Catholic Church in Emairete. As he told me in 2000, "there are 2,118 Christians here [in Monduli Juu], and I taught them all!" These days, he taught about thirty students a year for a two-year course of study before baptism. He thought that it was "absolutely necessary" for a catechist, in addition to being a good teacher, to "know how to give good advice, to be sympathetic, to be patient." For example, "when no one shows for class, or only a few, you need to call them and talk to them individually about why they didn't attend." He spoke fondly of the many Spiritans he had worked with, including most recently Father Christy, whom he claimed to have "trained." "I advise the priests," he explained, "on the community, about Maasai life. They do almost nothing without consulting me first." Diocesan priests, however, posed some problems, since "we have to support them with food and clothes. It is difficult. . . . It is better to be with the missionaries." "Even we catechists," he continued, "have to raise livestock and farm, since we only get a small bit from the church."

In 2000, Mwalimu Daniel was still the primary catechist in Emairete, but another young man, who I will call Mwalimu "Francis," had also started working as a catechist. Morani and I interviewed Mwalimu Francis one day in his tiny store, which displayed a few dusty packets of soap, some matches, and candies. A curtain divided the room, where Mwalimu Francis's "bedroom"—a cot and some blankets—was visible in the back. According to Mwalimu Francis, he attended primary school in Emairete, where he was taught religion by Mwalimu Daniel and baptized by Father Tunney in 1984 when he was in Standard 6. He said that he was baptized "because I was pulled by a calling, God called me. I heard it while I was being taught at school. I believed his words and teachings." "After I was baptized, I was circumcised," he said, "So I followed the ways of *ilmurran* for a while. After I returned from the Eunoto ceremony, then I turned toward God." He received First Communion in 1994 and started working as a catechist in 1999.

He decided to become a catechist because of a calling he felt when he was baptized: "something touched my spirit. I felt God's words: 'You will become a servant of God to serve other people.'" He had attended some catechetical seminars, including a "one-month seminar on spiritual matters," and planned to participate in more. In 2000, Mwalimu Francis taught people studying for baptism and First Communion, and led services. He worked in Emairete, Embopong' (and the other localities that comprised Mfereji), Mti Mmoja, and Nado Soitok. He traveled everywhere by foot and received only a small allowance (*posho* in Swahili) for his work, "not enough money to do anything."

Mwalimu Francis was very frustrated by the disparities he perceived between the importance of the work of catechists and the lack of adequate compensation that they received. "Without catechists, there would be no church!" he exclaimed. Morani, my research assistant, interjected that he was surprised that such a wealthy church as the "Roman Catholic" could not afford to at least buy bicycles for its catechists to use in their work. "Bill [Father Christy] and other *wazungu* [whites] couldn't do their work without me," replied Mwalimu Francis, shaking his head in agreement:

> They don't speak the language, so how could they teach anything in a place like Mfereji—they need me and other catechists to translate for them. Meanwhile they drive cars and motorcycles and I walk miles to Embopong' and other places to teach and for services. The bishop is starting to take us seriously, but it is hard work. No one could do it without a calling—you work day after day virtually for free, and yet you still have to find food and make a living to raise your family.

Later, Morani told me that Mwalimu Francis had come from an extremely poor Maasai family, where his father did not have even one cow. Mwalimu Francis married an Arusha woman who lived near Monduli town and they soon had a child, but her family was unhappy. They did not approve of him as a husband because he was so poor and was Maasai rather than Arusha. Eventually, by demanding more bridewealth than Mwalimu Francis or his family could pay, they forced her to move back home with their child.

Mwalimu Moses Lengaa, the Mti Mmoja catechist, told a similar story of being called by God. In 2000, Mwalimu Moses (he took Moses as his baptismal name) helped me with some of my interviews, so I visited him often. On the day I was supposed to interview him, I arrived early to his modest homestead. I found him busy getting dressed in neatly pressed slacks and a shirt and combing his hair. He invited me into his house, which was a thatched mud hut with a wooden bed, some stacked-up wooden chairs, a wooden and glass cupboard, and a wooden coffee table. His wife Teresia brought us tea and sliced white bread, and sat in on our interview. They treated each other with tremendous respect and kindness (at least when I was present), and seemed to have a marriage premised on equality and love. (I had in fact witnessed the blessing of their marriage by Father Kohler after they, and their youngest son, were baptized at the 1992 Easter service—they named their son "Kohler.") At the time, they were thrilled because their oldest daughter had just given birth, so they were now grandparents. They were both Arusha. Moses had studied through Standard 5, and Teresia had worked for two years at the Catholic school for handicapped children outside of Monduli.

After Mwalimu Moses said a short prayer over the bread and tea, we began the interview. Mwalimu Moses said that he was initially attracted to the Catholic Church when he was "still a pagan" and the pope visited Tanzania in 1989. During a run-in with the police when he tried to visit Kenya without a passport, he prayed and prayed to God to help him, and attributed his release to God's intervention; "I realized that God listens to people at all times, when there are problems and good times." When he returned home, he talked to Teresia about joining the church, which was just starting in Mti Mmoja. Mwalimu Moses read the Bible and "other papers about the word of God." "I knew," he said, "that to get to God one followed the path of Jesus Christ by way of the church, so I joined the church." Mwalimu Moses began teaching even before he was baptized, and Father Kohler sent him to his first catechetical seminar in 1993. "Then I slowly, slowly, progressed until where I am now."

He outlined his weekly schedule. He had (or "took" as he put it) two free days a week—he took care of his personal affairs on market day, when no one was around, and rested on Wednesdays, when many people attended another large local market. On other days, he worked in his office at Mti Mmoja, or taught there or at Nadusoito, where he was helping to train a new catechist. Previously, he had worked in five outstations: Losengori, Ngir-ringiri, Mti Mmoja, Nadusoito, and Duka Mbovu, but fortunately "we found more catechists to help." So now he worked only in Mti Mmoja and Nadusoito. "I do all the teaching," he said, "and call the priest when people are ready to be baptized, or to give Eucharist or First Communion. I also teach the confirmation class and arrange for the bishop to confirm." "I myself," he stressed, "am the teacher for everyone." He prepared all of the classes himself. Although there was not a syllabus for adult instruction, they were preparing one based on the syllabus for primary school instruction. He was delighted that Father Christy was so accessible: "He meets with all of his catechists every two months as a group. . . . And he is close by for advice and instruction. He is also ready to come here rather than have you call to see him." He acknowledged that "some people wondered [about my work]. They say that I am wasting my time. But I have gained a wealth of the spirit instead of a wealth of the body."

These three men were each drawn to the church in different ways, but all shared a sense of calling to what was generally demanding, poorly paid work. They all acknowledged that they were paid only minimally for their efforts, but Mwalimu Francis, who suffered the most financial hardship, was the most vocal. Yet the mixture of being called to their work, the nature of their tasks, and the sacrifices demanded of them raised an ongoing debate within the church—was the work of catechists a "vocation," in which case they should do it for the glory of God with minimal or no compensation, or a "job," with the requisite need for adequate compensation? As Father Christy explained:

> Some people had the concept that catechists have a vocation, they are called from their local community, and therefore shouldn't be paid anything. Other people say that they should be compensated for the time they spent away from their farms and herds and what not. Some people say [that] these are my co-ministers, and I can't leave my co-minister—how can he preach when his children have no food?

There is no diocese-wide policy or standard for the support of catechists; most are dependent on the ability and willingness of their parishes to support them. According to Father Ned Marchessault, a long-time American Spiritan missionary, in 1960 the salary of catechists was linked to that of a Grade C teacher, which was about 350 shillings a month at the time, with a bag of maize selling for 35 shillings. In contrast, in 1992 he paid his catechists between 6,000 and 7,000 shillings a month at a time when a bag of maize sold for over 5,000 shillings. This drastic drop in the real value of their remuneration has produced a precarious and troubling situation, given the tremendous dependence of the diocese on the work of its catechists. "The diocese is very afraid of catechists," said Father Christy. "They know they can't live without them; they can't work without them. They are afraid of any commitment to them, because the diocese can't even support their diocesan personnel, so what can they do for catechists?"

Teaching Respect, Love, and Freedom

The three catechists that I have focused on—Mwalimu Daniel, Mwalimu Francis, and Mwalimu Moses—all had different relationships with and attitudes toward Maasai women and therefore the "church of women." Mwalimu Daniel, as a prosperous senior elder with four wives and thirteen children (in 1992), was a stereotypical patriarch in many ways. He was the unquestioned head of his household, who demanded respect and obedience from his wives and children. He expected similar respect and obedience from his primarily female students, all of whom had to treat him with the appropriate respect behaviors that were his due as a senior male elder. He was reputedly a strict but good teacher, who tolerated no challenges to his authority, wisdom, and position. As an older man, he followed most of the social and cultural practices of his generation, including polygyny, participation in all of the life-cycle ceremonies, and sponsoring of drinking fests for his age-mates.

In addition to his regular work, he also served as a counselor and advisor to many of the women. He thought that the status of women had declined and that many elder men treated them like "prisoners." So in addition to teaching his students about Catholic beliefs, practices, and prayers, he also taught the women "respect." In particular, if a woman was having domestic troubles, he worked with her "to understand why her husband beat her or ignored her, what was her mistake? Find her own faults first . . . think about what she did that day when her husband beat her or yelled at her." During the second year of instruction, he spent a lot of time teaching women "to live a life of happiness and faith . . . how to live happily with their husbands, children, and neighbors." At baptism, he advised their family and friends that the women "had changed their lives and their habits." In sum, Mwalimu Daniel clearly used his role as catechist and advisor to help "improve" women's lives, by which he envisioned teaching them to blame themselves for their situation and take responsibility to improve their relationships by being more obedient, respectful, and responsible. His objective, in other words, was to reproduce and strengthen the patriarchal relationships with which he was most comfortable.

Mwalimu Moses, in contrast, had embraced a very different model of marriage, and therefore appropriate gender roles for husbands and wives, than Mwalimu Daniel. As a strictly monogamist couple, Mwalimu Moses and Teresia shared a vision of the ideal relationship between a husband and a wife that was premised on mutual respect and autonomy. This was clear in their interactions: they always sat close together, they looked each other in the eyes when they spoke, and each spoke freely and openly in front of the other. Mwalimu Moses sometimes even helped Teresia haul water from a nearby dam, an arduous task that few Maasai or Arusha men would deign to help with. At one point, when we discussed Teresia's work at the Catholic handicapped school near Monduli, Mwalimu Moses said, "I agreed to let her work away from home, but people were stunned, as she was the first in the area to do such a thing, much less with handicapped people. She enjoyed it. Thus she speaks good Swahili, but doesn't know how to read or write." The school director even wanted to send Teresia to school, but "she says it is hard for her to learn at such an old age."

Mwalimu Moses thought that Maasai women were drawn to the church for two reasons: the "wretchedness of their lives" and "their great faith." "They see that when they are together they can help one another. When they share in the Word of God they can share in all of their work." He admired women for their faith and sympathized with many of their problems, especially *orpeko*. "Women are the foundation of the church," he told me one day. As such, he was always respectful and cordial to all of the women we met in our walks through the community, often engaging in the friendly teasing and banter that signaled familiarity and informality among Maasai. He had a reputation for being a gentle, patient teacher and was clearly supportive of women's leadership, as seen in his eager support of training Mwalimu Lea and two other female catechists. The only time I saw him assert his authority was during church services, in the presence of the priest and other men.

In contrast to Mwalimu Daniel's emphasis on teaching women "respect," Mwalimu Moses thought the most important lessons of the church were "love" and "freedom." Although many women in Mti Mmoja initially came to the church because they were sick with *orpeko*, once they were healed "they realized that they had found salvation." In contrast to the "dark way" (Swahili: *njia ya gizagiza*) of their homes, they found freedom in the church. He believed that participation in the church helped them with many domestic problems, such as "marital affairs, drunkenness, and being beaten by their husbands." "The church shows them that this is a bad way." He claimed that "the church" would call elder men in to talk about domestic problems, even if the men were not baptized. "The church is like a court. . . . It tells the truth: husbands should love their wives and wives should respect their husbands and love their children." He thought that many husbands were pleased with what their wives learned in church, "that through love they gained freedom." The men saw that women learned to "help themselves," to motivate others, to start businesses themselves. "They say that 'my wives have seen the light!'" In addition, women were able to travel and receive various forms of material assistance from church organizations such as ADDO and Caritas. He described how a delegation of women from the Mti Mmoja church went to greet the new bishop, and "they benefited from a broader vision" of the world.

Finally, as the account from Embopong' suggests, Mwalimu Francis's relationships with women were much more contentious. He was neither a prosperous senior elder like Mwalimu Daniel nor a respected (if not very wealthy) elder like Mwalimu Moses, but a poor young man who could not even support his own wife and child. As such, most women had no reason to respect him or even listen to him, and few women trusted him. This was clearly evident in the encounter I witnessed in 2000 in Embopong', where Nashioki publicly accused him of stealing the offerings and demanded that Father Christy replace Mwalimu Francis with a catechist dedicated to working full-time in Embopong'. Whatever women might have thought about Mwalimu Daniel and Mwalimu Moses, they would never have shared their concerns in such a public, direct, and confrontational manner that so clearly signaled disrespect. Women in Emairete treated Mwalimu Francis with similar, but subtler, disrespect. They often intentionally ignored his directions and demands (such as which songs to sing, or which key to sing them in) and ridiculed his attempts to assert his authority. "Who does that boy think he is?" they muttered among themselves.

Despite these difficulties, he spoke well of Maasai women, at least in our interview. Like Mwalimu Moses, he thought they were more sympathetic and open to God's calling than men: "they aren't stubborn, their hearts are not hard." But they were still subject to their husbands' authority at home ("the husband is the head of the homestead"). He hoped that the church would help to improve their relationships at home, even if their husbands were not Christians.

Outside the Church Looking In

But what of other Maasai men, those who have chosen not to participate in the "church of women"? How do they understand Maasai women's fervent embrace of the Catholic Church? Their responses ranged from respect to ridicule, depending in great part on the length of the time that the church had been actively present in their community. Men from Embopong', where the church had only had a short-term presence, tended to disparage the church and the women who participated in it. As one old man from Embopong' commented: "Women are just brought [to church] by other women. Nothing important happens there, nor do they receive anything. They only go there to be scattered about like goats and then to return." In 1992, a younger, unmarried man claimed that there was in fact no church in Embopong', and what there had been was merely a "church of women" (*kanisa oo ntasati*). He had seen no benefits in it, or he would have joined. But the priest had quit coming, and the women had returned to their homes. "How could a thing like that make people happy?" A middle-aged man curtly stated, "Women just go to waste time." Nonetheless, when Father Lobon missed a weekly instruction class in 1992, the women convinced two *ilmurran* to walk to Emairete to check on him and make sure that he was all right. (The young men ended up walking all the way to the fathers' house in Monduli only to discover that Father Lobon was fine but his car had broken down.) By 2000, some of the men in Embopong' had started to change their attitudes, but few had little time or interest in the church themselves.

In contrast, Maasai men in Emairete and Mti Mmoja, where the church had a longer presence, were more tolerant. Although not baptized themselves, most men accepted their wives' decision to attend instruction or be baptized. "I have agreed to let my wives attend; I don't condemn the church," said "Lepayian," an elder from Mti Mmoja. Some, such as "Toimon," who is quoted below, even encouraged their wives to participate. A few, such as "Lengong," a senior elder from Emairete, saw no value in the church, but let their wives participate anyway: "I think women just like to wash their clothes and dress up, there is nothing they follow there. . . . My wife goes to church but I never ask her about it. Even when she was baptized, I didn't attend. . . . I haven't seen anything good or bad come out of the church." Joseph thought that male attitudes were slowly improving: "Because the elders didn't want the women to go to church, but now they have come to realize that the women are told good things, even the same things they have been telling women at home. So now they agree, and a few of the men are even beginning to come to church."

Perhaps most surprisingly, like Lemenye (discussed above), many other members of the large Inkidong'i clan (the clan of the *iloibonok*) who lived in Emairete participated in the church, including several men. Even those Inkidong'i men who were not part of the church encouraged their wives and children to participate. As Toimon, a senior elder (of the Ilnyangusi age-set) from Emairete, explained: "I'm of the Inkidong'i clan and we are not baptized. But my wives are Christians and I don't get upset. Some are Lutheran and some are Catholic. I am the only one who hasn't entered the religion." As he elaborated in a subsequent interview in 2000, "I like it when people go to pray to Eng'ai as I do. They pray to Eng'ai in church just as I pray to Eng'ai in my religion. . . . I never prevented my wives from attending, they were among the first to join the church when it started. I mean, we heard about the goals of the church, and I heard they did good things. I would have been the first to join, but it didn't suit me." When asked why being an Inkidong'i prevented him from being baptized, he replied: "It is up to each person to decide. But Inkidong'is didn't even go to school. Now we have accepted it and my children go these days. And we have even come to accept Christianity now that we have seen that it is not like being saved [Pentecostalism], and it doesn't prevent us from following our traditions." For an *oloiboni* to approve of his wives' baptisms is remarkable, and a testament to women's success in overcoming men's prohibitions.

Ministering to the Church of Women

Although bewildered by the insistent participation of Maasai women, most Catholic missionaries have reluctantly accepted their participation, and adapted themselves accordingly. Their attitudes toward the "church of women," however, varied significantly. Father Hillman, who spent most of his time with schoolchildren, noted that "there were always more women," but it never concerned him. This gender differential, he explained, was "not just among Maasai, . . . [but occurred] everywhere in the world." He thought that Maasai society was patriarchal, Maasai women were discriminated against, and it was not his job to interfere: "It's a patriarchal society, I'm not here to turn them into something else. That's not what we are here for. But we would hope that the Gospel in their society would transform their outlook and give equal recognition to all members of society." Other missionaries, as described above, simply refused to "teach just women," claiming it would "divide the family" (MMJ/Jan. 1982–June 1983). Some just disparaged the "church of women," however, and felt the need for a church to be a proper "community" with proper (male) "leadership."

After years of teaching in one area, Father Kohler gave up, claiming there was a lack of interest and response: "We want some men in this community, [because] given the cultural thing the women can't carry the burden." As his comment makes clear, what was lacking was *male* interest and response; women alone were not enough. Or as he wrote in 1990 in his circular letter home about a Maasai village that he and others had been evangelizing for six years "where the men just have not been responsive": "As I am not keen on baptizing a Christian community of only women and youngsters I have been plodding along, waiting for some enthusiasm and simply interest to develop."[9] In our interview, he elaborated:

> I think baptism is SO important; it is an entry into the church community. If you don't have a church community, and no sorts of signs that it is going to be coming along any time soon, or [if you could have] just the individuals with certain skills and gifts, among them male leadership in the Maasai community, because the women can't do it. In a sense, they do do it, but I think it is an artificial church. And my experience with the Maasai thing is that the men can tell the women to do whatever they want them to do, and they have to do it. You know, "Go off and move the cows some place," [or] "we're going to cultivate the *shamba* [farm] today." "We've got Mass." "Too bad, cultivate the *shamba*." And that's the end of that. And if she's the key person, you know, if she's the leader of the singing or whatever it is, there goes your liturgy. Unless you've got other people who can substitute. Thank God that's what happening up there at Mti Mmoja. If one's not there, others seem to take over.

Father Kohler wondered whether such a "church of women" was also a community: "I baptized at Mti Mmoja because the group wanted it. . . . There was a community there, there was a context. It is a regular [pause] as formal a community as we have anyplace in Maasailand." Yet, "I'm not really terribly comfortable with that group." Furthermore, despite his somewhat positive comments about women's leadership abilities in the Mti Mmoja church, Father Kohler dismissed the female chairperson of the church (Esta) as "sort of" a leader, occupying the position only "because the men factor is only two or three people." In 1992, only one elder man regularly attended the church, but Father Kohler had appointed him, as the lone male elder, "the official prayer," even though "he's not very good" nor "a very influential sort of person." But, at least, he was a man (see fig. 5.2).

Fig. 5.2. The lone male elder in the Mti Mmoja congregation sits on the edge of a bench in the left foreground, with his eyes cast downward. He is surrounded by female congregants seated on the benches and floor. Father Kohler appointed him the "official prayer" of the church. Photo by author, 1992.

In contrast, Father Christy was more supportive of the church of women, acknowledging that women sought and found "community" through their participation in the church:

> They find [the church] as a place where they do have a voice, they do have an expression for their belief. They have an outlet. They have community. . . . Maasai women . . . even to visit each other in each other's *bomas* is frowned upon. And to a certain extent . . . if a woman comes and says "so and so has been doing this and that," her husband will say "Where did you hear that?" She'll say, "Well, I was over at Natamotisho's *boma*." And he says, "Why were you there? What reason? What purpose were you there? Were you just there to pass the time of day?" But [the church] gives them a sense of community, of empowerment, of spiritual nourishment.

Although he thought women's opportunities for leadership were "hindered by their gender," he recognized and accepted the many leadership roles that they did play in the church:

You are talking about [in] many places a "church of women," with maybe two or three men present in the church . . . and [the] role [of women] in front of other women is very accepted and very looked after. And leader of prayer in small Christian communities. We do have small Christian communities within the outstations, and most of them are headed by women. And . . . their leadership is accepted there. Parish councils have always looked for a man to be *mwenyekiti* [chairperson]; even if there is only one man in the parish, he'll be the *mwenyekiti*, but the rest of the parish council can all be women and function very well.

Father Christy was more frustrated with the lack of participation by men than with the enthusiastic participation of women. But he realized that by the time he began to work in Maasai evangelization, "this was an established fact."

Seeing the Light?

Clearly, the "church of women" was a much more complicated space than the phrase implied. In addition to Maasai women, Maasai men, Maasai children, other African adults and children, catechists, and missionaries all came together to teach, learn, and worship together. Some Maasai men, both young and old, were drawn to the Catholic Church by a range of complex and often contradictory reasons. Their stories evoke themes of faith, belief, and callings, but also customary aspirations for prestige and power, and modernist ambitions for education, authority, and new ways of being. Moreover, they illuminate the differences among Maasai men of not just age but education, wealth, attitude, and aspiration. Other men had no interest in the church, despite (or because of) its appeal to women. Generally, however, men's tolerance and even acceptance of the church of women seemed to increase with time, familiarity, and the increasing involvement of their mothers, wives, sisters, and daughters. Spiritan missionaries were similarly ambivalent—at once perplexed, frustrated, and resigned to the surprising form the Maasai church has taken, despite their concerted efforts to instruct, convert, and engage men.

POSSESSED BY THE SPIRIT

6

The word "conversion" implies transformation from one state to another, raising questions of motivation, meaning, power, and process. Who converts and why? Who does not convert? How do we trace and understand the dynamics of power when conversion occurs in a missionary context, as opposed to in areas in which the church is well established and Christian conversion and belief have become the unquestioned norm? More centrally, how do we explain the preponderance of female converts to Christianity in Africa and elsewhere, despite concerted efforts by most missionary groups to convert men?

This chapter analyzes why so many Maasai women (and so few men) chose to participate in the Catholic Church. I probe the different perspectives of Maasai men and women on conversion: why they converted or did not convert, the meanings of conversion, and their experiences of conversion. Questions of agency are central to these discussions, as illustrated by the concept of *oltau* (heart, spirit) as the agent of conversion and the role of *orpeko* (spirit possession) in "forcing" women to convert and enabling them to overcome the resistance of men. Spirituality and conversion were thus sites for struggles over gender relations, ethnic identities, and claims to power and moral authority. Although both men and women asserted the centrality of religious beliefs and practices to their sense of ethnic identity, I argue that involvement in the Catholic Church has enhanced women's spirituality, strengthened their sense of moral authority, and provided them with an alternative female community beyond the control of men. In contrast, most men have rejected women's more flexible notions of the relationship between ethnicity, culture, religion, and identity and have insisted that Catholic teachings and practices are contrary to "being Maasai."

Spiritual Natures

So why have Maasai women been so eager to join this "church of women," despite the objections of Maasai men and the reluctance of most Spiritan missionaries? Certainly the historic moment of the encounter was one factor, as missionaries intervened at a time when tensions between men and women over economic rights and political authority were high, and women were searching for individual and collective "healing." As discussed in chapter 1, by the 1950s the former complementary roles, rights, and responsibilities of Maasai men and women had been transformed into much more hierarchical and patriarchal relationships. Maasai men took advantage of the economic and political opportunities provided to them by British colonial practices to assert themselves as the household "heads," livestock "owners," and political leaders of their families and communities (Hodgson 2001a, 1999a). These slow and sometimes subtle social changes were intensified in the 1950s when the British suddenly accelerated their pressure on Maasai to "modernize," in part through the comprehensive objectives and coercive implementation of the Masai Development Plan. These included harsh demands that Maasai integrate themselves fully into the cash economy, improve the productivity and increase the sales of their livestock, educate their children, exploit the vast labor potential of *ilmurran*, replace their customary dress with Western clothes, and build and live in permanent settlements (Hodgson 2001a, 2000a). As a result of these changes, Maasai women lost economic and political power, social autonomy, and spatial mobility. Their domestic workloads increased, and they were excluded from the expanding opportunities for education and income generation. Not surprisingly, they became (and remain) bitter and resentful about their changed situation (Hodgson 2001a, 1999c).

But timing was only one factor. Unlike colonial administrators concerned with economic and political issues, Spiritan missionaries interceded in a realm—religion—where women felt empowered to assert themselves. As discussed in chapter 1, women perceived themselves (and were perceived by some men) as more religious, more prayerful, and therefore closer in spirit to Eng'ai. As "Nanne," a middle-aged woman, explained to Morani and me in 1992: "You men [referring to Morani] just don't want it. Why, for me there is usually not a day when I don't come out and pray to Eng'ai. Even when I'm sleeping I pray to Eng'ai. But you men pray to Eng'ai only if you have a problem. Why, I splash milk for Eng'ai every evening and morning." A number of Maasai men that I interviewed supported such a perspective,

211

explaining women's attraction to the church as part of their superior spiritual nature, which manifested itself in their inherent kindness, empathy, and compassion. In contrast, they argued, Maasai men were prone to anger and violence. As Thomas, a Catholic Maasai who had studied at Oldonyo Sambu Junior Seminary, explained to me:

> Maasai women are and have always been more spiritual than men; it is their nature. Women are just more compassionate—if someone is hurt or hit, women aren't violent, men are. I would be in there fighting and hitting someone and a woman would be trying to stop the fight, crying and pleading. For example, I recall one time there was a thief—he was a stranger, and we men were beating him for stealing. The women cried and pleaded with us to stop. "What will his mother say?" "Leave him alone, give him a chance!" and so on. We killed him, and they sobbed, "Oh his poor mother, here she is going about her work and she doesn't know that her son is dead!" One woman was so upset by the killing that she died of a heart attack right on the spot.

Steven echoed Thomas's explanation. He compared the way men and women treated cattle: "I will beat cattle, move them from one point to another. And then sometimes I am angry, I shout a lot. . . . But once livestock come back to the homestead, the relationship changes, very nice . . . there is a lot of cuddling [by women]." "Women," he continued, "are more like priests in their work and relationships than men. They are more spiritual people than men. [They have] *huruma* [Swahili for "sympathy, mercy, pity"], they have more sympathy than anyone else."

"[The] trust [that women have in Eng'ai] and all of the things that they do makes them closer to Eng'ai than men," explained "Solomon," a baptized and highly educated Maasai man who worked as a primary school teacher.

Women's spiritual superiority and close relationship to Eng'ai were premised in great part on their roles as mothers, as the creators of new life. As Solomon remarked: "Only women know the pain and suffering (and half death) of giving birth. We men are not allowed nearby. We are told about some of the things that happen, but not all of them. Women pray there, and talk to Eng'ai in the ways they know: 'Ehh, Eng'ai, we ask for peace when the women give birth, no problems.' . . . Because the women know about all the problems that can happen." For example: "When I advise women with problems to go to the hospital to give birth, they tell me that they have been doing these things [giving birth] for a long time. Eng'ai is there. 'You are now a big man but even you were born in this very way, so don't have any doubts because Eng'ai is there and She helps children to be born, not like cattle have calves. Eng'ai Herself is doing the work.'"

Like Solomon's mother, a skilled local midwife, Maasai women served as the midwives—literally and figuratively—between Eng'ai and Her people. Eng'ai gave women—and not men—the power to create new life on earth, a power central to their greater religiosity and spirituality, and therefore their interest in Christianity. As the Spiritans eventually discovered, much to their chagrin, religion was a female-dominated domain of belief and practice among Maasai.

As the above explanations suggest, the concepts of spirit and spirituality were central to understanding Maasai ideas of religion and conversion. Maasai spoke of these in terms of *oltau* (pl. *iltauja*), a Maa word that was often translated as heart, soul, spirit. It was at once a unique, inner, non-material essence bequeathed to each person by Eng'ai and, as such, their closest connection to Eng'ai: "Everyone is born with their own *oltau*." Like Western and Christian notions of "spirit," *oltau* resided in individual bodies, but was not contained by them. As "Naishepo," an older woman from Mti Mmoja who was adamantly not a Christian, told us: "Eng'ai created me, and you know that Eng'ai gave you the *oltau* that you have, so if She wants to slaughter a chicken, you slaughter a chicken, because She gave it to you. She gave you the *oltau* that you have, because Eng'ai is the reason you are even walking around." A person's *oltau* could influence their actions, forcing them to do things or go places they might not otherwise choose. Moreover, people could improve or worsen their *iltauja* through their practices, in part by "opening" or "closing" their *iltauja* to Eng'ai: "Eng'ai helps people especially if you open your *oltau* to Her."

In addition to being an agentive force, *oltau* was also the locus of moral value. A good *oltau* was described as being black in color (*oltau orok*), "because black is the color of Eng'ai." In contrast, a bad *oltau* was red. Certain people were referred to as having "black spirits" because they were perceived as kind, generous, respectful, and moral, with no malice or evil in their hearts, actions, or intentions. Usually these were elder men and women who had proved themselves by a lifetime of good actions, but occasionally younger men and women were praised in these ways. Men selected by their *ilmurran* age-mates to become *ilaunoni* (the ritual representatives of their age-set) had black spirits, as did elder men and women who led important ritual delegations. Other men and women were said to have "red spirits," because they were selfish, greedy, malevolent, and mean. I often heard residents of Emairete describe Mary in such terms, in part because she was always fighting—with her neighbors over alleged infractions of her land boundaries, with the village council to demand more land, with the schoolteachers over their treatment of her children, with the women's grinding machine committee over money, and so forth. Their venom was only fuelled by her financial autonomy, social independence, and comfortable wealth. Similarly, "Simon," one of the wealthiest men in Emairete, was also charged with having a "red spirit" because he refused to share his wealth according to customary kinship, age-set, clan, and patron-client relations. In the case of both Mary and Simon, accusations of having a "red spirit" were not a critique of their wealth, but of their selfish, greedy refusal to share their wealth according to customary principles of redistribution. In other words, being wealthy was not in itself an immoral state. Rather, how a person used his or her wealth determined whether or not they were characterized as moral or immoral, as having a black or red *oltau*.

As the discussion of women's greater spirituality implies, the *iltauja* of men and women had different characteristics. In general, women's spirits were described as closer and more open to Eng'ai, while men's *iltauja* were more distant and closed. As a result, women's *iltauja* were more flexible and open to new experiences than men's. As Letani commented, "Women are very quick to change their *iltauja*, while men are very hard-headed (*megol ilukuny*)." Similarly, as Esta said before, "It is women who were able to see that there was light (*ewangan*), and we tried to persuade the men, but they got stuck, so therefore there are only a few these days [in church]."

Many Maasai men made similar comments about their inflexibility and unwillingness to change, but they often spoke in terms of their *oregie*, a Maa word that means culture and customs, instead of their *iltauja*. In contrast to women, they were unwilling to change their culture, which they saw as incompatible with Christianity. "Men like you who have been educated," said elderly "Lesinon," gesturing to Morani, "you have seen that many things in Maasai culture are nonsense in today's world. But we old men have failed to throw away our culture completely; we are still living in our culture." Even young men such as "Sipai" acknowledged the friction between Christianity and their "culture": "I didn't want to be baptized because of my culture; I am very much a Maasai." Some men confused the teachings of different denominations, especially as to their acceptance or rejection of Maasai cultural practices. As "Lepayian," a male elder from Mti Mmoja, explained:

> I agreed to let my wives attend; I don't condemn (*meeta eng'ongoni*) the church. But I don't go to church because of all their rules—such as tobacco. The church won't let me chew tobacco, but I am used to it. But a person who goes to church can't use tobacco. And many times, if a child is born, the church won't allow you to slaughter for the mother. Or if a cow dies unexpectedly, the church

won't let you eat the meat because its throat wasn't cut. How can I live without
these things that I am used to?

When I asked how he had learned about these rules, he replied, "I learned
them from people who went to church. And once I heard them I decided
that I couldn't give up my culture, which was given to me by Eng'ai."

For men like Lepayian, their sense of being Maasai was grounded in
and expressed through their cultural practices. Moreover, they justified their
firm embrace of a fairly static notion of culture with claims that their culture
was a gift from Eng'ai.[1] It was their culture, not their spirit, which prevented
them from joining the church. As Father Donovan recounted many years
ago:

> One elder told us he was very eager to become a Christian, but he would find
> it very difficult to give up all of his cattle. We asked him why he thought he
> had to give up all his cattle to become Christian, and he answered, "But isn't
> your religion the religion of the poor, the religion of the Swahilis (a Masai
> term for all non-Masai), the religion of those tribeless, wandering people who
> live near all the government centres through Masailand?" (Donovan 1967: 209)

A similar perspective was reflected, as discussed in chapter 5, in the dis-
courses and debates about Maasai men such as Joseph and Steven who,
because of their education, work, dress, and Christianity, were considered
ormeek. Several men spoke explicitly about the stigma associated with being
a Christian and therefore an *ormeek*, implying that Christianity challenged
the dominant norms of Maasai masculinity (Hodgson 1999b). The strong
embrace of the churches by women only fuelled such associations and men's
reluctance to participate. As "Lemali" wondered, "There are so many women,
do you think I could be with all of those women?"

In Search of Healing

The concept of *oltau*, especially its gendered dimensions and associations, is crucial to understanding an important aspect of the missionary encounter: how Maasai women overcame the objections of their husbands and
fathers to join the church. Despite the evident attraction of women to Christianity once first the *boma* approach and then the individual approach enabled
their participation, many Maasai men were initially reluctant to allow their
wives and daughters to attend instruction and forbade them to be baptized
in either the Catholic or Lutheran church. As with their sons, men feared
that conversion would separate women irrevocably from Maasai culture.

They tried to assert their authority and prevent women's involvement, and mocked those who considered attending as *emeeki* (female *ormeek*). Unwilling to directly challenge men, women resorted (whether intentionally or not) to an indirect means of overcoming their objections—*orpeko*. *Orpeko* was understood by Maasai as a sickness of the *oltau* caused by the influence of (or possession by) an evil spirit (often identified as satan [*esetan*]), which manifested itself in an array of physical ailments and actions.[2] Briefly, when sick with *orpeko*, a woman could demand anything and everything from her husband and family, including permission to attend baptismal instruction and church. Since the only permanent means to either cure or prevent *orpeko* was to be baptized in the Christian churches, other Christian women usually took possessed women to church for instruction, baptism, and permanent healing (see also Hurskainen 1985a, 1985b).[3]

The account of Namanak, recorded by Peterson in 1971, is a typical example:[4]

> During a pregnancy she lost a child. She felt an intense burning under and around her womb and right up her back to her head. At times she would feel something covering her head. She would also get extreme headaches that would drive her mad. Often she would be in a stupor, shaking and then throwing herself on the ground. The above symptoms occurred about twice daily.
>
> Due to the nature of the symptoms the elders decided she was crazy and that a spirit was involved. . . . [After sending her to an *oloiboni* whose ministrations failed to cure her, and watching her condition deteriorate] the elders decided to send her to another *oloiboni*. She, however, refused to go because she had heard from Masai Christian women . . . who had been cured that Christianity was the only true cure. The elders consented so she went to church in about 1966. She was taught by a [Lutheran] Maasai evangelist . . . and then baptized on the 24th of September 1967.
>
> As soon as she began baptismal instruction, she started improving as far as the shaking, the burning sensations in the groin and the headaches. All of these symptoms left her before baptism. She still had occasional problems mentally, i.e., confused thinking, amnesia. These mental lapses continued until baptism.
>
> The day before baptism when she first heard that she was to be baptized, all the original symptoms returned in full—yelling, dancing, shaking, burning sensations. They continued until the moment when she was baptized (first application of the water). Afterwards she became normal and has been so since that time. When she was baptized, she said she felt a heavy feeling pass over her and then afterwards she felt very relaxed.
>
> She said, "I've seen the greatest power of Christ. Others who haven't realized it are fools." She also said she'd seen others die from demons. She felt if it hadn't been for the church she would have been dead today. (Peterson 1971: Case 8)

Namanak's narrative of her symptoms, their onset after a troubled pregnancy, the impotence of the *iloibonok* in curing her, and the healing power of Christian baptism were repeated in most of the accounts I heard or read about. As "Naisatot," a young married woman from Embopong', told me in 1992:[5]

> Men just don't want it [baptism]. There are men, for instance, like mine, who insult the church and say "*Shie,* child, where are you going? Church? And what do you intend to find there? Have you changed? Have you become an *emeeki?* If you go, you'll leave a bad omen here."
>
> But they all have to put you in that house of Eng'ai (*ena aji Eng'ai*) on the day when satan (*esetan*) comes inside you. If you are unable to cook his porridge and he is stricken by hunger, then he says, "*Shie,* yesterday I slept without eating, perhaps my wife is crazy with *orpeko,* let me take her to church."
>
> And he doesn't know what else to do to cure her. I mean, he left her for a long time until the day when he missed his food because satan prevented her from cooking. Then and only then did he take her [to church]. But when he takes her, she will embarrass him there since she might jump about and tear off her clothes. But he left her [at home] without taking her so she could pray to Eng'ai when her spirit was still good (*supat oltau*); he left her until she got blemishes on her spirit (*oldoai oltau*), then and only then did he take her.

Like Koko Nayieu, Koko Naomon, and many other women whom I interviewed over the years, Naisatot and Namanak joined the church to rid themselves of an "illness" (*emuoyian*) over which they felt they had no control and for which they found no other source of relief.

Significantly, as missionaries began to teach and evangelize new groups of Maasai, *orpeko* soon followed. Peterson (1971), Hurskainen (1985a, 1985b, 1989), and Hodgson (1997) have documented that a resurgence of *orpeko* accompanied the intensified evangelization efforts of both Lutherans and Catholics in the 1950s and 1960s, and continues today.[6] Gradually, as Maasai men realized that instruction, baptism, and ongoing participation in the Christian churches was the only permanent "cure" for *orpeko,* they reluctantly allowed their wives and daughters to join the churches. These days men speak of putting (*etipika*) their sick wives in church, and it is often enough for women today to merely invoke the possibility of *orpeko* to receive permission. As one elder man explained:

> There is a sickness (*emuoyian*) that has spread into this area recently that was not here before, this thing called *esetan,* this *orpeko.* It hasn't entered men, but women. But when you take a woman to the *oloiboni* he says, "She is cursed." And if you take her to another, "She is cursed." *Basi,* . . . this wisdom of Christians showed that a thing called the church (*ekanisa*) could heal (*eishiu*) this sickness. When we put women in there they were healed; really it helped them.

Shie, why else would so many have joined? Also, it is said that a healthy person who is baptized cannot be possessed.

As this man's comments reveal, Maasai associated *orpeko* with devastation and disease, and often alluded more obliquely to the "sickness" (*emuoyian*) that had come from the outside and afflicted only women, primarily those of child-bearing age.[7] As in the case of Namanak, the symptoms of *orpeko* included assorted body pains, physical fits, nightmares, listlessness, apathy, all of which could of course be attributed to other ailments. What is important is that other women, usually Christian women, *named* the afflicted woman's symptoms as *orpeko;* the ability to "name" *orpeko* was simultaneously an assertion of power, the recognition of a common condition, and the first step toward healing.

As I have argued elsewhere (Hodgson 1997), the symptoms of *orpeko* expressed, in embodied terms, women's consternation over their economic disenfranchisement, political marginalization, and increased workloads and isolation. But *orpeko* also provided a means to address and "heal" their situation by reinforcing relationships among women who worked to heal one another and by facilitating their participation in the Christian churches. By resorting (whether consciously or unconsciously) to claims of spirit possession, Maasai women were able to overcome any reluctance on the part of men to allow them to join the church.[8]

The themes of involuntariness and lack of agency evoked repeatedly in early and contemporary accounts of *orpeko* are critical. The ambiguity and ambivalence of *orpeko* in terms of women's agency and intentionality enabled women to displace responsibility for joining the church from their wishes to the desires of their *iltauja,* the actions of satan, and the decisions of men. As a result, Maasai women got what they wanted—to attend instruction and participate in the church—without directly challenging the authority of Maasai men.

Spiritan missionaries had (and still have) varying attitudes toward *orpeko.* Some discounted it as "foolishness" on the part of women, while others worked hard to help sick women.[9] I witnessed many cases of *orpeko* inside and outside of the church, and noted the different responses of the priests, catechists, and parishioners. During the Easter baptism presided over by Father Kohler in 1992, for example, several women had fits during the service. As one woman sat on the floor with her legs extended, her legs started trembling, she began moaning in a rhythmic low groan, and her upper torso swayed up and down. Then she collapsed in a heap on the floor. "Quit that

Fig. 6.1. A Maasai woman collapses into an acute *orpeko* attack just before she was supposed to be baptized in Mti Mmoja. Her friends struggled to pull her onto the soft grass as she flailed her rigid arms and legs and moaned in a low, rhythmic growl. Photo by author, 1992.

foolishness!" yelled Father Kohler. He asked people to carry her outside. Several women helped her outside, then held her on the ground. She was still in a trance-like state, staring off into the distance with her eyes rolling around. As she slowly regained her composure, still shaking with tears coming from her eyes, she cried out to "bring water!" A woman asked me for water, which I quickly brought from the car. Later, just before the baptismal water touched her, another woman flung her arms back and fell into a trance (fig. 6.1). As with the first woman, she started shaking and moaning in a low, rhythmic growl. Several women quickly grabbed her and pulled her on to the soft grass, where she thrashed around, then lay shaking and trembling. Father Kohler lost his patience: "Quit this nonsense! This is not the place for this silliness, it is disrespectful!" Eventually, some other women helped her sit up, and one of them kept hitting her on the back, saying, "Get out! Get out!" When another woman went into a fit just before being baptized as well, Father Kohler was furious. After yelling at the women, he stormed into the church to calm down, leaving the remaining baptismal candidates in line, confused and apprehensive. As soon as Father Kohler resumed the baptisms, another low groan was heard from inside the church, and the woman was carried to the back room of the church. By the end of the service, I counted five women lying in the grass around the church recovering from *orpeko* fits.

When I interviewed Father Kohler about a week later, I asked for his views on *orpeko*. "I'm not very sympathetic," he said, deadpan. We both laughed.

"I noticed," I replied.

"Body language, huh?" he quipped. "I just don't want to encourage it, especially because the group knows that that's not acceptable behavior." He continued:

> My experience has been that people are looking for attention. A step of baptism, you know, we have the anointing business and so on, oftentimes that is sufficient. Oftentimes just to pray over people. And God bless them. In several situations where a woman would throw a fit, other women would just gather around, the nurturing sort of thing, and form a circle. Whether it was a natural configuration or just what they did. And kind of soothe and sing and cluck, cluck, cluck and soothe the person down. And if people needed a prayer, as I said, I would go over and pray, or put my hands on, or the group would pray, . . . or the anointing. . . . So the person feels they are getting something, a blessing of some sort, a religious moment for them. And as often as not, that was sufficient, it took care of them.

He thought that certain kinds of music triggered the fits, and gave several examples from his experience. He also wondered about the similarities with the ritualized fits (called *mori*) that *ilmurran* used to express extreme emotions by eating certain kinds of plants. In general, while he agreed that women probably could not control their fits, he thought that it was a means to get attention, "a totally exploitative sort of thing on the part of the women." "Any number of guys," he added, "have come here asking that their women be baptized because [they] are sick with *orpeko*."

Like Father Kohler, most Spiritans dismissed any suggestion that *orpeko* was a form of satanic possession, explaining it instead as a dramatic attempt by disenfranchised women to demand resources and attention from their husbands (as Lewis 1971 and others have argued). They therefore refused to baptize sick women who had not completed religious instruction classes. In contrast, many Lutherans supported (if not promoted) the idea that *orpeko* was a form of satanic possession (Benson 1980; cf. Meyer 1999). Consequently, they often baptized sick women on the spot to heal them, which led to bitter accusations by some Catholics that the Lutheran church was spreading stories and fear of *orpeko* among Maasai in order to coerce Maasai to be baptized as Lutherans (e.g., Kane 1995: 10–11). For example, as already quoted in chapter 4, an American Spiritan working in Mti Mmoja in the early 1980s complained in the mission journal one day that "it seems to me that the Lutherans are trying to build the church on fear of the devil taking possession of women" (MMJ/Jan. 1982–June 1983).

The male catechists were often more sympathetic to the women, in part because they knew many of them as family members, friends, and neighbors and saw the daily consequences of their suffering. Mwalimu Daniel attributed *orpeko* to women's sufferings and their declining status:

> A woman is a person who is not respected as she deserves as a person, as a human. Instead, she is a person . . . with a very low status. She is treated like a prisoner by most elders, like a prisoner. So I usually ask her some questions about her life, how she lives at home, any problems, what hurts her, how many children does she have, does she even have any children, what is her relationship like with her husband, does her husband like her, help her, give her clothes?

Once he understood the particulars of her situation, he then tried to teach her to not be afraid of her situation, to treat her husband and family with "respect," and to change her attitude and practices so that she could live more happily with her husband. He was adamant, however, that all women seeking baptism to cure *orpeko* complete the full two years of instruction.

Mwalimu Moses offered similar explanations for the sources of *orpeko*. He believed that baptism cured women because "they realize that they are free. . . . They hear the Word of God, they sing with their friends, and they are happy. They learn to speak successfully with their husbands, to discuss ideas, to share concerns. . . . They learn to be free in their interactions." "Before," he continued, "they were tied up by the chains of satan (Swahili: *minyororo ya shetani*), but now they are free. They understand that they are children of God, and there is a great freedom with God by way of Jesus Christ."

Whatever the theological differences between Catholics and Lutherans, priests and catechists, *orpeko* was intimately connected, in the minds of Maasai, to *oltau*. Recall the following explanation from one of the earlier accounts: "But he left her [at home] without taking her so she could pray to Eng'ai when her spirit was still good (*supat oltau*); he left her until she got blemishes on her spirit (*oldoai oltau*), then and only then did he take her." *Orpeko* was therefore a sickness of the spirit, of one's *oltau*, which could be healed (or prevented) only by baptism and participation in the Christian church. "Do you think I want satan to come inside me?" asked "Naini," in response to a question about why she had joined the church. When men tried to prevent them from joining the church, women's *iltauja* sickened, with severe consequences for the daily lives and livelihoods of men. *Iloibonok* were unable to cure the illness, and "even the government," as Mwalimu Francis declared, "didn't have medicine to cure *orpeko*!" Only the priests and churches—through instruction, baptism, and continuing pastoral care—were able to heal women's spirits.

One God, One Spirit, Many Churches

As the analysis of *oltau* and *orpeko* indicates, conversion (*airuk:* to believe, to agree) itself was therefore perceived as a process occurring by the desire of a person's *oltau*, rather than their will or mind. As "Martha," an elderly woman, explained, "No one is forced to convert; each person comes when his/her spirit agrees (*oltau lenya loiruko*), then s/he says I will go to church and get baptized." Many Maasai confirmed this idea of *oltau*, saying that their *oltau*, their spirit, decided, their spirit led them to church. "My *oltau* wanted to go to church," explained Esta, "so I went and was baptized." Thus, in contrast to Father Donovan's rhetoric about the power of community over the individual, many people, of all ages, spoke of conversion to Christianity as a matter of individual choice. No one was forced by another person to convert, nor was anyone forbidden to convert. "It is just up to each person to decide," said Mwalimu Francis. Women, however, as discussed above, usually had to have their husband's or father's permission to attend instruction and services. But in the aftermath of *orpeko*, few men dared to refuse.

Differences in the *iltauja* of men and women were also a frequent explanation for the gendered differences in church participation. Women (and some men) claimed that women's *iltauja* were more open to Eng'ai, closer to Eng'ai, while "the spirits of men don't want to go to church." Women's spirits, in contrast, with their close links to Eng'ai, were drawn to these new religious teachings and novel sacred spaces where Eng'ai, they believed, was present and worshipped. They described a yearning, a desire, an uncontrollable urge, to join the church, all driven by their *oltau*; "my *oltau* demanded that I go to church!" "I went to instruction because my *oltau* wanted to go (*oltau lai oltaiyieu*)." In contrast, some men also invoked their *oltau* as a reason they had not participated in Christianity: "My *oltau* was not interested."

In general, Catholic Maasai were very tolerant of those Maasai who were not interested in the church. The problem, many explained, was that their *oltau* had not yet led them to church, "their *oltau* won't let them." Some, like Letani, offered more pluralistic views: "Those who go to church think they have found the true way to God, and those who don't go to church think they have found the true way. But there are many religions, and each one says that it is the true way." Others, such as Koko Nayieu, attributed it to their lack of knowledge: "It is just ignorance that keeps people from going to church. I mean, if you knew that there was a place that you could go to rid your body of disease, wouldn't it make sense for everyone to get together and go, without leaving anyone behind?" And some, such as Maria, saw the work of satan at hand. While she agreed that some Maasai just did not recognize the importance of church, others had attended instruction, but were "prevented from coming [to church] by satan."

Churches of God

According to the Maasai women we interviewed, conversion to Christianity enhanced their already substantial spiritual life by providing yet another place to sing and pray to Eng'ai: "When we stay in the homesteads we are singing, and all the songs we sing are for Eng'ai. When we go to church we are still singing the same songs for Eng'ai" (cf. Hurskainen 1985a: 42). Or as elderly "Koko Namunyak" explained to me one evening in her home:

> I started going to church because of the changes that have occurred. In the past, Maasai only prayed to Eng'ai, and people went to worship at the *oreteti* trees. They prayed when children were born, at circumcision ceremonies, and at all times that they needed Eng'ai. But now things have changed—people say they are going to church to pray to Eng'ai. . . . I don't care where people go to pray, whether Maasai places or the church: I like to pray in all places at all times.

Similarly, Koko Naserian told me that "I went to instruction because it was about praying to Eng'ai and I like to pray to Eng'ai since I pray all the time. And so we gather together in the church to pray." Several Maasai compared the church to the *oreteti* tree, which they argued was "the Maasai church."

As the comments by Koko Namunyak and Koko Naserian suggest, missionary adaptations of Christianity to Maasai religious and cultural realities (and Maasai adaptations of Christianity) in first the *boma* approach and then the individual approach had been so successful (or, depending on one's perspective, such failures) that few people perceived any significant difference between Eng'ai and the Christian God or between the prayers and rituals of Maasai religion and Catholicism. As another woman explained:

> It is all the same since the Maasai agree that you can go to church by your own abilities (*inkidimat*) while another can say I am not going to church, but will stay home to pray to my God, that God of the past of the Maasai. I mean, formerly, didn't we always have people who didn't go to church? But Eng'ai still gave them life? But another person can say that s/he will go to church to pray (*asai*) to Eng'ai so that Eng'ai will give her/him a bright spirit (*oltau owang'*).

Or as "Nashie," a young woman from Mti Mmoja, summed up: "All ways [of prayer] are fine, they are similar. I mean, it is the same God who is being prayed to."

"When I go to church I pray in the same way that I pray at home," explained Koko Nayieu. At least one person noted an important difference between Maasai and Christian prayers: "The Christian prayers are very, very long!"

Although the central theological difference between the Christian and Maasai faiths was the belief in Jesus and his message, Jesus was rarely mentioned in the many conversations and interviews that I held with Maasai over the years about their beliefs and practices. Jesus was not unknown, but was primarily discussed and remembered according to ideal Maasai values, as the "good son" who cared for and respected his mother, Mary. Because the bonds between Maasai women and their adult sons were one of the most important ties in Maasai social life, Jesus was principally understood through his relationship to Mary, rather than, for example, as part of the trinity of the Holy Spirit and God.

Instead, the main differences that people remarked upon were spatial and temporal aspects having to do more with the form of Catholicism than its content. In contrast to short, personal prayers said throughout the day or collectively at celebrations and gatherings, the church provided a regular time and space for people to gather together and pray. Some Christian women such as Maria preferred the regular, collective prayers facilitated by the church; "I prefer going to worship Eng'ai in large groups in church." But Naishepo, an older unbaptized woman in Mti Mmoja, disagreed: "They [Christians] believe that you have to get together to see Eng'ai, but we believe that even when you are walking in the plains alone you can pray to Eng'ai, at dawn you pray to Eng'ai, when you go outside to milk and spill the first milk for Eng'ai you are praying." Most Christian women, however, did both, praying together at church services, but continuing to pray individually throughout the day and collectively at ceremonies and celebrations.

To some extent, men and women associated these features of the church with other social changes such as schools, markets, and new styles of dress and ornamentation. As "Koko Naisandi" summarized, "The ways of worshipping these days have become modern ways." Like several other older women, she then listed related changes in clothing (from skins to cloth to dresses), ornaments (less beadwork), and other aesthetic practices (such as a decline in piercing and extending earlobes). For some adherents, conversion thus entailed new modes of consumption and dress.

Another aspect of the "modern" way of worshipping was language. A number of female parishioners in Emairete complained about the increasing use of Swahili prayers and songs, which they could not understand, in the service. "So if you go there and you don't know Swahili, what have you gone there to do?" wondered Koko Naomon. "I didn't participate for a long time because I don't understand Swahili, I don't know how to read, I don't know how to sing the songs that the young people know."

In addition to language, the Catholic Church's request for money was another "modern" difference that troubled some parishioners. They complained about the large sums of money demanded for collections and contributions to ceremonies and feasts: as Koko Naomon grumbled, "[The Emairete Catholic Church] is a place to steal people's property from them. I mean, there is always collection of money, every day, and people who don't have any money have problems. They don't prevent the poor from coming, but you go and find out that you have lost one hundred, two hundred [shillings]." Naoyeyio shared her concerns, noting that the expected weekly contribution had risen from two hundred shillings to five hundred shillings.

God the Father and Mother

As noted above, few Maasai noted any differences between Eng'ai and the Christian God. Like Maria, many stated that "I think the Maasai God and the Christian God are the same; there is no difference." "It is the same God," said Koko Naserian, an elderly woman in Mti Mmoja. Joseph, however, was one of the few who disagreed: "No, [they are] not the same. Because some Maasai worship trees (irkeek), and some worship (eserem—"to praise, to honor") iretet (oreteti trees), others mountains. But, as I've seen, it is because they were seeking those ways to find God, but now they see that

225

they can do it in the church, which is the reason that many have returned to church." Similarly, Koko Naomon sadly stated that "these days the Maasai God is no longer here, only the God of the church. . . . You don't pray to two gods, you pray to the God of the church and give up the other God."

Ironically, in contrast to Spiritan arguments about the differences between Eng'ai and the Christian God (see chapter 3), some Maasai argued that they thought that Eng'ai was more hopeful and forgiving than the Christian God. Steven, for example, found the Christian ideas of punishment and guilt, and especially of hell, "a little bit threatening." In contrast, he explained, once you were punished for a bad deed in Maasai society, "There is no problem anymore. You are finished." Although he agreed that Catholics had procedures to request and receive forgiveness, he still thought that there was "a lot of hope in our [Maasai] way of praying. And I want to be a hopeful person, not the one who feels 'oh, today I did this and I feel so bad about it.' " He then described, as an example, the recent payment of forty-nine cattle made in compensation for the murder of one Maasai man by another in a nearby homestead. With the final transfer of cattle, the grievous incident was forgiven by all.

Finally, despite Christian references to God as male, as Our Father, all the Maasai Christians I interviewed continued to refer to and understand Eng'ai in primarily female terms. "I think Eng'ai is a woman," stated "Sekot," an elder man from Mti Mmoja. Many spoke of Eng'ai as both male and female, father (*menya oltungani*) and mother (*ngotonye oltungani*), while others, when questioned, spoke of Eng'ai as female, as the creator and nurturer of the world and all of its people. "Eng'ai is a person who is our Father and our Mother," said "Lepopo," a baptized senior elder from the Inkidong'i clan who lived in Emairete. "We respect Her/Him more than any person, we fear Her/Him a lot, just like our father and mother." "I pray to Eng'ai because I know that She has power over everything, children, cattle, and your life as well" said Maria, a young Catholic woman from Emairete.

Spaces of Wisdom

In general, Maasai men and women described church as a place where one could study new things and gain wisdom (*eng'eno*). Women said that they learned about the "word" of God (*ororei lEng'ai*), as well as increased awareness about gender relations: "If you are ignorant you go to get instruction there. You'll like it there, and you'll come to see how your husband treats you, and once you have seen, you will understand that what they do is stupid. . . . There is much wisdom there." Men agreed that women gained wisdom by going to church, although one older man qualified his remark: "I haven't seen them get wiser than male elders." One old man, not baptized himself, but with many baptized wives and children, explained: "It helps the women who know how to read. And for those who don't know, those who follow the ignorant ways of the past, some want wisdom so that they can see the way to pass (*enkitoi naaim*)."

When I asked people to be more specific about what they had learned from the church, most replied with a list of specific moral precepts such as Naini's: "I learned to stop hating, to love my neighbors, to quit desiring the property of others, to stop stealing, to quit being selfish, and to stop cursing people." Other moral lessons that people (especially former students of Mwalimu Daniel) mentioned were not to use God's name in vain, to treat people with love and respect, and not to sleep with other men's wives. Some said that they only learned "various prayers to worship Eng'ai, that's all." In general, they were taught, according to Koko Naomon, to "give up all of these things and accept Jesus."

At least one older woman, however, who sought baptism because she was sick with *orpeko*, found instruction classes less than stimulating. "I dozed off when people were being asked questions," said Koko Naomon. "Then they woke me: 'Mama, who gave birth to Jesus?' 'Christmas,' I answered. Now they tease me all the time, 'Who gave birth to Jesus?' 'Christmas,' I tell them."

These comments suggest that, in contrast to the predominantly male spaces of schools, women have taken over the churches as their own institutions of learning, their "schools." (One man, when discussing the church, even used the word for school, *eshule*, derived from the Swahili *shule*.) When, as part of the individual approach, missionaries shifted the site of Christian instruction and celebration to accessible spaces outside the homestead, these religious spaces became public, visible signs of women's religiosity. The eventual construction of church buildings made the churches seem even more like schools, and further solidified women's access to and control of these newly created public spaces beyond the control of their husbands and fathers. Women in many Maasai communities, including Mti Mmoja, took primary responsibility for building the churches (which, ironically, occasionally served as temporary school buildings).

Moreover, the format of religious instruction classes and the liturgy, as detailed in chapter 4, treated participants very much like students, with the catechist (or occasionally priest) teaching them weekly lessons, challenging them to identify the themes and morals of religious stories, requiring them to memorize prayers and songs, coaxing them to practice reciting prayers in front of one another, and even urging them to compete for plastic rosaries! There was clearly a progressive socialization of men and women into the normative routines of Catholic liturgy, prayer, and worship. This included teaching them appropriate behavior during services. As Koko Naomon recalled, "When Father Nangoro was there, he would say 'Ladies, prayer time is prayer time, not time for drinking *uji* [a thin broth made from flour and milk] or spitting. You can't just enter church and leave again. You enter the church and stay until the end.' "

Gender, Culture, and Conversion

Clearly, whatever the missionaries intended to communicate with their instruction, presence, and preaching, their message was received and interpreted in diverse ways that sometimes differed significantly from their intentions (cf. Landau 1991). Although it is difficult to generalize from individual narratives and case histories, some patterns do emerge. Perhaps most importantly, the Catholic Church has meant very different things to Maasai men and women, depending not just on their gender, but on their age and aspirations. Many women understood and approached the church as a spiritual place, another place to worship Eng'ai. Drawn by their spirits, their *iltauja*, some suffered from *orpeko*, a terrible sickness of the spirit, when their husbands and fathers initially refused to let them participate. But once *orpeko* helped them overcome their menfolk's objections, they joined the church in large numbers, so that it became known as the "church of women" in many places. Through the church, the women found not only Eng'ai, but also healing, wisdom, and community in difficult times.

Most Maasai men, in contrast, felt no such attraction to the church. For them, the church was less a place of the spirit than a harbinger of unwanted cultural change. Despite all of the Catholic Church's efforts at inculturation, these men perceived a fierce incompatibility between "being Maasai" (or at least being a Maasai man), and "being Christian." Not all men shared these views, however. Some respected older men, free from any pressure to conform to the preferences of their peers, were drawn, like women, to the church by their spirits. In addition, an increasing number of younger, educated men embraced the church for both spiritual and cultural reasons. Like women, many said that their spirit was called to the church by Eng'ai. Unlike women, however, most of these men saw the church as a "modern" spiritual place, with its books, language, *wazungu* (whites), leadership roles, money, and more. In many ways, they were attracted to the very same modernist associations of the church that repelled their elders.

Both men and women asserted the centrality of their religious beliefs and practices to their sense of ethnic identity. But while women embraced Christianity as an extension and enhancement of their spirituality, many men retained a fervent resistance to Catholic teachings and practices as contrary to their "culture," to "being Maasai." Conversion for them was a cultural, not spiritual, matter. These men rejected women's more flexible notions of the relationship between ethnicity, culture, religion, and identity, and used their opposition to Christianity to reinforce their cultural and ethnic boundaries.

In contrast, conversion to Christianity enabled women to become more religious and thereby further accentuate their moral differences from men. One woman we interviewed implied that men, like wild animals, had no spirits: "Our [women's] spirits (*iltauja*) just love [the church]. I mean, if I only knew how to seize/obey (*aibung'a*) my spirit even more, I would do so. But a man is just a wild animal (*olowuaru*) at all times." The invocation of men as wild animals suggested a sharp moral critique of the changes in Maasai gender relations, simultaneously casting men's increased political and economic control as evil and an affront to Eng'ai and affirming the moral superiority of women in the face of such betrayals. Women's outright rejection of men's assertions of patriarchal privilege was also seen in their shifted allegiance from *iloibonok* to Catholic priests as their diviners and healers. By emphasizing their moral and spiritual superiority to men, Maasai women advanced a female vision of "being Maasai" that was in marked contrast to male perspectives and challenged male authority and control.

TOWARD A MAASAI
CATHOLICISM?

7

If the presence of the Catholic Church, and its enduring embrace of inculturation as an approach to instruction, theology, liturgy, and everyday interactions, has not produced many changes in Maasai beliefs about God/Eng'ai, has it produced something that might be called "Maasai Catholicism"? What about its influence on Maasai practices not just within the church, but beyond the church as well? Have Maasai ceremonies, rituals, and cosmological beliefs changed since they were first documented in the late 1800s and early 1900s? What have been the changes, if any, for Maasai gender relations, as women have tried to strengthen their spiritual and moral authority through their embrace of the church as a space for female communion and community in the face of continuing economic and political disenfranchisement?

Blurring the Boundaries

The acceptance of Maasai customs and ceremonies by the Catholic Church was one of the most common reasons given for its success. As Joseph, the young storekeeper and church secretary in Mti Mmoja commented, "there is not a lot of hassle in the Catholic Church; the church permits you to do many things. But other churches have lots of harsh rules even though they promote the word of God. . . . The Catholic Church permits everything that is part of Maasai customary practices." This was in sharp contrast, he claimed, to the Pentecostals, who "prevent[ed] you from wearing your customary clothes," and the Lutherans, who "prohibit everything, including suffocating animals even though that is part of our tradition." Sekot, the grandson of a famous Maasai leader, shared these views: "The Catholic Church has spread a lot among Maasai because the Catholics don't care about a person's culture, even if you have ocher on and [wear] your own [customary] clothes." "I follow Maasai customs as usual," said Sinyati, the leader of a small Christian community in Mti Mmoja.

As these comments suggest, despite the presence and popularity of the Catholic Church as a venue for interacting with Eng'ai, most women (and men) still participated in the customary rituals, prayers, and rites described in chapter 1. If anything, the validation of many of these practices and beliefs by Catholics has imbued them with even greater meaning, relevance, and potency. Moreover, Maasai women continued to serve as ritual experts and organizers. The ongoing centrality of women to the memory, organization, and practice of rituals was very clear in several of my interviews with Maasai men, both educated and illiterate. As I interviewed Sekot one day in his senior wife's home, he constantly asked her about the order and content of the various life-cycle rituals. "What's the next ritual?" "Then what happens?" She quietly answered each question, with no hesitation and full knowledge. Similarly, when I asked Steven, the former catechist, about various myths and rituals in our second interview, he regretted his mother's absence: "I wish my mother were around today . . . [she] knows all these very well!"

Trees of God

Prayers, worship, and ceremonies at *oreteti* trees, for example, remained a vibrant practice among Christians and non-Christians. They were still considered "trees of Eng'ai" (*olchani lEng'ai*), sacred places where men and women could pray to and petition Eng'ai either individually or collectively. In 2000, Sekot was kind enough to escort me to a famous *oreteti* tree that sits on the slopes of Monduli mountain between Mti Mmoja and Emairete. We stopped on the way to pick up "Lepayian," a man from Ngorongoro, because he had participated in a collective ritual several years ago at the *oreteti* tree to ask for rain.

As I recorded in my field notes: Crouching over, we slowly entered a tunnel in the thick canopy, where trees and branches had been bent over the years to form a natural entryway. The dirt path was well worn, footprints still visible in the dust. After about 100 yards, we made a sharp descent along a dirt path into a gully. The air was cool and calm as we walked down, approaching the *oreteti* tree from behind. "This is our church, the Maasai church," proclaimed Sekot proudly and reverently, as we rounded the corner to the front of the tree, set near the edge of a dry riverbank. The tree was really many small trees that had grown up together, clustered here and there, with openings in between. The branches/roots grew out of high branches to the ground, like long tendrils. Earlier, Sekot had told me that there were eight doors to the church, so people could approach or weave through each of them (eight is also an auspicious number for Maasai). The tree(s) rose up very high and very wide, a beautiful, awesome sight—more like a cathedral than a church. There were two other *oreteti* trees nearby, but both men told me that this was the most holy (see fig. 1.1).

After gazing at the tree, Sekot collected some long green grass and handed it to each of us, saying that it would be appropriate to pray. Lepayian went first. Dividing the grass into each of his hands, he walked up to the tree and held his hands out while making a simple prayer for his cattle, children and wives, and rain. He then laid the grass in his right hand down in front of one set of tree roots, and the other in front of a left-hand set of tree roots, then walked back to us. Sekot approached next, holding the grass in the same way, and laying it down in the same spots once he was done praying. I was last, feeling a bit awkward but respectful as well. I copied all of their movements with the grass, including laying it down in the same place. Both men were eager to know what I thought, and I told them the truth—that it was an awesome and holy place, and it certainly felt like there was a special power there. I thanked them profusely for showing it to me.

According to the men, Maasai men and women would come here alone or in groups to pray for things such as children, more cattle, rain, and the like. Even Arusha believed in and worshipped this tree. Sekot told me that he had come to this tree when he was a young *olmurran*, all alone, to pray to Eng'ai. Other people visited and slept overnight under the tree.

Lepayian described the ritual he had participated in about five years before:

> There had been no rain, and it was decided to send a delegation to pray to Eng'ai here at the *oreteti* tree. We were almost one thousand men and women of all ages, chosen by the people because we were perceived as good, with no grudges or problems with others. The women stood in a group to the left of the tree [if you are facing it], singing their prayer songs, and the men stood in a group to the right. A very old, respected man stood in front of the tree (or sat on the ancient stool that was nearby—once three-legged, now two-legged), leading the ceremony. Eventually, the men and women formed two separate lines, and walked in and out of the "doorways" singing and praying. The old man applied a mixture of *chokaa* [chalk] and fat from the slaughtered ox on each person—marking the women's foreheads, and the men's left upper arms. Back to the right of the tree, near where the men stood, was where they slaughtered—one ox and three sheep, all supposed to be the finest beasts available, given by good, generous people. The animals were roasted on long skewers over

the fire, and the skewer sticks still remain, about ten of them propped up against the other *oreteti* tree. During the ritual, four *kibuyas* [calabashes] (two of honey beer, two of milk) were presented to Eng'ai and left at the *oreteti* tree. After more prayers and eating the roasted meat, everyone left.

"Lengare," a senior elder from the rainmakers clan who lives in Emairete, described his organization of and participation in similar rituals at the *oreteti* tree to beseech Eng'ai for rain. According to people in Emairete, Lengare had special powers to successfully pray for rain and to find lost cattle. Like the ritual described by Lepayian, the ceremonies involved delegations of men and women, the slaughtering of sheep, offerings of honey beer, milk, and water, singing, and praying. Lengare led similar delegations to Oldoinyo Leng'ai. When asked why he had these special gifts, Lengare explained that he belonged to the Ilmoingo clan, who had received these powers from Eng'ai. He was "an expert" among his clan members, an expertise that was inherited through the male line: "My father was the expert in his time and he taught me. . . . I will teach [my son]."

"How is your clan different from the Inkidong'i clan?" I asked.

"I don't really know," he replied. "But if you look we are equivalent. Therefore if an *oloiboni* fails in his work, he can say go find a person from the Ilmoingo clan like me and he will do your work of making offerings. Or at other times the rain refuses to come but if I wake up and go pray it rains."

Ceremonies of Life and Death

In addition to the *oreteti* tree, Maasai men and women continued to organize and participate in the many life-cycle ceremonies described in chapter 1. I observed and participated in many of these over the years, including ceremonies to celebrate and bless childbirth, naming, male and female circumcision, certain stages of age-set promotion such as the drinking of milk by a man in front of his wife, courtship, and marriage. I also witnessed collective rituals to plead to Eng'ai for rain, bless meetings and decisions, and settle disputes. At dawn, I watched Maasai women throw their first milk on the ground for Eng'ai and mutter prayers as they milked their cows. During the day, I heard many impromptu prayers, praise songs, and blessings as women went about their work. Men opened and closed collective gatherings with prayers to Eng'ai. Older men offered occasional blessings and prayers on my behalf and that of others they encountered throughout the day. Before I finally had children, I endured endless small rituals as elder women spat on their hands, rubbed my belly, and prayed for an end to my hopelessly (to them) barren state:

"May your belly become round and full with Eng'ai's bounty."
DH: Eng'ai!
"May Eng'ai bless you with many children."
DH: Eng'ai!
"May you become the mother of *ilmurran*."
DH: Eng'ai!

And so on. When I finally had my first son, Luke, and brought him to Tanzania in the summer of 2000, he and I were both regaled with showers of spit and streams of blessings and prayers by most women and some male elders.

All of these occasions, of course, were discrete, unique performances whose content and format varied by place, people, and time, yet they cumulatively and collectively revealed key continuities with—and significant divergences from—past patterns and principles as described for the late nineteenth and early twentieth centuries in chapter 1.

One important continuity was the ongoing centrality of Maasai women as the "behind-the-scenes" planners and organizers of ritual events, keepers of ritual knowledge, and sometimes vital ritual actors. When questioned about the details of most life-cycle ceremonies, many women responded with elaborate, step-by-step guidelines for the form and content of the ceremonies, while most men just gave me abbreviated answers with the name of the ceremony and its purpose. In practice, I observed women telling men and sometimes other women (usually younger women) where to stand, what to do, and even what to say during certain ritual occasions. For example, at a naming ceremony for "Sinoti," a young woman, prior to her circumcision, I watched the elderly "Koko Nanu" order the younger women and men about as they slaughtered a cow, roasted and distributed the meat, and prepared for the ceremony. That evening, as we sat inside around the hearth, Koko Nanu carefully explained to Sinoti how to hold her hands as Koko Nanu poured a small bit of milk from a calabash into her palm, drank the milk, then crossed her hands and repeated the process so that she drank twice from each palm. Koko Nanu then directed Sinoti to pour the milk as Koko Nanu crossed her palms and drank the milk two times from each palm. Koko Nanu then instructed the elder men who were present to begin to suggest teasing names until they finally said the name that Koko Nanu had suggested earlier.

Women coordinated the proceedings at both male and female circumcision ceremonies, in addition to preparing the food and alcohol (men usually roasted the meat, however). Although women did not witness the actual cutting at male circumcision, they formally opened the ceremony in the morning, helped to prepare their sons for their ordeal, ensured that the guests were welcomed and cared for, watched warily from their doorways as the circumcision took place, trilled their praiseful blessings once the cutting was completed, and welcomed their sons into their homes to feed them and help heal their wounds. When I attended the circumcision of Koko Naserian's grandson (together with two other boys) in 1987, she seemed to be everywhere at once, directing her sons and daughters-in-law, greeting visitors, scolding noisy children, advising her husband on the placement of the hide on which the boys would be circumcised, encouraging her grandson, shuttling the women to their houses so that the cutting could begin, and ensuring that everything and everyone followed the proper procedures and protocols.

Similarly, women were central to the many naming, blessing, and circumcision ceremonies that I attended. At the female circumcision ceremony for the daughters of a wealthy widow named Mary (which is described in more detail in Hodgson 2001a: 241–249), delegations of singing women met the guests, women prepared and served the food, women supervised and sanctified the actual circumcision (which men were not allowed to witness), ululating their praise and encouragement once the operation was complete. Throughout the festivities, especially when delegations of *ilmurran* from neighboring communities arrived, adult women danced and sang in groups, praising Eng'ai, and asking Her to bless Mary and her daughters. They also sang the praise songs for different age-sets of men, including the *ilmurran*. At one point, Mary and her close friend "Sidai" each grabbed one of the two *elaitin* trees planted outside Mary's kitchen and began to dance and jump around wildly, spurred on by the singing and approving taunts and laughter of a surrounding group of women. Other women, including the circumciser and Mary's sister, also took turns holding on to the trees while dancing raucously. The dancing and singing went on into the wee hours of the morning.

Another significant continuity was the use of grass, water, milk, spittle, and other signs of blessing. Even in ceremonies created to accommodate the changing social and political circumstances of Maasai, these symbols were deployed to bless and sanctify. In 1986, my husband and I were invited to attend the blessing ceremony of Lepilall ole Molloimet, a Maasai man who had just been reelected as the member of Parliament representing Monduli District. After a long, dusty drive to the village of Sinya, near the Kenyan border, we were greeted by a group of Maasai women dressed in their finery, singing songs of welcome and praise. As soon as Lepilall arrived, a low stool was brought out for him to sit on. Sheaves of fresh grass were put on his shoulders, and four elder men approached him. Each man held a calabash filled with milk, with fresh green grass stuffed into the top. As the men circled Lepilall, one chanted a prayer to Eng'ai (asking Eng'ai to watch over him, to bless his endeavors, and so forth) while the others responded "Ng'ai." At the same time, they all drank from their calabashes and spit on Lepilall, spraying him with milk (fig. 7.1). At the end, a group of nearby women ululated and sang several praise songs.

As Lepilall dried himself off, we joined a group of elder men who were sitting under the shade of a large acacia tree. As Lepilall walked over, the men shuffled around until they formed a V-shape—the man sitting at the point of the V had his back to the tree, and the two lines of men radiated outward, seated according to hierarchies of clan and seniority. A group of women sat close together slightly behind and to the left side of the men, and a group of *ilmurran* sat behind them to their right. Two low stools were provided for my husband and me to sit facing the group on their left side. First, Lepilall was given several gifts—a stool (a symbol of elderhood), a short carved stick with a knob on top (an elder's stick), and two goats. Then he addressed the men and women. He thanked the community for the blessing, their gifts, their votes, and their continuing support. He then spoke of his ambitious political plans to solidify the rights of Maasai to land, to bring *maendeleo* (the Swahili word for development) to the community, especially a permanent water source and working health clinic, and to ensure that Maasai interests were well represented in Parliament. Afterward, we joined Lepilall and many of the elder men in the home of one of his supporters, as platters of roasted meat, pilau (an Indian dish of rice, potatoes, meat, and spices), fried bananas, bottled beer, and soda were served.

A few aspects have changed, however. Several elite, educated Christian Maasai now send printed invitations in English and/or Swahili to invite family, neighbors, and friends to certain ceremonies. Mary circulated printed invitations to her daughters' circumcision ceremony, which prompted some people to call it a *sherehe ya karatasi*, or "paper party." Others wondered why the celebration had two tiers of guests—the "special guests," who sat in the living room and were served the best food, and everyone else, who had to

Fig. 7.1. Lepilall ole Molloimet being blessed by four elder men in Sinya after winning his recent reelection as member of Parliament for Monduli District. The men are praying to Eng'ai as they sprinkle milk on Lepilall, using calabashes stuffed with grass. Photo by author, 1986.

237

eat outside. They contrasted it with another female circumcision that had happened the same day in a neighboring homestead where everyone was welcome and shared the same food, drink, and social space.

These days, the Catholic priests and/or catechists also participated in many "customary" Maasai ritual celebrations. In the past, Spiritan missionaries often attended female and especially male circumcision ceremonies (including those of the children of *iloibonok*), male age-set promotion ceremonies such as Eunoto and Ilongesherr, and even women's feasts and fertility rites.[1] Occasionally they would offer to bless the ceremonies, which at least one Spiritan claimed "people appreciate[d]" (LMJ/19 Oct. 1967). Usually, however, they were just honored spectators, more interested in watching and taking pictures than participating. Only a few, such as Father Herbert Watschinger, a German Spiritan who also was a trained doctor and ran a Catholic hospital near Loliondo, took (or tried to take) more engaged roles. In May of 1965, according to the mission journal, "a crowd of Maasai women showed up dancing and praying for children. So Father Watschinger put in a plug for the hospital and took them all to the church to pray" (LMJ/31 May 1965). Just a few weeks later, when Father Watschinger and some other Spiritans attended a female circumcision ceremony, they were informed that the ceremony was cancelled because the "necessary mama" (the circumciser) did not show up. As recounted in the journal, "Father Watschinger's offer to officiate [that is, to circumcise the girl] was thoroughly considered but ultimately rejected as an infringement on certain prerogatives" (LMJ/13 June 1965). Nonetheless, the fact that he even offered to perform this central ritual role suggests not just a tolerance but an encouragement of Maasai rituals.

Over the years, Spiritan priests have increasingly been more active in not just attending, but participating in, these ceremonies. They regularly bless the participants and outcomes, and occasionally assist in officiating them. Some Spiritans, such as Father Christy, have even come to interpret certain Maasai rituals in Christian terms. For example, Father Christy told me that he thought that the *orkiteng lolbaa* ceremony (which he translated as the "bull of injury" ceremony) was in many ways a renewal of marriage vows between a man and his senior wife, so "if there is a Christian man who is slaughtering the bull, I'll change my schedule, I'll go there. I'll be present. I'll bless him. I'll bless the bulls. I'll show my commitment to them."

Similarly, catechists have always attended local ceremonies in their capacity as community members. But, like the priests, in recent years they have taken increasingly more active roles that expressed and reinforced their power and authority as Catholic catechists. Mwalimu Daniel attended most of the ceremonies that took place in Emairete and offered, when requested, a Christian blessing. At the circumcision ceremony for Mary's daughters, Mwalimu Daniel was the first male elder to bless the girls in a prayer session in the late afternoon. As he recited prayers in Maa to Eng'ai for the girls' health, wealth, fertility, and well-being, the other male elders responded "Ng'ai." Once he was finished, three other male elders, none of whom were Christians, took turns blessing the girls, so that a total of four (a propitious number) prayed for them. Finally, Mwalimu Daniel said some final prayers on their behalf as he spit on them with water and used his hands to wipe the water on their bodies from top to bottom as they stood uncomfortably with their arms crossed in front of them.

The rituals that seemed to have changed the most dramatically under the influence of the Catholic Church were those associated with death and the treatment of dead bodies. In contrast to the customary practice of leaving dead or dying people (except for respected elder men and occasionally women) in the bush for hyenas and other wild animals to dispose of, most Maasai Christians now chose to bury their dead in a formal funeral ceremony. But, despite the Christian promises of heavenly redemption and glory in the afterlife, the lurking fear of death, dying, and especially corpses remained.

Early one morning as I was typing my field notes in my room in Emairete, a group of junior elders came to see me. In contrast to the usual exchange of jovial greetings and news, they were silent and subdued. Quietly, my friend "Legol," who was also the church secretary, explained that "Peter," one of Wanga's sons, had been killed the night before in a tragic accident in which he had fallen off one of the overloaded pickup trucks that regularly clamored up the steep mountain road to Emairete. The young driver had misjudged his gears, and the truck slid backward and overturned on the boy. Would I be willing to drive with them to the morgue in Monduli to recover Peter's body for a proper burial in Emairete? I was distressed by the news, as I not only knew and liked Peter, but had grown very close to his father, Wanga, a baptized Catholic and renowned and respected *olaigunani* (customary leader) in the village (see Hodgson 2001a: 93–99).[2] I agreed to help, and the men accompanied me on the trip to Monduli. As we waited for the police to finish their paperwork, two of the men walked to a nearby store to buy a sheet in which to wrap the body. Then a local government official walked up and asked if we planned to bury Peter in a coffin. "No," replied "Legol," "the sheet will do." "How can you not bury the child in a coffin?"

responded the official, who was quite agitated. Legol apologized and eventually the official walked away. "It is tough teaching the Maasai to be Christians," Legol explained to me. "In the past they would just throw their dead into the bush, so that even convincing them to bury the dead was a big improvement." "Just yesterday," he added, "there was another death and the Maasai just wanted to leave the body with the police to dispose of. They are so scared of corpses." After the men wrapped the body in the sheet and laid it into the back of my Land Rover, we drove back up the mountain.

As we approached Wanga's homestead on the far side of the crater, I saw that a large hole had been dug in the bushes about twenty yards from the houses. About fifty *ilmurran* and junior elders were gathered at the site, and women silently peeked at me from the doorways of their homes. A discussion ensued among Legol and a few other men about whether the burial site was appropriate and what the next step should be. Most of the *ilmurran* stood by quietly, facing away from the corpse and grave, and covering their heads and mouths with their shoulder cloths.

As the men continued their discussions, an *olmurrani* walked over and told me that Wanga wished to see me. Wanga was seated on a stool outside his favorite wife's house, surrounded by several of his age-mates. He stood up when I approached, shook my hand, and thanked me profusely for helping to retrieve the corpse. I told him how sorry I was for what had happened. He explained that he had had a premonition yesterday, as his stomach felt bad and even his *oltau* was shaking. Peter had been returning from a trip to buy bean seeds for the small farm he planted to support his education. He used the profit from his harvest to purchase his uniform, books, and supplies. Wanga and I sat together quietly for a while and watched a line of schoolchildren bringing water and firewood to Peter's mother. "Don't be so sad," he advised me. "It was Eng'ai's plan, only Eng'ai knew. We all die someday, but Eng'ai is there."

After a while, Wanga told me that since Peter was baptized, he wanted him to have a Christian burial. "But Father Lobon is not here and Mwalimu Daniel has hurt his back and cannot walk here. Would you be willing to give him a ride here in your car?" I agreed, but first asked to visit Peter's mother to give my condolences. About fifteen women, including one of the local schoolteachers, were seated quietly outside her house. They had removed all of their jewelry and were dressed in dark cloths. Peter's mother sat sadly in the doorway of her home, held closely by several other women. After I told her how sorry I was, one of her co-wives served me some tea, and then I walked back to my car.

When I arrived, accompanied by Legol, at Mwalimu Daniel's homestead, Mwalimu Daniel was seated outside with two elders. After greetings, I sat down and listened to the sometimes heated exchange between Lengai and Mwalimu Daniel. Mwalimu Daniel was furious. "The whole funeral is improper! They should have a coffin for the boy! They should have sent notice to Father Lobon yesterday so that he would be here! I can't go, I really can't go. My back just hurts too much." "But it was a priest who suggested that we ask you to officiate," replied Legol. "Which priest?" asked Mwalimu Daniel. No one answered. "Just bury him as you had planned," advised Mwalimu Daniel. "But he was baptized!" pleaded Legol. Finally Mwalimu Daniel relented, but muttered that he would have to change his clothes (he was wearing several pieces of cloth and wrapped in a blanket) and get his Bible, holy water, and other things.

As Mwalimu Daniel walked off, an elder man yelled at Legol, "You shouldn't have brought the body back here! You should have just left it at the police station to be buried. Once the boy was dead, he was just dead and there was nothing else that could be done about it." Legol did not reply, but just stared sadly at the ground. After Mwalimu Daniel returned in his gray, pressed pants and a collar shirt, he told me that we had to drive to the church to pick up his vestments, Bible, and holy water. When we finally drove up to Wanga's homestead, Father Lobon arrived in his car. As I walked up to sit on the slope above the grave, Mwalimu Daniel and Father Lobon dressed in their white vestments and conferred on the order of service.

Father Lobon called everyone to gather, and sent an elder to get Wanga. Only men attended the funeral. The few women who had been peering at the grave had covered their heads and walked away when Father Lobon and I drove up. Father Lobon greeted everyone, then recited prayers for the body in Swahili, which Mwalimu Daniel translated into Maa. He blessed the grave as he poured holy water on it. Several men brought Peter's body over and placed it in the grave. He was laid on his left side, with his head facing the crater and his knees bent. Everyone present threw a fistful of dirt on him, and then several men grabbed shovels to fill the grave. They poked some branches into the dirt to mark the grave. Finally, Father Lobon borrowed a *rungu* (short stick carried by male elders) and used it to make the sign of the cross over Peter's grave. He poured some more holy water over it, and then laid some green grass on top.

241

Men of God

One major change that has occurred, in part because of the influence of the Catholic Church and other churches, is a greatly diminished respect for and use of *iloibonok*. I expected negative attitudes about *iloibonok* from Catholic Maasai, many of whom noted that the only thing that the Catholic Church forbade them to do was to consult *iloibonok*. "The *iloibonok* don't help us Christians with anything!" Or as Solomon, himself an Inkidong'i stated, "These days they are just businessmen!" But I was surprised at the prevalence of derogatory comments from non-Christian Maasai. Many men and women spoke of the *iloibonok* as cheaters and liars, who just pretended to throw stones and make medicine in order to earn money and gifts to feed themselves. "The rocks they read are just like those found in riverbeds!" snorted "Lengong," an unbaptized elder (Makaa age-set). "We call them *iloibonok*," muttered Naishepo, an unbaptized woman, "but I think that they are *setan* because they are people just like you but if they want to curse you they can steal your *oltau* and Eng'ai lets it happen. . . . If we could forget the *iloibonok*, we would forget them, but they are *setan*." Many called them sorcerers (*olasakutoni*, pl. *ilasakutok*) rather than healers. A few, such as "Koko Nanyorre," a very old unbaptized woman who was the wife and mother of *iloibonok*, were more circumspect: "They help and they don't help. My son in this homestead was an *oloiboni*. But in our homestead, we didn't have medicine for cursing (*sakut*), we only had medicine for divination, we didn't have the materials to kill a person. . . . There are many *laibons* now, many are evil, but many are good too. . . . But most of their work is cheating people; they can't save a person's *oltau*."

Moreover, only a few Maasai thought that *iloibonok* had any special relationship with Eng'ai.[3] Most noted that Eng'ai had created them and given them some unique powers, but "they have the same relationship to Eng'ai as anyone else." Eng'ai had, in fact, created everyone, bestowing unique gifts and abilities on everyone. "I think," mused Lepopo (himself a member of the Inkidong'i clan), "in the past when Eng'ai created them they were people with wisdom, but they took that wisdom given by Eng'ai to cheat people." Some Catholics thought that consulting with *iloibonok* was evidence of worshipping two gods; "I don't go to the *oloiboni*, I can't worship two gods (*enkaitin are*), only one." Others, such as Lemenye, disagreed: "[*Iloibonok*] don't help with anything. Even when they make their medicine they ask for Eng'ai's help, so they can't be Eng'ai if they are invoking Eng'ai!" For a few, such as Koko Naisandi, however, the efficacy of *iloibonok* was just a matter of faith: "*Iloibonok* help those who believe, but many don't believe these days because they have gone to school."

Several Christian women stated very frankly that they had more faith in the power of the church to heal and help them than in the *iloibonok*, in part because of the inability of *iloibonok* to cure *orpeko*. As "Nashipai," a young woman in Mti Mmoja who claimed that she "was forced to be baptized because of a sickness . . . that took over my body called *orpeko*," stated: "I saw that the church had more power to heal than the *iloibonok*. The *orpeko* never came back. I still go to church." Like other women suffering from *orpeko*, "I went to church to be cured because I saw other people going and getting cured." Similarly, Maria, the choir leader in Emairete, noted that "before the church came no one knew its importance; we only had the *iloibonok*. But when the church came we threw out the *iloibonok* and the church became our healer [here she used the Maa word *oloiboni*] that we depended on."

Everyone, Christian and non-Christian, was much kinder in their judgments of Catholic priests. Most Maasai men and women whom I interviewed recognized the imperfections of individual priests, but were reluctant to criticize them since they were "men of God." As Joseph summarized, "they all did good work, although each one had his own methods; some were nice and others were mean, but in the end they all explained matters of God." People spoke highly, however, of a few priests who they thought were particularly respectful and helpful, and criticized some others who seemed rude and disinterested. As Sarah, the educated and baptized daughter of a wealthy Inkidong'i elder, said diplomatically, although she thought that all the priests who had worked in Emairete had been fine, she wanted "true priests who follow the rules of God and help people to learn about God."

Prophets of Continuity and Change

One of the most remarkable signs of the influence of the Catholic Church among Maasai in Tanzania (or, conversely, the appeal of the church for some Maasai) was the appearance, in the early 1990s, of a Maasai prophet and Maasai prophetess whose visions from Eng'ai called for all Maasai to become Catholics.[4] Although both lived near the Ngorongoro Crater, far from the Monduli area, everyone in Emairete, Mti Mmoja, and Embopong' had heard about their messages from Eng'ai. In September 1992, I traveled with Father Ned Marchessault, an American Spiritan missionary who was based at Endulen Catholic mission in the Ngorongoro Conservation Area, to meet and interview Nailepo, the prophetess, and then Ashumu, the prophet. We were accompanied by Nailepo's sister Katasi (whom Father Marchessault had been helping in various ways) and my good friend Trish McCauley.

Nailepo lived with her parents, sister, and new baby in a homestead in Nairobi, on the edge of the Rift Valley wall overlooking Oldoinyo Leng'ai. After a long drive around Embegai Carter to the school at Nairobi, we parked the car and met Mwalimu Lengiriaa, the local catechist. After some milkless tea and white bread lathered with margarine, we filled our water bottles and set off on our journey. We walked for over an hour on a long, extremely dusty path, passing occasional homesteads, most with small gardens. Katasi walked quickly ahead to announce our arrival.

On our journey, Father Marchessault shared what he knew about Nailepo. She started having visions from Eng'ai when she lived near Loliondo with her husband. Her reputation as a prophetess grew until she had quite a large following of people who visited her to hear her revelations. She sent messages to Father Marchessault several times to ask to meet with him, but car trouble and other commitments prevented him from seeing her. She eventually left her husband and moved back to her father's homestead at Nairobi. She finally met Father Marchessault and requested instruction. Mwalimu Lengiriaa taught everyone in the homestead for two years, and then Father Marchessault baptized them in June 1992.

Nailepo was unusual in several ways. Not only was she one of the very few female Maasai prophets ever known, but by becoming pregnant she also defied customary protocols that required prophets to lead simple, celibate lives. Initially, news of her pregnancy and the eventual birth of her child harmed her reputation. In time, however, according to Father Marchessault, people began to think better of her, arguing that obviously Eng'ai had wanted Nailepo to have a child, so if the child was a gift from Eng'ai, then how could they think badly about Eng'ai's gift? Father Marchessault also thought that her recent baptism had helped her reputation. Since her baptism, Nailepo often preached at the Nairobi Catholic Church and administered the sacraments to the congregation. Father Marchessault also occasionally took Nailepo (and Ashumu) to speak at his other churches, where they were very well received. This practice contrasted with the usual customs of prophets, who rarely traveled or stayed in other homesteads. Instead, they usually waited for people to visit them in their homes or met at central locations where everyone could congregate.

As, covered with black dust from head to foot, we neared her homestead, eight women formed a group just outside the thorn gate and began singing Christian Maa songs to welcome us. After shaking hands with each of us in greeting, they led us into the homestead. Nailepo was standing inside, dressed in a black polyester gown, and wrapped by a leather shawl sewn throughout with cowry shells. I was surprised by her youth; she seemed no older than twenty. When I later took her picture (fig. 7.2), she pulled out a large necklace that had been tucked under her skin—a five-inch-square piece of leather covered with cowry shells, from which hung a large, cream-colored crucifix. After I gave Nailepo the two kilos of sugar and the biscuits that I had brought as a gift, her mother welcomed us to her house, where she served us *kule naoto* (curdled milk) and then milk tea. Before we drank, Nailepo's father said a brief prayer.

For our interview, Nailepo sat on a skin inside the cattle kraal, with Katasi seated on the skin to her right side. I sat on a log to the right of Katasi, and Mwalimu Lengiriaa (who was helping me translate because of dialectic differences) sat to Nailepo's left. Because we had no established rapport, except through our mutual relationship with Father Marchessault, Nailepo's responses were short and to the point, but still informative.

Nailepo explained that Eng'ai began to speak to her when she was still a child: "The words would come into my body at night, when I was sleeping."[5] She sensed that a presence had taken over her being: "The breath I was breathing and my body weren't my own." During these revelations, her body became very cold, and suddenly she was filled with words that came from some unknown place, the "Word of Eng'ai" (*Lororei L'Engai*). These visitations continued once she was married and moved to her new husband's homestead near Loliondo.

Eng'ai told her that many current Maasai practices were nonsense: "Maasai have no more *enkanyit*. They do not help one another and fight one another all the time." Consequently, they needed to change their lives in many ways. *Ilmurran* should stop stealing cattle and smallstock because it was a sin: "If you steal from a homestead, you leave the children crying [with hunger]." Or the sheep that was stolen may be the very one a man was preparing to slaughter for his wife who had just given birth. "Married women and ilmurran should stop sleeping together. . . . When you see someone who is hungry, give them cattle." In general, Eng'ai said that Maasai should follow the "ways of love. Like my mother who gave birth to me, which was an act of love." Moreover, Maasai needed to be educated, to go to school, and to learn Swahili.

Fig. 7.2. Nailepo, a Maasai prophetess, stands to the left of her sister Katasi (*photo right*) in the cattle kraal of her father's homestead in Nairobi. Nailepo is dressed in a black gown, covered by a black leather cape with double rows of beaded cowry shells stitched in rectangular patterns. Photo by author, 1992.

Initially, "people were very surprised. They were suspicious that I was really Eng'ai. But Eng'ai told me to share Her message without being afraid. My *oltau* directed me, and I became a prophet." Although people began to believe her and more and more came to see her, her husband was upset by her visions and status. "He beat me and even cut me with a knife because of the Word of Eng'ai," she said, showing me two scars. Eventually, Nailepo left him and returned to her father's homestead.

In time Eng'ai's message was that she and all Maasai should "accept Jesus." "So when I went to hear Father [Marchessault] preach, when I heard him from afar even before I saw him, the words he said were the very ones that I had heard [from Eng'ai]." Eng'ai then told her to prepare for baptism, and she was baptized in June 1992 after two years of instruction. "After my baptism, I was rid of satan and I was better able to tell the difference between good and evil." Around the same time as she was baptized, Nailepo gave birth to a baby. As she explained, "Eng'ai directs me to do everything, even to give birth. . . . No one tells me what I can or can't do, but the breath/ words of Eng'ai guide me. Everything that I want to do, Eng'ai wants to do." Although when I interviewed her she was still in postpartum seclusion, she felt a "strong urge" to preach the Word of Eng'ai, even if that meant leaving her child behind. "If Father [Marchessault] agrees, I'll go with him now." These days, she strongly believed that "the right path is the path of Jesus; baptism is good." "Now I follow Eng'ai while Maasai just follow stupid things and bad things like *iloibonok*."

Ashumu's visions from Eng'ai were filled with both similar and different messages. I interviewed him the next day at Endulen Catholic mission. Like Nailepo, Ashumu was quite young, and was an *olmurrani* (a Landiss) at the time. He was dressed as an *olmurrani* in a red cloth wrap, with a red blanket draped around his shoulders (fig. 7.3). His hair was cut short, but not shaved like some elders' or worn long like many *ilmurran*. Since he was waiting for us when we arrived from the long trip to Nairobi, Father Marchessault offered to show him and his brother a movie while I rested, ate, and prepared for the interview. The movie was *The Life of Christ*, which was filmed among Maasai in Tanzania a few years ago by a German Spiritan father and later dubbed in Maa. Ashumu had been pestering Father Marchessault to see it, and Father Marchessault had just received a copy.

According to Father Marchessault, Ashumu was a well-known prophet. He received delegations (*olamal*, pl. *ilamal*) from Kiteto, Loliondo, and all Maasai areas. Many of the *ilamal* were made up of women who came singing and bearing gifts. In return, Ashumu would pray for them and bless them.

247

Fig. 7.3. Ashumu, a Maasai prophet, stands to the left of his brother (*photo right*), with his eyes looking down. Photo by author, 1992.

Father Marchessault thought that Ashumu and Nailepo were liked and respected not only for their visions, but for their extremely gentle and humble personalities. Father Marchessault first met Ashumu when he appeared in church a few years ago. The next time Ashumu came to church, Father Marchessault asked him to preach. Ashumu requested catechetical instruction, which he followed, and he was baptized in 1990. These days, according to Father Marchessault, when people came to Ashumu seeking help, he often told them to go to church.

In contrast to Nailepo, Ashumu gave long, detailed answers to most of my questions.[6] His first vision from Eng'ai came when he was an *olmurran*. One day, as he was going to an *olpul* (an extended meat-eating feast held by *ilmurran* and their *intoyie* girlfriends), he felt a "cold wind" in his body, even though it was a warm day. At the same time, the cattle they were herding became sick, and starting peeing everywhere. "I felt trouble in my *oltau*." He went to confer with an *oloiboni*, who was his friend, about his illness and the sick cattle. After throwing stones to divine the cause of the problem, "he told me my cattle were cursed, . . . and I was cursed. . . . He gave me some medicine. When I returned to the cattle, many had been slaughtered and people were eating the meat. I didn't eat anything; my stomach hurt, and I felt dizzy." After falling down twice, he began trembling and shaking fiercely, and everyone ran away. Some friends took him and washed his body with water, but it did not help. "I couldn't talk; I felt crazy." His friends gave him medicine, then *mori* (an herbal soup drunk by *ilmurran* as a purgative), and poured more water over his head, but nothing helped.

As his friends discussed taking him to the hospital in Moshi, Ashumu suddenly felt very tired, as though he needed to sleep:

> I wanted to sleep in my bed. Then everything felt very dark (*enaimin enaimin*). I was like a person who walks from the bright outdoors into a dark house. Then everything changed as if I was dreaming. I entered a land of shining light (*enkop naong*). There was a sea of water that shimmered so brightly, as if the sun and the water were one, that it hurt my eyes. That was Eng'ai. She greeted me: "You have come to visit my land today? Do you wish to stay?" I replied that I did not want to stay in a land without trees or people. "But this is the land of the people of Jesus who have no sins. When they died they came here. They have shimmering clothes, clothes like the sea, and they are very tall. Look how it rains here." And suddenly there was a tremendous downpour.[7]

More miraculous visions followed, and then Ashumu woke up. He told the woman in whose house he was staying about his visions, and asked her to tell his friend to prevent it from raining that day or Ashumu would die. "*Oi Enkiteng' Esupat*" (O Great Cow), she replied, "he has been cursed."

> Suddenly it started to rain, and it became very dark, just as it had before my vision. I don't know if anyone else saw it; I think that only I did. The woman was busy cleaning her calabashes. Eng'ai had shaken my *oltau*. Eng'ai returned and asked more questions, including: "Why aren't you following the words and example of Jesus?" I saw all of this while I was sleeping and my body was shaking.

Once he woke up he felt fine, like a normal person—"no shaking, no craziness."

At first, according to Ashumu, he wanted to keep these visions a secret. "But Eng'ai told me I had to share the revelations. She told me to slaughter a bull. People would come and I should share the meat with them." Eng'ai told him to hold the feast at a place called Olomuratii, where some *iloibonok* used to live. "So we moved, held the feast, and a delegation (*olamal*) came to visit. And then more words came to me."

In time, Ashumu became accustomed to these visions, which always began with the sense that Eng'ai's breath (*enkiyang'et*) had come inside him. "When the breath of lightness that was Eng'ai came inside me, I was no longer afraid." Eng'ai's message often focused on Jesus: "Tell people that Jesus will come and tell people about the church. Tell them that Jesus will come to Maasailand. They should accept and follow him." Despite (or because of these visions), Ashumu began to feel troubled: "In my *oltau*, I knew that something was not right, that I had not followed Eng'ai's words. I was not happy, I didn't feel well, I did not have a good life."

"Is that why you were baptized?" I asked.

"Yes, the breath came and told me to get baptized," he replied.

> Eng'ai said, "Many have accepted me. You will lead them until you have been baptized. If you decide to be baptized, you will be in Jesus' hands." And it was as Eng'ai said. . . . A man called Olonyokie came, then [Father Marchessault] visited our homestead. Eventually we were baptized. We understood that these were the people that Eng'ai had told us about. . . . When they came, we knew they would come. We knew they were people of God [*iltunganak l'Eng'ai*].

In response to a series of questions about the similarities and differences he saw between Maasai and Catholic religious beliefs and practices, Ashumu replied that they were very similar. "Eng'ai is the God of everyone. She never said I am the God of the church or I am the God of the Maasai. She just talked about Jesus." There were some problems with Maasai these days, he explained: "They no longer get along . . . they don't love one another." When I asked if he planned to remain unmarried and celibate, he responded that he had never heard that there were any prohibitions against sex or marriage for prophets. "No one told me that I couldn't marry. . . . If you don't then you have a cold house. It is far better to stay together with someone." Like Nailepo, he believed that all Maasai should go to school. Even though he had never attended, he planned to educate all of his children, both boys and girls.

Toward the end of the interview, I asked him if he had any questions for me. "Yes," he said, "I have a problem and I would like your advice." About two months ago, a group of *Walokole* (the Swahili word for "saved one," that is, Pentecostals) visited him. "They told me to leave the bed of darkness for the bed of light." Among other things, they told him that his visions and prophecies were from satan and he should quit sharing them. Moreover, the sheepskin that he was wearing and the stick that he carried were also satanic. To save himself, he should get rid of the skins and stick and wear cloth. "I did what they said because I had accepted the church. But I have felt terrible ever since. And the breath of Eng'ai has not spoken to me since then either. My *oltau* told me to wear sheepskins, but the Walokole told me not too. They said that they were teaching the truth."

He was clearly very upset and confused by the loss of his powers and the accusation of the Walokole that he was spreading the message of satan, not Eng'ai. "Have you discussed this with Father Marchessault?" I asked. "No, he is always so busy that we don't have time to talk." I suggested that since our interview was almost over, I could briefly explain the problem to Father Marchessault, and perhaps he could talk to Ashumu that afternoon. Ashumu agreed and he and Father Marchessault had a long private talk. Afterward, Father Marchessault said that he planned to call a meeting of the council of Maasai elders to discuss the problem. He said that he told Ashumu that it was odd: here Ashumu was preaching to Maasai not to give up their traditions, yet he was willing to give up the traditional attire of a prophet? He said that he also told Ashumu that most people were not happy at times during their lives, especially Jesus.

Of One in the Spirit?

And so the borders between the church of the Catholics and the church of Maasai, between "culture" and "religion," were often blurred and sometimes contested. But the melding of practices and beliefs was not smooth, universal, or fixed. Rather, like all "religions," it was a dynamic process that was, and will continue to be, always in the making, shaping and shaped by changing social, political, and economic dynamics.

Perhaps understandably, Maasai experienced more ambivalence in choosing to *change* certain practices (such as those surrounding death and the treatment of corpses) than in merely *adding* new practices (such as collective prayers in churches) to their repertoire. Christian funerary and burial practices revealed the changes and continuities in Maasai life, and signaled the ongoing challenges to the production of Maasai Catholicism. When elder Catholic men such as Wanga insisted on burying their children in the ground according to Christian protocols, they met with a range of reactions, from support to disbelief to disapproval from their families and neighbors. Moreover, some fellow Christians felt that their efforts were not quite good enough—no wooden coffin, no timely notice to the priest, no clear sense of the appropriate procedures.

Peter's funeral also showed the enduring salience of certain patterns of gendered associations and practices: Maasai women, as the embodiment of Eng'ai's powers of fertility and reproduction, avoided any direct involvement in the funeral. Their avoidance of any association with death was marked not just socially, but also spatially in the distance that they kept from the body and grave. Instead, their responsibilities lay with Peter's mother, in collectively supporting her in her grief, mourning, and eventual healing. Their collective concern and care for her was similar in many ways to how I had seen groups of women care for and heal women suffering from *orpeko*.

The visions and conversions of the Maasai prophets, Nailepo and Ashumu, perhaps most clearly troubled and challenged any "boundaries" between Maasai religion and Catholicism. Building on a long history of prophets, they channeled messages from Eng'ai about the state of the present and the hope for the future. Maasai in the present had changed; they did not get along, they were no longer respectful, they did not love one another. Yet the future that Nailepo and Ashumu prophesied to remedy this situation incorporated seemingly contradictory continuities and changes: Maasai should return to their "traditional" ways of love and respect, but they should also go to school, convert to Catholicism, and follow the ways of Jesus. The implication, of course, is that the ways of Jesus were one and the same with the "traditional" ways of Maasai, a message that at once reinforced and undermined the assumptions and objectives of inculturation: If Maasai were already living (or had once lived) a Christian life, why the need to formally convert to Catholicism? Moreover, by supporting, sanctioning, and even encouraging Nailepo and Ashumu to preach during church services, Father Marchessault conferred a legitimacy on them as both Maasai prophets and Christian prophets that collapsed the two prophetic traditions into one: Were Ashumu and Nailepo just the most recent prophets from a lineage that began long ago in Jerusalem? Ashumu's encounter with a group of Pentecostals who denounced him, his prophecies, and his dress as satanic starkly illustrates how the precepts and practices of Catholic inculturation could be viewed as heresies by other Christian denominations.

Against Inculturation

Not all Maasai, however, supported inculturation and the continuity of Maasai ritual practices. In recent years, there have been struggles among Maasai Catholics over inculturation and the boundaries between Maasai culture and Maasai religion (much less Catholic culture and Catholic religion). Some Catholics, especially educated, younger men, criticized the Catholic Church for embracing and promoting Maasai customs; they desired neat boundaries between "being a Maasai" and "being a Christian." They wanted a more standard service, strict observance of Catholic teachings (including monogamy), and less incorporation of what they saw as outdated customs, traditions, and symbols. Many of these men were sensitive to critiques by Lutherans and Pentecostals that the Catholic Church promoted "pagan" (and even "satanic") practices. In Emairete, the tension between those who appreciated the "Maasai" church and those who wanted a more "modern" church was played out in ongoing critiques of and disputes between the two catechists. Mwalimu Daniel was a member of an older generation and a central figure in the development, practice, and promotion of inculturation. As a result, in recent years he had been accused by some younger, educated men of being a hypocrite because he participated in customary ceremonies, had more than one wife, and even, it was rumored, consulted with *iloibonok* on occasion. Mwalimu Francis, in contrast, was very critical of inculturation (for which there is now a Swahili word: *utamadunisho*). He thought that it "brought problems":

> *Wazungu* (whites) want to learn the history of Maasai from long ago. But if they bring those beliefs to believers, then there seems to be no difference [between Maasai religion and Christianity]. The practices that we left behind are reinstated. This creates problems between believers and non-believers, because believers thought they'd left those customs behind. But now we have turned back. So those non-believers think that Christianity is just like their faith.

He noted three practices that he found particularly disturbing. The first was the use of the white chalk "that *iloibonok* use" in services, because of its "associations with witchcraft." The second was the use of milk and honey beer, "especially honey beer because drunkenness is such a problem here." Finally, he disliked the use of cowskins, as they were also associated with *iloibonok*. Christians, he concluded, "say that we have returned to our pagan ways." Thus, although inculturation practices were responsible, in part, for the large number of converts to Catholicism (as opposed to the less tolerant attitudes of the Lutherans), they have also fostered, among parishioners (and between them and their catechists), fierce debates and even divisions about culture, religion, and tolerance that were deeply intertwined with issues of modernity and social change.

In contrast, some men who had been ardent supporters of the Catholic Church have now decided that the church has not done enough to incorporate and respect Maasai religious and cultural practices and beliefs. Steven, for example, the former catechist who once spoke of himself as a "very, very dedicated Catholic" when he was a young man (chapter 5), has become increasingly disenchanted with the Catholic Church because of what he perceives as its dismissive attitude toward Maasai culture. He has, in fact, left the church altogether. Now he just prays in his house and has rediscovered and reinvigorated his knowledge and practice of Maasai cultural and religious ways: "I go by what the Maasai culture says, go strongly into that now. . . . I am a Maasai, it is my culture; you may not like it, but that is the way it is."

He is not alone in his growing distance from the Catholic Church. Other educated Maasai men with similar backgrounds have now left the church, especially those who have become involved in the indigenous rights movement and have embraced a much more politicized concept of culture and cultural change (Hodgson 1999e, 2001a, 2002). Although many owed their education to Christian missionaries, they simultaneously blamed them for disparaging and changing their "culture" either directly through preaching against certain practices and beliefs or indirectly through their support of modernization through education. The prevalence of this attitude was clear at an important conference I attended in 1991, the First Maasai Conference on Culture and Development.[8] The organizers insisted that no missionaries would be allowed to attend, except Father Hillman, who submitted a paper on the "pauperization" of the Maasai in Kenya (Hillman 1991, later revised and published as Hillman 1994b). Other Maasai have made symbolic changes to note their disaffection, most notably by rejecting their Christian baptismal names and reinstating their Maasai names.

These contemporary debates about inculturation among some Maasai Catholics, especially educated Maasai men, point to some of the tensions described previously: Is inculturation perhaps just a form of colonial "cultural preservation," a strategy to keep Maasai "traditional" in a world of rapid modernization? Or is it an insidious way to subtly and slowly introduce cultural and religious changes that ultimately (and intentionally) undermine customary Maasai practices and beliefs?

Perhaps most importantly for the arguments of this book, why are the merits, problems, and assumptions of inculturation argued about primarily if not solely by Maasai men, and not women? Is this just another instance of the culturally recognized "flexibility" of Maasai women and "hard-headedness" of Maasai men? Or does it point to their differential engagement with and experience of the church, a relationship not just shaped by gender but inflected by class as well? If, as I have argued, most Maasai women (and some uneducated men) were drawn to the spirit and teachings of the Catholic Church, while most educated Maasai men were attracted to its structure and modernist associations, then these categories of congregants already had distinct perspectives on Maasai culture and therefore inculturation. The Catholic Church's calculated acceptance and incorporation of Maasai religious and cultural practices both inside and outside the church minimized any distinctions between "Catholic culture" and "Maasai culture." As a result, most Maasai women saw few obstacles to adopting Christian practices (such as collective, regular prayer in a common space) in order to expand their spiritual repertoire. But for educated men who identified "being Catholic" with "being modern," the insistent presentation of Christian beliefs in Maasai cultural forms was perceived as at best patronizing, and at worst insulting. Still other educated men, armed with an increasingly politicized sense of Maasai cultural identity in the face of enduring cultural disparagement, social hostility, and economic and political disenfranchisement by first colonial powers and now postcolonial elites, thought that the Catholic Church had not done enough to respect and reinforce Maasai cultural practices. Ironically, the views of these educated men echoed those of the many uneducated Maasai men, young and old, who had avoided any involvement with the Catholic Church precisely because they thought it challenged and would therefore change their "culture." These debates about the merits of inculturation point to the ongoing dynamism of the relationship between missionaries and Maasai, one in which deliberations and disagreements about the very definition of "culture" are central.

If one product of these encounters is in fact something we might call "Maasai Catholicism," it is crucial to understand that both terms of the phrase are historically contingent and temporally particular. The dominant meanings and manifestations of "being Maasai" and "being Catholic" in everyday life have changed and will continue to change, in part through their ongoing juxtaposition with one another, but also because of the continuing prosaic and poetic struggles of men and women, believers and non-believers, missionaries and catechists, to define the terms and outcomes of the encounter. Although religious change and conversion are always processes of becoming, they are neither linear nor unidirectional. As the case of Steven, once a fierce believer in the Catholic faith and now an equally strong advocate of Maasai rituals, suggests, people's religious practices and beliefs may change over time, belying any static notion of "syncretism" (cf. Taylor 1996; Werbner 1997).[9]

CONCLUSION

From the perspective of the Spiritan missionaries, their evangelization efforts among Maasai in Tanzania have been a legacy of frustration, even failure: from schools to *bomas* to individuals, they concentrated their efforts on attracting and converting men, but ended up mainly converting women. Insisting on a vision of community, whether as a *boma* or as a village, that included both men and women, they found themselves teaching and ministering to a community of women. Trying to develop male leadership among Maasai, they were dismayed to find women emerging as leaders. And seeking to enforce the power of elder men, they inadvertently subverted their power by providing an outlet for women to escape their control.

Incorporating gender into our analysis of this missionary tale of "frustration" and "failure" enables us to understand and explain this paradoxical outcome in a different manner. Catholic evangelization, baptism, and creation of churches provided fresh sites for the ongoing contestation and production of Maasai gender relations, including struggles over the gendered meanings of authority, morality, and ethnic identity. At a time when Maasai men, despite their differences, were consolidating their political-economic power, Catholicism offered them few attractions. Conversion was perceived as a rupture and threat to the dominant ideology of "being Maasai men," and male converts were disparaged as *ormeek*, as non-Maasai "others." Although the school and individual approaches allowed men to ignore missionary interventions, the *boma* approach brought the Catholic message and messengers into their homesteads. Unwilling to directly prohibit missionary activity, men expressed their disinterest through avoidance and absence.

In contrast, missionary interventions complemented and expanded the spiritual dimension of female roles in Maasailand. By providing women with an expanded spiritual platform from which to launch their critiques of men, they enabled women to reaffirm and reinforce their claims to spiritual and moral superiority in opposition to the increasingly material interests of men. Once first the *boma* approach then the individual approach enabled women to participate, they responded eagerly and persistently to these new opportunities for spiritual engagement and female fellowship. Conversion enhanced their already substantial spiritual practice by offering new forms of spiritual expression and healing. By rejecting the authority of the *iloibonok* and assuming the powers of healing for themselves and Christian missionaries, women challenged male assertions of power and authority.

Although conversion can be understood as the product of a convergence of cultural, historical, and political-economic factors, this book demonstrates that it is crucial to integrate the mediating role of social factors such as gender (or race, class, ethnicity) into the analysis. We can no longer assume that the experience of men—whether of missionization, conversion, or faith—represents the normative or "generic" model. Instead, following Peterson (2001: 489), we must explore how conversion can serve as a "grammar of ethnic and gendered debate." In the Maasai case, incorporating gender into theories of conversion enables a richer understanding of the conversion process, attuned to the complicated intersections of expressive as well as instrumental concerns that were simultaneously constrained and enabled by historical events and processes, including the directives of Vatican II, colonial and postcolonial state policies, forced villagization, ethnic ideologies and images of "being Maasai," and the gender, age, and residence restrictions implicit in the school and *boma* approaches. Conversion entailed different motivations as well as different meanings for men and women. In turn, these gendered motivations and meanings shaped the shifting contours of the missionary encounter and produced the seemingly paradoxical outcome. In seeking to possess the power of the spirit, Maasai women displayed their own powers and spirit, to the reluctant acquiescence of Maasai men and the astonished dismay of Spiritan missionaries.

Perspectives

So how does this study contribute to the study of gender, power, and mission? Clearly we must begin to rethink and rewrite studies of gender that ignore issues of spirituality and religious practice and belief. Gender ideologies, relations, and practices encompass and express a range of power relations among and between men and women that go beyond just the economic, political, and social. As the Maasai case demonstrates, attention to the spiritual aspects of those relations can complicate any easy understanding of gender inequality. Moreover, spiritual beliefs and practices may be central to the production, reproduction, transformation, and negotiation of gendered identities, of masculinities and femininities. As such, they can then serve as a site of struggle or sustenance. This is not, however, a call for ungrounded accounts of some supposed "universalized female spiritual essence" (Shaw 1995: 74), but for careful, empirical studies that probe and problematize these possibilities.

Such an approach has significant implications for rethinking dominant ideas about the forms and nature of power. Feminist anthropologists and others have long challenged normative Western assumptions about power, such as the assumed superiority of the public domain over the domestic (including the very composition and creation of these two domains), of formal over informal leadership, and of the "status" of so-called First World women over Third World women. Yet these debates, like most analyses of gender, still revolve around the economic, political, and social dimensions of people's lives. What happens, then, when we add spiritual power into this mix? For Maasai women, their unique, gender-based spiritual connection to Eng'ai was central to their sense of identity as Maasai, as women, and, eventually, as Catholics. It was also a domain of their lives where they experienced and expressed significant power—the power of procreation, of responsibility for mediating between Eng'ai and humans, and of upholding the moral order. Moreover, all this occurred in a historical context where they had lost substantial economic and political rights and autonomy . . . to men. At the same time that women resisted and protested the increasing secularization of their everyday world, they retained and strengthened their connections to the sacred. They also struggled to defend their vision of the moral order, a vision premised on gender complementarity, mutual respect, and the fusing of sacred and secular.

These perspectives on gender and power also provide new insights into the study of mission and its components—evangelization, instruction, baptism and other sacraments, liturgy, worship, and leadership. Gender was central to all of these arenas, in terms of the assumptions, ideas, and practices of missionaries, catechists, and Maasai men and women. Moreover, although spirituality and religion were most salient to the encounter between Spiritan missionaries and Maasai, they were intimately intertwined with and shaped by political, economic, and social relations of power between and among Spiritans, Maasai, and other actors, such as neighboring Chagga and Tanzanian elites. These gendered encounters were dynamic sites of change and struggle, as all involved influenced, and were influenced by, their involvement in the creation of local churches.

Despite these insights, however, it would be foolish to reduce the religious experiences and encounters of men and women to mere power struggles among themselves or with other political entities such as the colonial and postcolonial state (cf. Ranger 1986). As many of the accounts in the book attest, Maasai men and especially Maasai women were attracted to the church because of their faith. Faith, like morality and spirituality, is not inherently political, but may become politicized in a context of change and challenge. Although the *effect* of the conversion of so many women to Christianity was to challenge and perhaps rework gender relations, it is not clear at all that this was their intention. The centrality of *orpeko* and *oltau* to their narratives of conversion further complicates any easy attribution of intention or agency. Morality and spirituality may have served, at times, as sites for the exertion and expression of power and authority, but neither is simply reducible to power (cf. Lambek 2000). Like all purely instrumental perspectives, such a narrow, impoverished view of human experience ignores the complicated, layered meanings, practices, and contexts that shape and are shaped by human interactions.

Finally, the particular configuration of gender and power relations in missionary encounters is historically contingent and ever changing. Most of the men and women whom I interviewed for this book were among the first generations of converts. The comparisons among Maasai in Emairete, Mti Mmoja, and Embopong' suggest that the appeal of the church, the reasons for conversion, and the perspectives of men and women will change over time, especially as the church becomes more established and being a Christian becomes more the norm than the exception. Thus, while the gendered differences in the meaning and practice of conversion seemed especially stark during the period covered by this book, this may well change with shifting concerns and contexts.

Futures

This book has described the first fifty years of the encounter between Maasai and Spiritan missionaries in Tanzania, but the encounter continues. What lies ahead for the "church of women"? Will women retain their control of the church? Will the collective power and vision women have discovered in the church serve as a platform for future organizing, protest, and action?

Or will the gendered nature and form of interest and participation change as more and more children, girls and boys, are educated, become *ormeek*, and are either baptized by their parents or choose to be baptized themselves? (The statistics in 1992 from Emairete suggest an increasing gender parity at least in the baptism of future generations, but such numbers say little about who will remain active in the church as adults.) If so, will women seek alternate venues for or modes of healing?

What of the future of inculturation as an approach? Will it fade away with the decline of expatriate mission priests? Or will Maasai priests embrace and rework it as their own, to form a different kind of Maasai Catholic Church? What will be the role of Maasai catechists in such debates? Although they valiantly continue their work, often under dire circumstances, their demands for increased recognition and resources have become more vocal in recent years. Will the new female Maasai catechists change the nature of these discussions, and even the content and form of instruction and pastoral care?

These are just some of the many questions and challenges that lie ahead for the Maasai church. I have been fortunate enough to witness the past twenty years of its formation, to know many of the Maasai, missionaries, catechists, and others involved, and to study the previous history. Now I, like others, am curious to see its future.

Notes

Introduction

1. The topics of missionization, conversion, and religious change have long intrigued anthropologists and historians studying Africa. For key overviews of this work, see Barrett (1968), Beidelman (1974), Blakeley et al. (1994), Hastings (1967, 1976, 1979, 1994), Horton (1967, 1975a, 1975b), Isichei (1995), Shorter (1978), Strayer (1975, 1978), Spear (1999), and Spear and Kimambo (1999).

2. These recent contributions include Grosz-Ngate and Kokole (1997), Hodgson (2000b, 2001a, 2001b), Hodgson and McCurdy (2001), and Lindsay and Miescher (2003).

3. This is a vast literature. See, for example, Atkinson et al. (1985), Holden (1983), King (1995), Sered (1992, 1994, 1999), and Swatos (1994). For Africa, see Berger (1995), Burton (1991), Hackett (1985, 1987, 1995), and Jell-Bahlsen (1998).

4. For general models and theories of conversion, see Hefner (1993), Rambo (1982, 1993), and Tippett (1977). Studies of conversion in Africa that ignore or downplay gender include Butselaar (1981), Carmody (1988, 1989), Comaroff and Comaroff (1991), Horton (1967, 1975a, 1975b), Isichei (1970), Kaplan (1985), and Rounds (1982). Gender (and other social differences) are considered by Gabbert (2001), Green (2003), and Peel (2000).

5. In an endnote, Rambo mentions several recent studies that do consider women's experiences, including Brereton (1991), Davidman (1991), and Juster (1989), none of which explores the issue in the context of missionary settings.

6. Isichei, for example, argues that "in societies where resources and power were controlled by older men, women, like the young, had less to lose by change" (1995: 239; cf. Comaroff 1985: 150). Furthermore, women were "empowered by church support" to reject unacceptable marriages, pray for help from infertility and sickness, and seek protection from witches (Isichei 1995: 240). In "Were Women a Special Case?" Hastings argues that churches, whether mainstream or independent, appealed to women because they offered "specifically female freedoms" surrounding issues of childbirth, marriage, and autonomy (Hastings 1993: 122). Similarly, Paul Landau contends that women's greater participation in Christian churches throughout southern Africa was "a means of self-protection and mobilization; it re-gendered, and encroached upon the public, social sphere of human activity" (1995: 109).

7. Neckebrouck (1993, 2002) reviews these diverse explanations of Maasai "cultural conservatism" and alleged resistance to Christian evangelization.

8. For anthropological and historical studies of Christian and Islamic evangeliza-

tion among other East African pastoralists, see Aguilar (1995), Burton (1985), Fratkin (1991), and Lienhardt (1982). For missionary perspectives on Maasai evangelization, see Donovan (1967, 1978), Kiel (1997), Klobuchar (1998), Mtaita (1998), and Priest (1990).

9. Where possible, I use the accepted spelling "Maasai," although "Masai" is retained when used in the original sources and titles.

10. This history is recounted in great detail in Hodgson (2001a), especially chapters 1–3. Primary sources include Baumann (1894), Hinde and Hinde (1901), Hollis (1905, 1910, 1943), and Merker (1910 [1904]).

11. Much of the debate is about the relative roles of language, livelihood, social institutions, cultural practices, political systems, and so forth in defining an "ethnic group." As with all ethnic groups, however, Maasai identity is historical (its meaning, referents, and constituents change over time), relational (defined in part through contrast to other groups), and contextual (claims to being "Maasai" vary according to situation, historical moment, and political-economic context). My designation of people as Maasai is based on their representation as such in historical documents and, in the contemporary period, on their self-identification as Maasai. See Hodgson (2001a: 167–171) for more discussion on this, especially as to the relationship between "Maasai" and "Arusha."

12. I draw on the following important sources for this early history: Bernsten (1976, 1979a, 1979b, 1980), Galaty (1993a), Sommer and Vossen (1993), Sutton (1990, 1993), and Waller (1978, 1985a, 1985b, 1988).

13. The names of clans and sub-clans varied by place, historical moment, and section. Also, Maasai often used the terms *inkishomi* and *ilgilat* interchangeably. For lists of names recorded in the late nineteenth century, see Hollis (1905: 260–261), and Merker (1910 [1904]: 16–18). See Mol (1996: 20–21) for a historical chart that shows the mythical birth order of the clans.

14. There have been numerous efforts to reconstruct the names and initiation periods of male age-sets. See, for example, Bernsten (1979a: 83–93), Fosbrooke (1948), Hollis (1905: 262–263), Jacobs (1968), Mol (1977: 17–18). Spencer (1976, 1988) offers some of the most rich and interesting, if ahistorical, analyses of the functions and meanings of male age sets.

15. See Hollis (1905: 260–261) and Merker (1910 [1904]: 16–18) for a list of section names. Kisongo Maasai are the largest section in Tanzania, and the focus of my contemporary ethnographic research.

16. See Hodgson (2001a), Koponen (1996, esp. 24–25), and Waller (1988) for more detailed discussions of these crises and their effects on Maasai society and livelihoods.

17. Officially, Tanganyika was a protectorate, not a colony, and the British were only caring for it under a Permanent Mandate granted by the League of Nations, not ruling it for their own self-interest. Unofficially, this distinction made little difference, except perhaps, as some have argued, to minimize British interest in developing social services and commercial infrastructures.

18. Several Lutheran "bush" primary schools were established in the early 1930s, and a Native Authority–financed primary school was opened in 1937 in Monduli, the district headquarters of Masai District (Hodgson 2001a).

19. Administrators specified that one "educated" Maasai from each area had to be appointed to the MFC, "a step which it is hoped will enable the council to keep abreast of new developments" (Northern Province Annual Report 1954: 85).

20. These measures were sanctioned, in part, by the recommendations of the Report of the Arusha-Moshi Land Commission (1947), more familiarly know as "The Wilson

Report." For a more detailed account of the post–World War II period, see Hodgson (2000a, 2001a).

21. The following is a summary of findings that are documented in detail in Hodgson (1999a, 2000a, 2001a).

22. Examples of such rulings include the codification of "traditional" Maasai customs for marriage, bridewealth, and divorce; an agreement to shorten the period of "warriorhood" to three years; and attempts to force *ilmurran* to clear tsetse-infested bush. See, for example, Tanzania National Archives (TNA)/17/250/2/5, Sheria za Ndoa (Marriage Laws), 20 July 1950; TNA 17/250/1/7, Masai Custom to Be Followed in the Hearing of Cases, 1950; and, generally, Memoranda of the Olkiama meetings in TNA/471/949 and Arusha Branch of the TNA (ATNA)/284/II.

23. This brief overview of complicated social changes should not be interpreted as romanticizing the "traditional" past or demonizing the present, but as a summary of the marked historical shift from complementarity to hierarchy as the dominant principle of Maasai gender relations.

24. Goody (1961) offered an interesting earlier discussion. Important recent contributions to these debates include Asad (1993 [1982]), Brenner (1989), Lambek (2002), and Landau (1999).

1. "Oh She Who Brings the Rain"

1. This story is compiled from a version written by Alais ole Morindat and those reported to me by several informants. Alais first told me about Kunguru, and I asked subsequent interviewees in 2000 about her story (I had already completed many of the interviews). I have found no mention of this story in other published sources.

2. The problems of evidence in historical studies of precolonial African religions are discussed in Baum (1999) and Ranger and Kimambo (1972).

3. Hollis relied on Justin Ol-omeni (also known as Lemenye), a baptized man who was born a Parakuyo but raised by a Maasai family after he was captured in a raid (Fosbrooke 1955 and 1956).

4. For example, Baumann (1894) read Thomson (1968 [1885]) and Hollis read Merker (1910 [1904]), Baumann (1894), and other earlier sources.

5. Thus, although Merker (1910 [1904]) offers important early ethnographic glimpses of Maasai gender relations and religious practice, his explication of Maasai religion is deeply influenced by Christian categories and precepts—such as guardian angels, heaven, paradise, hell, and so forth—that neither I nor other scholars or missionaries have ever heard Maasai speak of.

6. Jan Voshaar is a former Catholic missionary priest from The Netherlands who worked primarily among Maasai in Kenya—from 1962 to 1966 in Kilgoris and 1969 to 1974 in Loita, with a study visit in 1977–1978 with Kisongo Maasai in Emairete (Voshaar 1998a: 16). Voshaar was transformed by his work with Maasai, so much so that he left the priesthood, researched and wrote a Ph.D. thesis (or "Doctorale Scriptie") (Voshaar 1979) analyzing Maasai religious thought and practices, and then revised and expanded his thesis into a book (Voshaar 1998a) that is in part a vehement defense of the spirituality and morality of Maasai religion and an attack on most missionary assumptions and practices.

7. The work of Tord Olsson (1977, 1989), for example, while fascinating, is very generic and essentializing. He provides no sense of which section or community of Maasai

he is talking about or where, when, or how he collected his information. Although I wrote and emailed him to inquire as to these details, he never responded.

8. To minimize confusion, especially in later chapters that discuss the similarities and differences between Eng'ai and God, I will try to use "Eng'ai" when referring to the Maasai deity, and "God" when referring to the Christian God. I will, however, retain "God" when it is used in the excerpts or comments of others to refer to Eng'ai.

9. Based on his studies of Atuot, Dinka, and Nuer in southern Sudan, Burton (1982, 1991) argues for the centrality of female principles to all Nilotic religions.

10. For a fascinating discussion of the relationship between Maasai concepts of time and space, see Rigby (1983).

11. Like many Maa words, *Eng'ai* has several accepted spellings, including *Ng'ai*, *Nkai*, and *Enkai*.

12. Others who argue that Eng'ai is predominantly a female deity include Voshaar (1998a: 130–143) and Hillman (1993: 51–53). Many early reports also described Eng'ai as female, including Baumann (1894: 163), Eliot (1905: xviii, 1966 [1905]: 140), and Johnston (1886: 417, 1902: 830).

13. I purposefully avoid using "heaven" in my discussion of Maasai religion because of its Christian associations.

14. Nonetheless, some Christian authors and other scholars insisted on calling Eng'ai "He" (e.g., Bernsten 1979a: 113; Merker 1910 [1904]: 204). Benson (1974: 81), drawing on Mpaayie, claims that in the case of the word Eng'ai, the feminine "En" denotes an abstract noun, and should not be perceived as implying that Eng'ai is feminine. But the predominance of female metaphors and forms of address for Eng'ai suggests otherwise.

15. This myth is also a rationale for why Maasai have and love cattle (and, according to some, e.g., Krapf 1968 [1860]: 359, believe that stealing cattle from others is fine since Eng'ai gave all cattle to Maasai and Dorobo are destined to be hunter-gatherers).

16. See, for example, Eliot (1966 [1905]: 140–141), Kipuri (1983: 29–30), Merker (1910 [1904]: 205–206), and Mol (1996: 3–4). Other missionaries and scholars, however, claim to have never heard of such a distinction (Voshaar 1998a: 131; EH/28 [Interview with Father Eugene Hillman, C.S.Sp., on February 12, 2000, in Sarasota, Florida. References to the interview transcript are abbreviated as EH/page number]). Most of my Maasai informants mentioned the distinction, but it is hard to determine if this was learned from their oral traditions or missionary teachings.

17. Johnston (1902: 830–831) told a long origin story about four deities that ruled the world—one black ("full of kindness towards humanity"), another white (called Eng'ai, who held himself aloof, but was in fact, god or goddess of the Great Firmament), a gray god (who was "wholly indifferent to the welfare of humanity"), and a red god ("who was thoroughly bad") (see also Hinde and Hinde 1901: 99–100). After the birth of the first Maasai, the gods quarreled and most died, leaving the white god, Eng'ai (the black god died after founding the ruling family of *iloibonok*).

18. Other stories of Naiterukop appear in Hollis (1905: 270, 1943: 122), Johnston (1886: 418), and Thomson (1968 [1885]: 260). Johnston (1886: 418) acknowledged that Naiterukop was female.

19. This may be the same figure that Krapf (1968 [1860]: 360) calls "Njemasi Enauner," who was married to a woman named Samba. Through the "intercession" of Eng'ai, Samba gave birth to a number of children, "the progenitors of Wakuafi and Maasai." Krapf makes no mention, however, of Njemasi being hairy or a half-beast.

Merker (1910 [1904]: 210) claimed that Nenauner was "a male demon . . . whose body is as hard as stone, and therefore invulnerable, who had the head of a beast of prey, and whose feet are armed with claws. He lurks by the paths and calls passers-by by their names that he may then tear in pieces and devour all who come up to him." See also Chanel (1900: 172) and Hurskainen (1990: 69).

20. For examples, see French-Sheldon (1892: 380, 383), Hinde and Hinde (1901: 103–104), Hollis (1905: 288–290), Merker (1910 [1904]: 102, 124), and Thomson (1968 [1885]: 260).

21. Some of these practices may have been learned from neighboring, conquered, or incorporated groups, including the Tatoga, who had a custom of "tying grass" for ritual protection against Maasai raids (Bernsten 1979a: 31).

22. My analysis here challenges that of Århem (1990), who ignores and devalues the sacred roles and powers of Maasai women. According to him, milk was only "ordinary" food as compared to the "extraordinary" food of roasted meat that was associated with men, the public realm, and major rituals. See also Talle (1990).

23. For examples, see Chanel (1900: 165–166), French-Sheldon (1892: 383), Hollis (1905: 315–316), Johnston (1902: 833), and Mallett (1923: 279–280).

24. See, for example, French-Sheldon (1892: 383), Hollis (1905: 322), and Merker (1910 [1904]: 102).

25. Dallas (1931) described one sacred *oreteti* tree at Oldenyesha in Tanzania. He and Maguire (1931) also discussed the remarkable capacity of *oreteti* trees for retaining rainwater in their cavities.

26. Galaty (1983: 367) has argued convincingly that sacrifice (*empolosata*) among Maasai is signaled by suffocating an animal, as opposed to the "ordinary" technique of slaughtering an animal by cutting its neck with a knife. Moreover, according to Burton (1991: 87), "sacrifice by suffocation in the Nilotic world may well be understood (and thus intended) as a mode of promoting life" by killing the animal in a manner that keeps its blood and bodily fluids in its body.

27. For a detailed examination of the colors and shapes used in shield designs, see Merker 1910 [1904]: 78–83, including a table of 19 shields.

28. For more information on the significance of colors in Maasai beadwork, see Klumpp (1987), Klumpp and Kratz (1993), and Kratz and Pido (2000).

29. Merker (1910 [1904]: 153–156) lists some of the hand signs used for numbers.

30. See Hurskainen (1990) for a detailed (if sometimes overstated) analysis of Maasai (especially Parakuyo) "numerical symbolism."

31. For more on the principle of symmetry as expressed in contemporary Maasai rituals, see Galaty (1983). Hurskainen (1990) analyzes other dualisms in Maasai symbolism and cosmology, as does Århem (1990).

32. I am grateful to Misty Bastian for pushing me to develop some of these ideas about the centrality of literal and metaphoric umbilical cords.

33. For more on these terms, see Mol (1977: 126; 1996).

34. Maasai, as Krapf (1854: 24) noted, were disdainful of other ways of praying: "The Wakuafi take great offence at the Suahilis turning their backside toward heaven by bowing their foreheads to the ground in prayer. Why do you, say they, turn your backside to god?"

35. Similar themes were expressed in the prayer-songs recorded by Voshaar (1998a) in the early 1970s from Maasai women in Kenya and Tanzania.

36. Mbatian is the only *oloiboni* who was prayed to in this way, according to the

accounts I have read. Chanel (1900: 168) reported that even seven or eight years after Mbatian's death this prayer was still being repeated. My interpretation is that this one-of-a-kind prayer reflected more about Mbatian's unique power and influence than that of *iloibonok* as a group.

37. For a comparative perspective on *iloibonok*, see Fratkin (1979), and Anderson and Johnson (1995) more generally for the history and role of prophets in certain African societies. See also Peristiany (1975).

38. Bernsten (1979a: 121–128) offers compelling evidence that many of them were probably Kikuyu (see also Fosbrooke 1948: 14, 21–22). Farler (1882: 734), however, claimed that Mbatian was the son of Suberti, a Mgogo "who acquired great influence by claiming magical powers, . . . married the local chief's daughter, and formed a strong government, which he bequeathed to his son Mbatian" (see also his comments in Last 1883: 541). Merker (1910 [1904]: 19) provided a longer lineage, but acknowledged that "The Masai cannot tell one much about the pedigree of the ol oibonok." Fosbrooke (1948: 3, 12) dates the "discovery" of the first *oloiboni* to about 1640. Jacobs (1965: 20) states that the first ritual expert was Sitonik, the third on Hollis's list.

39. Hollis (1905: 325–326), however, claimed that Kidongoi was the son of "E-Sigiriaishi ('The Somali'), the son of Ol-le-Mweiya." Ol-le-Mweiya, according to Hollis's informants, "came down from heaven [*eng'ai*] and was found by the Aiser clan sitting on top of their mountain. He was such a small person that he was first believed to be a child. He was taken by the Aiser clan to their kraal, where it was discovered he was a medicine-man [*oloiboni*]. He married and had issue." Fosbrooke (1948: 12, 13) repeats this genealogy. According to Jacobs (1965: 321), however, Ole Mweiya is not a proper name but refers to "the first one" in stories where the proper name is unknown.

40. Thomson (1968 [1885]: 247), for example, reports a version of this myth in which Kidong'oi figures as part-human, part wild-animal, and is described as the ancestor of all Maasai, not just Iloibonok: "The primal ancestor of the Masai was one Kidenoi, who lived at Donyo Egèrè (Mount Kenia), was hairy, and had a tail. Filled with the spirit of exploration, he left his home and wandered south. The people of the country, seeing him shaking something in a calabash, were so struck with admiration at the wonderful performance that they brought him women as a present. By these he had children, who, strangely enough, were not hairy, and had no tails, and these were the progenitors of the Masai."

41. Their liminal status, as Bernsten (1979a: 113–114) among others has noted, was parallel to that of Maasai blacksmiths (*ilkunono*), who formed a distinct occupational group. Their "otherness" was marked socially and physically in many ways, notably that they lived apart from and did not intermarry with other Maasai clans. But, like *iloibonok*, they wielded the capacity for powerful curses and blessings.

42. Merker (1910 [1904]: 18, 22) called these two types by different names, distinguishing the *oloiboni* ("the chief") from an El goiatek [*olkuyatiki*] as the more minor "medicine man," both of the Inkidong'i sub-clan. He also noted that the Ilkiboron of the Ilmollelian clan were known for their rain-making powers (Merker 1910 [1904]: 22). Fosbrooke (1948: 13–15) includes a third type that he suggests was mid-range in skills and prestige between minor and major *iloibonok*.

43. Much has already been written about the struggle between Lenana and Sendeu for primacy as the primary Oloiboni after the death of their father, Mbatian, including stories of betrayal and deceit. One result of their rivalry was that Lenana remained and was recognized as the Oloiboni in British East Africa (later Kenya), while Sendeu moved

to German East Africa (later Tanganyika) (Bernsten 1979a ; Merker 1910 [1904]: 19; Waller 1995). The Tanganyikan government gave Parit, the son of Lenana, a club made from rhino horn in recognition of his role as chief. Upon his death, the club was given to his successor, Mbeiya, and came to be regarded, at least in British eyes, "as the emblem of the office of the Laibon." Webster, Provincial Commissioner, Northern Province to Chief Secretary, Dar es Salaam, 12 May 1928, TNA, 69/47/MS/2.

44. Other spellings include *inkoiantik, ilkuyantik, ilgoiatik, ilkuyantik.* In the contemporary period, the term *ilkuyatik* is also used to disparage minor *iloibonok* as "charlatans" or "quacks" (Spencer 1991: 334; Mol 1996: 217).

45. Bernsten (1979a) convincingly argued that the successful successor son chosen by a major *oloiboni* was usually an *olmurrani* at the time of his father's death.

46. Interestingly, in light of the above discussion of Maasai associations of hair with the wild, Merker (1910 [1904]: 147) claimed that the men of the Ilkiboron section were the only Maasai who did not remove their facial hair because "they would lose their power, especially their supernatural power of bringing or withholding rain."

47. In a similar vein, Kipuri (1989) argues that the emergence of *iloibonok* as a distinct lineage of men claiming a special relationship to Eng'ai introduced new, unfamiliar hierarchies into Maasai social organization, which in turn led to the transformation of gender complementarity into gender inequality.

48. Hinde and Hinde (1901: 72), however, mention that barren women visited Oloiboni Lenana to request his assistance in overcoming their infertility (see also Shaffer 1985: 46–47).

49. For example, Merker (1910 [1904]: 159–160) listed them as the short rains (*oldumeril* [*oltumeret*]), the short dry season (*engokwa* [*enkokua*]), the long rains (*olairodjerod* [*oloirujuruj*]), and the long dry season (*olameii* [*olameyu*]). But see Hollis (1905: 333–334).

50. Merker (1910 [1904]: 205–206), however, disagreed. He argued that Maasai believed that their souls went to the "next world," where they were judged by God and sent to either "Paradise" (full of "luxuriant pastures," "fat stock," plenty of water, "a superabundance of the best food," and so forth) or "a dreary waterless waste." Since there are no confirming sources of such beliefs in either the past or the present, I think this is an example of Merker's desire to present further evidence for his belief that Maasai were descended from the tribes of Israel.

51. See, for example, Baumann (1894: 163), Hollis (1905: 304–305), Johnston (1902: 828), Last (1883: 532), Merker (1910 [1904]: 200–203), and Thomson (1968 [1885]: 259).

52. Merker (1910 [1904]: 201), in contrast, claimed that mourning occurred only after the death of an adult man.

53. Conversely, a miscarriage or stillbirth was perceived as a punishment by Eng'ai for some offense by the woman or close family member (Merker 1910 [1904]: 51).

54. This ceremony was supposed to occur when the child was still small, but could happen when they were older. It had to occur, however, before a child could be circumcised (Hollis 1905: 294).

55. Mol (1977: 110–111) and Merker (1910 [1904]: 58–60) listed common Maasai names.

56. Children continued to acquire new names throughout their lives, beginning with a second name from their father, other family names, public names, married names, the names of their children, and so forth.

57. The following is a synthesis of the accounts described in Hollis (1905: 296–299), Merker (1910 [1904]: 60–67), and Bagge (1904). See also Beadnell (1905), Leakey (1930: 189–191), and Storrs-Fox (1930: 448). Jacobs (1965: 287–288) provides a more recent account of a male circumcision ceremony among Kisongo Maasai.

58. Merker (1910 [1904]: 62–65), in fact, described large groups of boys being circumcised together.

59. Whitehouse (1932/1933), for example, described how selected uncircumcised boys, dressed in short cloaks made from black calfskins with their heads covered with ocher, traveled to different homesteads to demand that the elders agree to "open" the circumcision of a new age-set.

60. The preliminary rituals included the "horn-of-the-ox" ceremony (*emowuo olki-teng'*), which among the Purko and Kisongo sections was held first by members of the Ilkeeyonyukie section (see also Leakey 1930: 188–189). According to Bernsten (1979a: 64): "The ceremony took its name from the attempt of the young men to seize and maintain their grasp on the horn of a young bullock." Other preliminary ceremonies are discussed in Hollis (1905: 294–296) and Merker (1910 [1904]: 60–62).

61. Among the Naivasha Maasai, however, the girl wore a string of cowry shells on her forehead (Bagge 1904: 169).

62. Bernsten (1979a: 106, n.34) argues, however, that the derivation of *olaunoni* and *Eunoto* is from the other meaning of *aun*, which is "to shave." Thus the *olaunoni* was the first to be shaved by his mother at Eunoto, "the shaving ceremony." For more contemporary accounts of the Eunoto ceremony that differ from those discussed here, see Galaty (1983), Benson (1974), and "Eunoto" ca. 1915, pp. 77–83 of Dr. E. A. Lewis Deposit, Mss. Afr. s1241, Rhodes House Library [RHL], Oxford [hereafter, Lewis Deposit]. For pictures of different Eunoto ceremonies that took place in the 1950s, see Hamilton (1963), "Masai Initiation Ceremonies" (1949–1950), and Queeny (1954). Flatt (1973) offers a symbolic analysis of the ritual.

63. The following day, according to Hollis (1905: 300–301), a black bullock with a white neck and belly was chosen for slaughter. The elder men placed its horn in a large fire, and then called the *ilmurran* to grab the horn as the fire was dying down. The first *olmurrani* to find it held it out in his arms, shouting, "I have finished it." The Eunoto feast was then finished.

64. Although Merker and Hollis made little mention of these aspects of the ceremony, more recent accounts suggest that they were in fact central to the ritual and have a long history. I therefore draw on some of these sources, including Storrs Fox (1930), Benson (1974), and Galaty (1983).

65. See descriptions in Galaty (1983: 375–376), Hollis (1905: 301), Spencer (1988: 159), Storrs-Fox (1930: 453), and cover of Spear and Waller (1993).

66. Thus, for example, according to Lewis: "At the Ol-Ngesherr festival in January 1908 which took place on the Kasserian [Kiserian] River near [Oloibon] Lenana's kraal the elders circumcised in 1896 took the name Il-talala." "Ol'Ngesher," p. 80 of Lewis Deposit.

67. Lewis Deposit, p. 80.

68. In addition to arranged marriages, elopement between lovers also occurred. If successful, the couple was recognized as married and there were no wedding feasts (Merker 1910 [1904]: 46).

69. Krapf (1854: 24) also used *esetan* for witchcraft, claiming that "when the Wak-uafi see a book, they take it for esétan or witchcraft." Last (1883: 531) wrote that "Es-

satan" referred to "the source of evil," as opposed to "Engai . . . as the source of good." In his brief vocabulary list, however, he translated "esatan" as "witchcraft" (1883: 536).

70. According to Merker (1910 [1904]: 221), killing a non-Maasai was not understood as a transgression and therefore did not require compensation.

71. These were similar to Pokot "shaming parties" (Edgerton and Conant 1964).

2. Men of the Church

1. In the United States, the Spiritans have also historically been known as the Congregation of the Holy Ghost and the Immaculate Heart of Mary, or the Congregation of the Holy Ghost, or just the Holy Ghost Fathers and Brothers. In 2002, they decided to change their name to the Congregation of the Holy Spirit to more clearly reflect the translation of "St-Esprit" from French. Spiritan priests and brothers have the abbreviation "C.S.Sp." at the end of their names.

2. This vision, or charism, distinguishes Catholic missionary orders from one another (see Shapiro 1981).

3. Unless otherwise noted, the following history is based on Koren (1983).

4. Father Poullart des Places was born to extremely wealthy parents in Brittany, France, in 1679. Despite his privileged upbringing and the desires of his parents, he felt called to religious work and training. In the course of his own studies, he supported many destitute seminarians, which led him to form his own seminary. Because of the work of running the seminary and some theological qualms, he delayed his own ordination until 1707, just two years before his death in 1709 (Gobeil 1985; Koren 1983; Michel 1985).

5. Father Libermann was born Jacob Libermann in Alsace, France, in 1802. Although his father was an Orthodox Jewish rabbi, Libermann converted to Catholicism and was baptized in 1826 and ordained in 1841. He formed the Society of the Immaculate Heart of Mary to minister to newly freed slaves in Haiti, Reunion, and Mauritius. Surprisingly for the founder and later superior of a missionary congregation, he never went overseas himself, and died in 1852 (Koren 1983; Tenailleau 1985; Tillard 1985).

6. As Koren (1983: 292–294) documents, a few Spiritans had visited and worked in the United States as early as 1794 or 1795. Several U.S. dioceses invited Spiritans to join them, especially in the 1850s and 1860s, but there were not enough priests to accept these offers.

7. Pope Gregory XV started Propaganda Fide in 1622 to coordinate and supervise missionary work. As a "sacred college" headed by a cardinal prefect and comprising almost 30 cardinals, its responsibilities included the assignment and categorization (as a mission, prefecture, vicariate, or diocese) of missionary territories, selection of mission leadership, and supervision of mission affairs (Kieran 1966: 4–7, 37–38). According to Kieran, Propaganda Fide preferred to assign "untouched" territories to new missionary orders. Propaganda Fide also advised missionaries on the often difficult questions of faith, morality, and practice that emerged from their encounters with diverse societies (Kieran 1966: 44). Only in 1969 did Propaganda Fide, now renamed the Congregation for the Evangelization of Peoples, abolish the *jus commissionis* that entrusted entire dioceses to particular missionary societies (Koren 1983: 496).

8. Important overviews of mission history in East Africa include Oliver (1965), Sahlberg (1986), and Wright (1971).

9. Among other crops, the Spiritans introduced coffee into East Africa, where it flourished, especially in Kilimanjaro. The planting and care of coffee therefore became a

key part of the curriculum in many Spiritan schools, assisting in the spread of coffee cultivation among Africans (Kieran 1969b).

10. These organizations, founded in 1822 and 1842 respectively, collected money from Catholic laity for the express purpose of helping to spread the Catholic faith through the financial support of missions.

11. The Society for the Propagation of the Faith published a journal, *Annales de la Propagation de la Foi*, and a popular magazine, *Mission Catholiques*, that had a large readership. Holy Childhood's journal was called *Annales de l'Oeuvre de la Sainte-Enfance*.

12. These included Kilema in 1891, Kiboscho in 1893, Rombo in 1898, Uru in 1911, and Mashati in 1912 (Gogarty 1927: 37–38).

13. Including Arusha in 1907.

14. The northern line was started by the Germans in 1891. But funding difficulties, conflicting priorities, war, and other problems made progress slow and intermittent; the railway did not reach Moshi until 1911 and Arusha until 1930 (Iliffe 1969: 14, 103; 1979: 303).

15. Father LeRoy was an avid amateur anthropologist intent on learning about and analyzing "primitive religions" (LeRoy 1909). To this end, he was the founder of *Anthropos*, an anthropology journal for missionaries (LeRoy 1906).

16. Similarly, in 1906, Bishop Shanahan of southern Nigeria, himself a Spiritan priest, took money sent by Propaganda Fide in Rome to ransom slaves, and used it to begin building an extensive school system in southern Nigeria (Donovan 1978: 6; Kohler 1977a: 1; GK/3).

17. According to Kieran (1966: 333), the Germans praised Spiritan work only in so far as it was perceived to help the "Motherland" by providing education and economic training to further the material and moral progress of Africans.

18. Kieran (1966: 219) mentions reports of a community in Kilimanjaro attacking and expelling their catechist, and another community where few students attended the school because the catechist was disliked.

19. Walker (1933: 168–169) describes some of the upheavals suffered by the Vicariate of Kilimanjaro during the First World War.

20. According to Kieran (1966: 71–75), the employment of nuns in the mission fields was still a rare practice at this time, and caused some administrative difficulties.

21. They were Father Thomas Harris, Father John Todorowski, and Father Patrick McCarthy (Koren 1994).

22. For more on the Arusha and their relationship to Maasai, see Hodgson (2001a) and Spear (1993, 1997).

23. These days, according to Father LeClair "the Principal Superior proposes and the Bishop of the Diocese appoints, and gives the fathers faculties, that is, permission to administer the sacraments in his diocese" (LeClair 1993: 197–198).

24. "Arusha Becomes Archdiocese." *USA Eastern Province Newsletter* 27(4):2.

25. In 1862, the British and French both signed a declaration recognizing the independence of the Sultans of Muscat and Zanzibar and pledging to "seek no territorial advantage" in their dominions (Bennett 1963: 57).

26. Bennett (1963: 73) claims that certain Spiritans at Bagamoyo violated the policy by helping the Germans in several ways, including spying on rebel Arab forces.

27. This policy was formalized in Kenya (then called British East Africa) in a 1910 circular called "Land Grants to Missions in the Native Reserves" (Kieran 1966: 282).

28. As a result, for example, the American-dominated Catholic Vicariate of Kili-

manjaro had a much more tenuous relationship with the British colonial administration than the British-run Church Missionary Society in Kaguru described by Beidelman (1982).

29. Interview with Father Eugene Hillman, C.S.Sp., on February 12, 2000, in Sarasota, Florida. References to the interview transcript are abbreviated as EH/page number. Unless otherwise noted, all quotations ascribed to Father Hillman are from this interview.

30. Profession Day has since been moved to August 22, the Feast of the Immaculate Heart of Mary (LeClair 1993: 15).

31. Interview with Father Girard Kohler, C.S.Sp., on April 29 and May 9, 1992, in Monduli, Tanzania. References to the interview transcripts are abbreviated as GK/page number. Unless otherwise noted, all quotations ascribed to Father Kohler are from these interviews.

32. Father Hillman attributes this "influential theology of grace" to Karl Rahner, whom he read and met with during Vatican II (Hillman 1994a: 163).

33. He recognized that certain practices such as polygyny could be interpreted in different ways. As he noted, "I had angry reactions from women in this country [the United States] about the fact that I wrote a book which was not condemning polygamy. . . . But I always thought African women weren't at all [upset by it]. . . . And it is to the advantage of a wife to have co-wives because they share the work. Maasai have nice customs in that regard. Like if a woman is unable to have a child of her own, she'll be given one of the children of [another wife]."

34. A version of the paper was published the following year in *Concilium*, an international theological review, and received national attention, including an overview in *Time* magazine ("The Case for Polygamy," 1968). Subsequently, the paper became the basis of his Ph.D. dissertation in social ethics, which was later published as *Polygamy Reconsidered* (1975).

35. Interview with Father William Christy, C.S.Sp, on July 11, 2000, in Monduli, Tanzania. References to the interview transcript are abbreviated as WC/page number. Unless otherwise noted, all quotations ascribed to Father Christy are from this interview.

36. According to Father Christy, a census of church members found over 80 different ethnic groups (WC/2).

37. The "catechumenate" refers to the "period between a prospective convert's application to become a Christian and his actual baptism. Its conditions and length depended on the vicars apostolic appointed by the Holy See, but the Spiritan Generalate counseled against two extremes: on the one hand, that of admitting people after insufficient instruction (which could result in many baptisms but few true Christians) and, on the other, that of demanding so much that it discouraged most candidates and thereby rendered the mission's work fruitless" (Koren 1983: 449–450). Sometimes the appropriate length of the period was decided by bishops, sometimes by individual priests (Koren 1983: 450).

3. Evangelizing "the Maasai"

1. This and subsequent excerpts from LeRoy are my translation from the original French.

2. Until the late 1990s, there was one Maasai Deanery, but the new archbishop, Father Lebulu, much to the distress of some priests, divided it into three Maasai deaneries representing different geographical areas (WC/30).

3. The examples of such verbal and visual images of Maasai are numerous. See Hodgson (2001a) for an overview of the written accounts, as well as Knowles and Collett (1989).

4. Even scholars of missionaries such as Oliver uncritically repeat these stereotypes. He refers to Maasai as "predatory" (Oliver 1965: 28) and "the most warlike of tribes" (1965: 41).

5. One commentator claims, however, that some of the children were actually traded by their Maasai parents to Chagga for food, and the Chagga in turn sold them to the missionaries for approximately three pieces of cloth valued at 10 rupees, or 14 francs, each (Chanel 1900: 85).

6. Father Kilasara was born in approximately 1916 in Kilema, less than a mile from the mission. He attended St. James Junior Seminary and Our Lady Queen of Angels senior seminary in Kilimanjaro, and was ordained in 1944. After working for the diocese for eight years, he joined the Spiritans and made his vows in Ridgefield in 1953. He studied canon law for two years in Rome, then returned to work in the Vicariate of Kilimanjaro. He was ordained as bishop in 1960, but served for only six years because of bad health. He resigned in 1966 and died in 1978 (Koren 1994: 523).

7. *Monduli Mission Journal,* Volume I, 1957–87. References to the journal are abbreviated as MMJ/date of entry. I am grateful to Father Girard Kohler for giving me permission to copy and quote from the mission journal and baptismal registers of Monduli Mission. Father Ed Kelly opened the mission with Father Hillman, and served as the superior.

8. *Loliondo Mission Journal,* 1956–1970/Background. Copy available in Bethel Park archives. Hereafter referred to as LMJ/page number.

9. The application was originally submitted in 1952 and finally granted in 1956 (Anon. 1970: 1). Because of this delay, the first fathers' residence in Masai District was actually opened the year before in the town of Loliondo, near the Kenyan border (GK/ 2).

10. Father Dennis Vincent Durning was born in Philadelphia in 1923. After following the usual series of studies at Cornwells, Ridgefield, and Ferndale, Father Durning was ordained in 1949 and assigned to Kilimanjaro District in 1950. He was assigned to Mashati and Arusha before moving in 1957 to Loliondo, where he undertook first-evangelization work with Maasai. He served as bishop of Arusha Diocese for 26 years, from 1963 until his resignation in 1989. For the last few years of his term, he was the last non-African bishop serving in Tanzania. After his resignation, he took over a small parish in the neighboring Diocese of Mbulu, where he worked until his death in 2002 (Koren 1994: 500; Durning 2002). I worked very closely with Bishop Durning during my three years with ADDO, and have fond memories of his humility, sense of humor, and vision. We remained friends and correspondents until his death in 2002.

11. Father Donovan's description of a missionary emphasizes the image of the missionary as solitary hero: "a missionary is essentially a *social martyr,* cut off from his roots, his stock, his blood, his land, his background, his culture. He is destined to walk forever a stranger in a strange land. He must be stripped as naked as a human being can be, down to the very texture of his being" (Donovan 1978: 193, emphasis in original; cf. Beidelman 1974: 242–243).

12. This is calculated from a population census taken in 1967 which found a population of 104,313 (MMJ/28 Mar. 1968, lists data from "Population Census taken in 1967").

13. Masai Reserve was renamed Masai District in 1926.

14. In particular, large groups of Arusha were resettled after the 1947 Wilson Report found that Maasai had land "plenty and to spare" and therefore advocated, in part, moving some of the more "productive" Arusha farmers from the "agricultural slum" of Arusha District to Masai District (Hodgson 2001a: 111–12; Report of the Arusha-Moshi Land Commission 1947).

15. Pels (1999) offers a fascinating study of what he calls the "politics of presence" avowed by Dutch Spiritan missionaries in Uluguru, Tanzania.

16. Father Hillman also received financial support from a "Mission Club" that he formed in the late 1950s. He asked members to "make the sign of the cross once a day as a prayer for the Church in Africa" and to offer one dollar a month for his mission. In return, he wrote monthly letters about his work and travels. Typed mimeo and letters in "Masai Mission, 1952–," Archives of the Spiritans U.S. Eastern Province, Bethel Park, Penn. [hereafter Bethel Park], File 21C-32.

17. The mission journals for the two other Catholic missions in Masai District at the time, Kijungu and Loliondo, are full of the same litany of school-related tasks, problems, and concerns. *Kijungu Mission Journal* [KMJ], LMJ.

18. As visitors to Simanjiro in 1960 described it, the school was a simple group of buildings set in the open plains: "The wide blue skies and the endless tawny plains of Simanjiro dwarf the school: bare red earth and five small buildings, iron-roofed, mud and wattle walled. There are two classrooms with half-walls, wooden benches and a blackboard; a dormitory and a living-room; a small dispensary and a three-roomed house for the teacher. The long plum of dust heralding Father Hillman's arrival brings everyone out into the baked earth clearing. He shakes hands with the two young African teachers who wear British-style long khaki shorts and socks, neat white shirts, knotted cravats. Then the children cluster round him, each gently butting their shaven heads against him in traditional greeting, all shy smiles and soft words" (Moss and Moss 1960: 6).

19. As of 1958, Monduli mission was running three dispensaries, in Simanjiro, Sunya, and Gelai (MMJ/7 Nov. 1958; 6 Dec. 1958). Father Kohler justified the church's involvement with dispensaries by the need for the "sheer . . . physical survival" of converts and potential converts: "If you get any kind of influence with anybody and they drop dead on you, then you've wasted your time. . . . If we are going to erect a church, we need some people who are somehow . . . alive physically and mentally." Other dispensaries in Masai District were run by the Lutheran church and the Masai Native Authority (later the Masai District Council).

20. Masai District Book [MDB]/145, 147, Reel 5, Cooperative Africana Microfilm Project [CAMP]. Although the Lutheran church has been quite active in Maasai are they have only recently made occasional forays into Emairete, Mti Mmoja, or Embopong'. For more on the history of Lutheran efforts to evangelize Maasai, see Parsalaw (1999), Benson (1970, 1974), Kiel (1997), Klobuchar (1998).

21. SOAS Archives/International Missionary Council/Conference of British Missionary Societies/Box 249, "East Africa—Tanganyika"/File F, "Missionary Rivalry: Assignment of 'Spheres.' "

22. An application for land on which to build a fathers' house in 1952 was not granted until 1956, however (Anon. 1970: 1).

23. Father Hillman noted that there were, of course, exceptions, such as a British veterinary officer who was "very outspoken in helping [Maasai] organize politically and create a consciousness of losing their land."

24. MMJ/26 July 1960, 13 Jan. 1963, 26 Mar. 1964, 5 Mar. 1967, 22 Oct. 1968. The school was finally built in Simanjiro by the Catholic Church in 1987, when I was the coordinator of ADDO.

25. First interview with Daniel Logolie, 14 Oct. 1992. References to the interview transcript are abbreviated as DL1/page number, and are my translation from the original Swahili. Unless otherwise noted, all quotations ascribed to Mwalimu Daniel are from this interview. I follow Tanzanian practice of using the honorific *Mwalimu* (teacher) to refer to Daniel and the other catechists. I use *Mwalimu* throughout the book to designate catechists and distinguish them from regular parishioners and catechumens.

26. The complicated but essential role of African catechists and evangelists in the missionary encounter has been woefully understudied. Landau (1995) is an important exception. See also Beidelman (1982) and Hastings (1994).

27. Although some Catholic sisters (both Euro-American and Tanzanian) eventually began to work in Maasailand as nurses, and later teachers and development workers, they were concentrated in Catholic hospitals and schools. No Catholic sisters worked in the Monduli area during this period.

28. As Father Hillman explained, "in our schools, if some of the kids were Lutherans, then a Lutheran pastor would come, or a Lutheran catechist. . . . So in a Lutheran school, Catholics would theoretically have access to those kids."

29. See also interview, by telephone, 10 July 1994, with Saning'o Milliary, a former Maasai diocesan priest who worked in the Diocese of Arusha. Hereafter SM.

30. MMJ/14 Mar. 1966; MMBR/12 June 1968; 28 Mar. 1970; EH/10.

31. Daniel Lolgolie described how he was chased, caught, and forced to begin primary school by a headman named Sirowei: "We were out herding. Jumbe [Headman] Sirowei, who died recently, was the *jumbe* during that period, which was still the colonial period before independence. He would walk among the herds. If he saw cattle, he would approach them. If he saw two children [herding], he would take one. But if he just saw one child herding, he would leave him. Well, we were three children. So I . . . I mean, if you saw the *jumbe*, that *jumbe* who had a special hat, well you knew he was the *jumbe*. We were told that, if you saw a person wearing a hat, run! Because he is the *jumbe*. So when I saw him—[DH: Was he Arusha or Maasai?] Maasai. We ran. I went into the small bushes and hid myself. The others ran. He saw that only two were running so he knew that one had hid himself. He went around and around, and finally caught me. Then we went to the cattle herd. He didn't only tie your hands so you couldn't run, but also tied you up back here so that he could drive you like cattle. . . . Seven of us were taken to school that day. [DH: Straight?] Straight, without passing our homes. [DH: *Oya!* Did you cry?] I cried a lot. Anyways, we were taken, we were given food. We met lots of students, since it was a boarding school. . . . The next day, my father came and found me. But that was it. It was the rule. The DC [District Commissioner] had decided to send the *jumbe*, so there was no asking why this particular child was in school. And so I started school."

32. Father Vincent Donovan was born in 1926, ordained to the priesthood in 1953, and assigned to the Vicariate of Kilimanjaro in 1956. His initial postings included running the catechetical training center at Usa River in 1962. His work with Maasai began in 1965, when he was assigned to Loliondo mission. He was forced to return to the United States in 1973 because of health problems, after which he held a series of administrative positions in the U.S. Eastern Province and pastoral positions serving var-

ious congregations. He also wrote several books and articles during this period (Koren 1994: 538; Donovan 1978, 1989, 2000).

33. His frustration with the schools was shared by other Spiritans at the time. As Father Raymond Buchler wrote in 1966 in the *Kijungu Mission Journal*, "We're having second thoughts on all the schools in Masai land. Up until now the Masai parents have resisted schools with all their power. We have not been able to establish the Church through the schools and we know that as representatives of the school system we are resented" (KMJ/Jan. 1966).

34. I lived at Oldonyo Sambu Seminary from 1985 through 1987, and taught English to Form 2 and Form 6 in 1985–1986.

35. For a discussion of polygamy as a source of friction between Africans and missionaries, see Ekechi (1970).

36. MMJ/2 Sept. 1965, 18 Oct. 1966; Kohler (1977a: 413), cf. LeClair (1993: 113–115).

37. According to one entry in the Monduli mission journal: "Father V. Donovan is having success in Loliondo area and is to baptize a large number of adult Masai!" (MMJ/Dec. 1966). Moreover, at a 1966 meeting in Monduli in which Father Donovan described his new approach, the Spiritans in attendance reached "unanimous agreement that this was to be stressed in the future" (LMJ/18 Oct. 1966).

38. MMJ/6 Oct. 1966; 13 Oct. 1966, May 1969–Jan. 1970, Aug. 1970; Donovan (1978: 9).

39. Father Poirier was born in 1937 in Bay City, Michigan. After completing his studies at the Spiritan Junior Seminary in Ann Arbor, Cornwells, Ridgefield, and Ferndale, he was ordained in 1963. He was sent to Tanzania in 1964, where he first worked as an assistant at Kijungu mission in Masai District. From 1971 to 1975 he served as head of Monduli mission, then moved to Kitwai, Kijungu, and finally Simanjiro. In 1983 he left Africa because of illness, and took up pastoral work in Texas and California, primarily among Mexican migrants (Kane 1995; Koren 1994: 593).

40. Father Mort Kane, an American Spiritan who worked with Maasai in Tanzania for many years and spent his last years supervising a training center for Maasai catechists, provides a more detailed description of Father Poirier's methods (Kane 1995).

41. In 1967, a meeting of diocesan priests limited the "direct apostolate to adults" to the Kijungu and Loliondo areas and firmly decreed that "All direct boma preaching in the Arusha area to stop!" (MMJ/30 Aug. 1967).

42. Most of the adult men who sought baptism were already seen as *ormeek*. Ndangoya, the male elder of the first *boma* that Father Donovan baptized "as a community," was in fact an educated Maasai from Kenya who had served for years in the Masai Native Authority. He was once praised by the British for being "a strong supporter of discipline and progress" (Northern Province Annual Report 1949: 70). Not surprisingly, given his rhetorical reinforcement of the untouched "noble savage" image of Maasai, Donovan mentions none of these details about Ndangoya in his account.

43. At present, *boma* teaching continues in some Maasai areas, maintained by the few Spiritans still working in the area who adopted the approach in the late 1960s and early 1970s, as well as by some Spiritan and diocesan priest newcomers.

44. The first Maasai priest in the Diocese of Arusha, Father Fred Oloshiro, was ordained in 1976 (Kohler 1977a: 410). Olle Timan (1987) describes some of the tensions between missionaries and Diocesan priests in the diocese of Arusha.

45. Joe Herzstein and Mortimer Kane, "Report to Chapter in 1996 of East Africa Province by Tanzania Group-Arusha." Bethel Park, no file information.

46. Ibid.

47. Missionaries and theologians have written extensively about the concept (e.g., Hillman 1993; Luzbetak 1961, 1988; Waliggo et al. 1986), but for more anthropological studies, see Kozak (1993), Sanneh (1989), and Shorter (1978, 1988).

48. Other denominations, such as the Lutherans, have also proposed similar ideas, often called "incarnation" and "contextualization" (Mtaita 1998). Mtaita argues that "contextualization" is more theological, in contrast to "inculturation," which is more cultural and anthropological (1998: 72).

49. The Anglican Church was similarly strict in its cultural prohibitions on the dress, practices, and beliefs of converts, at least in the late 1950s in Kaguru, Tanzania (Beidelman 1982: ch. 6, esp. 135–136).

50. Key works on these issues of translation and cultural form in the mission context include James (1998), Keane (1997), Lienhardt (1982), and Rafael (1987, 1993).

4. THE CHURCH OF WOMEN

1. Unfortunately, the mission journal was not kept up from 1970 to 1975. One reason, according to a Spiritan who was working in another Maasai area during the same period, was that the resident Spiritan intentionally failed to keep the journal in order to minimize evidence that he was baptizing polygamists in Emairete (MMJ/1975, "Transcribed from Rev. Butts' notebook").

2. The church was built, in part, to honor Edward Sokoine, who had been gathering money and construction materials before his death. After his death, his family and supporters urged the diocese to continue raising funds to build the church, and contributed toward the effort one million shillings from the almost eight million shillings they received as *rambirambi* (Swahili for "condolence gifts") (GK/30–31). The rest of the money was raised from the Capuchins, Missio-Germany, and the Koch Foundation in Florida (GK/31).

3. The following statistics are compiled from the Emairete Baptism Register, 1972–present (EBR/date); Monduli Mission Baptism Register, vols. I–III, 1958–present (MMBR/date); and a census of all individuals (1,974 adults and children) and households (454) residing in the three communities undertaken Feb.–April 1992. The census included questions on whether an individual was baptized (and if so, by whom and when) and their religious affiliation. From 1986 to 1992, the gender difference in adult baptisms is easy to perceive, as adults were baptized at Easter and children at Christmas.

4. In 1992, the conversion rate was approximately 500 shillings for a dollar, so 50 shillings was equivalent to about 10 cents.

5. Although my friend had forewarned me about the impending ceremony and invited me to attend, he never knew when it was going to happen until Koko Naserian and her delegation appeared on his doorstep. By then it was too late to tell me. I only learned the details the next morning (but not his daughter's new name—he had forgotten it! "Ask my wife," he advised.).

6. Father Christy told me later that he had in fact witnessed this ritual. Morani also described a similar ritual that he had observed in Emairete: four newly married women without children were dressed in black and rolled back and forth in the rain pond.

A black sheep, given by someone with a reputation for generosity, was then slaughtered.

7. Although there was regular social interaction between the two homesteads, I suspect that the physical separation marked the ambivalent and suspicious attitudes most Maasai held about members of the Inkidong'i clan and the long-standing preference of most Inkidong'i to live by themselves.

8. Even unbaptized women drew on the rich canvas of Christian concepts to embroider and enliven their praise songs. As I was half-heartedly listening to a group of unbaptized Maasai women sing in my car one day as we trekked across the bush from a water tank, I suddenly realized that they were blessing me and thanking me for the ride by invoking the many spiritual attributes of "Yesu" (Jesus in Swahili and now Maa).

5. Being a Man in the Church of Women

1. For other accounts of Maasai men who became Christians, see King's (1971) biography of Molonket Olokorinya ole Sempele, a Keekonyokie Maasai who became a leading member of the African Inland Mission (AIM) in Kenya in the early 1900s (see also Mullenix and Mpaayei 1984), and Fosbrooke's (1955 and 1956) translation of the autobiography of Justin Lemenye, an Ilparakuyo who was captured and raised by Maasai in Tanzania.

2. LMJ/24 Aug. 1959; MMJ/26 Aug. 1959, 27 Aug. 1959. In May 1957, the British created a "Chief's Convention" in an unsuccessful effort to appeal to older, more conservative constituencies and institute a more gradual transition to independent rule. They feared the more rapid, radical model for independence supported by the Tanganyika Africa National Union (TANU) and its leader, Julius Nyerere (Hodgson 2001a: 122–126; Iliffe 1979: 535).

3. See, for examples, entries from 1959 to 1961 in MMJ.

4. For example, Chief Mbarnoti asked the Catholics if they would provide a medical sister to take over the Native Authority dispensary in Loliondo and several other dispensaries. MMJ/14 Nov. 1960.

5. Letter by Edward Ole Mbarato, ca. 1960, Bethel Park, File 21 C-32–17.

6. Victor Kimesara, "A Masai Looks Back," ca. 1960, Bethel Park, File 21C-32–10a.

7. For more on Oltimbau, see Hodgson (2001a: 116, 120–121) and Jacobs (1965: 333).

8. For more about Mary, see her profile in Hodgson (2001a: 241–249).

9. Father Girard Kohler Letters, Summer 1990 [hereafter GKL].

6. Possessed by the Spirit

1. In my earlier book (Hodgson 2001a), I argue that this fierce embrace of a very fixed idea of Maasai "culture," or at least Maasai masculinity, was itself a historical product of the colonial and postcolonial encounter.

2. The etymology of the term *esetan* is unclear. Although I think that Maasai adopted it from the Swahili word for "satan" under Christian influence, the Swahili term has antecedents in Arabic, suggesting the possibility of an even earlier adoption into Maa.

3. The Maasai case is very different from most African contexts, in which possessed women join spirit cults to engage and appease their spirits, but are never able to permanently get rid of them (e.g., Boddy 1989).

4. I am grateful to David Peterson for giving me permission to copy, use, and quote extensively from his unpublished manuscript.

5. For more information about *orpeko,* see Hodgson (1997) and Hurskainen (1985a, 1985b, 1989).

6. The earliest cases were reported to have occurred when Maasai dispersed toward the coast of Tanzania as a consequence of the "disasters" of the 1890s. A few cases were also reported during the 1930s (Hurskainen 1989: 141–142). In 1966, Spiritans noted that Wagogo living in Kibaya saw baptism as a way of "being freed from the Ol Pepo" (KMJ/Jan. 1966).

7. No other factors, according to Hurskainen's study, were significant predictors, including clan membership, number of children, economic status of the household, and relationships with co-wives and husband (1985a: 24–26).

8. Although I present a brief and therefore seemingly more instrumental account of *orpeko* in this chapter, I have argued elsewhere that we need to explore spirit possession also in terms of its relationship to the cultural meanings, social relations, and historical context of the wider society. In other words, we must understand its form, content, and context, not just its function (Hodgson 1997, 2001a).

9. The increasing prevalence of *orpeko* among Maasai, and differing attitudes of the Catholic and Lutheran churches, even prompted the churches to jointly commission a study of the phenomenon in 1982 by the anthropologist Arvi Hurskainen (1985b). See also Peterson (1985).

7. Toward a Maasai Catholicism?

1. These visits are noted throughout the journals for all three Maasai missions. See, for example, LMJ/3 Oct. 1962 (when Father Tunney went to a "women's feast and fertility rite" in Sukenya); LMJ/24 Apr. 1963 (when a Spiritan priest, two Catholic sisters, Father Hillman, and Father Hillman's sister attended the circumcision ceremony of two Maasai girls); and LMJ/12 Mar. 1959 (when some Spiritans attended an Eunoto ceremony near Loliondo).

2. I briefly describe the funeral and burial in Hodgson (2001a: 93–94).

3. In contrast to the work of Schoffleleers (1982, 1989), no Maasai Christians associated *iloibonok* with Jesus. But see the work of Henschel (1991), a German Spiritan who draws on the parallels between life as depicted in the Old Testament and that of Maasai to suggest in print and film that "Christ was Maasai."

4. Earlier that year, another Maasai prophet had similar visions calling for Maasai to become Lutherans, prompting a mass baptism near Loliondo (Klobuchar 1998: 191–197).

5. Interview with Nailepo by author at Nairobi, Tanzania, on September 23, 1992. The interview was taped and transcribed. Unless otherwise noted, all subsequent quotations attributed to Nailepo are from this interview.

6. Interview with Ashumu by author on September 24, 1992, near Ngorongoro, Tanzania. The interview was taped and transcribed. Unless otherwise noted, all subsequent quotations attributed to Ashumu are from this interview.

7. I have edited and abbreviated the original transcript in this and the following paragraphs.

8. This conference, especially its gender dynamics, is described in more detail in Hodgson (1999e).

9. For a thoughtful overview of current debates on syncretism, see Stewart and Shaw (1994). Peel (1967) raised some of these points in a much earlier article. See also Aguilar's (1995) study of "reconversion" among Muslim Waso Boorana pastoralists in Kenya.

Bibliography

Primary Sources

Maasai Census

Basic social and economic data were collected in 1992 through a census of all households (454) and individuals (1,974) in the three communities. The questions included the following: Have you ever been baptized? If so, when? If so, by whom? Which religion?

Maasai Interviews (including catechists)

These comprise four sets of interviews:

(1) 150 semi-structured interviews conducted in 1992 and 1993 with a stratified random sample based on gender and age of five members of each gender/age category in each of the three communities of Emairete, Mti Mmoja, and Embopong'. Among the broad range of topics covered in these interviews were questions about Maasai religion, the Catholic Church, spirit possession, and missionaries. The interviews were taped and transcribed, and sections were translated into Swahili. Since those questioned wished to remain anonymous, they are identified by pseudonyms.

(2) Life history interviews were conducted in 1992, 1993, 1995, and 2000 with men and women of different ages in all three communities. The interviews were taped and transcribed, and sections were translated into Swahili. All those questioned who wished to remain anonymous are identified by pseudonyms.

(3) Semi-structured interviews were conducted in 2000 with twenty-four key men and women of different ages in all three communities, both Catholics and non-Catholics. These questions probed aspects of Maasai religious belief and practice, the relationship between Christianity and Maasai religion and culture, the history of the Catholic Church in their area, and the gender dynamics of the contemporary churches. The interviews were taped and transcribed, and sections were translated into Swahili. All those questioned who wished to remain anonymous are identified by pseudonyms.

(4) Catechists who worked or had worked in the communities and surrounding areas were interviewed in 1992, 1997, and 2000. They were Daniel Lolgolie (who was interviewed in 1992 and 2000), Moses Lengaa (2000), "Francis" (2000), "Steven" (2000), and Thomas Porokwa (1997). These interviews were taped and transcribed.

281

Bibliography

Spiritan Interviews (all agreed to be identified by name)

Christy, Father William, C.S.Sp. [WC]. 11 July 2000. Monduli, Tanzania.
Hillman, Father Eugene, C.S.Sp. [EH]. 15 February 2000. Sarasota, Florida.
Kohler, Father Girard, C.S.Sp. [GK]. 29 April 1992 and 9 May 1992. Monduli, Tanzania.

Other Related Interviews (all agreed to be identified by name)

Benson, Reverend Stanley and Marie [SB, MB]. 20 April 2001. St. Peter's, Minnesota.
Milliary, Saning'o [SM]. 10 July 1994 and 16 July 1994, by telephone in the United States.

Mission Journals

Kijungu Mission Journal [KMJ], 1962–1979. Copy available in Bethel Park archives.
Loliondo Mission Journal [LMJ], 1956–1970. Copy available in Bethel Park archives.
Monduli Mission Journal [MMJ], Volume I, 1957–1987. Copy in author's possession, made from originals available at Monduli mission.

Missionary Correspondence

Circular letters, Father Girard Kohler to supporters and friends, 1990–1993, 2001–2003 [GKL]. Copies in author's possession.

Baptismal Registers

Emairete Baptismal Register, 1972–1993 [EBR].
Monduli Mission Baptismal Register, 1958–1993 [MMBR].

Archives Consulted

Archives of the Archdiocese of Arusha; Arusha, Tanzania [Arusha Diocese].
Archives of the Spiritans U.S. Eastern Province; Bethel Park, Pa. [Bethel Park].
Cooperative Africana Microfilm Project, United States [CAMP].
East African Collection, University of Dar es Salaam.
School for Oriental and Africa Studies; London, England [SOAS].
Tanzania National Archives, Arusha [ATNA].
Tanzania National Archives, Dar es Salaam [TNA].

NEWSLETTERS, PERIODICALS

Endulen Mission newsletters.
Flying Medical Service newsletters.
Spiritan News (East African Province, then Kilimanjaro District).
USA Eastern Province Newsletter, Congregation of the Holy Spirit.

SECONDARY SOURCES

Abbott, Walter, and Joseph Gallagher, eds. 1966. *The Documents of Vatican II.* New York: Guild Press.
Aguilar, Mario I. 1995. "African Conversion from a World Religion: Religious Diversification by the Waso Borana in Kenya." *Africa* 65(4): 525–544.
Allen, Roland. 1962 [1912]. *Missionary Methods: St. Paul's or Ours?* Grand Rapids, Mich.: Eerdmans.

Anderson, David M., and Douglas H. Johnson, eds. 1995. *Revealing Prophets: Prophecy in Eastern African History.* London: James Currey.

Anonymous. 1970. "History and Policy of Monduli Mission." Typed insert in *Monduli Mission Journal.*

Århem, Kaj. 1989. "Why Trees Are Medicine: Aspects of Maasai Cosmology." In *Culture, Experience and Pluralism: Essays on African Ideas of Illness and Healing,* ed. Anita Jacobson-Widding and David Westerlund. Stockholm: Almqvist and Wiksell.

———. 1990. "A Folk Model of Pastoral Subsistence: The Meaning of Milk, Meat and Blood in Maasai Diet." In *The Creative Communion: African Folk Models of Fertility and the Regeneration of Life,* ed. Anita Jacobson-Widding and Walter Van Beek. Stockholm: Almqvist and Wiksell.

———. 1991. "The Symbolic World of the Maasai Homestead." In *Body and Space: Symbolic Models of Unity and Division in African Cosmology and Experience,* ed. Anita Jacobson-Widding. Stockholm: Almqvist and Wiksell.

Asad, Talal. 1988. "Towards a Genealogy of the Concept of Ritual." In *Vernacular Christianity: Essays in the Social Anthropology of Religion,* ed. Wendy James and Douglas Johnson. Oxford: Journal of the Anthropological Society of Oxford.

———. 1993 [1982]. "The Construction of Religion as an Anthropological Category." In *Genealogies of Religion: Discipline and Reasons of Power in Christianity and Islam.* Baltimore: Johns Hopkins Press.

Atkinson, C., et al. 1985. *Immaculate and Powerful: The Female in Sacred Image and Social Reality.* Boston: Beacon Press.

Bagge, S. 1904. "The Circumcision Ceremony among the Naivasha Masai." *Journal of the Anthropological Institute of Great Britain and Ireland* 34: 167–169.

Barrett, David B. 1968. *Schism and Renewal in Africa: An Analysis of Six Thousand Contemporary Religious Movements.* Nairobi: Oxford University Press.

Baum, Robert M. 1999. *Shrines of the Slave Trade: Diola Religion and Society in Precolonial Senegambia.* New York: Oxford University Press.

Baumann, Oscar. 1894. *Durch Massailand zur Nilquelle: Resien und Forschungen der Massai-Expedition des deutschen Antisklaverei-Komite in den Jahren 1891–93.* Berlin: Dietrich Reimer.

Beadnell, C. Marsh. 1905. "Circumcision and Clitoridectomy as Practised by the Natives of British East Africa." *British Medical Journal* (April 19, 1905): 964–965.

Beidelman, T. O. 1974. "Social Theory and the Study of Christian Missions in Africa." *Africa* 44(3): 235–249.

———. 1982. *Colonial Evangelism.* Bloomington: Indiana University Press.

———. 1999. "Altruism and Domesticity: Images of Missionizing Women among the Church Missionary Society in Nineteenth-Century East Africa." In *Gendered Missions: Women and Men in Missionary Discourse and Practice,* ed. Mary Taylor Huber and Nancy Lutkehaus. Ann Arbor: University of Michigan Press.

Bennett, Norman R. 1963. "The Holy Ghost Mission in East Africa: 1858–1890." *Studies in East African History.* Boston: Boston University Press.

Benson, J. Stanley. 1970. "Christian Communication among the Masai." *Africa Theological Journal* 4: 68–75.

———. 1974. "A Study of the Religious Beliefs and Practices of the Maasai Tribe and the Implications on the Work of the Evangelical Lutheran Church in Tanzania." Master's thesis, Northwestern Lutheran Theological Seminary (St. Paul, Minnesota).

————. 1980. "The Conquering Sacrament: Baptism and Demon Possession among the Maasai of Tanzania." *Africa Theological Journal* 9: 52–61.

Berger, Iris. 1995. "Fertility as Power: Spirit Mediums, Priestesses and the Pre-colonial State in Interlacustrine East Africa." In *Revealing Prophets,* ed. David M. Anderson and Douglas H. Johnson. London: James Currey.

Bernsten, John. 1976. "The Maasai and Their Neighbors: Variables of Interaction." *African Economic History* 2: 1–11.

————. 1979a. "Pastoralism, Raiding and Prophets: Maasailand in the Nineteenth Century." Ph.D. dissertation, Department of History, University of Wisconsin–Madison.

————. 1979b. "Maasai Age-Sets and Prophetic Leadership: 1850–1910." *Africa* 49(2): 134–146.

————. 1980. "The Enemy Is Us: Eponymy in the Historiography of the Maasai." *History in Africa* 7: 1–21.

Bianco, Barbara. 2000. "Gender and Material Culture in West Pokot, Kenya." In *Rethinking Pastoralism: Gender, Culture and the Myth of the Patriarchal Pastoralist,* ed. Dorothy L. Hodgson. Oxford: James Currey.

Blakeley, Thomas D., Walter E. A. Van Beek, and Dennis L. Thomson, eds. 1994. *Religion in Africa: Experience and Expression.* London: James Currey.

Boddy, Janice. 1989. *Wombs and Alien Spirits: Women, Men and the Zar Cult in Northern Sudan.* Madison: University of Wisconsin Press.

Bowie, Fiona. 1993. "The Elusive Christian Family: Missionary Attempts to Define Women's Roles: Case Studies from Cameroon." In *Women and Missions: Past and Present,* ed. Fiona Bowie et al. Providence: Berg.

Bowie, Fiona, Deborah Kirkwood, and Shirley Ardener, eds. 1993. *Women and Missions: Past and Present.* Providence: Berg.

Brenner, Louis. 1989. " 'Religious' Discourse in and About Africa." In *Discourse and Its Disguises: The Interpretation of African Oral Texts,* ed. Karin Barber and P. F. de Moraes Farias. Birmingham: Center for West African Studies, University of Birmingham.

Brereton, Virginia Lieson. 1991. *From Sin to Salvation: Stories of Women's Conversions, 1800 to the Present.* Bloomington: Indiana University Press.

Broch-Due, Vigdis. 2000. "The Fertility of Houses and Herds: Producing Kinship and Gender amongst Turkana Pastoralists." In *Rethinking Pastoralism in Africa: Gender, Culture and the Myth of the Patriarchal Pastoralist,* ed. Dorothy L. Hodgson. Oxford: James Currey.

Brusco, Elizabeth. 1994. "Missionaries of Liberation? Gender Complementarity in Colombian Pentecostal Leadership." In *The Message in the Missionary: Local Interpretations of Religious Ideology and Missionary Personality,* ed. Elizabeth Brusco and Laura F. Klein. Studies in Third World Societies 55. Williamsburg, Va.: College of William and Mary.

Burton, John W. 1982. "Nilotic Women: A Diachronic Perspective." *Journal of Modern African Studies* 20(3): 467–491.

————. 1985. "Christians, Colonists, and Conversion: A View from Nilotic Sudan." *Journal of Modern African Studies* 23(2): 349–369.

————. 1991. "Representations of the Feminine in Nilotic Cosmologies." In *Body and Space: Symbolic Models of Unity and Division in African Cosmology and Experience,* ed. Anita Jacobson-Widding. Stockholm: Almqvist and Wiksell.

Butselaar, G. Jan van. 1981. "Christian Conversion in Rwanda: The Motivations." *International Bulletin of Missionary Research* 5: 111–113.

Carmody, Brendan. 1988. "Conversion and School at Chikuni, 1905–39." *Africa* 58(2): 193–209.

———. 1989. "Mission Primary Schools and Conversion: Help or Hindrance to Church Growth?" *Missiology* 17(2): 177–192.

"The Case for Polygamy." 1968. *Time,* May 10, p. 114.

Chanel, M. Joseph. 1900. *Voyage au Kilima Ndjaro.* Paris: Extrait du Bulletin Trimestriel de l'Association des Anciens Élèves de l'École des Hautes Études Commerciales.

Christian, William A. 1981. *Local Religion in Sixteenth Century Spain.* Princeton, N.J.: Princeton University Press.

Christy, William, C.S.Sp. 2001. "Greetings from Arusha." In "Mission Diary" section of *USA Eastern Province Newsletter* 29(1): 3.

Comaroff, Jean. 1985. *Body of Power, Spirit of Resistance.* Chicago: University of Chicago Press.

Comaroff, Jean, and John L. Comaroff. 1991. *Of Revelation and Revolution: Christianity, Colonialism, and Consciousness in South Africa.* Vol. 1. Chicago: University of Chicago Press.

Comaroff, John L., and Jean Comaroff. 1997. *Of Revelation and Revolution: The Dialectics of Modernity on a South African Frontier.* Vol. 2. Chicago: University of Chicago Press.

Connell, R. W. 1987. *Gender and Power: Society, the Person and Sexual Politics.* Stanford, Calif.: Stanford University Press.

Cooper, Frederick, and Ann Stoler, eds. 1997. *Tensions of Empire: Colonial Cultures in a Bourgeois World.* Berkeley and Los Angeles: University of California Press.

Dallas, Douglas. 1931. "The Sacred Tree of Ol Donyesha." *Man* 31: 39–41.

Davidman, Lynn. 1991. *Tradition in a Rootless World: Women Turn to Orthodox Judaism.* Berkeley and Los Angeles: University of California Press.

di Leonardo, Micaela, ed. 1991. *Gender at the Crossroads of Knowledge.* Berkeley and Los Angeles: University of California Press.

Dirks, Nicholas, Geoff Eley, and Sherry B. Ortner, eds. 1994. *Culture/Power/History.* Princeton, N.J.: Princeton University Press.

Dolan, Rev. Thomas A., C.S.Sp. 1953a. "Cowboys of Tanganyika: The Masai-I." *Mission News,* pp. 3–4.

———. 1953b. "Cowboys of Tanganyika: The Masai-II." *Mission News,* pp. 10–11.

———. 1953c. "Cowboys of Tanganyika: The Masai-III." *Mission News,* pp. 18–19.

Donovan, Vincent, C.S.Sp. 1967. "Preaching the Gospel to the Masai." *AFER-AMECEA Pastoral Institute* (Gaba) 9: 204–215.

———. 1978. *Christianity Rediscovered.* Chicago: Fides/Claretian.

———. 1989. *The Church in the Midst of Creation.* Maryknoll, N.Y.: Orbis.

———. 2000. Obituary. *USA Eastern Province Newsletter* 28(3): 5.

Durkheim, Emile. 1947. *The Elementary Forms of the Religious Life.* Trans. George Simpson. New York: Free Press.

Durning, Dennis, C.S.Sp. 2002. Obituary. *USA Eastern Province Newsletter* 30(2): 3–4.

Edgerton, Robert B., and Francis P. Conant. 1964. "*Kilipat:* The 'Shaming Party' among the Pokot of East Africa." *Southwestern Journal of Anthropology* 20: 404–418.

Ekechi, E. K. 1970. "African Polygamy and Western Christian Eurocentrism." *Journal of African Studies* 3: 329–349.

Elbourne, Elizabeth. 2002. *Blood Ground: Colonialism, Missions, and the Contest for Christianity in the Cape Colony and Britain, 1799–1853*. Montreal: McGill-Queen's University Press.

Eliot, Charles. 1905. "Introduction." In Alfred C. Hollis, *The Masai: Their Language and Folklore*. Freeport, N.Y.: Book for Libraries Press.

———. 1966 [1905]. *The East Africa Protectorate*. London: Frank Cass.

Etherington, Norman. 1977. "Social Theory and the Study of Christian Missions in Africa: A South African Case Study." *Africa* 47: 31–40.

Farler, J. P. 1882. "Native Routes in East Africa from Pangani to the Masai Country and the Victoria Nyanza." *Proceedings of the Royal Geographical Society* 4(12): 730–742, 776 (map).

Flatt, Donald C. 1973. "The Cross-Cultural Interpretation of Religion in Africa." *Missiology* 1(3): 325–341.

Fosbrooke, H. A. 1948. "An Administrative Survey of the Masai Social System." *Tanganyika Notes and Records* 26: 1–50.

———. 1955 and 1956. "The Life of Justin." *Tanganyika Notes and Records* 41: 31–57; 42: 18–30.

Foucault, Michel. 1972. *The Archaeology of Knowledge and the Discourse on Language*. Trans. A. M. Sheridan Smith. New York: Pantheon Books.

———. 1978 [1976]. *The History of Sexuality*. Vol. 1. Trans. Robert Hurley. New York: Vintage Books.

———. 1979. *Discipline and Punish: The Birth of the Prison*. Trans. Alan Sheridan. New York: Vintage Books.

Fratkin, Elliot. 1979. "A Comparison of the Role of Prophets in Samburu and Maasai Warfare." *Senri Ethnological Studies* 3: 53–67.

———. 1991. "The Impact of Christian Missions." In *Surviving Drought and Development: Ariaal Pastoralists of Northern Kenya*. Boulder, Colo.: Westview Press.

French-Sheldon, Mrs. 1892. "Customs among the Natives of East Africa, from Teita to Kilimeglia, with Special Reference to Their Women and Children." *Journal of the Royal Anthropological Institute of Great Britain and Ireland* 21: 358–390.

Friedman, Greg, O.F.M. 1980. "No Baggage—Just the Gospel." *St. Anthony Messenger* 88(3): 12–19.

Gabbert, Wolfgang. 2001. "Social and Cultural Conditions of Religious Conversion in Colonial Southwest Tanzania, 1891–1939." *Ethnology* 40(4): 291–308.

Gaitskell, Deborah. 1979. "Christian Compounds for Girls: Church Hostels for African Women in Johannesburg, 1907–1970." *Journal of Southern African Studies* 6: 44–69.

Galaty, John. 1983. "Ceremony and Society: The Poetics of Maasai Ritual." *Man* 18(2): 361–382.

———. 1993a. "Maasai Expansion and the New East African Pastoralism." In *Being Maasai*, ed. Thomas Spear and Richard Waller. London: James Currey.

———. 1993b. "The Eye That Wants a Person, Where Can It Not See? Inclusion, Exclusion, and Boundary Shifters in Maasai Identity." In *Being Maasai*, ed. Thomas Spear and Richard Waller. London: James Currey.

Geertz, Clifford. 1973. "Religion as a Cultural System." In *The Interpretation of Cultures*. New York: Basic Books.

Gobeil, Maurice, C.S.Sp. 1985. "Claude Francis Poullart des Places: A Life-Experience under the Breath of the Spirit." *Spiritans Today* 4: 29–48.

Gogarty, H. A., C.S.Sp. 1927. *Kilima-njaro: An East-African Vicariate*. New York: Society for the Propagation of the Faith.

Goody, Jack. 1961. "Religion and Ritual: The Definitional Problem." *British Journal of Sociology* 12: 142–164.

Green, Maia. 2003. *Priests, Witches and Power: Popular Christianity after Mission in Southern Tanzania*. New York: Cambridge University Press.

Grosz-Ngate, Maria, and Omari H. Kokole, eds. 1997. *Gendered Encounters: Challenging Cultural Boundaries and Social Hierarchies in Africa*. New York: Routledge.

Gulliver, Philip. 1969. "The Conservative Commitment in Northern Tanzania: The Arusha and Masai." In *Tradition and Transition in East Africa*, ed. Philip Gulliver. London: Routledge and Kegan Paul.

Hackett, Rosalind. 1985. "Sacred Paradoxes: Women and Religious Plurality in Nigeria." In *Women, Religion and Social Change*, ed. Yvonne Yazbeck Hadad and Ellison Banks Findly. Albany: State University of New York Press.

———. 1987. "Women as Leaders and Participants in the Spiritual Churches." In *New Religious Movements in Nigeria*, ed. Rosalind Hackett. Lewiston, N.Y.: Edwin Mellen Press.

———. 1995. "Women and New Religious Movements in Africa." In *Religion and Gender*, ed. Ursula King. Oxford: Basil Blackwell.

Hamilton, Claud. 1963. "The 'E-Unoto' Ceremony of the Masai." *Man* 63: 107–109.

Hastings, Adrian. 1967. *The Church and Mission in Modern Africa*. London: SPCK.

———. 1976. *African Christianity*. New York: Seabury Press.

———. 1979. *A History of African Christianity 1950–1975*. Cambridge: Cambridge University Press.

———, ed. 1991. *Modern Catholicism: Vatican II and After*. London: SPCK.

———. 1993. "Were Women a Special Case?" In *Women and Missions: Past and Present*, ed. Fiona Bowie et al. Providence: Berg.

———. 1994. *The Church in Africa, 1450–1950*. Oxford: Clarendon Press.

Hauge, Hans-Egil. 1979. *Maasai Religion and Folklore*. Nairobi: City Printing Works.

Hefner, Robert W., ed. 1993. *Conversion to Christianity: Historical and Anthropological Perspectives on a Great Transformation*. Berkeley and Los Angeles: University of California Press.

Henschel, Johannes. 1991. *Christus wurde Maasai: Kirche unter den Nomaden in Ostafrika*. Mainz, Germany: Matthias-Grünewald-Verlag.

Hillman, Eugene, C.S.Sp. 1966. *The Church as Mission*. London: Sheed and Ward.

———. 1968. *The Wider Ecumenism: Anonymous Christianity and the Church*. London: Burns and Oates.

———. 1975. *Polygamy Reconsidered: African Plural Marriages and the Christian Churches*. Maryknoll, N.Y.: Orbis.

———. 1989. *Many Paths: A Catholic Approach to Religious Pluralism*. Maryknoll, N.Y.: Orbis.

———. 1991. "The Pauperization of the Maasai." Paper presented to the First Maasai Conference on Culture and Development in Arusha, Tanzania.

———. 1993. *Inculturation Applied: Toward an African Christianity*. New York: Paulist Press.

———. 1994a. "My Pilgrimage in Mission." *International Bulletin of Missionary Research* 18(4): 162–166.

———. 1994b. "The Pauperization of the Maasai in Kenya." *Africa Today* 41(4): 57–65.

Hinde, Sidney Langford, and Hildegarde Hinde. 1901. *The Last of the Masai*. London: William Heinemann.

Hinfelaar, Hugo F. 1994. *Bemba-Speaking Women of Zambia in a Century of Religious Change (1892–1992)*. Leiden: Brill.

Hobley, C. W. 1911. "Further Researches into Kikuyu and Kamba Religious Beliefs and Customs." *Journal of the Royal Anthropological Institute of Great Britain and Ireland* 41: 406–457.

Hodgson, Dorothy L. 1996. " 'My Daughter . . . Belongs to the Government Now': Marriage, Maasai and the Tanzanian State." *Canadian Journal of African Studies* 30(1): 106–123.

———. 1997. "Embodying the Contradictions of Modernity: Gender and Spirit Possession among Maasai in Tanzania." In *Gendered Encounters: Challenging Cultural Boundaries and Social Hierarchies in Africa*, ed. Maria Grosz-Ngate and Omari Kokole. New York: Routledge.

———. 1999a. "Pastoralism, Patriarchy and History: Changing Gender Relations among Maasai in Tanganyika, 1890–1940." *Journal of African History* 40(1): 41–65.

———. 1999b. " 'Once Intrepid Warriors': Modernity and the Production of Maasai Masculinities." *Ethnology* 38(2): 121–150.

———. 1999c. "Women as Children: Culture, Political Economy and Gender Inequality among Kisongo Maasai." *Nomadic Peoples* (n.s.) 3(2): 115–130.

———. 1999d. "Engendered Encounters: Men of the Church and the 'Church of Women' in Maasailand, Tanzania, 1950–1993." *Comparative Studies in Society and History* 41(4): 758–783.

———. 1999e. "Critical Interventions: Dilemmas of Accountability in Contemporary Ethnographic Research." *Identities* 6(2/3): 201–224.

———. 2000a. "Taking Stock: Ethnohistorical Perspectives on State Control, Ethnic Identity, and Pastoralist Development in Tanganyika, 1940–1961." *Journal of African History* 41(1): 55–78.

———, ed. 2000b. *Rethinking Pastoralism in Africa: Gender, Culture and the Myth of the Patriarchal Pastoralist*. Oxford: James Currey; Athens: Ohio University Press.

———. 2001a. *Once Intrepid Warriors: The Cultural Politics of Gender, Ethnicity and Maasai Development in Tanzania*. Bloomington: Indiana University Press.

———, ed. 2001b. *Gendered Modernities: Ethnographic Perspectives*. New York: Palgrave.

———. 2002. "Precarious Alliances: The Cultural Politics and Structural Predicaments of the Indigenous Rights Movement in Tanzania." *American Anthropologist* 104(4): 1086–1097.

Hodgson, Dorothy L., and Sheryl McCurdy, eds. 2001. *"Wicked" Women and the Reconfiguration of Gender in Africa*. Portsmouth, N.H.: Heinemann.

Hodgson, Dorothy L., and Richard Schroeder. 2002. "Dilemmas of Counter-Mapping Community Resources in Tanzania." *Development and Change* 33(1): 79–100.

Hoehler-Fatton, Cynthia. 1996. *Women of Fire and Spirit: History, Faith, and Gender in Roho Religion in Western Kenya*. New York: Oxford University Press.

Holden, Pat, ed. 1983. *Women's Religious Experiences: Cross-Cultural Perspectives*. London: Croom Helm.

Hollis, Alfred C. 1905. *The Masai: Their Language and Folklore*. Freeport, N.Y.: Book for Libraries Press.

———. 1910. "A Note on the Masai System of Relationship and Other Matters Connected Therewith." *Journal of the Royal Anthropological Institute* 40(21): 473–482.

———. 1943. "The Masai." *Journal of the Royal Anthropological Institute* 42(167): 119–126.

Horton, Robin. 1967. "African Conversion." *Africa* 41(2): 85–108.

———. 1975a. "On the Rationality of Conversion, Part I." *Africa* 45(3): 219–235.

———. 1975b. "On the Rationality of Conversion, Part II." *Africa* 45(4): 373–399.

Huber, Mary. 1988. *The Bishop's Progress: A Historical Ethnography of Catholic Missionary Experience on the Sepik Frontier.* Washington, D.C.: Smithsonian Institution Press.

Huber, Mary Taylor, and Nancy C. Lutkehaus, eds. 1999. *Gendered Missions: Women and Men in Missionary Discourse and Practice.* Ann Arbor: University of Michigan Press.

Hunt, Nancy Rose. 1990. "Domesticity and Colonialism in Belgian Africa: Usumbura's Foyer Social, 1946–1960." *Signs* 15(3): 447–474.

———. 1999. *A Colonial Lexicon of Birth Ritual, Medicalization, and Mobility in the Congo.* Durham, N.C.: Duke University Press.

Hurskainen, Arvi. 1985a. "Tatizo la Kushikwa na Pepo Umasaini Tanzania" [The Problem of Spirit Possession in Maasailand, Tanzania]. Helsinki. Privately circulated paper, commissioned by the Catholic and Lutheran churches, Tanzania.

———. 1985b. "Epidemiology of Spirit Possession among the Maasai in Tanzania." *Africa Theological Journal* 14(3): 161–173.

———. 1989. "The Epidemiological Aspect of Spirit Possession among the Maasai of Tanzania." In *Culture, Experience, and Pluralism: Essays on African Ideas of Illness and Healing,* ed. Anita Jacobson-Widding and David Westerlund. Uppsala: Almqvist and Wiksell International.

———. 1990. "Formal Categories of Maasai Symbolism." In *From Water to World-Making: African Models and Arid Lands,* ed. Gísli Pálsson. Uppsala: Scandinavian Institute of African Studies.

Iliffe, John. 1969. *Tanganyika under German Rule 1905–1912.* Cambridge: Cambridge University Press.

———. 1979. *A Modern History of Tanganyika.* Cambridge: Cambridge University Press.

Isichei, Elizabeth. 1970. "Seven Varieties of Ambiguity: Some Patterns of Igbo Response to Christian Missions." *Journal of Religion in Africa* 3: 209–227.

———. 1993. "Does Christianity Empower Women? The Case of the Anaguta of Central Nigeria." In *Women and Missions: Past and Present,* ed. Fiona Bowie et al. Providence: Berg.

———. 1995. *A History of Christianity in Africa: From Antiquity to the Present.* Grand Rapids, Mich.: Eerdmans.

Jacobs, Alan H. 1965. "The Traditional Political Organization of the Pastoral Maasai." D.Phil. thesis, Oxford University.

———. 1968. "A Chronology of the Pastoral Maasai." In *Hadith I.* Kenya: East African Publishing House.

James, Wendy. 1998. "Uduk Faith in a Five-Note Scale: Mission Music and the Spread of the Gospel." In *Vernacular Christianity: Essays in the Social Anthropology of Religion,* ed. Wendy James and Douglas H. Johnson. Oxford: Journal of the Anthropological Society of Oxford.

Jell-Bahlsen, Sabine. 1998. "Female Power: Water Priestesses of the Oru-Igbo." In *Sisterhood, Feminisms and Power: From Africa to the Diaspora,* ed. Obioma Nnaemeka. Trenton, N.J.: Africa World Press.

Johnston, Harry. 1886. *The Kilima-Njaro Expedition: A Record of Scientific Exploration in Eastern Equatorial Africa.* London: Kegan Paul, Trench.

———. 1902. *The Uganda Protectorate.* Vol. 2. New York: Dodd, Mead.

Jules-Rosette, Bennetta, ed. 1979. *The New Religions of Africa.* Norwood, N.J.: Ablex Publishing Co.

———. 1987. "Privilege without Power: Women in African Cults and Churches." In *Women in Africa and the African Diaspora,* ed. Rosalyn Terborg-Penn, Sharon Harley, and Andrea Benton Rushing. Washington, D.C.: Howard University Press.

Juster, Susan. 1989. " 'In a Different Voice': Male and Female Narratives of Religious Conversion in Post-Revolutionary America." *American Quarterly* 41: 34–62.

Kane, Mortimer F., C.S.Sp. 1995. "A Golden Key for Evangelization." Manuscript. Spiritan Archives, Bethel Park, 36F-4A. Photocopy in author's possession.

Kanogo, Tabitha. 1993. "Mission Impact on Women in Colonial Kenya." In *Women and Missions: Past and Present,* ed. Fiona Bowie et al. Providence: Berg.

Kaplan, Steven. 1985. "The Africanization of Missionary Christianity: History and Typology." *Journal of Religion in Africa* 16: 166–186.

Keane, Webb. 1997. "Religious Language." *Annual Review of Anthropology* 26: 4–71.

Kelly, Joseph, C.S.Sp. n.d. "Moshi Centenary Is Spiritans', Too." *Congregation of the Holy Ghost Newsletter.*

———. 1999. "Too Young to Quit." *USA Eastern Province Newsletter* 27(3): 2.

———. 2000. "Still US East's Youngest." In "Mission Diary" section of *USA Eastern Province Newsletter* 28(2): 3.

Kiel, Christel. 1997. *Christians in Maasailand: A Study of the History of Mission among the Maasai in the North Eastern Diocese of the Evangelical Lutheran Church in Tanzania.* Makumira Publication 9. Erlangen, Germany: Erlanger Verlag für Mission und Ökumene.

Kieran, J. A. 1966. "The Holy Ghost Fathers in East Africa, 1863–1914." Dissertation, University of London.

———. 1969a. "Some Roman Catholic Missionary Attitudes to Africans in Nineteenth Century East Africa." *Race* 10(3): 341–359.

———. 1969b. "The Origins of Commercial Arabica Coffee Production in East Africa." *African Historical Studies* 2(1): 51–67.

———. 1971. "Christian Villages in North-Eastern Tanzania." *Transafrican Journal of History* 1(1): 24–38.

King, Kenneth J. 1971. "A Biography of Molonket Olokorinya ole Sempele." In *Kenya Historical Biographies,* ed. Kenneth King and Ahmed Salim. Nairobi: East African Publishing House.

King, Ursula, ed. 1995. *Religion and Gender.* Oxford: Basil Blackwell.

Kipuri, Naomi. 1983. *Oral Literature of the Maasai.* Heinemann: Nairobi, Kenya.

———. 1989. "Maasai Women in Transition: Class and Gender in the Transformation of a Pastoral Society." Ph.D. thesis, Temple University.

Kirby, Jon. 1994a. "Cultural Change and Religious Conversion in West Africa." In *Religion in Africa: Experience and Expression,* ed. Thomas D. Blakely, Walter E. A. Van Beek, and Dennis L. Thomson. London: James Currey.

———. 1994b. Review of Eugene Hillman, *Toward an African Christianity: Inculturation Applied. International Bulletin of Missionary Research* 18(3): 138.

Klein, Laura. 1994. " 'Timid Women Do Not Make Good Missionaries in Alaska': Gender and Mission in Southeastern Alaska." In *The Message in the Missionary: Local*

Interpretations of Religious Ideology and Missionary Personality, ed. Elizabeth Brusco and Laura F. Klein. Studies in Third World Societies 55. Williamsburg, Va.: College of William and Mary.

Klobuchar, Jim. 1998. *The Cross under the Acacia Tree: The Story of David and Eunice Simonson's Epic Mission in Africa.* Minneapolis: Kirk House Publishers.

Klumpp, Donna. 1987. "Maasai Art and Society: Age and Sex, Time and Space, Cash and Cattle." Ph.D. thesis, Columbia University.

Klumpp, Donna, and Corinne Kratz. 1993. "Aesthetics, Expertise and Ethnicity: Okiek and Maasai Perspectives on Personal Ornament." In *Being Maasai: Ethnicity and Identity in East Africa,* ed. Thomas Spear and Richard Waller. London: James Currey.

Knowles, Joan, and David Collett. 1989. "Nature as Myth, Symbol and Action: Notes towards a Historical Understanding of Development and Conservation in Kenyan Maasailand." *Africa* 59(4): 433–460.

Kohler, Girard, C.S.Sp. 1977a. "Tanzania: The Apostolate to the Masai." *Fides* 2818: 410–414.

———. 1977b. "Apostolate among a Nomad Tribe in Africa: The Masai Tribe in Tanzania." *Christ to the World* 6: 398–402.

———. 2002. "Libermann." *USA Eastern Province Newsletter* 30(1): 2.

Koponen, Juhani. "Population: A Dependent Variable." In *Custodians of the Land: Ecology and Culture in the History of Tanzania,* ed. Gregory Maddox, James Giblin, and Isaria Kimambo. London: James Currey.

Koren, Henry J., C.S.Sp. 1983. *To the Ends of the Earth: A General History of the Congregation of the Holy Ghost.* Pittsburgh: Duquesne University Press.

———. 1994. *Spiritan East Africa Memorial, 1863–1993.* Bethel Park, Pa.: Spiritus Press.

Kozak, David. 1993. "Ecumenical Indianism: The Tekakwitha Movement as a Discursive Field of Faith and Power." In *The Message in the Missionary: Local Interpretations of Religious Ideology and Missionary Personality,* ed. Elizabeth Brusco and Laura F. Klein. Studies in Third World Societies 55. Williamsburg, Va.: College of William and Mary.

Krapf, J. Lewis. 1854. *Vocabulary of the Engútuk Eloiköe or of the Language of the Wakuafi-Nation in the Interior of Equatorial Africa.* Tübingen: Lud. Fried. Fues.

———. 1968 [1860]. *Travels, Researches and Missionary Labours during an Eighteen Years Residence in East Africa.* 2nd ed. London: Frank Cass.

Kratz, Corinne, and Donna Pido. 2000. "Gender, Ethnicity and Social Aesthetics in Maasai and Okiek Beadwork." In *Rethinking Pastoralism in Africa: Gender, Culture and the Myth of the Patriarchal Pastoralist,* ed. Dorothy L. Hodgson. Oxford: James Currey.

Labode, Modupe. 1993. "From Heathen Kraal to Christian Home: Anglican Mission Education and African Christian Girls, 1850–1900." In *Women and Missions: Past and Present,* ed. Fiona Bowie et al. Providence: Berg.

Lambek, Michael. 2000. "The Anthropology of Religion and the Quarrel between Poetry and Philosophy." *Current Anthropology* 41(3): 309–320.

———. 2002. "General Introduction." In *A Reader in the Anthropology of Religion,* ed. Michael Lambek. Oxford: Blackwell.

Landau, Paul Stuart. 1991. "Preacher, Chief and Prophetess: Moruti Seakgano in the Ngwato Kingdom, East-central Botswana." *Journal of Southern African Studies* 17(1): 1–22.

————. 1995. *The Realm of the Word: Language, Gender, and Christianity in a Southern African Kingdom*. Portsmouth, N.H.: Heinemann.

————. 1999. " 'Religion' and Christian Conversion in African History: A New Model." *Journal of Religious History* 23(1): 8–30.

Larsson, Birgitta. 1991. *Conversion to Greater Freedom: Women, Church, and Social Change in North-Western Tanzania under Colonial Rule*. Uppsala: Uppsala University.

Last, J. T. 1883. "A Visit to the Masai People Living beyond the Borders of the Nguru Country." *Proceedings of the Royal Geographic Society* 5(9): 517–543, 568 (map).

Leakey, L. S. B. 1930. "Some Notes on the Masai of Kenya Colony." *Journal of the Royal Anthropological Institute of Great Britain* 60: 185–209.

LeClair, Richard J., C.S.Sp. 1993. *Kibo! Speak My Song*. Self-published.

LeRoy, Alexandre. 1906. "La Rôle Scientifique des Missionaires." *Anthropos* 1(1): 3–10.

————. 1909. *La Religion des Primitifs*. Paris: Gabriel Beauchesne.

————. 1914. *Au-Kilima-ndjaro*. Paris: Souvenir Africain.

Lewis, I. M. 1971. *Ecstatic Religion: An Anthropological Study of Spirit Possession and Shamanism*. Middlesex: Pelican.

Libermann, François Marie Paul. 1962–1964. *The Spiritual Letters of the Venerable Francis Libermann*. Pittsburgh: Duquesne University Press.

Lienhardt, Godfrey. 1982. "The Dinka and Catholicism." In *Religious Orientation and Religious Experience*, ed. J. Davis. London: Academic Press.

Lindsay, Lisa A., and Stephan F. Miescher, eds. 2003. *Men and Masculinities in Modern Africa*. Portsmouth, N.H.: Heinemann.

Listowel, Judith. 1965. *The Making of Tanganyika*. London: Chatto and Windus.

Ludwig, Frieder. 1999. *Church and State in Tanzania: Aspects of a Changing Relationship, 1961–1994*. Leiden: Brill.

Luzbetak, Louis J. 1961. "Toward an Applied Missionary Anthropology." *Anthropological Quarterly* 34(4): 165–176.

————. 1988. *The Church and Cultures: New Perspectives in Missiological Anthropology*. Maryknoll, N.Y.: Orbis Books.

Macdonald, Lieutenant-Colonel J.R.L. 1899. "Notes on the Ethnology of Tribes Met With during Progress of the Juba Expedition of 1897–99." *Journal of the Royal Anthropological Institute of Great Britain and Ireland* 29 (3/4): 226–247.

Maguire, R. A. J. 1931. Letter re: "Masai Water Trees." *Man* 31: 142–143.

Mallett, Marguerite. 1923. *A White Woman among the Masai*. London: T. Fisher Unwin.

Margetts, Edward L. 1963. "On the Masai E-Unoto." *Man* 63: 190–191.

"Masai Initiation Ceremonies." 1949–1950. *East African Annual* 1949–1950: 54–55.

Merker, Moritz. 1910 [1904]. *Die Masai. Ethnographische Monographie eines ostafrikanischen Semitenvolkes*. 2nd ed. Berlin: Dietrich Reimer.

Meyer, Birgit. 1999. *Translating the Devil: Religion and Modernity among the Ewe in Ghana*. Trenton, N.J.: Africa World Press.

Michel, Joseph, C.S.Sp. 1985. "The Sources of Poullart des Places's Spirituality and the Origins of His Work." *Spiritans Today* 4: 9–27.

Mol, Frans. 1977. *Maa: A Dictionary of the Maasai Language and Folklore*. Nairobi: Marketing and Publishing.

————. 1996. *Maasai Language and Culture Dictionary*. Limuru, Kenya: Kolbe Press.

Moss, Barbara. 1999. " 'And the Bones Come Together': Women's Religious Expectations in Southern Africa, c. 1900–1945." *Journal of Religious History* 23(1): 108–127.

Moss, John, and Bini Moss. c. 1960. "Mission for the Masai: Article with Photographs." Typescript available in Bethel Park Archives 21C-32–14.

Mtaita, Leonard A. 1998. *The Wandering Shepherds and the Good Shepherd: Contextualization as the Way of Doing Mission with the Maasai in the Evangelical Lutheran Church in Tanzania, Pare Diocese.* Erlangen, Germany: Erlanger Verlag für Mission und Ökumene (Makumira Publication Eleven).

Mullenix, Gordon R., and Rev. John Mpaayei. 1984. "Matonyok: A Case Study of the Interaction of Evangelism and Community Development among the Keekonyokie Maasai of Kenya." *Missiology* 12(3): 327–337.

Musisi, Nakanyike B. 1999. "Morality as Identity: The Missionary Moral Agenda in Buganda, 1877–1945." *Journal of Religious History* 23(1): 51–74.

Naas, Eef A. H., C.S.Sp. 1971. "Christian Communication among the Masai." *Africa Theological Journal* 4: 56–67.

Neckebrouck, Valeer. 1993. *Resistant Peoples: The Case of the Pastoral Maasai of East Africa.* Rome: Editrice Pontificia Universita Gregoriana.

———. 2002. *Les Maasai et le Christianisme: Le Temps du Grand Refus.* Leuven: Peeters.

Northern Province Annual Reports, Tanganyika. Dar es Salaam: Government Printer.

Oliver, Roland. 1965. *The Missionary Factor in East Africa.* London: Longmans.

Olle Timan, Fr. Matthew [Mathai]. 1987. "An Analysis of the Causes of Tension between Local Clergy and Missionaries in Arusha Diocese." Mimeo in author's possession.

Olsson, Tord. 1977. "The Social Usage of Mythical Elements among the Maasai." *Temenos* 13: 118–127.

———. 1989. "Philosophy of Medicine among the Maasai." In *Culture, Experience and Pluralism: Essays on African Ideas of Illness and Healing,* ed. Anita Jacobson-Widding and David Westerlund. Stockholm: Almqvist and Wiksell.

Parsalaw, Joseph Wilson. 1999. *A History of the Lutheran Church, Diocese in the Arusha Region from 1904 to 1958.* Erlangen, Germany: Erlanger Verlag für Mission und Ökumene (Makumira Publication Twelve).

Peel, J. D. Y. 1967. "Syncretism and Religious Change." *Comparative Studies in Society and History* 10(1): 121–141.

———. 1995. "For Who Hath Despised the Day of Small Things? Missionary Narratives and Historical Anthropology." *Comparative Studies in Society and History* 37(3): 581–607.

———. 2000. *Religious Encounter and the Making of the Yoruba.* Bloomington: Indiana University Press.

Peligal, Rona Elayne. 1999. "Spatial Planning and Social Fluidity: The Shifting Boundaries of Ethnicity, Gender and Class in Arusha, Tanzania, 1920–1967." Ph.D. thesis, Columbia University.

Pels, Peter. 1997. "The Anthropology of Colonialism: Culture, History, and the Emergence of Western Governmentality." *Annual Review of Anthropology* 26: 163–183.

———. 1999. *A Politics of Presence: Contacts between Missionaries and Waluguru in Late Colonial Tanganyika.* Amsterdam: Harwood Academic Publishers.

Peristiany, John G. 1975. "The Ideal and the Actual: the Role of Prophets in the Pokot Political System." In *Studies in Social Anthropology,* ed. J. H. Beattie and R. G. Lienhardt. Oxford: Clarendon Press.

Peterson, David. 1971. "Demon Possession among the Masai." Manuscript in author's possession.

Peterson, Dean. 1985. "Spirit Possession among the Maasai in Tanzania." *Africa Theological Journal* 14(1): 174–178.

Peterson, Derek. 2001. "Wordy Women: Gender Trouble and the Oral Politics of the East African Revival in Northern Gikuyuland." *Journal of African History* 42(3): 469–489.

Peterson, Derek, and Jean Allman. 1999. "Introduction: New Directions in the History of Missions in Africa." *Journal of Religious History* 23(1): 1–7.

Poirier, Father Ralph, C.S.Sp. 1974. "Christ Makes Sense." Manuscript available on Father Poirier's website: http://www.ralphcssp.hispeed.com/sense.htm. Downloaded September 14, 2001. Typescript copy in Bethel Archives.

———. 1984. "Christ before Literacy." Manuscript available on Father Poirier's website: http://www.ralphcssp.hispeed.com/literacy.htm. Downloaded September 14, 2001. Typescript copy in Bethel Archives.

Priest, Doug, Jr. 1990. *Doing Theology with the Maasai*. Pasadena: William Caren Library.

———. 1991. "Do the Maasai Know God? An Exercise in Cultural Exegesis." *African Theological Journal* 20(2): 81–88.

Queeny, Edgar Monsanto. 1954. "Spearing Lions with Africa's Masai." *National Geographic* 104(4): 487–517.

Rafael, Vicente L. 1987. "Confession, Conversion, and Reciprocity in Early Tagalog Colonial Society." *Comparative Studies in Society and History* 29: 320–339.

———. 1993. *Contracting Colonialism: Translation and Christian Conversion in Tagalog Society under Early Spanish Rule*. Durham, N.C.: Duke University Press.

Rambo, Lewis. 1982. "Current Research on Religious Conversion." *Religious Studies Review* 8(2): 146–159.

———. 1993. *Understanding Religious Conversion*. New Haven, Conn.: Yale University Press.

Ranger, T. O. 1986. "Religious Movements and Politics in Sub-Saharan Africa." *African Studies Review* 29(2): 1–69.

Ranger, T. O., and I. N. Kimambo, eds. 1972. *The Historical Study of African Religion*. Berkeley and Los Angeles: University of California Press.

Report of the Arusha-Moshi Land Commission. 1947. Dar es Salaam: Government Printer.

Reusch, Richard. n.d. "Masai Circumcision, Its Meaning and Origin." 8 pages of typescript, in Hans Cory files 371, East Africana Collection, University of Dar es Salaam.

Rigby, Peter. 1981. "Pastors and Pastoralists: The Differential Penetration of Christianity among East African Cattle Herders." *Comparative Studies in Society and History* 23(1): 96–129.

———. 1983. "Time and Historical Consciousness: The Case of the Ilparakuyo Maasai." *Comparative Studies in Society and History* 25(3): 428–456.

———. 1985. *Persistent Pastoralists: Nomadic Societies in Transition*. London: Zed Books.

———. 1992. *Cattle, Capitalism, and Class: Ilparakuyo Maasai Transformations*. Philadelphia: Temple University Press.

Rounds, John C. 1982. "Curing What Ails Them: Individual Circumstances and Religious Choice among Zulu-Speakers in Durban, South Africa." *Africa* 52(2): 77–89.

Sahlberg, Carl-Erik. 1986. *From Krapf to Rugambwa: A Church History of Tanzania*. Nairobi: Evangel Publishing House.

Sanneh, Lamin. 1989. *Translating the Message: The Missionary Impact on Culture*. Maryknoll, N.Y.: Orbis.

Schoffeleers, Matthew. 1982. "Christ as the Medicine Man and the Medicine Man as Christ: A Tentative History of African Christological Thought." *Man and Life* 8(1/2): 11–28.

———. 1989. "Folk Christology in Africa: The Dialectics of the Nganga Paradigm." *Journal of Religion in Africa* 19(2): 157–181.

Scott, Joan. 1988. *Gender and the Politics of History.* New York: Columbia University Press.

Sered, Susan. 1992. *Women as Ritual Experts: The Religious Lives of Elderly Jewish Women in Jerusalem.* New York: Oxford University Press.

———. 1994. *Priestess, Mother, Sacred Sister: Religions Dominated by Women.* New York: Oxford University Press.

———. 1999. *Women of the Sacred Groves: Divine Priestesses of Okinawa.* New York: Oxford University Press.

Shaffer, Ruth T. 1985. *Road to Kilimanjaro.* Grand Rapids, Mich.: Four Corners Press.

Shapiro, Judith. 1981. "Ideologies of Catholic Missionary Practice in a Postcolonial Era." *Comparative Studies in Society and History* 23(1): 130–149.

Shaw, Rosalind. 1990. "The Invention of 'African Traditional Religion.'" *Religion* 20: 339–353.

———. 1995. "Feminist Anthropology and the Gendering of Religious Studies." In *Religion and Gender,* ed. Ursula King. Oxford: Basil Blackwell.

Shorter, Aylward. 1978. *African Culture and the Christian Church.* London: Geoffrey Chapman.

———. 1988. *Toward a Theory of Inculturation.* London: Geoffrey Chapman.

Sommer, Gabrielle, and Rainer Vossen. 1993. "Dialects, Sectiolects, or Simply Lects? The Maa Language in Time Perspective." In *Being Maasai,* ed. Thomas Spear and Richard Waller. London: James Currey.

Spear, Thomas. 1993. "Being 'Maasai,' but not 'People of the Cattle': Arusha Agricultural Maasai in the Nineteenth Century." In *Being Maasai,* ed. Thomas Spear and Richard Waller. London: James Currey.

———. 1997. *Mountain Farmers: Moral Economies of Land and Agricultural Development in Arusha and Meru.* Oxford: James Currey.

———. 1999. "Toward the History of African Christianity." In *East African Expressions of Christianity,* ed. Thomas Spear and Isaria Kimambo. Oxford: James Currey.

Spear, Thomas, and Isaria N. Kimambo, eds. 1999. *East African Expressions of Christianity.* Oxford: James Currey.

Spear, Thomas, and Richard Waller, eds. 1993. *Being Maasai: Ethnicity and Identity in East Africa.* London: James Currey.

Spencer, Paul. 1976. "Opposing Streams of the Gerontocratic Ladder: Two Models of Age Organization in East Africa." *Man* (n.s.) 11: 153–175.

———. 1988. *The Maasai of Matapato: A Study of Rituals of Rebellion.* Bloomington: Indiana University Press.

———. 1991. "The Loonkidongi Prophets and the Maasai: Protection Racket or Incipient State?" *Africa* 61(3): 334–342.

Stewart, Charles, and Rosalind Shaw, eds. 1994. *Syncretism/Anti-Syncretism: The Politics of Religious Synthesis.* London: Routledge.

Storrs-Fox, D. 1930. "Further Notes on the Masai of Kenya Colony." *Journal of the Royal Anthropological Institute of Great Britain and Ireland* 60: 447–465.

Strayer, R. W. 1975. "Mission History in Africa: New Perspectives on an Encounter." *African Studies Review* 19: 1–15.

———. 1978. *The Making of Mission Communities in East Africa.* London: Heinemann.

Sutton, John. 1990. *A Thousand Years in East Africa.* Nairobi: British Institute in Eastern Africa.

———. 1993. "Becoming Maasailand." In *Being Maasai,* ed. Thomas Spear and Richard Waller. London: James Currey.

Swaisland, Cecillie. 1993. "Wanted—Earnest, Self-Sacrificing Women for Service in South Africa: Nineteenth-Century Recruitment of Single Women to Protestant Missions." In *Women and Missions: Past and Present,* ed. Fiona Bowie et al. Providence: Berg.

Swatos, William H., ed. 1994. *Gender and Religion.* New Brunswick, N.J.: Transaction Books.

Talle, Aud. 1987. "Women as Heads of Houses: The Organization of Production and the Role of Women among the Pastoral Maasai in Kenya." *Ethnos* 52(1–2): 50–80.

———. 1988. *Women at a Loss: Changes in Maasai Pastoralism and Their Effects on Gender Relations.* Stockholm: Stockholm Studies in Anthropology.

———. 1990. "Ways of Milk and Meat among the Maasai: Gender Identity and Food Resources in a Pastoral Economy." In *From Water to World-Making: African Models and Arid Lands,* ed. Gísli Pálsson. Uppsala: Scandinavian Institute of African Studies.

———. 1998. "Female and Male in Maasai Life: Aging and Fertility." In *The Politics of Age and Gerontocracy in Africa: Ethnographies of the Past and Memories of the Present,* ed. Mario I. Aguilar. Trenton, N.J.: Africa World Press.

Tate, H. R. 1949–1950. "Three East Africans of Mark." *East African Annual* 1949–1950: 44–48.

Taylor, William B. 1996. *Magistrates of the Sacred: Priests and Parishioners in Eighteenth Century Mexico.* Stanford, Calif.: Stanford University Press.

Tenailleau, Bernard, C.S.Sp. 1985. "Father Libermann's Spirituality." *Spiritans Today* 4: 49–76.

Thomson, Joseph. 1968 [1885]. *Through Masai Land.* London: Frank Cass.

Tillard, J. M. R., O.P. 1985. "Father Libermann's Missionary Intuition." *Spiritans Today* 4: 77–94.

Tippett, Alan R. 1977. "Conversion as a Dynamic Process in Christian Mission." *Missiology* 5(2): 203–221.

van der Veer, Peter, ed. 1996. *Conversion to Modernities: The Globalization of Christianity.* New York: Routledge.

Voshaar, Jan. 1979. "Tracing God's Walking Stick in Maa: A Study of Maasai Society, Culture and Religion." Doctorale scriptie, Catholic University of Nijmegen, The Netherlands.

———. 1998a. *Maasai: Between the Oreteti-Tree and the Tree of the Cross.* Kampen, The Netherlands: Kok Publishers.

———. 1998b. "Heaven and Earth: A Probe into Maasai Reality." *Studies in Interreligious Dialogue* 8(2): 133–154.

Wakefield, Thomas. 1870. "Routes of Native Caravans from the Coast to the Interior of Eastern Africa." *Journal of the Royal Geographical Society* 40: 303–339.

Waliggo, J. M., A. Roest Crollius, T. Nkeramihigo, and J. Mutiso-Mbinda. 1986. *Inculturation: Its Meaning and Urgency.* Kampala: St. Paul Publications.

Walker, Reginald F., C.S.Sp. 1933. *The Holy Ghost Fathers in Africa: A Century of Missionary Effort*. Blackrock College, Ireland: Senior House of Studies.

Waller, Richard D. 1978. "Lords of East Africa: The Maasai in the Mid-Nineteenth Century (c. 1840–c.1885)." Ph.D. thesis, Cambridge University.

———. 1985a. "Ecology, Migration and Expansion in East Africa." *African Affairs* 84(336): 347–370.

———. 1985b. "Economic and Social Relations in the Central Rift Valley: The Maa-Speakers and Their Neighbours in the Nineteenth Century." In *Kenya in the Nineteenth Century*, ed. Bethwell Ogot. Nairobi: Anyange Press.

———. 1988. "Emutai: Crisis and Response in Maasailand 1883–1902." In *The Ecology of Survival: Case Studies from Northeast African History*, ed. Douglas Johnson and David Anderson. Boulder, Colo.: Westview Press.

———. 1995. "Kidongoi's Kin: Prophecy and Power in Maasailand." In *Revealing Prophets: Prophecy in Eastern African History*, ed. David Anderson and Douglas Johnson. Athens: Ohio University Press.

———. 1999. "They Do the Dictating and We Must Submit: The African Inland Mission in Maasailand." In *East African Expressions of Christianity*, ed. Thomas Spear and Isaria Kimambo. Oxford: James Currey.

Werbner, Richard. 1997. "The Suffering Body: Passion and Ritual Allegory in Christian Encounters." *Journal of Southern African Studies* 23(2): 311–324.

Whitehouse, L. E. 1932/1933. "Masai Social Customs." *Journal of the East Africa and Uganda Natural History Society* 47/48: 146–153.

Williams, Peter. 1993. " 'The Missing Link': The Recruitment of Women Missionaries in Some English Evangelical Missionary Societies in the Nineteenth Century." In *Women and Missions: Past and Present*, ed. Fiona Bowie et al. Providence: Berg.

Wright, Marcia. 1971. *German Missions in Tanganyika 1891–1941*. Oxford: Oxford University Press.

Index

Italicized page numbers indicate illustrations.

afterlife, 46–47, 144, 267n50
age-grades, 7–8
age-sets, 7–9, 36, 46, 49, 57–60
agriculture: Maasai practices, 7, 13, 179; Spiritan interest in, 73, 104–105
alcohol, 19, 89, 192, 194. *See also* honey beer
Allen, Roland, 90, 126–127
Alsace, 70, 72, 83
altars, 142, 152, *162,* 174
amulets, 30, 37, 39, 43–44, 63, 64
anger, 31–32, 34, 62. *See also* red
Anglican church, 85, 159, 276n49. *See also* Church Missionary Society
Anglo-German agreement of 1890, 10, 83
"Anna," *163*
anthropology, 88, 101, 270n15
Archdiocese of Arusha, 82–83. *See also* Diocese of Arusha
Århem, Kaj, 49–50, 265n22
arrows, 52, *53*
Arusha Diocesan Development Office (ADDO), 94, 204
Arusha people, 80, 96–97, 113, 146, 148, 158, 170, 200, 273n14
Arusha town, 80, 82–83, 89; map of, *81*
ashes, 34, 39
Ashumu (prophet), 244, 247–251, *248,* 252
attendance, church, 137–138, 149, 150, 153, 161, 165, 166, 182–183, 197

Bagge, S., 51, 55
baptism, 78, 92, 96, 98, 103–104, 121–122, 125, *145,* 148–149, 153, 158–164, 167, 169, 170, 173, 174, 175–176, 191, 199, 202, 207, 216, 219–220, 244, 247, 250
Barsai, 31–32
bathing, 52
Baumann, Oscar, 27, 41
beads, 32, 33–34, 51, 58
beauty, 57
beliefs, 14–15, 19–20, 21–67, 91–92, 154–158, 166–169, 177–180, 188–206, 214–215, 223–229, 230–243. *See also* conversion; Eng'ai; faith; inculturation

Bennett, Norman, 83
Benson, Pastor Stanley, 24–25, 264n14
Berlin Act of 1885, 83
Bernsten, John, 7, 40, 41, 43, 58, 60
betrothal, 60
Bible, 131–133, 142, 152, 200, 241
birds, 31, 52
bishops, 80, 189. *See also specific names*
black, 7, 22, 23–24, 31, 32–33, 36, 39, 48, 50, 51, 54, 60, 66, 152, 175, 213, 245, 276n6; ritual dress, *42, 53, 246*
blessings, 25–27, 30, 31, 32, 45, 50, 58, 59, 233, 235–236, 239; blessing ritual, *237*
blood, 28, 32–34, 48, 50, 51, 52, 55, 64, 66
blood brotherhood, 28, 32
blood money, 35, 64–65, 226
blood revenge, 64–65
bodies, 47, 51, 213
bones, 52
bovine pleuropneumonia, 10
bows, 52, *53,* 64
boys. *See ilayiok; isipolio*
branding irons, 60
breasts, 37
Brennan, Father Joseph, 190
brideservice, 153
bridewealth, 58, 60, 199
British colonial rule, 10, 189–190, 262n17; policies toward Maasai, 10–11, 211; and slavery, 76; and Spiritans, 83–85, 117. *See also* colonialism
Bura Catholic mission, 78
Burton, John, 22, 23, 46, 264n9, 265n26
Butts, Father Robert, 135, 149
Byrne, Father Joseph, 79, 80, 88–89, 110

Carmody, Brendan, 5
catechesis, 73, 78, 88–89, 103–104, 121–122, 136–137, 146, 157, 167, 169, 171–173, 179, 182, 191, 198, 201, 202, 216, 227–228, 244. *See also* evangelization

Index

catechists, 16, 70, 76–77, 103, 110, 114–144 passim, 150, 152, 176–177, 186–187, 188–189, 197–204, 216, 238–239, 260, 274n25; female, 138, 186–187. *See also specific names*

catechumenate, 271n37

Catholic church, 1, 5, 15, 141–142, 167, 243, 252–255. *See also* Spiritans; and specific churches, missions

Catholic Teacher's Training College (Singa Chini), 79, 116, 198

Catholic Theological Union (CTU), 100, 101

cattle, 8, 22–23, 26, 27, 28, 31, 32–33, 37, 44, 50, 56, 58, 59, 60, 212, 232, 248, 264n15. *See also* hides; livestock; milk; pastoralism

ceremonial hut, 58

Chagga, 78, 89, 97, 101, 110, 188

chalk, 32, 34, 51, 56, 59, 232, 253; ritual chalk markings, *33, 53*

Chanel, Joseph, 71–72, 109–110

charcoal, 34

childbirth, 50–51, 57, 212–213, 244, 247

children, 21, 25, 46–47, 109–110. *See also ilay-iok; intoyie*

choirs, 150, 152, 175, 191

choke law, 138, 140

Christian, William, 15

Christian villages, 73, 74–75

Christianity, 5, 15

Christy, Father William, 69, 99–105, 151–153, 164–166, *165,* 173–177, 181, 182, 183, 191, 194, 198, 199, 201–202, 204, 208–209, 238

Church Missionary Society, 72

"church of women," 2, 17, 145–187, 205, 209

circles, 30, 35, 37, 46–47, 50, 54, 59, 61, 220; circular ritual marking, *33. See also* female imagery; rings

circumcision, 25, 28, 32, 51–57, 235, 236, 238, 239

clans, 7, 8, 262n13. *See also* Ilkiboron sub-clan; Inkidong'i clan; Laiser clan

clergy, 70, 76–77, 79. *See also* diocesan priests; Spiritans; specific names

clothing, 32, 33, 51, 52, 55, 56, 58, 63, 128, 142, 150, 160, 193, 211, 225, 230, 241, 245

clouds, 32

coffee, 78, 269n9

coldness, 51, 55, 248

colonialism, 44, 83–85, 88–89, 117. *See also* British colonial rule; German colonial rule

colors, 23–24, 31–34. *See also* black; red; white

comets, 31–32

Commenginger, Father August, 74

communion, 164, 176, 196. *See also* First Communion; mass services

community, ideas of, 125, 134–135, 138, 208–209

compassion, 212

complementarity, 22, 35–36, 45–46, 57, 61–62, 67, 211

confiding of missionary territories, 72, 84. *See also* Propaganda Fide

confirmation, 152–153, 166, 176, 191; instruction, 137–138, 201

conflict resolution, 7, 8, 58, 203–204

Congregation of the Holy Spirit. *See* Spiritans

conversion, 1–2, 4–6, 193, 200, 210–229 passim, 256–257, 261n4. *See also* beliefs

cords, 22–23, 24, 30, 36, 63, 64. *See also* lines; *osotua*

Cornwells seminary, 87–88, 100

corpses, 47–48, 239–241

cowry shells, 61, 43, 245, *246*

creation, 22, 34, 46

culture, 88; and conservatism, 6, 12, 149; and religion, 16, 68, 114, 122, 129, 142–144, 214–215, 252–255. *See also* inculturation

curses, 30, 44, 45, 62, 242, 248. *See also iloi-bonok*

Dallas, Douglas, 30, 265n25

danger, 58

Dar es Salaam, 72

darkness, 22, 249

dawn, 30, 34, 37

daytime, 46

death, 32, 43, 44, 46–49, 71, 144, 239–241, 251–252

deCourmont, Bishop John Marie, 74

Del Mestri, Archbishop, 92

descent, 7

development, 115; Catholic initiatives, 94, 117, 189, 204; colonial projects, 11–12, 85; postcolonial projects, 128–129, 236. *See also* Arusha Diocesan Development Office; dispensaries; education

diet, 58, 59, 65. *See also* meat; milk

diocesan priests, 82, 140, 198. *See also specific names*

Diocese of Arusha, 71, 80–83, 99–100, 107, 111, 127–128, 139; map of, *81. See also* Archdiocese of Arusha; Vicariate of Kilimanjaro; specific missions

Diocese of Mbulu, 82, 272n10

Diocese of Moshi, 80–83, 127, 189; map of, *81*

Diocese of Same, 82. *See also* Same Prefecture

direct evangelization. *See* first evangelization

directionality, 34–35. *See also* east; left-side; north; right-side; south; west

disasters of 1883–1992, 10, 109

disk (teaching tool), 131–134, *132,* 144, 152, 165, 169, 177

dispensaries, 78, 116, 170, 273n19
District of Kilimanjaro (of the Spiritans), 80–81
diviners, 20, 41–43, 248. *See also iloibonok*
Dolan, Father Thomas, 108
domestic sphere, 1, 13, 49, 50–51, 55–56, 136
Donovan, Father Vincent, 89, 95, 99, 104, 114, 125–139 passim, 215, 222, 274n32, 275n37
dreams, 42, 43, 245, 247, 248–250
drought, 26, 31, 153, 166
dryness, 34
Duka Mbovu, 200
dung, 39, 55, 64
Durkin, Father Egbert, 89
Durning, Bishop Dennis, 80–83, 111, 139, 189, 272n10
dusk, 34, 37

earth. *See enkop*
east, 34–35, 47
East African Province (of the Spiritans), 82, 102, 140
Easter, 91, 97, 159–164, 173, 179–180, 183, *184, 185,* 218–220
ecumenism, 90–91, 169
Edoinyo e Moruak, 60
education, 70, 73, 74–79, 84–85, 111, 115–124, *119,* 125, 128, 136, 146, 153, 170; of girls, 78–79, 122–124, 153, 192, 193, 198, 226–228, 240, 250, 274n31
Edward, Mwalimu, 97, 160–164, *163*
elaitin tree, 51, 157, 235
elders (male), 8, 9, 12, 46, 135–136, 193–194, 207, 208, *237. See also Eunoto* ritual; *ilpiron; Olong'esherr* ritual
elites, 73, 113, 124, 128, 236–237, 252–255
Eluwai, 149
Emairete, 19, 95, 107, 122, 124, *137,* 146–158, 205–206, 213, 214; map of, *147*
Emairete Catholic church, 17, 94, 137–138, 139–140, 146–158, *148,* 186, 191, 193, 197–199, 253–254, 276n2
Embopong', 107, 149, 170–180, *178,* 204, 205; map of, *147*
Embopong' Catholic church, 17, 140, 170–180, 181, 194
encounters, 15–18, 68, 255, 256–257
Endulen Catholic mission, 99, 244, 247
enemies, 26, 34, 38, 43
Eng'ai, 14, 22–67 passim, 91, 129, 144, 154, 156, 158, 167, 169, 179, 183, 186, 191, 206, 211–229 passim, 231–251 passim, 258, 264nn8,11,12,17
Enguiki, 149
enkaji, 8, 77, *163, 185*
enkanyit (respect), 9, 32, 57, 184, 194, 195, 196, 202, 204, 221, 245
enkop (land, earth), 22, 29

enturuj (taboo, forbidden), 35, 65
enyorrata (love), 167, 168, 203–204, 245
Erhardt, J. J., 72
esetan, 15, 44, 63, 167, 216, 217, 242, 268n69, 277n2. *See also orpeko;* sorcery
Esta, 161, 165, 166–167, 181, 184–185, 207, 214, 222
Etherington, Norman, 5
ethnicity: and conversion, 2; and evangelization, 97; and religious change, 14–15, 21; and spirituality, 2. *See also specific groups*
Eucharist, 101. *See also* communion; First Communion
Eunoto ritual, 57–59, 199, 268n62
evangelization: approaches to, 1, 15–16, 17, 70, 73, 106–141; boma approach, 1, 125–139, 146, 148, 158, 159; and gender, 1–2, 4, 117–118, 121–124, 134–139, 140–141, 256–257; individual approach, 1, 139–141, 146, 148, 159, 171–173; preevangelization, 113–115; school approach, 1, 74–79, 84–85, 115–124, 125, 170; studies of, 4. *See also* baptism; catechists; conversion; disk; Spiritans
evil, 63–64, 250–251. *See also esetan;* sorcery
evil eye, 64

faith, 103–104, 195, 203, 242–243, 259
Farler, J. P., 41
fat, 32, 33, 47, 48, 59, 61, 232
fear, 144
feathers, 31, 52, *53,* 56
female imagery, 22–23, 35–36. *See also* circles; Eng'ai; Naiterukop
fertility, 22, 26, 30, 31, 32, 37, 50–51, 54, 55, 56, 61, 65, 91–92
fighting, 26, 52
fingers, 63
fire, 34, 35, 39, 52
First Communion, 150–151, *151,* 199
first evangelization, 95, 101, 102, 107, 140. *See also* Embopong' Catholic church
forgiveness, 26, 30, 32, 62, 65, 226
Fosbrooke, H. A., 41
France, 69, 72
"Francis," Mwalimu, 152, 173–177, 198–199, 201, 204, 222, 253
French-Sheldon, M., 26, 32
funerals, 47–48, 239–241, 251–252

Galaty, John, 58, 59, 265n26
gender: in African studies, 2–3; assessing inequality, 3–6, 45–46; changes during colonial period, 12–13, 211; and conversion, 4–6, 256–257; and decision making, 8–9; dominance of political-economic perspectives, 3, 5; and evangelization, 1, 2, 4, 117–118, 121–124,

Index

gender (*continued*)
134–139, 140–141, 256–257, 258–259;
and history, 3; and power, 3–6, 17, 19–
20, 257–259; in precolonial period, 7–
10; and rituals, 25–40, 46–67, 230–241;
and scale, 3; and spirituality, 2, 3–6, 17,
21, 45–46, 66–67, 210–229 passim, 256–
259
German colonial rule, 10; and slavery, 76; and
Spiritans, 83–84
Germany, 72
gifts, 44, 58, 60, 61, 119, 173, 179, 236, 245.
See also bridewealth; *osotua*
girls. *See intoyie*
goats, 31, 32, 43, 48, 64, 236
God, 152, 155, 158, 200, 224, 225–226, 243,
250, 264n8. *See also* Eng'ai
Gogarty, Father Henry, 77, 79, 84, 109
grass, 22, 25–28, 30, 37, 38, 48, 56, 63, 91,
142, 232, 235–236, 241
graves, 47–48
Gray, Robert, 88
greetings, 9, 195
Greiner, Johann, 72
Gulliver, Philip, 6

hail, 32
hair, 25, 41, 49, 51, 52, 55, 56, 59, 266n40,
267n46
Harris, Father Thomas, 270n21
Hastings, Adrian, 1, 4, 261n6
Haya, 5
healing, 28, 56, 215–222, 243. *See also iloibonok; olcani*
Hearn, Father Edward, 94
heart. *See oltau*
heaven, 48, 264n13
hides, 9, 33, 39, 47, 48, 51, 55, 56, 58, 59,
61, 66, 142, 152, 157, 165, 245, 250,
253
Hillman, Father Eugene, 69, 86–93, 99, 104,
108, 110–124 passim, *116, 120,* 146,
188–190, 197–198, 206, 254,
273nn16,18
Hinseley, Apostolic Delegate Arthur, 76
Hollis, Alfred, 20, 21–67 passim, 262n3
Holy Childhood, 73–74, 270n11
holy people, 20, 46, 58, 62. *See also ilaunoni*
homesteads, 8, 125, 129–130, 136, 177
honey, 28, 48, 60
honey beer, 28, 37, 39, 43, 46, 50, 51, 56, 58,
233, 253
horn-of-the-ox ritual, 268n60
Horton, Robin, 5
hospitals, 73, 76, 78, 111
houses. *See enkaji*
hunting, 170
Hurskainen, Arvi, 35, 278n9

ilaigwenak, 8, 9, 124, 134–135, 193, 239
ilamala (delegations), 19, 31, 35, 36–37, 183,
185
ilaunoni, 33, 57–58, 213, 268n62
ilayiok, 6, 9, 60, 89, *116, 120*
Ilkiboron sub-clan, 45, 48, 266n42, 267n46
ilkunono (blacksmiths), 266n41
Ilmoingo clan, 233
ilmurran, 7, 9, 12, 19, 20, 31, 34, 39, 44, 45,
52, 54, 57, 65, 109, *137,* 155, 166,
171, 191–192, 193, *194,* 199, 205, 211,
220, 234, 235, 240, 245, 247. *See also
Eunoto* ritual
iloibonok, 12, 19–20, 26, 37, 40–46, *42,* 47–48,
49, 51, 54, 57, 63–64, 156, 191, 193,
206, 216, 217, 233, 242–243, 248, 253,
257. *See also specific names*
Iloikop, 7
ilpiron ("fire-stick" elders), 58–59
inculturation, 88–89, 92–93, 104, 129, 141–
144, 154–155, 157–158, 182, 223, 225,
230–243, 251–255, 260
inheritance, 7
Inkidong'i clan, 20, 40–41, 44, 45, 146, 153,
177, 191, 206, 226, 233, 242–243,
277n7. *See also iloibonok*
inside, 55
insults, 62–63
intoyie (girls), 9, 175
Isichei, Elizabeth, 261n6
isinkoliotin, 37–38, *38,* 39–40, 50, 51, 59, *184,
185,* 232–233, 235
isipolio, 31, 51–52, *53,* 56. *See also* circumcision
Islam, 119

Jacobs, Alan, 61, 88
jealousy, 172
Jesus, 121, 192–193, 200, 224, 227, 247, 249–
251, 252, 278n3
Johnston, Harry, 28–29, 41–42, 43, 48, 108,
264n17
"Joseph," 166, 190–191, 195, 205–206, 225–
226, 230, 243

Kane, Father Mortimer, 104, 135–136, 149,
275n40
Katasi, 244–247
Kelly, Father Edward, *137*
Kelly, Father Joseph, 104
Kenya, 7, 10
Kerio, 6
kerygma, 129–134, 141
Kibosho Catholic mission, 78, 79, 270n12
Kibosho seminary, 88–89
Kidongoi, 40–41, 266nn39,40
Kieran, J. A., 69–80 passim, 141
Kierie, Peter, 159–164
Kijungu Catholic mission, map of, *81*
Kikatiti Catholic mission, 101–102

Kikuyu, 20
Kilasara, Bishop Joseph, 110, 272n6
Kilema Catholic mission, 71, 74, 78, 79, 109, 188, 270n12; map of, *75*
Kimesera, Victor, 190
kinship, 9, 33–34
Kipuri, Naomi, 62, 267n47
Kisongo section, 60
Kiteto District, 113; map of, *112*
Kohler, Father Girard, 69, 89, 90, 94–99, 107–141 passim, 149, 159–164, *162, 163,* 182, 186, 200, 207, 218–220
"Koko Naisandi," 225, 242–243
"Koko Namunyak," 223
"Koko Nanu," 234–235
"Koko Nanyorre," 242
"Koko Naomon," 157–158, 225, 226, 227, 228
"Koko Naserian," 164, 168–169, 193, 223, 225, 235
"Koko Nasisi," 174
"Koko Nayieu," 155–156, 223, 224
Krapf, J. Lewis, 24, 41, 63, 72, 264n19
Kunguru, 19–20, 66–67
Kwavi, 7, 63–64

Laiser clan, 48
Laiser, Father John, 150
land alienation, 12, 13, 113, 128–129
Landau, Paul, 14, 261n6
language, 87–88, 95, 101, 109, 143, 150, 152, 156, 160, 175, 199, 225, 236, 241
Larsson, Birgitta, 5
Lashaine plains, 41, 146, 150; map of, *147*
Last, J. T., 47
laypeople, 70
Lea, Mwalimu, 186–187, 203
leadership, 8–9, 117–118, 138, 183–187, 195, 196–197, 207, 208–209. *See also ilaig-wenak; ilaunoni;* Kunguru
Leakey, L. S. B., 48, 52
leather. *See* hides
Lebulu, Archbishop Josephat, 82, 102, 271n2
LeClair, Father Richard, 87
Le-eyo, 46–47
left-side, 8, 36, 47, 48, 59, 196, 232, 241
"Legol," 239–241
"Lemali," 215
"Lemenye," 183, 191–192, 206, 242
Lemenye, Justin, 277n1
Lenana, Laibon, 41, *42,* 266n43
Lengaa, Mwalimu Moses, 162, 164–168, *165,* 187, 199–201, 203–204, 221
"Leng'ai," 173–174
"Lengare," 19, 233
Lengiriaa, Mwalimu, 244–247
"Lengogo," 153, 154
"Lengong," 205, 242
"Lepayian," *29,* 205, 214–215, 231–233

"Lepilall," 19, 183, 193–194, 195
"Lepopo," 226, 242
LeRoy, Father Alexander, 74, 76, 78, 108–109, 270n15
"Lesinon," 214
"Letani," 191, 195, 214
"Leyio," 173–176, 194–195
Libermann, Father François Marie Paul, 69–70, 98–99, 269n5
life, 46–47
lightning, 31–32
liminal states, 25, 32, 56, 266n41. *See also isi-polio*
lines, 35, 46–47, 51. *See also* cords; male imagery
lions, 31
literacy, 73, 130–134, 138, 156
liturgy, 142, 161, 165–166, 182, 227–228. *See also* inculturation; mass services
livestock, 9, 10, 12, 13, 25, 31, 58, 60, 211. *See also* cattle; goats; hides; milk; pastoralism; sheep
Livingstone, David, 72
Lobon, Father Simon, 150, 171–173, 174, 176, 177, 179, 180, 181, 205, 240–241
localities, 8, 9
Lolgolie, Mwalimu Daniel, 118, 122, 146–149, 152, 153, 155, 186, 196–198, 202, 204, 221, 239, 240–241, 253, 274n31
Loliondo Catholic mission, 95, 125, 189; map of, *81*
Loljuju, 25
Lolkisale mountain, 91
Losengori, 200
"Loserian," 177, 179
love. *See enyorrata*
Lukanima, Bishop Fortunatus, 82
Lutheran church, 5, 72, 90, 96, 110, 116–117, 119, 121, 142, 150–151, 154, 158–159, 169, 174, 216, 217, 220–221, 230, 253, 262n18, 273n20, 276n48. *See also specific names*

Maa language, 36–37, 109, 130, 136, 150, 165
Maasai: and colonial rule, 10–13; early history, 6–10; as ethnonym, 7, 262n11; origins of, 6–7; religious beliefs and practices of, 14–15, 19–20, 21–67, 91–92, 154–158, 166–169, 177–180, 188–206, 214–215, 223–229, 230–243; social organization, 7; and Spiritans, 98, 106–144, 145–153, 158–166, 170–177; stereotypes of, 6, 20, 97, 107–109, 114, 190; studies of, 5–6
Maasai Deanery, 107, 140, 271n2
Maasindat. *See* OlMaasindat
Madagascar, 72
Maitumbe, 24

Index

Makumira Lutheran seminary, 90
male imagery, 35–36
Mandera Catholic mission, 78
Marchessault, Father Ned, 99, 201, 243–251, 252
"Maria," 150, 182, 223, 224, 225, 226, 243
marriage, 7, 8, 33, 44, 56, 60–61, 98, 113, 123, 199, 238, 250. *See also* polygyny
"Martha," 222
"Mary," 196, 213–214, 235, 236–237, 239
Mary (mother of Jesus), 177, 224
Masai Development Plan, 211
Masai District, 6, 89, 110, 111, 113, 190; map of, *112*
Masai Federal Council, 12, 113, 189, 190, 262n19. *See also* Masai Native Authority; *Olkiama*
Masai Native Authority, 12. *See also* Masai Federal Council; *Olkiama*
Masai Reserve, 10, 113; map of, *11*
Mashati Catholic mission, 270n12
mass services, 150–153, 159–166, 173–177, 182, 196. *See also* liturgy
"Mateo," Mwalimu, 152, 153
Mauritania, 72
Mbarnoti, Boniface, 188–189
Mbarnoti, (Chief) Edward, 188–190
Mbatian, Laibon, 38, 40, 41, 44, 45, 48, 265n36, 266n38
Mbeiya, Laibon, 266n43
McCarthy, Father Patrick, 270n21
meat, 9, 39, 52, 63, 66
medicine. *See olcani; sakut*
men: as fathers, 50, 54, 56–57, 60; as fathers-in-law, 60; as husbands, 60, 63; as sons, 57, 60, 63; religious beliefs and practices of, 25–67 passim, 188–206, 214–215, 223–229, 230–243. *See also* elders; *ilmurran*
menstruation, 55
Merker, Moritz, 21–67 passim, 78, 263n5, 264n19
Meru people, 110
Mfereji, 170. *See also* Emairete
midwives, 50, 213
milk, 9, 26–27, 30, 32, 37, 38, 48, 50, 51, 52, 55, 59, 61, 91, 142, 171, 211, 224, 233, 234, 235–236, 245, 253
missiology, 87–88, 92–93, 100–101, 126. *See also* evangelization; theology
missionization. *See* evangelization
Mlelia, Chief, 78
mobility, 9, 13, 52, 56
moeties. *See Odomong'i; Orokiteng'*
Mol, Father Frans, 262n13
Molloimet, Lepilall ole, 236, *237*
Mondul Juu Parish, 99, 100, 102–103, 107, 149–150. *See also* Emairete Catholic church

Monduli Catholic mission, 16, 89, 94–95, 102, 110–113, 117, 119–120, *120, 121,* 135, 189, 198; map of, *81*
Monduli District, 41, 89, 113, 236; map of, *112*
Monduli Juu, 19
Monduli mountain, 111, 113, 146, 170, 231; map of, *112*
Monduli town, 41, 89, 97, 102, 111–113, 180, 192, 239–240; maps, *112, 147*
months, 46
moon, 35, 46–47, 50
morality, 3, 5, 17, 62–66, 109, 213–214, 227, 229, 257–258, 259
Morani, 173–176, 199, 211, 214
Moshi town, 74, 82–83
Mount Kilimanjaro, 31, 71, 74
Mount Meru, 31, 74, 80
mountains, 30–31, 40–41, 225. *See also specific names*
mourning, 25, 48–49, 239–241
Mtaita, Leonard, 276n48
Mti Mmoja, 107, 135–136, 158–169, 192, 205–206, 213, 221; map of, *147*
Mti Mmoja Catholic church, 17, 97, 158–169, *160,* 181, 190, 200, 204, 207, *208,* 227
Mto wa Mbu Catholic mission, 102
Munsch, Father Aloyse, 77, 78
murder, 35, 64–65, 212, 226
myths, 22–23, 40–41, 46–47, 142

Naas, Father Everhard, 130–131
Nadusoito, 200
Nailepo (prophetess), 243–247, *246,* 252
"Naini," 222, 227
"Naisatot," 217
"Naishepo," 213, 224, 242
Naiterukop, 24–25, 31, 46–47
Namanak, 216–217
naming, 50–51, 59, 98, 169, 234–235, 254, 267n56
Nangoro, Father Benedict, 153, 157, 168, 228
"Nanne," 211
"Nanyore," 172, 174
"Naoyeyio," 186
"Nashie," 224
"Nashioki," 174–177, 204
"Nasidai," 177–180, *178*
"Nashipai," 243
nationalism, 128–129
nature, 25–32, 46
Ndangoya, 275n42
Neckebrouck, Valeer, 6, 261n7
Nenauner, 24–25
Ngiringiri, 200
Ngoilenya, 151
Ngorongoro District, 113, 243; map of, *112*
Ngoto Nemasi, 45
Nicene Creed, 142, 172

Njui, Clement, *120*
north, 34–35, 37, 39, 47
Northern Province, 74
novitiate, 71, 87, 95, 100
numbers, 34–35, 42–43, 59, 232, 233, 234, 239
Nyerere, President Julius, 128–129, 139

oaths, 63–64
ocher, 33, 34, 59, 61, 230
Odomong'i, 7, 36
offerings, presentation of, 150, *151*, 153, 164, 196, 225
Ol gurugur, 31–32
olcani (healing medicine), 28, 40, 46, 63
Oldoinyo Leng'ai, 31, 233, 244; maps of, *11*, *112*
Oldonyo Sambu Junior Seminary, 116, 128, 150, 193, 212
Ole Sempele, Molonket Olokorinya, 277n1
Oliver, Roland, 72, 76–77, 78, 272n4
Olkiama, 113
olkishiroto, 65
OlMaasindat, 22–23, 24
oloirishi, 65
Olong'esherr ritual, 57, 59–60
Oloshiro, Father Fred, 188, 191, 275n44
olpul, 175–176, 248
Olsson, Tord, 263n7
oltau, 17, 48, 154, 167, 179, 181, 192, 194, 210, 213–223, 228–229, 240, 242, 248–250, 259
Oltimbau, 193
Operation Imparnati, 139, 146
ordeals, 63–64
ordination, 71, 95, 102
oreteti trees, 28–30, *29*, 36, 169, 223, 225, 231–233
origin myths, 24–25
orkiteng' lentomono ritual. *See* naming
orkiteng lolbaa ritual, 59, 238
ormeek, 12–13, 122, 130, 193, *194*, 215, 216, 217
ornaments, 36, 39, 47, 48–49, 51, 52, 55, 57, 58, 60, 142, 157, 225, 240. *See also* beads
Orokiteng', 7, 36
orpeko, 15, 17, 156, 157, 159, 203, 210, 216–222, *219*, 227, 228–229, 243, 252, 259
orphanages, 73, 109–110, 188
osotua, 27, 36, 176
outside, 51

parables, 130, 172
Parakuyo, 7
Parit, Laibon, 19, 266n43
pastoralism, 6, 7, 12, 128. *See also* cattle; goats; hides; livestock; milk; sheep
peace, 25–27, 32

peace, sharing of the, 142, 164, 176, 196
Pels, Peter, 273n15
Pentecostal church, 120, 154, 169, 170–171, 206, 230, 250–251, 252, 253
"Peter," 239–241, 251–252
Peter, Mwalimu, 157
Peterson, David, 216
Peterson, Derek, 257
plantations, 73, 78
Poirier, Father Ralph, 89, 131–134, 144, 146, 148, 170, 275n39
polygyny, 8, 92, 124, 271n33, 276n1. *See also* marriage
popes, 15
Poullart des Places, Claude-François, 69, 269n4
power: and color red, 34; and gender, 3–6, 17, 19–20, 257–259
prayer festivals, 39–40
prayers, 36–40, 47, 50, 51, 57, 156, 169, 171–172, 174–176, 211, 223–225, 232, 233–234, 239, 265n34. See also *isinkoliotin*; rituals
preevangelization, 113–115
Prefecture of Zanguebar, 72
procreation, 36, 50–51, 56–57
profession, 71, 87, 100
Propaganda Fide, 72, 76, 79, 269n7, 270n16
prophets, 20, 32, 41–42, 45, 243–251, 252. *See also* Ashumu; *iloibonok*; Nailepo
propitiousness, 34–35, 47. *See also* numbers
public sphere, 13, 49, 51, 56

raids, 38, 44. *See also ilmurran*
railroad, 74; map of, *75*
rain, 22, 23, 31, 42, 43, 45, 46, 156, 175, 249
rainbows, 31–32
Rambo, Lewis, 4
Rebmann, Johann, 72
reconciliation, 62
red, 7, 23–24, *29*, 33–34, 36, 152, 213–214, 247
religion: and culture, 16, 68; definitional issues, 13–14; as dynamic, 14–16, 21, 24; and nature, 25–36, 46–47; as school subject, 118–119. *See also* beliefs; conversion; evangelization; faith; inculturation; prayers; rituals; spirituality
religious movements, 5
research methods, 16
residence patterns, 8
resources, access to, 8, 9
respect. *See enkanyit*
Reunion, 72
Reusch, Pastor Richard, 52–53
Rigby, Peter, 6, 264n10
right-side, 8, 36, 37, 39, 40, 48, 51, 59, 196, 232
rinderpest, 10, 109

Index

rings, 39, 59, 175, 179

rites of passage. *See* rituals

ritual knowledge, 56–57, 61–62, 231, 234–235

rituals, *237;* and auspicious numbers, 35; circularity of, 46–47; classifications of, 49–50; continuities and changes in, 155, 157, 230–255; fertility, 30, 31, 91–92; of forgiveness, 26, 32; and gender, 50–62; for peace, 25–27; for rain, 26, 175, 232–233, 276n6. *See also* blessings; childbirth; curses; death; *Eunoto* ritual; horn-of-the-ox ritual; inculturation; liminal states; mourning; naming; *orkiteng lolbaa* ritual; *Olong'esherr* ritual

Robert, Father Michel, 102, 104

Roimen, *120*

Rombo Catholic mission, 79, 270n12

rosaries, 174–175, 192

sacraments, 157–158

sacredness, 4, 14, 25–36 passim, 61–62, 67, 258. *See also oreteti* trees

sacrifice, 31, 32, 48, 49, 66, 265n26

St. James Catholic seminary, 79

St. Mary's Catholic seminary, 87

St. Patrick's Teachers' Training School. *See* Catholic Teacher's Training College

St. Theresa's Catholic church, 89

sakut (harmful medicine), 43–44, 242

salvation, 126, 144

Samburu, 7

Same Prefecture, 80; map of, *81. See also* Diocese of Same

sanctuaries, 142, 149

Sangale, Father Moses, 191

"Saning'o," 177

"Sarah," 153–155, 243

Satorelli, Archbishop, 92

seasons, 46, 50

sections, 8

secularity, 4, 14, 61–62, 67, 258

Sekenan, 45

"Sekot," *29,* 226, 230–233

seminary, 71, 87–88

Sendeu, Laibon, 41, 266n43

Senegal, 72

sermons, 142, 152, 161–162, 166, 175–176

sexual intercourse, 52

sexuality, 52–53, 56, 58, 60, 65

Shanahan, Bishop, 270n16

sheep, 31, 39, 60, 61, 66, 165, 175, 232

shields, 34, 89, 142

sickness, 28, 32–33, 39, 63, 216, 217–218, 248–249. *See also* healing; *olcani; orpeko*

"Sidai," 235

Simanjiro Animal Husbandry School, 191

Simanjiro School, 116, *116, 119,* 121, 123, 273n18

"Simon," 214

Singa Chini, 79

"Sinoti," 234–235

Sinyati, 166, 167–168, 231

"Sipai," 214

Sisters of the Precious Blood, 78

skulls, 48

sky, 22, 24, 29, 31, 34

slaughter, 9, 50, 55, 59, 61, 234, 249, 265n26

slavery, 70, 73, 76

small Christian communities, 166, 168, 186, 209

smallpox, 10

smoke, 39

snakes, 31, 48

Society for the Propagation of the Faith, 73–74, 270n11

Society of the Holy Heart of Mary, 69

Sokoine, Edward, 124, 150, 189, 190, 276n2

"Solomon," 212, 242

song-dances. *See isinkoliotin*

songs, 37, 46, 142, 161, 164, 165–166, 171–171, 174–176, 182, 223, 245, 277n8

sorcery, 44, 63–64, 167, 242. *See also esetan; iloibonok*

soul. *See oltau*

south, 34–35

spears, 35, 52, 89, *116*

Spencer, Paul, 44, 45, 262n14

spirit. *See oltau*

spirit possession. *See orpeko*

Spiritan Associates, 94

Spiritans, 1–2, 15, 17, 269n1; African, 80–82; American, 70–71, 79–80; and colonial rule, 83–85; English, 89; French, 72, 83–84; German, 72, 83–84; history of, 68–105; Irish, 79, 84; and Maasai, 98, 106–144, 145–153, 158–166, 170–177, 206–209, 218–221, 238, 256–257; training of, 71–72, 87, 95, 99, 100–101. *See also specific names*

spirituality, 2, 3–6, 17, 21, 45–46, 66–67, 210–229 passim, 256–259. *See also iloibonok*

spittle, 27–28, 39, 50, 62, 234, 235–236, 239

"Steven," 119–120, 121, 134, 137, 192–193, 212, 226, 231, 253–254, 255

sticks, 35, 52, 60, 236, 241

stomach, 32

stones, 25, 42, 43, 48, 54

stools, 58, 60, 64, 142, 232, 236

Storrs-Fox, D., 28, 52, 59

Sultan of Zanzibar, 83

sun, 35, 39, 46

Swahili language, 95, 128, 150, 157, 193, 225

Swahili people, 12, 117, 128, 215

swords, 35, 52

symmetry, 35

taboo. *See enturuj*

Tanga Province, 74

Tanga town, 75
Tanganyika Africa National Union (TANU), 190
Tanzania, 1, 7, 10, 128; map of, *112*
teachers, 114, 121; female, 138. *See also* catechists
Teresia, 200, 203
theology, 88–90, 92–93, 95, 126, 182. *See also* preevangelization
"Thomas," 142, 212
Thomson, Joseph, 27, 38, 40, 41, 44, 47, 108
thunder, 23, 31–32
tobacco, 60, 179, 214
Todorowski, Father John, 270n21
"Toimon," 205, 206
traders, 9, 13, 179–180
transgressions, 62–66
translation, 23, 24, 142, 143, 172, 199. *See also* catechists
transportation, 114–115, 172, 176, 199, 239, 240
trees, 28, 225. *See also elaitin* tree; *oreteti* trees
Tunney, Father Thomas, 89, 153, 198
Turnbull, Governor Richard, 189

umbilical cord, 36. *See also osotua*
United States Eastern Province (of the Spiritans), 71, 80–82, 98, 140, 189–190
Usambara mountains, 74
Uru Catholic mission, 270n12

van der Veer, Peter, 5
Vatican, 15, 70
Vatican Council (Second), 85, 93, 94, 99, 100, 104, 105, 127–128, 129, 138–139, 142
vessels, 142
vestibules, 149
vestments, 142, 151, 152, 161, *162,* 165, *165,* 174, 241
Vicariate of Bagamoyo, 79
Vicariate of Kilimanjaro, 74–80, 84, 87, 110; map of, *75*
Vicariate of Zanzibar, 79, 141
villagization. *See* Operation Imparnati
visions, 245, 247, 248–251
vocations, 201–202

Voshaar, Jan, 22, 24, 263n6

Waller, Richard, 6, 40
Walokole. See Pentecostal church
Wanawake Wakatoliki wa Tanzania (WA-WATA), 183, 186
Wanga, 239–241, 251
water, 23, 25–26, 51, 55, 59, 219, 239, 249
Watschinger, Father Herbert, 238
wealth, 44–45, 213–214
weddings, 60–61
west, 34–35
wetness, 22
white, 23, 29, 31, 32, 40, 41, 52, 56, 59, 60; white ritual markings, *33, 53*
White Fathers and Sisters, 5
Whitehouse, L. E., 43
widows, 48, 98, 168, 186–187, 196
wild animals, 24–25, 31, 41, 47, 229, 239
wilderness, 57. *See also* outside
wind, 32, 248
wisdom, 226–228, 242
womb, 66
women, *38,* and aging, 8; and baptism, 1, *184, 185;* barren women, 31, 55, 157, 234; control of houses, 8; and conversion, 4–6, 210–229; as daughters, 60; and evangelization, 1; as mothers, 50–52, 54–57, 58–59, 60, 63, 92, 168, 212–213; as mothers-in-law, 60; and prayer, 36–40, 91; religious practices and beliefs, 25–67 passim, 91–92, 154–158, 166–169, 177–180, *208,* 223–229, 230–243; responsibilities of, 9; and spiritual power, 2, 21–67 passim, 210–229, 256–257; symbolic associations of, 25–27; as traders, 9, 13, 179–180; as wives, 58, 60, 63, 172. *See also* gender; midwives; widows
World Vision, 170–171
World War I, 10, 78, 79, 84
World War II, 12, 85

years, 46

Zanzibar, 72

DOROTHY L. HODGSON

is Associate Professor and Graduate Director in the Department of Anthropology at Rutgers University, New Brunswick, New Jersey, where she is affiliated with the Center for African Studies and the Women's and Gender Studies Department. She is author of *Once Intrepid Warriors: Gender, Ethnicity, and the Cultural Politics of Maasai Development* (Indiana University Press, 2001); editor of *Gendered Modernities: Ethnographic Perspectives* and *Rethinking Pastoralism in Africa: Gender, Culture, and the Myth of the Patriarchal Pastoralist;* and co-editor of *"Wicked" Women and the Reconfiguration of Gender in Africa.*